IN A LEAGUE OF THEIR OWN

IN A LEAGUE OF THEIR OWN

Cricket & Leisure in 20th Century Todmorden

Freda, Malcolm & Brian Heywood

Supported by
The National Lottery®
through the Heritage Lottery Fund

heritage
lottery fund

UPPER CALDER VALLEY
PUBLICATIONS
2011

First published in 2011
by Upper Calder Valley Publications

ISBN
Paperback 978-0-9547146-4-2
Hardback 978-0-9547146-5-9

Printed by
The Amadeus Press, Cleckheaton BD19 4TQ

Contents

Preface and Acknowledgements

In a League of Their Own continues Todmorden's cricket and leisure-time story from *Cloth Caps and Cricket Crazy: Todmorden and Cricket 1835-1896*, published in 2004. It is the fifth local history book to grow from Hebden Bridge WEA Local History Group (originally a Leeds University tutorial class), which became the Upper Calder Valley History Group (UCVHG).

The first of the group's books was *Pennine Valley: A History of Upper Calderdale*, published in 1992. Following this *A History of Todmorden* was produced for the centenary of the creation of the Borough of Todmorden in 1996, written by Bernard Jennings, Freda and Malcolm Heywood with illustrations by the late Laurence Greenwood. Next came *Cloth Caps and Cricket Crazy: Todmorden and Cricket 1835-1896*, published in 2004 and written by Freda and Malcolm Heywood with help from their son, Brian. Recounting the birth and growth of Todmorden Cricket Club and of parallel organised leisure pursuits against a backdrop of Victorian trends and influences, *Cloth Caps and Cricket Crazy* told the story to 1896, leaving much material on the cutting room floor and the 20th century unexplored.

In a League of Their Own brings the story up to date, relating events and developments in local cricket and other leisure pursuits through the often turbulent, ever-changing and increasingly frenzied 20th century to the present day.

Between *Cloth Caps* and *In a League of Their Own*, Freda and Malcolm Heywood wrote *Todmorden Hippodrome: One Hundred Years of Theatre*, published for the Centenary of the Todmorden Hippodrome Theatre in 2007.

Further spin-offs from *Cloth Caps* are National Curriculum local history schemes of work for primary schools, based on the histories of sports' clubs, written by Brian Heywood. Originating as part of the University of Huddersfield's Lottery-funded Cricket Heritage Project, the first schemes were for amateur cricket clubs. Schemes have since been written for several professional clubs in the Football League and in the Rugby Football League.

The UCVHG authors are grateful to the Heritage Lottery Fund for its support in helping to fund *In a League of Their Own* and for encouragement and guidance from their staff at Leeds. The UCVHG members wish to thank those who supported their application for a grant: Gary Borrows, Head of Calderdale Libraries, Museums and Arts; Dr Peter Davies, University of Huddersfield; Duncan M Warburton, Lancashire Cricket League; Professor Bernard Jennings, Professor Emeritus Hull University; Sheila Tordoff, Editor, Todmorden News and Hebden Bridge Times; and Peter Cockcroft, Todmorden Information Centre Trust.

The authors are privileged to have the guidance of Professor Bernard Jennings, who has read the script, made corrections, and made suggestions for improvement, especially in emphasising the economic and social background to the themes. Our thanks and best wishes go to Bernard and to Jean, his wife, for their friendship and encouragement.

In addition to detailed research into newspapers, books and other publications, the authors have conducted a limited survey, and interviewed many people whose stories and recollections have been woven into the themes of the book. Others have generously contributed in script and many have supplied photographs to illustrate the text.

We, the authors, thank all those who so willingly contributed information and/or illustrations.

We are especially grateful for the co-operation of Todmorden High School, where we conducted our 2009 survey with Year 9. Particular thanks go to Mr Duerden for overseeing the completion of the questionnaires and to Year 9 pupils for their friendly and positive response. We also thank all those Senior Citizens who completed questionnaires, members of: Age Concern and the luncheon clubs at Roomfield House and St Michael's Church, Cornholme; Todmorden Antiquarian Society; St Mary Choir; Todmorden Cricket Club Beer Festival; University of the Third Age and the many who invited us into their homes.

For their help, access to their archives and for illustrations, we thank the staff of:

Todmorden News/Advertiser (TN, TA), pp84, 85, 109, 144, 155, 160, 194, 201, 211, 214, 317, 327;
The Halifax Courier (HC), pp143, 153, 191, 218, 329, 345, 347, 350;
The Lancashire Evening Telegraph (LET), pp248, 251, 252, 263, 272, 273, 276, 277, 309, 316, 325, 326, 328, 333;
Rotherham Advertiser;
Sunday Graphic, pp94, 102;
Todmorden, Calderdale, Burnley, Manchester and Rotherham libraries;
Accrington Cricket Club, p31;
Bridgeholme Cricket Club;
Burnley Football Club p138;
Calderdale Council Young People's Service;
The University of Huddersfield Cricket Heritage website, www.ckcricketheritage.org, pp33, 318, 351, and Rugby Football League Archive, p132;
Incredible Edible Todmorden and website, p344;
Lancashire Cricket League and website, www.lancashireleague.com;
Rawtenstall CC for the 1949 film 'Cricketers All', pp241, 246;
Todmorden OAK;
Todmorden Angling Society;
Todmorden Antiquarian Society, p37;
Todmorden Community Band;

Todmorden Cricket Club;
Todmorden Golf Club;
Todmorden Harriers;
Todmorden Amateur Operatic and Dramatic Society, pp219, 345;
Todmorden Information Centre;
Todmorden Natural History Society;
Todmorden Photographic Society;
Todmorden Scouts, Guides, Cubs and Brownies;
Todmorden Sports Centre;
Todmorden and Walsden website;
Vale Youth Club;
Walsden Cricket Club;
and especially Roger Birch for supplying and enhancing photographs, pp3, 12, 15, 26, 28, 29, 40, 41, 60, 115, 118, 129, 131, 133, 134, 136, 137, 140, 154, 157, 165, 166, 167, 169, 173, 176, 177, 178, 179, 180, 181, 182, 183, 185, 186, 187, 188, 190, 192, 195, 198, 205, 207, 210, 213, 217, 218, 231, 236, 239, 245, 248, 250, 298, 300, 315, 335, 347.

Regarding the many themes which the book explores, the following generously gave their time to contribute information, some in writing, others orally (some of which was recorded), for which we are very grateful: Ibrar Ali, Rachael Barber, Ray Barber, Brian Binns, Michael Bourne, John Brierley, John Cockcroft, Neil Dansie (South Australia), Ian Duffield, Peter Eastwood, Michael Endley, Alan Fiddling, Rowena Goldthorpe, Mandy Goth, Maurice Greenwood, Ian Griffiths, David Hatton, Jack Jarman, Terry Halstead, John and Elizabeth Hodgson, Joe Jennings, Lauren Jeska, Lyndsey Kerr, Dorothy Kershaw, Peter Lever, John McGrath, Phil Morton, Dave Payne, Barrie Pickles, Robert Priestley, Andrew Savage, Ian Smith, Robert Smith, Arthur and Alice Stansfield, Colin and Jean Sutcliffe, Will Sutcliffe, Harry and Joy Tootell.

The following have supplied and allowed us to reproduce their photographs to illustrate the book, or helped in some other way, for which we thank them: Ian Bailey, Marion Bednall, p224; Andy Betteridge (*HC*); Estelle Brown; Sheila Brown; Barry Bruce, p21; Mary Clear; John and Jacqueline Cockcroft, p168; Betty Crabtree, pp196, 197, 200, 210; Margaret Crowther, pp46, 116, 146, 147, 148, 153, 177, 205, 221, 343; Maurice Davies; Paul Dawson p349; Peter Devine, p313; Ian Duffield, pp53, 116, 139, 142; Peter Eastwood, p187; Abigail Fairbank; Mary Findon; David Frith, pp13, 27, 45, 56, 64, 73, 108, 254, 270; John Greenwood (*TN*); John and Helen Greenwood, p98; Maurice Greenwood; the late John Grundy, p291, 293; Bert Hanson, p339; David Hanson (*HC*); Alan Heywood; Jessica Heywood; Nathan Heywood; Alan Hitch, p63; John Hodgson, p172; Stanley Hollows, pp119, 122, 126, 274; Shirley Horsfall, p199; Peggy Horsfield, p159; Edward Lea, p175; Verna and Brian Mitchell, p170, 202; Anne Morris, Violet Noble, pp170, 206; Derek Parker, p88; Barrie Pickles, pp149, 150, 151, 152; Paul Plunkett (*LET*), Robert Priestley, Sarah and Stuart Priestley, p89; Freda Proctor, p204; Keith Raistrick;

Steve Riley; Peter Roberts; Albert Ross; Andrew Savage, p232; Julian Shackleton, pp230, 240; Issy Shannon, p184; Robert Smith, p346; Nigel Stockley, pp79, 330, 341; Jean and Grenville Stretton, pp61, 66, 70, 243, 312; Allan Stuttard, pp10, 18, 59, 94, 103; Andrew Sutcliffe; Anita and Keith Sutcliffe, p108; Ben Sutcliffe; Neville Sutcliffe, pp238, 280, 282, 286, 298, 305, 310, 332, 333, 352; Will Sutcliffe, p164, 175; Abigail Webb, p348; Julia Whelan, p145; Elizabeth Whittaker, pp82, 86, 288, 289; John Wild and Douglas Wilson, pp141, 174.

Other illustrations:
pp 45, 64, 96, *The Book of Cricket*, Denzil Batchelor, The Sportsman's Book Club 1953;
p 77, *Cricket in the Leagues*, John Kay, Eyre & Spottiswoode, London 1970;
p 93 Jul 1982, p104 Aug 1982, p250 Apr 1979, *The Cricketer International*;
p 229 Nov 1981, *Wisden Cricket Monthly*;
p 97, *A Cricket Pro's Lot*, F Root 1987;
p 227, *The Book of Cricket*, Sir Pelham Warner, Sporting Handbooks Ltd 1946;
p 258, *Flying Stumps*, Ray Lindwall, Stanley Paul & Co Ltd 1952;
p 262, *A Typhoon Called Tyson*, F Tyson, Sportsman's Book Club 1962;
p 264, *Happy Go Johnny*, Robert Hale Pub 1957;
p 269, *100 Years of Cricket*, Ammonite Press 2008.

We thank the owners of material listed in the references. Our thanks also go to John Kettley for writing the thoughtful and entertaining Foreword and to Robert Priestley for the artistic and eye-catching end-papers.

We hope that the statistics section will be of interest to many Todmorden families, as it includes the name of every cricketer to represent Todmorden's 1st XI since 1897 when the club first played in the Lancashire League. The membership of the Lancashire League has, incredibly, remained unchanged ever since, its fourteen clubs truly engaging *In a League of Their Own*.

Every effort has been made to contact copyright holders. We apologise for any omissions and may be contacted at Upper Calder Valley Publications.

Foreword to *In a League of Their Own*
by John Kettley

Freda, Brian and Malcolm maintain an insatiable appetite for writing based on their passion for the history of Todmorden together with the people and sporting achievements for which this part of the Calder Valley is rightly proud.

I was drawn to chapter 8 in their previous book 'Cloth Caps and Cricket Crazy' in which they refer to the lack of any organised winter sport in the area despite cricket being already well established by the middle of the 19th century as a summer recreation. In 1864 nearby Littleborough and Rochdale organised a cricket match on a frozen Hollingworth Lake. Such was the popularity of the summer game that even during the bleak mid-winter a cricket match would still prove enormously popular since football and rugby were scarcely considered locally as competitive pastimes. Unsurprisingly I was very interested to learn of the severe cold that year which clearly allowed such an event to be played. It was with some amazement that driving past the same Hollingworth Lake in late December 2010 it was again frozen in many places although I doubt that 'Health and Safety' would allow a repeat almost one hundred and fifty years later!

Todmorden officially joined the Lancashire Cricket League in 1897 but almost inevitably the weather played a big part in their early days, in fact the first match against East Lancs on 17th April was a complete washout. Seven days later they travelled to Rishton where they were trounced, bowled out for 36, but again the weather conditions were intolerably wet for batting so I blame nature for this inauspicious introduction to the 'big time'. For more than a century I would be the first to admit that many fixtures in the Lancashire League, but particularly at Centre Vale in Todmorden, the weather has often conspired against one team or another. The first season I remember watching cricket was 1961 when Frank Tyson, England and Northants, was employed for £800 as the professional. It was a truly awesome sight seeing one of the fastest bowlers in the world in full swing, even though the damper pitches of the Lancashire League subdued the 'typhoon'. The following season Des Barrick, also from Northants, replaced Tyson but a good season was marred by the bizarre events of the Worsley Cup Final away to Johnny Wardle's Nelson. Rain prevented a conclusion to the match and the trophy was shared by each club for six months. Twelve months later the final again involved Todmorden, this time against Rishton at home but with the same professional in opposition as Johnny Wardle had changed clubs in the winter. I remember being at the match although I refuse to be blamed for the rain interruptions which meant the game drifted over two Sundays and into the Tuesday evening!

Fittingly Todmorden won the match because Wardle always said that 'this was the most attractive ground in the League'.

Some years later I played fairly regularly for the seconds and thirds although my ambitions far outweighed my potential. Due to holiday commitments I was drafted into the first team when Peter Marner, Lancashire and Leicestershire, was the professional. Sadly not a ball was bowled, not a penny taken at the gate - it rained all day and my chosen career was already impinging on my sporting pastimes.

In my own book 'WEATHERMAN' I make constant references to weather events throughout my lifetime and also the great cricketers I did eventually play alongside, including Peter Lever of Lancashire and England who enjoyed two full seasons in the Todmorden first team in 1958-59.

It was a great honour when in 2000 I was asked by BBC Television to return to my home area and record a piece for 'Songs of Praise'. The programme would be shown on Mothers' Day but it was still mid-winter when I walked in the shadow of Stoodley Pike above Mankinholes with snow on the ground and a bitter wind whistling across the fields. Yes I was home, and the weather was as unkind as I always remembered it, but there was also warmth in the town and the people. During the interview with Kevin Woodford I recalled the character of the Todmorden community – their pride and resolution but also their stubborn nature when they fight for what was is right and proper. The John Fielden doctrine lives on and with it the will to succeed, whatever the elements or even the rest of Britain throws at them.

In this skilfully produced book the authors have encapsulated many of the characteristics for which 'Tod' folk are renowned. Their quest to be the best and their determination to build a cricket club to be proud of are catalogued in great detail decade by decade. Similar fortitude is written about in other sporting activities and social topics over the same period, including football, music and drama. There is also a mention of the competitive art of 'knur and spell', a Pennine pastime probably dating back to the 14th century which is now rarely seen and remains a non-Olympic sport!

Coming up to date Todmorden remains a focus for walkers, harriers and anglers but has also been seen on several television programmes under the banner 'Incredible Edible Todmorden'. So, despite the obvious drawbacks of the West Yorkshire weather from time to time it is now recognised as a leading centre for growing your own food, and long may it continue.

Todmorden was the start of a journey for me having lived, studied and enjoyed playing sport in the town but despite its geographical position at the head of the Calder Valley it will never be the 'end of the line'. There will always be stories to tell to match the anecdotes and documentary evidence included in this book. It serves as a fascinating account of the sporting and cultural life of Todmorden in the 20th century and I am proud to have been a small cog in the family of its inhabitants.

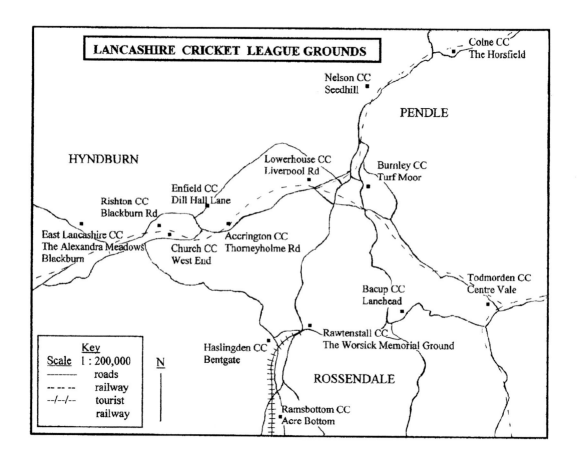

LANCASHIRE CRICKET LEAGUE GROUNDS

Colne CC
The Horsfield

Nelson CC
Seedhill

PENDLE

HYNDBURN

Lowerhouse CC
Liverpool Rd

Burnley CC
Turf Moor

Enfield CC
Dill Hall Lane

Rishton CC
Blackburn Rd

East Lancashire CC
The Alexandra Meadows
Blackburn

Accrington CC
Church CC   Thorneyholme Rd
West End

Todmorden CC
Centre Vale

Bacup CC
Lanehead

Rawtenstall CC
The Worsick Memorial Ground

Key
Scale 1 : 200,000   N
------   roads
-- -- --   railway
--/--/--   tourist
          railway

Haslingden CC
Bentgate

ROSSENDALE

Ramsbottom CC
Acre Bottom

Chapter 1

In a League of Their Own

The Lancashire Cricket League holds a world record for longevity. Since Todmorden rejoined in 1897, the same fourteen clubs have competed unchanged to the present day, only a two-year suspension during World War I breaking the sequence.

In 1897 Todmorden was a town of 26,000 inhabitants, basking in the pride of achieving borough status and their cricket team's success as 1896 Champions of the Central Lancashire League. Todmorden's first season in the Lancashire League was eagerly anticipated and speculation focused fiercely on the team's prospects. Competition 'of very superior character to any included in the Central Lancashire League' was predicted, and Todmorden's standing as a Yorkshire club and Central Lancashire League champions was expected to intensify competition.

This was the second time Todmorden had joined the Lancashire League, but the first time they would play in it. This is borne of the club's reluctance to join the stampede to form leagues in the early 1890s. In October 1890 they were founder members of the Lancashire League (initially known as the North East Lancashire Cricket League), only to resign in February 1891 before a game had been played.

At that time Todmorden was happy with its enviable list of challenge matches, as club matches were called before leagues became the vogue. The town's position on the Lancashire/Yorkshire border allowed a unique combination of opportunities and the club's 1891 programme ran to 39 matches, including trips to play Manchester at Old Trafford, Bradford at Park Avenue and Leeds at Headingley, all just a train journey away along valleys which converge at the town's centre. During that summer, however, it became clear that challenge match opponents would be increasingly unavailable as their league fixtures took priority. Threatened with isolation, Todmorden had little choice but to join the league cricket bandwagon. In late summer 1891 they became founder members of the South East Lancashire Cricket League along the Rochdale valley to the south west, which in 1893 was renamed the Central Lancashire Cricket League (CLL).

Ironically, Todmorden's initial reticence about league cricket has given the club unique status as a founder member of the two leagues which - using annual coverage in *Wisden* as an authoritative benchmark - became cricket's most famous of the 20th century.

As the new South East Lancashire League (CLL) had only nine clubs giving a programme of 16 matches, Todmorden briefly had the best of both worlds, being able to retain a decent number of challenge matches. After a complacent first season, Todmorden enjoyed considerable success, finishing as runners-up to Rochdale in 1893, 94 and 95. These two clubs enjoyed an almost unhealthy dominance, and the Todmorden supporters began to eye the stiffer competition in the Lancashire League.

On 4 March 1896 the Todmorden committee applied to join the Lancashire League for the 1897 season and the club was formally accepted at the next League meeting, effectively filling the vacancy left by Bury's resignation in 1894.

So Todmorden began the 1896 season knowing it would be their last in the Central Lancashire League. For the first time, the club was able to field its best players of the

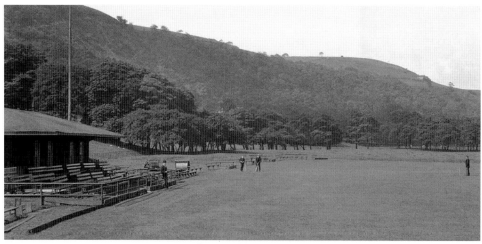

Centre Vale c1900
The ground is virtually a continuation of the Centre Vale Estate.

era in the same team. Four former club professionals (pros), Fred Blakey, Jonas Clegg junior, Johnny Horsfall and John Crabtree, formed a powerful nucleus backing two highly effective and complementary professionals. These were pace bowler William Wilkinson and left-arm spin-bowling all-rounder William Finney, ex-county professionals with Nottinghamshire and Leicestershire respectively. Todmorden swept all before them. On 22 August the town celebrated becoming an independent borough and the Charter Day procession was gilded with the Central Lancashire League trophy, won with an ease that inspired great optimism about the club's prospects in the Lancashire League. The popularity of cricket in Todmorden, as reflected in a commemorative booklet to celebrate the successful team, had reached a new height.

By mid-June 1896, with the title virtually assured, the two professionals were re-signed 'at their present terms'. Both Finney, at £3 5s, and Wilkinson, at £3 per week, earned more pro-rata than their team mate John Crabtree, headmaster of Roomfield Senior School Boys' Department and paid an annual salary of £130, or £2 10s, per week.

The professional cricketers' financial situation was nevertheless precarious, dependent on finding employment outside the 22 week season and on their physical well-being. For Finney there were tough times ahead. Around New Year 1897 he suffered a serious leg injury and later that month two club officials visited him in Leicester Infirmary. The surgeon confirmed that Finney would be unable to play in the coming season. The talented all-rounder had played his last match for Todmorden.

Finney's request that Todmorden 'would do something for him as benefit or some other way' indicated his plight and a collection for him at an early season match at home to Haslingden raised £8 15s. Finney had recovered sufficiently to attend the home match against Rishton on August Bank Holiday weekend when a second collection raised £10 11s 9d. The club made the combined collections up to £20, around 30% of the salary Finney would have received for playing the full season. Fortunately Finney was able to resume his career and returned north in 1900 as professional for Great Harwood.

A replacement was recommended by the fearsome Leicestershire fast bowler Arthur Woodcock, who had played in Finney's testimonial match at Todmorden in 1895. Secretary JT Postlethwaite travelled to Darlington to interview Edward Hall. An

Todmorden 1st XI 1897
L-R Row 3 (back): JW Crabtree, E Halliwell, J Horsfall, E Hall (pro),
Row 2 (middle): S Hudson, F Helliwell, J Clegg, F Blakey, W Sutcliffe,
Row 1 (front): W Wilkinson (pro), F Taylor

attacking batsman and right-arm fast bowler, Hall had recently returned to England from America. He had emigrated to Canada in 1880 and played with the Toronto club before succeeding Woodcock as coach to Haverford College in the USA. Postlethwaite secured Hall's signature for £2 15s per week.

At the Centre Vale ground everything was in place for the opening match against East Lancashire on Saturday 17 April - and it rained! The match was abandoned, and Todmorden's Lancashire League debut was delayed until they took the field at Rishton seven days later. The home attack was spearheaded by their 23 year-old professional, the great SF Barnes. For a League characterised, probably like no other in any sport, by the contest of local amateur against world-class international, this was indeed an appropriate beginning.

> More than six feet tall with high, wide, rugged shoulders, deep chest, long arms and strong legs, he was perfectly built to be a bowler...he made himself into a right-arm fast-medium bowler. ....He himself is content that he was essentially a spin bowler, that his movement through the air was, in modern technical language, swerve – obtained by spin - rather than 'swing', which derives from the 'seam-up' method. Certainly he made the ball move both ways through the air, and...he bowled both the off-break and the leg-break.[1]

When Barnes, at the age of 56, was playing for Wales, Bill Bowes, Yorkshire and future England fast bowler, was with the opposing MCC team. The two met for the first time and Bowes later wrote:

> I remember wondering who the old man was... My wondering increased as he slowly prepared for action. Ankle straps, knee bandages, a thigh bandage, a wrist strap, a body belt - good heavens! (I thought) was there no end to the paraphernalia?...Very soon, when I discovered who he was, I regarded him with greater veneration, well merited by the unforgettable bowling treat that he gave me. He had a beautiful length, varied his speed, bowled a leg-break and off-break and had the MCC scratching about like a lot of old hens.[2]

No respecter of authority, Barnes' county and international appearances punctuated a career spent mainly playing league cricket, which paid better. In the Lancashire League, Burnley, Church and Rawtenstall, where he bowed out in 1933 at the age of 60, all benefited from his services.

Rishton's combination of Barnes (6 for 13) and his fellow professional Daff Whittaker (3 for 14) was far too much for Todmorden and, batting in poor light on a wet and deteriorating pitch, they were bowled out for 36 in reply to Rishton's 118, a 'miserable exhibition' which 'came as a great surprise'.[3]

Edward Hall,
TCC pro 1897

Exciting home wins in May, by 5 runs against Lowerhouse, 177 to 172, and by one wicket against Haslingden chasing 188, boosted morale. Thus encouraged, the club arranged cheap tickets with the railway company for the remaining away matches, supporters to travel either with the players or by any train between 1pm and 2.15pm.

This involved some convoluted routes, and the metaphorical wheels came off on the 40 mile round trip to Rawtenstall, only seven miles away, on 7 July. Having arrived at Rochdale on time, the connection to Bury was late, causing them to miss the train from Bury to Rawtenstall. A later train took them as far as Ramsbottom, from where the team hailed a horse-drawn wagonette and arrived in Rawtenstall 45 minutes after the scheduled start. What the supporters did is not recorded, but those who made it were amply rewarded, first by controversy as Jonas Clegg junior 'protested very strongly' when given out caught behind, then by some brilliant batting as Edward Hall hit Todmorden's first Lancashire League century. Scoring 'at a phenomenal rate', Hall struck an unbeaten 103 out of 268 for 7 declared, Rawtenstall replying with 170 for 7. The train journey home was made via branch lines to Bacup and Rochdale which were closed in the 1950s.

Todmorden's first amateur century in the Lancashire League came seven days later, John Crabtree hitting 119 not out as Todmorden passed Bacup's 156 all out without loss. The game continued to allow Johnny Horsfall to complete his half century, extending the partnership to 179, a club and League record which remained until Crabtree (89) and Jim Crossley (143) added 184 for the first wicket at Colne in 1900. Interest in

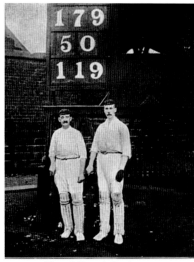

Horsfall and Crabtree:
record opening partnership of 179

cricket was never higher according to the *Todmorden Advertiser* of 4 June 1897, and on Saturday evenings excited crowds awaited the results of away matches which were communicated by telegram, known as 'the wire', and posted in Mr Wolfenden's shop window on North Street. In August 1900 supporters were in 'high glee' as the wires read 'Todmorden 117, Ratcliff 58, Accrington 18 for six wickets'.

> This meant a draw greatly in their favour - a sort of moral victory. It was discussed with evident delight, the only question being - who could have bowled so well? Judge the disappointment and changed expression when the players returned home later in the evening. They were congratulated on their splendid bid for victory. At first the players took it as so much sarcasm, but they saw that whilst the congratulations might be well meant, they were based on a false report...the telegrams should have read 'Accrington 118 not 18'. Many people are still unconvinced it was not a hoax of some of the players or post office officials.[4]

Being associated with the team's successes was good for trade, particularly in the local hostelries. The proprietors of the York Hotel, Mr and Mrs Singleton awarded a gold medal for the batsman with the highest average, won in 1897 by veteran batsman Jonas Clegg junior. They also promised to entertain the team to dinner if they won the League, but were not called upon to honour this as Todmorden finished a disappointing eleventh with 5 wins and 8 defeats from their 26 matches.

In contrast to the first team, the 2nd XI followed their Central Lancashire Junior League titles of 1894, 95 and 96 with further success. The Lancashire League's 2nd XIs played in two sections at this time and Todmorden, winning their's with ease, met the other section winners, Burnley, in the final. Walter Leslie Greenwood, whose forte was medium-pace bowling, hit 63 out of Todmorden's 213 all out before Arthur Girling took six wickets to rout Burnley for 105. In recognition of their four consecutive titles, Lancashire League President and founder, James Sutcliffe, presented the 2nd XI with gold medals at the club's annual dinner.

The 2nd XI's successes continued. They won their section in four of the next five seasons and the final against the winners of the parallel section, Rawtenstall in 1899 and Enfield in 1902. The latter triumph was celebrated in style. The team and supporters visited the Load of Mischief - a favourite watering hole close to Enfield's Dill Hall Lane ground - for tea and speeches. Afterwards they displayed the cup on a wagonette, pulled by four Belgian horses to Accrington, where they boarded the Todmorden train. Alighting at Stansfield Hall station, since demolished, they were greeted by a huge crowd and the Todmorden Brass Band, which led the team's wagonette on a parade of the town, terminating at the White Hart Inn.

President of the local Calder Valley League, Jeremiah Crossley, painted a vivid picture of the occasion in his speech at the following week's Calder Valley Cup final between Hebden Bridge Liberals and Mytholmroyd St Michaels, played at Centre Vale:

> When the Bill for closing all textile industries at twelve o'clock on Saturdays was before the House of Commons, Mr Ritchie [Home Secretary in Lord Salisbury's government 1900-02]...somewhat facetiously spoke of it as the 'football stop'. Of course, when he made that remark he could not have been thinking of Todmorden...because if there was one thing...that laid hold of Todmorden, it was not football but cricket. They had proof of that the previous week. They would not soon forget the triumphal procession, the enthusiastic welcome given to our lads on the previous Saturday night, as they drove through the town holding aloft the trophy they had so honourably won, and the thousands of people that lined the streets, and, with feelings of pride, responded in chorus to the strains of music, *See the Conquering Hero Comes*. The fact was that

cricket...had come to play a large part in the summer pastimes of the young life of the English nation.[5]

Todmorden's depth of talent owed much to the Calder Valley Cricket League, which included teams from just about every small community around Todmorden and Hebden Bridge in the upper Calder Valley. Usually rooted in a Sunday school or factory, many of their grounds were rough fields on the moors with a few, such as Eastwood, Harley Wood and Cornholme, in the valley bottom. Most of these teams had 2nd XIs who played in the Todmorden and District League and the Hebden Bridge League, so that the area had, in effect, a primitive pyramid structure, with Todmorden and Walsden (a member of the Central Lancashire League from 1893) at the top, creaming off the best talent.

Unlike the ECB's proposed pyramid imposition of the 1990s, the local district league structure evolved from vast numbers who were inspired to play. In an age when life was experienced almost exclusively within the town, watching top tier club cricket at Todmorden and Walsden helped to fire enthusiasm, and in 1896 there were 47 teams playing between Todmorden and Mytholmroyd, six miles into Yorkshire.

Both Walter Leslie Greenwood, who played for Todmorden Church, and Arthur Girling who played for Cornholme and Harley Wood came to Todmorden via the Calder Valley League. A popular fast bowler, Girling enjoyed a prolific 1897 in the 2nd XI, including a best of 8 wickets for 7 against Accrington 2nd XI. This won him the *Sunday Chronicle*'s weekly bowling prize, the illustrated book of *Famous Cricketers and Cricket Grounds*, one of a spate of cricket books published at this time. League cricket's impact on the national press, in addition to the comprehensive reports of local papers, reflected and encouraged interest, the game benefiting from an increasing number of people who could read, following the introduction of compulsory free schooling by the 1870 and subsequent Education Acts.

In 1898 Arthur Girling was appointed, from 44 applicants, as professional and groundsman at Batley Cricket Club. He moved on to Cheetham Hill, Padiham and Allerton, where he played against Shelf in the Bradford League's first Priestley Cup final in 1904. The following year he began a long association as professional and groundsman at Skipton in the Airedale and Wharfedale League.

Girling's failure to break into the 1st XI at Todmorden can be explained by a number of factors. The presence of two professionals, both of whom bowled, limited opportunities for the amateurs. Fred Blakey, a former professional, was also an established bowler, taking 66 Lancashire League wickets in 1897. Unforced team changes were rare as selection almost mirrored the rigid English class system. Being a regular member of the first or second team was a gauge of a player's cricketing class and Todmorden's championship winners of 1896, for the time being, had almost unquestioned 1st XI status.

The youngest member of that side, batting all-rounder Frank Taylor, was another product of the Calder Valley League. In 1897, less than a year after joining Todmorden, he was selected for Yorkshire Colts - effectively the county's 2nd XI. A string of consistent scores, achieved with a style 'very highly spoken of in the Yorkshire papers', failed to win him a place in the 1st XI and his county hopes appeared distant when, scoring only 21 runs in his first seven innings of 1898, he suffered the indignity of demotion to Todmorden's 2nd XI. Pitches were very wet, everyone was struggling for runs - Todmorden were bowled out for less than 90 in five of the first six matches - and Taylor took his demotion badly. He immediately moved to Walsden and, with weather and pitches improving, hit an unbeaten 82 against Padiham on debut. He briefly returned to Todmorden in August but a month later signed as one of Walsden's paid men for 1899 to begin a career as a club professional.

Professionals were the burning issue in the Lancashire League. Speaking at Todmorden's annual dinner in 1897, James Sutcliffe was convinced that league cricket had created greater interest, encouraging clubs to improve their grounds and players to strive for victory. It had never been anticipated, however, that wages of professionals would rise so rapidly, and 'some check would have to be put on it'. He added that well established professionals were 'not so easy to deal with as the rising professionals'.[6]

A 'Reasonable Athletic' voiced an increasing complaint that professionals were contributing little apart from playing matches, 'the remainder of their time being, for the most part, passed in a lounging manner at the pubs'.

Interviewed in the *Todmorden Herald* in May 1900, Todmorden's Johnny Horsfall recalled proing at Barnsley in the early 1880s for 50 shillings a week plus a £15 benefit, 'a grand income...reckoned to be good pay at the time'. It was, though, paltry compared to the £6 - £7 per week paid to some professionals by the end of the century, which he regarded as 'all right if funds will allow it, for people...believe in paying a good price for a good man'.[7]

But funds could not sustain two professionals at these rates. In December 1897 Todmorden's League representative, Edward Crabtree, later Lancashire League President from 1921-46, suggested either restricting the amount paid to professionals or reducing the professionals from two to one per club. The latter idea culminated in a majority vote, in April 1899, to allow only one professional from the start of the 1900 season. The Central Lancashire League faced similar issues and in 1899 allowed clubs to have one or two professionals, clubs with one having the option of engaging a second when playing those with two.

Controlling professionalism remains one of the Lancashire League's aims and a perennial topic of discussion, generally over costs rather than as a matter of principle. The reduction to one professional was partly in response to a genuine concern about limited opportunities for amateurs, particularly in bowling, but mainly because two salaries were a burden on clubs' limited financial resources.

The decision was timely as 1900 brought a downturn in manufacturing that affected many organisations and societies. The Todmorden Musical Society, for example, reported a £50-£60 shortfall, and at their Annual General Meeting (AGM) Edward Crabtree saw clear parallels between music and cricket.

> The financial condition of the society was...discussed with the utmost care and minuteness. Edward Crabtree, whom we have not seen at a gathering of this kind for many years, being most conspicuous by his anxiety to effect economy...the payments of the professional artistes were scrutinised and analysed.[8]

The Musical Society Chairman was John E Craven, a former cricketer, and his calculated optimism was an effective foil for Crabtree's caution. He pointed out that the town's other societies - of which the cricket club was one - had also suffered, and he was confident the economic circumstances were only temporary.

The roles of both men at this meeting - Crabtree meticulous, earnest and practical, Craven dignified, shrewd and calming - are absolutely consistent with their contributions to cricket club affairs over many years.

The cricket club, meanwhile, had turned a credit balance of £116 in 1897 to a deficit of £130 in the atrocious weather of 1898 and the club remained in the red until 1908. The reduction to one professional made little impact as their costs spiralled. Two professionals plus a groundsman cost £155 in 1897, £201 by 1899, briefly dropped to

£148 with only one professional in 1900, but rose to £170 by 1903 - £15 more than the 1897 figure with one professional fewer.

Meanwhile members' subscriptions remained constant at around £140 but gates dwindled from £371 in 1897, to £227 in 1899 and only £195 by 1905. Finances were almost exclusively dependent on these two sources of income, so that the weather and the form of the team were crucial to solvency. Genuine supporters, then as now, had two basic emotional requirements of their team - 'make me happy and make me proud' - achieved partly by the manner of performance but primarily and often overwhelmingly by winning. After three consecutive defeats in mid-1897, the *Todmorden Advertiser* commented, 'Todmorden [supporters] like to see their team win and some will not go if they think the visitors will win'. In April 1901 the *Todmorden Herald* concurred: 'Points mean money and money means the prosperity of the club'. Todmorden, unfortunately, were dogged by inconsistency. In their first 16 seasons in the Lancashire League they finished no higher than fourth and no lower than eleventh, sitting between seventh and eleventh twelve times. Given this mediocre record, the team was top or bottom of the league in mid-season a surprising number of times, only to fall away or recover to a mid-table position. At no point did the club's finances benefit from a sustained title challenge.

Timely donations from Sarah Fielden of Centre Vale Mansion, widow of the club's founder, Sam, encouraged development of the ground and over two winters, 1898-1900, WH Wall, the club's professional in 1879, was employed to re-lay the south-west corner in front of the current car park.[9] The appointment of experienced Joshua Wadsworth as groundsman in April 1901 met with the approval of the *Todmorden Herald*.

> I hear that he has already made a stand against the liberty members take of travelling across the ground to and fro...Why not compel all to travel outside the limits of the playing area, and also forbid that stupid practice...after the conclusion of the first innings of people rushing up to the crease...trying to look wise, and posing as experts in their arguments as to the suitability of the ground for this bowler or that, when, in fact, they are quite ignorant on the subject...hundreds of spectators...have the strongest objection to this practice.[10]

The local constable had apparently failed in at least part of his 1900 remit to:

> ...preserve order and remove disorderly persons from the ground; to keep spectators on the National School side from encroaching on the ground between innings; to keep the wall clear on the road side and prevent boys from coming down the ridge onto the field.[10]

William Oakley, a Shrewsbury-born left-arm medium-paced bowler - who had played for Shropshire and in 1893-94 for Lancashire - created a good impression in a trial match against the Central Lancashire League XI in 1897, and was engaged in partnership with Oliver Griffin, a right-arm medium-paced bowler from Lancaster for 1898. Oakley was retained for 1899 and was joined by TO Thomas from Hereford. Given a net trial at the club, Thomas was described as a fast right-hand bowler with his arm going right over the shoulder in delivering the ball, a tacit acknowledgement that round-arm bowling was still practised. It was Thomas's first professional post and, as an unknown quantity, he was paid £60 to Oakley's £103. Thomas was not a success but returned to the League in 1903 with Rawtenstall, who finished bottom that year.

With the Lancashire League limiting clubs to one professional in 1900, Todmorden had decided by June 1899 not to re-engage either Oakley or Thomas. One contender for the position was Bacup professional Sam Moss. Reputedly the fastest bowler in

William Oakley, TCC pro 1898-99

Oliver Griffin,
TCC pro 1898

England and 'head and shoulders above every bowler in the league', he bowled Bacup to the Lancashire League title in 1899 and confirmed his class when, as substitute professional for Barnsley, he took all ten Huddersfield wickets, including nine clean bowled. Unfortunately for Moss, dubious bowling actions were a hot topic and he had one. Lancashire, whose former England paceman Arthur Mold was at the forefront of the latest 'throwing' controversy, would not countenance further trouble and rejected Moss. Todmorden took a similar view…

> …he missed the appointment at Todmorden by a narrow shave…he was in the habit of 'cobbing' the ball…for that reason Todmorden would have none of him.[11]

But for some Todmorden supporters, the chance of signing a League-winning bowler had been squandered, a view reinforced by Todmorden's visit to Bacup on 17 June 1899. 'Aw tell thee 'at he cobs 'em eawt, he doesn't bowl 'em,' said one indignant Todmordian, as Moss (6 for 31) skittled Todmorden for 67. 'That's reight enuff', said his mate, 's' long as he's doing it for Bacup; but aw wish we had him for Todmorden, cobbing or no cobbing.'

At the tea interval it was thought that:

> …Bacup had so easy a thing on that the betting chaps could do no business at any price…But wait a bit. Bacup started badly…the betting men suddenly became dumb…51 for 9…It was now a hundred to one in favour of 'Tormden'…Hargreaves came out with his heart in his mouth no doubt. Thousands of eyes were upon him. He had to get possession of his nerves…and he found them by striking his first ball to the boundary for four. Hats and caps went into the air! Hargreaves never tried to play the balls; he just struck at them wildly, madly, and after every stroke there came runs, amid the lusty plaudits of his supporters…he succeeded in slogging off the required runs in a few minutes. There never was such fun on the Bacup ground - from a Bacup point of view it was the finest termination of a match ever known. Hargreaves fairly plucked the game from the fire, and was carried shoulder high from the pitch.

Sam Moss, fast bowling pro at
Haslingden 1896-97; Bacup 1898-1900

From a Todmorden point of view they had
been beaten by the professional they were
refusing to sign and a 'slogging novice'.[12]

Moss re-signed for Bacup where he took 143
wickets in 1900, a club record which still
stands. If not Moss, it seems the Todmorden
supporters wanted to retain Oakley and in late
July, the *Hebden Bridge Times and Calder Vale
Gazette* reported: 'almost everyone is now
wishing Oakley had been re-engaged'.

The committee was under heavy fire, even
after signing the admirable Creighton. This was
Ernest Creighton, a model club professional
who had played at Todmorden from 1888-91
and in 1894, taking over 700 wickets with
canny left-arm spin. He was celebrated in verse
by the local press:

T'were better to wait on
A bowler like Creigh - ton
Than run out of your ground and get stumped

Of the 564 wickets he took in his first spell at
the club, Old Ebor, the journalistic sage of Yorkshire cricket, wrote:

I should think it would be very difficult to find a record for four consecutive years in
really good club cricket to equal this.[13]

Nevertheless, the punters were not happy.

Todmorden cricket followers have been affecting to be grieved because Creighton has
been chosen as...next year's pro, and have carried it so far as to withdraw their support
from the club.[14]

Creighton was professional at Ramsbottom in 1899 and Todmorden's visit there on
5 August had taken on extra significance. The committee must have had mixed feelings
when Oakley (6 for 38) bowled the home side out for 94. Creighton responded with 7
for 31, veterans Horsfall and Blakey 'the only ones who could tackle his deliveries', as
Todmorden were bowled out for 63.

Creighton gave practical and most emphatic reply to his Todmorden critics on
Saturday...he took seven of the Todmorden wickets, and virtually won the game for
his side. Creighton has won many a triumph in bowling; but he has never achieved
anything more timely than this.[15]

The affection for Oakley, who signed for Scarborough at the end of the season,
cannot entirely be explained by his competent match performances. A dedicated and
helpful coach, and an engaging personality in the town's public houses, his popularity
in Todmorden was confirmed when he returned as a substitute professional for
Rawtenstall in May 1901 and 'received a hearty welcome from his many friends'.[16]

This contrasts sharply with the 'abuse' that Creighton received from a section of
supporters on his return to the club in April 1900.[17] To his credit, he quickly appeased
his critics with 8 for 19 to bowl Church out for 49 in the opening match, and took 26

wickets in the first four matches, although only two of these were won. 'Now, you grumblers, tell me who can beat that!' demanded the *Todmorden Herald*.[18]

Conditions were not always so conducive to Creighton's bowling and at Nelson in May he:

> got 'whopped'…the ground was in fine condition for scoring, being as hard as iron…and he was not able to get much 'spin' on the ball[19]

The signing of Creighton quickly highlighted the need for a good wicketkeeper and as early as 9 May the *Todmorden Herald* commented:

> I am rather afraid Mitchell is not quite good enough behind the stumps…I have not the slightest doubt that if Hudson could be prevailed upon to once more don the gloves he would make a good substitute…I do not know why he does not as he is at present acting as such for the Todmorden Church CC…it is far more dangerous to act as stumper on these rough [Calder Valley League] grounds than…at Todmorden, where the balls can be relied upon to come true from the pitch.

JW Mitchell, an excellent all-round sportsman, who played professional rugby for Halifax, coped well with medium-pace, but his reliance on natural ability rather than technique was exposed when standing up to Creighton, and by August he had been replaced by Sydney Hudson, returning to the club where he had kept in 1897 and 98. This began a long family association with the club. The Hudsons - Sydney until 1905, followed by his son Harry - kept wicket for the 1st XI for the next 25 years.

Creighton's 108 wickets in 1900 could not compensate for the team's indifferent batting and Todmorden finished eighth. They did, though, have the chance to influence the destination of the championship in a potentially explosive final home match against title-chasing Haslingden. The visitors arrived on the back of controversy in their match at Nelson. Haslingden's professional Jack Usher had been fined £10 by the League for attempting to bribe Harry Riley the Nelson professional to do them 'a good turn' in the advent of a close finish. Angry recriminations escalated into scuffles between rival supporters in which the Nelson captain was injured, and Haslingden completed a five wicket victory against ten men.

These incidents were 'much alluded to' at Todmorden, but Usher was a popular professional and the match, for which several special trains travelled from Haslingden, passed without incident. Usher, who bowled slow left-arm spin, took 8 for 23 on his way to a season's tally of 143 wickets, a Lancashire League record, equalled by Sam Moss, which stood until 1964. Haslingden had won by 4.30pm, much to the delight of Todmorden Rugby Football Club which had delayed its kick-off until 5.00pm in the hope that supporters could attend both games. Todmorden cricketer and rugby half-back Johnny Ratcliff joined the crowd in dashing up Burnley Road to the Holme Field and scored a brilliant try as Todmorden beat Otley 16-0. Commenting on the Usher incident, the *Hebden Bridge Times and Calder Vale Gazette* opined:

> We are rather afraid that the tension in the Lancashire League is becoming too keen for the good of the game - too often cricket is sacrificed for points.

But for Haslingden, the points produced a considerable prize. They tied at the top of the League with Church, and the play-off at Accrington, which they won by 116 runs, attracted a crowd of 10,000 over the two days, enabling them to clear a crippling £200 debt.[20]

A further 96 wickets in 1901 took Creighton's Todmorden tally to 913, still over 200 more than anyone else has ever taken for the club. Towards the end of 1901 Lord

Hawke, with whom Creighton had played his handful of games for Yorkshire in 1888, used his influence to obtain a coaching position for the left-arm spinner in South Africa for the winter.

> Now that it is nearing the end of the season, and Creighton is about to leave...many cricket followers believe that a good man is being lost.[21]

Todmorden had replaced the traditional benefit match with a slight increase in Creighton's salary for 1901. This move was supported by many people who, during a downturn in trade, could not 'see where their obligation comes in, being called upon to support a player whose wages far exceed their own'. Creighton, however, had won people over to such a degree that the committee opened a testimonial fund for him and, at a farewell evening at the White Hart Hotel, John E Craven presented him with a 20 guinea gold watch, commenting:

> No professional cricketer who ever came to Todmorden gave more satisfaction regarding his deportment, private life and exertions on the field...he always did his best to win matches honourably.

The Reverend WA Fox and 1st XI captain John Crabtree testified to Creighton's 'irreproachable character and manly influence both on the cricket field and in the street'. Extremely moved by the compliments from the friends and colleagues he was leaving behind, Creighton thanked them but was 'unable to say more owing to his pent-up feelings'.

Creighton returned to Todmorden in June 1902 as substitute professional for Burnley and received a 'hearty welcome', and was once more resident in the town in 1906 and 07 as professional for Walsden.

After three seasons with only one professional, some Lancashire League clubs were prepared to go further and in September 1902 Burnley and Haslingden proposed having no professional after 1903. Burnley's League representative complained that:

> This Saturday professional business is simply killing off the object of the League 'to

Horse-Drawn Mower
The horse, with leather shoes, appears in TCC records from the 1880s to the 1920s.

foster and develop amateur talent'.

Professionals' wages had risen whilst their contribution to coaching and practice had declined, and he advocated clubs replacing them with two 'tutors' (coaches). Whilst the proposals had merit, they were also motivated by Burnley's dire financial circumstances. Todmorden had been similarly forthright in proposing all-amateur cricket in the pre-league days of 1870, when a flood left the club financially stricken and it was compelled to struggle through the next three seasons without a professional against clubs which employed one or more.

By 1902 Todmorden had changed their tune and, like most other Lancashire League clubs, rejected the Burnley proposal. Todmorden, although in debt, were coping financially and professionals such as Oakley and Creighton had contributed a great deal in coaching.

Burnley, meanwhile, had been grateful to receive a cheque of £100 from Lancashire CCC in October 1901 …

> …as a contribution towards the reduction of the debt on the club. The gift is an acknowledgement of the consideration shown by the Burnley Committee in releasing SF Barnes, who has gone to Australia [with MacLaren's England team], from his engagement to play with Burnley next season in order that he might regularly assist the county.

MacLaren, it would seem, found Barnes a handful. Towards the end of the tour as the team was crossing to New Zealand a storm arose. The boat was tossed about and as they feared for their lives MacLaren exclaimed, 'Well there's one consolation. If we go down that bugger Barnes will go down with us'.[22]

In June 1901 SF Barnes had featured in one of the Lancashire League's most extraordinary finishes when Todmorden, then bottom of the table, visited unbeaten Burnley, who were third. Burnley were strengthened by former Todmorden professional Edward Hall, now playing as an amateur. He had moved to Burnley in 1899 to establish a 'cricket and sports' outfitters' with the Burnley professional at that time Thomas Nicholson. Although the business failed, he continued to live in the town.

Chasing Burnley's 147 all out in two hours, Todmorden were well on course at 80 for 1 with an hour to play. But despite some brilliant stroke play by Johnny Ratcliff, Todmorden could barely maintain the required rate as Barnes reduced them to 124 for 6. Ratcliff, cleverly fed the strike by

SF Barnes, pro at Rishton 1895-99; Burnley 1900-01; Church 1904-05; Rawtenstall 1931-33

Creighton, took Todmorden to the brink of victory at 144 for 6, but with the clock approaching the 7pm closure the professional, attempting the winning hit, was caught from Barnes's final delivery. Walter Leslie Greenwood ran to the middle and scrambled a single off the second ball of what was sure to be the last over, bowled by Hall. Ratcliff was facing, three runs needed, when:

> …the umpire notified that time would be up with the delivery of the next ball - the third of the over. Thereupon Hall deliberately sent a wide…far out of the batsman's reach…the batsman never got within yards of the ball.

To Todmorden's dismay, the stumps were uprooted; the illegal delivery would not be re-bowled. Mayhem ensued and as the players returned to the pavilion:

> ...Hall was surrounded by a threatening crowd.
>
> The wildest excitement prevailed...one of Todmorden's supporters, having said something of an uncomplimentary character to one of the Burnley players, the latter evinced a desire to get at close quarters, but was prevented by a colleague.[23]

The *Todmorden Herald* reporter 'once more recalled the old days', referring to the decades of acrimony between the clubs following the Centre Vale riot of 1867, when the Burnley visitors were 'pitched bag and baggage over the low boundary wall which then existed into the turnpike road'. Adopting a concerned and placatory tone, he absolved the Burnley faithful and laid the blame firmly with Hall.

> ...it was very unsportsmanlike...it not only called forth the indignation of the Todmordians present, but of the home people as well.[24]
>
> It is regarded as a very mean and shabby piece of business. Hall was formerly pro at Todmorden, and that he should be capable of such a trick passes comprehension. Todmorden...complain that they were not given a fair sportsman's chance.[25]

As the dust settled, the umpire's interpretation of the rules came under the spotlight.

> The laws of cricket throw no light on the subject. However, to satisfy the desires of their supporters and...lay the facts before the League...Todmorden decided on Monday night to protest against the match. Their grounds of protest raise a novel precedent. They question whether the umpire should call time in the middle of an over - and further, they contend that what the umpire declared to be the last ball could not count, being a wide.[26]

That the rules did not cover such a circumstance seems incredible. Todmorden, for one, had been involved in a similar controversy in a challenge match against Oldham in 1893, the Todmorden umpire uprooting the stumps in mid-over with his side hanging on for a draw, nine wickets down.

The League committee did not change the result of the match, but 'regretted that the umpire did not compel the bowler to finish with a legitimate delivery'.[27] They later 'resolved that an over commenced before the expiration of time must be completed, unless a wicket falls, and that the umpire should announce the last over when it is to commence'.[28]

Hall, meanwhile, was suspended from the return match at Todmorden on 6 July. The 'discreditable incident' at Burnley helped to swell the gate to £47 10s, beating the previous best for 1901 by over £30, 'the one desire in the hearts of Todmorden people...to avenge the unsportsmanlike incident of the first meeting by a glorious victory'. It was an opportune occasion for Willie Stansfield, a medium-fast seam bowler who had come to Todmorden from Eastwood in the Calder Valley League, to produce the performance of his life. His career best 7 for 38 earned a collection of £6 6s - close to a professional's weekly wage - as Burnley were bowled out for 91. Barnes (3 for 36) made Todmorden fight all the way, but Jim Crossley (33) and young William Law (44 not out) secured a four wicket victory. When Law made the winning hit to end Burnley's 14 match unbeaten start to the season 'the pent-up feelings of the crowd were relieved, and the enthusiasm of the homesters was loud and long'.[29]

There were two unfortunate sequels to this incident. In early August Todmorden's home match against Bacup 'ended in uproar', with the visitors hanging on for a draw at 99 for 9.

Centre Vale c1910

> …it wanted six minutes to seven by the Parish Church clock, which is generally taken
> to regulate the cricket time. With the concluding ball of the over an appeal was made
> against one of the Bacup batsmen and immediately the umpires pulled up the wickets
> and the players rushed off the ground.

Most people thought Todmorden had won, many streaming off the ground 'shouting
with glee'. But the umpires had declared time up and the match drawn and when this
became known:

> …passion was roused and a crowd gathered in front of the pavilion, crying loudly that
> time had not expired.[30]
> …the spectators 'went for' the umpire - a Burnley man - whom they singled out as the
> cause of the mischief, and he had a lively time…He was hooted by the crowd who
> followed him down the road to the railway station, but the presence of two policemen
> prevented any violence.[31]

By June 1902 Todmorden could be forgiven if they thought the League's umpires
were conspiring against them. This time Todmorden were hanging on for a draw, albeit
quite comfortably at 132 for 7 in reply to East Lancashire's 187 for 8 declared, when
the clock struck seven. But as the game had commenced seven minutes late, 'this time
had to be made up'. Todmorden lost two wickets in the following over, eating
considerably into the seven minutes, and when number eleven Willie Stansfield reached
the middle 'he protested to the umpire that time was up'. The umpire, who had
officiated at Burnley twelve months earlier, insisted that 'the over must be finished',
ignoring the proviso about the fall of a wicket. Almost inevitably, Stansfield was bowled
from the final delivery and 'an indescribable scene followed'. Todmorden immediately
lodged a protest, but again it was to no avail.[32]

By 1900 Todmorden's chance of making an early impact on the Lancashire League
had gone. The 1st XI was growing long in the tooth and when they were bowled out for
40 by Bacup in May - a match which coincided with the standardisation of six ball overs,
replacing the usual five - the *Todmorden Herald* suggested it was time for change.

What a name our cricketers had a few years ago; why it was a name to conjure with, and their fame was known far and near. But alas!...the players who have for a long number of years been the mainstay of the team have completely lost the ability and dexterity...they have had their day and must obey nature's call.[33]

Lobs and Co's weekly column in the *Todmorden Advertiser* three months later was less diplomatic:

The Mayor of Todmorden recommends golf to old and used up cricketers as a means of relaxation and it forcibly applies to certain Todmorden cricketers.

The stalwarts of the 1896 Central Lancashire League winning team were nearing the end and a fortnight after Lobs and Co's cutting comment Johnny Horsfall and Jonas Clegg junior were left out of the team. At the end of the season these two and Fred Blakey all retired from first team cricket. These three former professionals had collectively contributed over 17,000 runs and over 900 wickets to Todmorden's cause since Horsfall's debut in 1871 and the hole they left could not be filled overnight. Horsfall continued to play with considerable success in the second team and Clegg, who became an umpire, briefly and unsuccessfully attempted a comeback in 1903.

Leaving Clegg out of the team was particularly difficult for the committee. The Clegg family's connection with the club went back 50 years and his father, Jonas senior, the club's patriarchal rock, remained 'the life and soul of the cricketing circle'.

It was just over a year since Jonas Clegg junior had played his last major innings for the club - 105 at Rishton against the seemingly ubiquitous SF Barnes.

The committee's pangs at calling time on Jonas junior's career were eased by the success of his benefit match, fittingly against Todmorden's oldest and fiercest rivals, Burnley, on 23 June 1900. Clegg was unable to repeat his feat against Barnes, who bowled him for seven as Todmorden lost by eight wickets, but for once the result was probably secondary.

'No-one is better deserving of a bumper than "Joany"!' proclaimed the *Hebden Bridge Times and Calder Vale Gazette,* and so it transpired. A crowd of 5000 paid £38 1s, which was doubled by subscriptions to a club record benefit of £76 18s 10d. At a special presentation evening Mayor Alderman William Ormerod declared this 'a tangible token of the club's appreciation of Mr Clegg's services to Todmorden cricket'.[34]

Jonas junior, 'the champion hitter', whose 178 at Milnrow in 1896 remains Todmorden's record amateur score, had no regrets about his cavalier, hard-hitting approach to batting. When John E Craven, in his day a most studious batsman, commented that Clegg should have 'cultivated a firmer defence' and at times 'forfeited his particular sense of enjoyment in order to save matches', Jonas riposted that 'nine-tenths of spectators would sooner see the ball knocked over the National School than the "bit of style" which Mr Craven used to have'.

TODMORDEN CRICKET CLUB.

GROUND REGULATIONS

CONDITIONS ON WHICH VISITORS AND MEMBERS ARE ALLOWED ON THE CRICKET GROUND.

1. Disorderly conduct, drunkenness, swearing, bad language, and gambling are forbidden on the ground.

2. Dogs are forbidden to be brought on the ground.

3. Visitors must not interrupt, interfere with, or annoy players, during practice or matches.

4. Obedience must be given to the orders of those in authority on the ground.

5. Every Committee-man, Field Captain, Team Captain, officer or servant of the Club, shall have power to remove or to order the removal of any DISORDERLY or DISOBEDIENT PERSON, or of any TRESPASSER, from the ground.

Visitors and Members are respectfully requested to co-operate with the officers in the maintenance of ORDER, FAIR PLAY, and RESPECTABLE CONDUCT on the ground, and to protect the property of the Club for the general good.

BY ORDER OF THE COMMITTEE.

Ground Rules, late 19th century

Jonas added that 'he should have great pleasure in continuing to play…but…perhaps he was getting too old, and he was quite willing to retire when the committee thought fit. They had some young players coming up and it was pretty near time they tried some of them'.

Long serving committeeman John Lord was delighted that the benefit was sufficient to 'help Jonas on life's road', but as talented vocalists Edward Crabtree and Ernest Creighton brought the happy evening to a close, no one could have anticipated just how traumatic Jonas's journey would be.

Four months after his partially enforced cricketing retirement, on New Year's Day 1901, Jonas's six-month old nephew - also Jonas Clegg - died of inflammation and collapse of the left lung. The following June Jonas's mother died and, within a month, his father, Jonas senior, 'the exceedingly popular father of Todmorden cricket', suffered 'an unexpected seizure…of the nature of a paralytic stroke' and passed away without regaining consciousness, aged 66. Jonas junior's younger

Jonas Clegg junior,
hard-hitting batsman scoring 7021
runs, 1875-1903

brother, Arthur, with whom he lived at Horsfall, was under treatment for heart disease and bronchitis and, on New Year's Eve 1905, collapsed in Halifax Road. He was lifted into a handcart and taken home but breathed his last en route. He was 27. The Clegg family's tragedies are a reminder of the still high mortality rate at the start of the 20th century, when life expectancy was just 46 and one in six children died in their first year.[35]

Amidst these traumas, Todmorden, with the rest of the country, went into deep mourning over the death of Queen Victoria on 22 January 1901. She was the only monarch most people had known, a 'comforting absolute in a period of great and sometimes alarming change'.[36] In local cricketing terms, her reign had covered the development from pastureland knockabout to an organised commercial sport and almost the entire history of Todmorden Cricket Club.

For cricket club members more than most, 1901 had an end of era feel. For the first time in half a century there was no Jonas Clegg in the Todmorden team and the passing of Jonas senior severed the last direct link with those who founded the club in 1835 and re-formed it in 1850. Making his debut in 1851, he enrolled his son as a member within an hour of his birth in 1861, played until 1880 and thereafter served in various official and unofficial capacities. The reporter of the *Todmorden Herald* remembered him as 'one of the men I knew and respected and, in their day, we as lads almost worshipped on the cricket field'.[37]

To the last he was an inspiration to any player who 'caught the genial eye and the encouraging nod…the staunch old supporter will henceforth be sorely missed on the Todmorden ground'.

The *Hebden Bridge Times and Calder Vale Gazette* of 29 June 1900 concurred:

> If there is one cricketing name which is better known than any other in Todmorden, that name is Jonas Clegg.

Chapter 2

Ground Rules

The team's transition was far from smooth following the retirements of Fred Blakey, Johnny Horsfall and Jonas Clegg junior, partly because an economic downturn demanded greater mobility of the workforce so that Todmorden could not establish a settled side. Johnny Ratcliff and Jim Crossley, the first of the next generation of batsmen to emerge, were also the first to leave.

In 1898 Ratcliff, a free-scoring batsman, had changed his job so that he could play for Todmorden but, needing to find new employment in 1902, he moved to Accrington and played there for two seasons. Travelling daily to Accrington was not an option at the start of the 20th century. Ratcliff returned to Todmorden and was made captain in 1904, but in 1910 he moved to the Vickers shipbuilding works at Barrow, only to find that the job was not what he expected. By 1911 he was working in Bedford where he played for the Queen's Works in the Bedford and District League, on one occasion being carried in triumph from the field by his team mates after contributing 5 wickets and a match-winning 86. Returning to Todmorden near the end of 1913, he scored 109 not out in the final match of the season at Enfield. Work recalled him to Bedford in 1915, ending his 1st XI days at Todmorden, but as late as 1929 he took over the captaincy of the 2nd XI, retiring in 1932.

Jim Crossley arrived from the local Lydgate and Harley Wood clubs, having helped the latter to the Calder Valley League title in 1897. He developed from a very leg-sided player, vulnerable to being lbw as he played across the line, to scoring stylishly and fluently all round the wicket.[1]

At Colne on Whit Monday 1900, Crossley, aged 22, hit a new record individual score for the Lancashire League, 143 not out, and set a new Lancashire League record partnership with captain John Crabtree of 184. Todmorden's 274 for 2 would remain the club's highest Lancashire League total until 1921 and Crossley's score a club record in the Lancashire League until 1938. It was not customary to collect for performances by the visiting team and when a request was made, Colne would only offer to allow one later in the match if no Colne player was likely to score 50. By then it was too late and the collections had to wait until Whit Friday when the return match was played, raising £2 for Crabtree and £3 4s for Crossley, who also received 'numerous other gifts in acknowledgement of his great feat'.[2]

Like Ratcliff, Crossley too moved to find employment in 1902. Nelson were the beneficiaries, where he joined another former Todmorden player, Ernest Wynne, who had played for Lancashire 2nd XI. When they opened the batting against Todmorden on Whit Monday 1903 one supporter jocularly asked, 'How soon are Tod going to be all out?' It was a pertinent enquiry. Crossley scored 105 not out, the second of three not-out innings that Whitsuntide in which he totalled 254 runs, receiving collections and talent money of over £20 and county-wide fame, with articles about him in the northern dailies.

Crossley and Wynne formed a formidable opening partnership and Nelson won the League in 1903. Both continued to serve the club well until 1920, receiving an annual hearty welcome from the Todmorden crowd who continued to take pride in their successes. Wynne, who played five seasons for Burnley in the 1890s, scored 6174 runs for Nelson from 1899 to 1920. Crossley scored 3462 runs and took 47 wickets with his occasional medium-pace bowling between 1903 and 1920.

The mobility of labour was not all one way, and Todmorden briefly enjoyed the services of HE Stanley, a private tutor who came to the town from Liverpool in 1901. A studious, patient batsman of sound technique, he built his innings by steady accumulation before accelerating to 'score with freedom all round the wicket…a delightful batsman to watch. Perhaps his best stroke is to leg - a regular Ranji glide'.[3] For three seasons Stanley was the team's most reliable batsman, hitting 1491 runs at an average of 26.63. In 1901 he played several match-winning innings and, in the opinion of the *Hebden Bridge Times and Calder Vale Gazette* on 26 September 1901, rescued the club's finances from early-season doldrums.

> There can be no doubt that the phenomenal success of Mr Stanley has proved a great draw, and has added materially to the coffers of the club.

Stanley returned to Liverpool after the 1903 season, his last season coinciding with the first of Edward B Shackleton, a solid opening batsman from Walsden, where his father John had been captain in the 1880s. Another to cut his teeth in the Calder Valley League, Shackleton began his career as a boy playing for Walsden St Peters and recalled his first match against Eastwood when he wore only one pad and had a bat with a piece cut off the bottom. The first ball hit him 'dead on the place made specially for chastisement and almost lifted him onto the wicket'; this was still below the top of the stumps and he was given out lbw.

He was well established in the Walsden team by 1903 and his move in mid-season was sudden and surprising, Todmorden benefiting from unrest which saw Walsden lose their best batsman Shackleton and their professional in the same week. The paid man, Wimpenny, resigned, as he was 'not going to be put upon by Walsden spectators who come on at half-time, pay half-price, and do more shouting than all the other spectators put together'. This cut little ice with the local press:

> He has not been at all successful…this is a poor sort of excuse…a professional will have to expect that kind of thing if he does not suit the spectators and make the wickets fly.[4]

Wimpenny, may have been no great loss, but Shackleton was. The professional can be replaced but top quality amateurs, the backbone of any successful side, are harder to come by. Shackleton became the mainstay of the Todmorden batting for the next 20 years.

Like the batting, Todmorden's bowling was also in a state of flux. Opening bowler Willie Stansfield arrived towards the end of 1900 and took the Lancashire League by storm in 1901 with 70 wickets, winning the League's bowling prize. Unfortunately he was hampered by injuries and returned to Eastwood in 1903, where he played for the rest of his career. Fred Eastwood was another medium pace one-season wonder, taking 35 wickets in 1906 including 8 for 46 against Burnley. Less spectacular but ever-present and reliable was Walter Leslie Greenwood who, in a career spanning 1894 to 1924, remained the main medium-pace back-up to the professional. Despite these three and the steady change bowling of all-rounders Albert Marshall and William Law, the medium-pace department was often threadbare. Todmorden did, however, produce three terrific left-arm spinners - all of whom played much of their careers as professionals in other leagues.

The first of these to emerge was the diminutive Percy Hollinrake who, influenced by

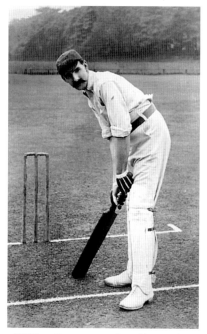

Creighton, spun the ball both ways, bowling orthodox finger spin and what would become known as a 'Chinaman', spinning in to the right-handed batsman from outside off-stump.

The team's transition after the turn of the century was not helped by Hollinrake's precarious health. He missed most of the 1901 season with illness and, still not fully recovered, 'yielded to the pleadings of his club-mates to turn out' in 1902.[5] As the season wore on he was 'unable to take the strain week-by-week'[6] and missed several matches, but still took 60 wickets - 46 more than anyone else - and was 'regarded as the best slow amateur bowler in the league'. One of only three amateurs to take two hat-tricks for Todmorden, he played his last match for the club in 1903 before moving as professional to Barnard Castle, then in County Durham, and subsequently to Barrow-in-Furness in the Ribblesdale League.

1905 saw the debut of Hollinrake's potential spin-bowling replacement, Walter Storah. Batting at number eleven, he made an inauspicious debut when he was timed out - still the only Todmorden

William Law, a genuine all-rounder, 1899-1920

batsman to be dismissed in this manner - as Todmorden were bowled out for 45 by Rishton. Storah took a few seasons to find his feet, but broke through in 1909 when he proved a far more effective slow bowler than professional James Meads. Meads had played three matches for Surrey in 1905 but his signing was, the committee admitted, 'a serious mistake', affording Storah 'unusual opportunities for an amateur bowler',

and he virtually carried the attack all season. From 1909 to 1911 he took 152 wickets but, unexpectedly, after a pre-season match against Walsden in 1912, he signed as their professional and enjoyed four successful seasons there.

Storah's departure gave twenty year-old Edwin Stansfield, another who spun the ball both ways, the chance to develop his left-arm spin and he took 288 wickets between 1912 and 1916. A good fieldsman and reasonable bat, Stansfield played a few matches for Yorkshire 2nd XI in 1914, taking 6 for 58 in a match against a Bradford League XI, and he became fiercely determined to earn his living from cricket.

> Stansfield is anxious to get out of the mill, and is so enthusiastic about his cricket that he carries a cricket ball always with him in order to experiment when an idea strikes him.[7]

After the war Stansfield played as a club professional, at Farnworth, Kearsley, Halifax, Slaithwaite, Queensbury and had five seasons at Walsden. In 1928 he returned as an amateur to Todmorden, where he

Walter Storah, a very successful spin bowler, 1905-26

Todmorden 1st XI 1904.
L-R Row 2: F Taylor, W Law, Walter Greenwood, ____, ____, W Huddlestone (pro), ____,
Row 1: H Hudson, EB Shackleton, JW Crabtree (c), WL Greenwood, ____.

played until 1933. He took a total of 1198 wickets for his various clubs, but this was not quite the end as, aged 52, he came out of retirement to help out towards the end of World War II, his Todmorden career thus spanning 37 seasons, 1908-44, the longest of any player.

Collectively the spin triumvirate of Hollinrake, Storah and Stansfield took 1258 wickets for Todmorden at about 13 runs each.

Both Hollinrake and Storah played alongside one of Todmorden's best professionals, William Huddleston, who held a mediocre team together from 1903 to 1905. Born at Earlstown near Warrington in 1875, Huddleston joined the Lancashire ground staff in 1899, making his debut that year against the Australian tourists.

An underrated right-arm medium-pace off-spin bowler, he was in and out of the county team for years, the notion being that, although nigh unplayable on sticky wickets, he bowled the ball too quickly and with too little variation in flight to be effective in dry conditions. Huddleston's experience against Warwickshire at Edgbaston in 1901 highlighted the issue. His friends had petitioned the committee to give him a fair chance on a good wicket and, against the wishes and judgement of Lancashire captain AC MacLaren, he was selected.

MacLaren's dogmatic captaincy made it a chastening experience. Huddleston bowled for most of the first day and by 4.30pm when MacLaren was being urged to give him a rest, he replied, 'My committee inform me that Huddleston's not had his fair chance on a good wicket, and that he's to be given a thorough trial. This is the best wicket in England, and I'm giving him a bloody thorough trial.' Huddleston bowled 55 overs on the first day and 80 in total, taking 3 for 187. No other Lancashire bowler took a wicket as Warwickshire declared deep into the second day at 532 for 4. It is questionable whether MacLaren would have dealt equivalent treatment to an amateur.

Huddleston must have wondered what he had come to at Todmorden after a debut in which he scored 29 out of 53 all out and took 8 for 18, yet still finished on the losing side as Lowerhouse scraped home by one wicket. Quickly established as a 'treasure of a professional'[8] his popularity peaked in May 1905 when his brilliant all round performance secured a home victory over Church. Huddleston hit 84 of Todmorden's 139 all out and, with Church cruising at 80 for 1, produced a spell of 7 for 14 to bowl the visitors out for 116. 'The way he knocked Sid Barnes…thrice out of the field filled the spectators with delight,' reported the *Hebden Bridge Times and Calder Vale Gazette*.

This contrasted with the concern caused by one of Huddleston's shots in 1903. On 31 July, practising about 30 yards from the boundary he mishit the ball into Burnley Road, striking a pedestrian, Mrs Sarah Broadbent, on the left ear. Cut and stunned, she required medical treatment and months later was still suffering dizziness. Consequently she sued the Todmorden committee for £25: 'for damages caused by the ball beyond the confines of the ground; and for the negligent act of its servant, a professional cricketer'. The club was represented by John E Craven at Todmorden County Court in what was regarded a test case concerning the liability of cricket clubs.[9]

Craven argued that: it was a pure accident; the committeemen were 'remote'; and conviction would have 'serious consequences' for Todmorden and cricket clubs in general. He won the case both at the local court and on appeal, the Lord Chief Justice concluding, 'a man playing cricket…had, without negligence, caused injury'. The club, however, faced substantial costs of £40. Craven, by taking a reduced fee, cut this to £30 and when Edward Crabtree, Todmorden's representative, appealed to the Lancashire League they agreed to pay half of this, as the outcome had implications for all clubs.

During his three seasons at Todmorden, Huddleston scored 1499 runs at an average of 24.57, including ten half centuries, took 249 wickets at 11.88 each, including five or more in an innings on twenty occasions, and held a remarkable 54 catches. Todmorden finished eighth, fourth and seventh as Huddleston comfortably kept the club's head above water.

He still played occasionally for Lancashire and whilst he was playing against Surrey at the Oval in 1904 Todmorden engaged their first overseas professional, Australian fast-medium bowler Alex Kermode, as his substitute for the visit to Enfield. Tall and strong, with a very high delivery and skilful variation of pace, Kermode had impressed AC MacLaren on England's 1901-02 tour of Australia and, after two matches for New South Wales, he took up MacLaren's invitation to emigrate to England and qualify for Lancashire. He forged a short and successful career with the county until 1908 before settling into life as a club professional. In 1910 Kermode played the first of his five seasons at Bacup, becoming the Lancashire League's first full time overseas professional along with Rawtenstall's professional of 1910, the splendidly named John Elicihs Benedict Bernard Placid Quirk Carrington Dwyer - known as 'EB' - an Australian pace bowler of Irish extraction.[10]

Kermode had a poor day as substitute professional for Todmorden, who lost to Enfield by seven wickets. He performed better a fortnight later when he took 8 for 71 for Mr Hornby's XI against a Lancashire League XI at the Blackpool Cricket Festival. William Huddleston was one of four professionals in the League team who were paid £4 10s with 'nothing to be deducted from their ordinary wages by the clubs in their absence', indicating that professionals' duties at their clubs during the week could be contractual and subject to financial penalty.[11]

After three seasons at Todmorden, Huddleston signed as professional for Church in 1906 and the county at last recognised his worth. Playing against Nottinghamshire in May he took 4 wickets for 5 runs in the first innings and 9 for 36 in the second, bowling them out for 52. Lancashire wanted him for their next match against Yorkshire but,

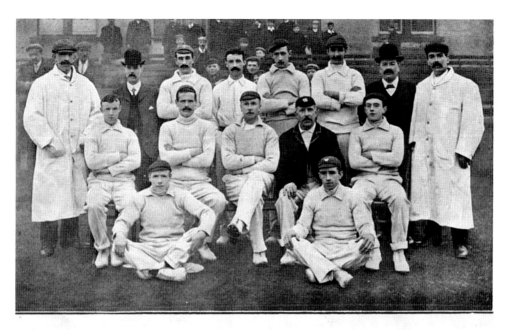

TODMORDEN C. C.—1907.

E. I'A LOWELL. J. RATCLIFFE. E. B. SHACKLETON. WM. GREENWOOD. W. LAW.
(Scorer).
WILF. GREENWOOD. W. I. GREENWOOD. J. W. CRABTREE. W. HALL. F EASTWOOD.
(Capt.) (Pro.)
E. HARGREAVES. H. HUDSON.

with a fixture on Whit Monday, Church refused. Lancashire persisted and during Todmorden's visit to Church on 21 July a telegram arrived asking Huddleston if he would leave Church and play for the county for the rest of the season. He and Church agreed this amicably and he signed off by scoring 48 of Church's 136 for 5 and taking 6 for 37 as Todmorden were bowled out for 99.

Huddleston was a member of the Lancashire side until the outbreak of war in 1914 and finished an impressive first class career with 685 wickets at an average of 17.57. He continued to visit Todmorden long after his time at the club. In October 1906, he married a Todmorden girl at the local Unitarian Church. She was Ellen Whitehead, daughter of Howorth, a tinplate worker.

In May 1905 the *Sports Telegraph* discussed the issue 'Should Boys Attend Lancashire League Matches?' This was prompted by problems at Nelson where boys and youths were 'indifferent to the comfort of others who had paid admission'. Some boys, ignoring all protests, invaded the playing area and interfered with the fielding. Nelson responded by banning all youths from matches. At the other extreme was Todmorden, where the Fielden's lease of the ground prohibited boys from attending matches and being members under the age of sixteen, conditions originating from a break-in at the pavilion in 1875. Todmorden would have welcomed boys if they could, arguing that gates would increase as some parents could not attend matches without bringing their children with them.

Boys were not the only cause of interruptions in 1905. At the benefit match for Church professional Sidney Barnes, for which he chose the visit of Todmorden on 5 August, inclement weather deterred neither the cricketers nor a company of artillery volunteers who were training in the next field. A constant, deafening bombardment ensued and smoke from the guns swept across Church's West End ground, causing the game to be suspended. One spectator, a veteran of the Boer War, mounted the railings and waved a white handkerchief on the end of his umbrella, calling out 'We surrender! We surrender!' which temporarily halted the firing. A less than satisfactory day for the great Barnes was complete when Todmorden won by 23 runs, their first victory in thirteen matches.

Todmorden turned to an archetypal old league professional in 1906, Walter Hall. Born in 1861 in Glossop, Derbyshire, his first professional engagement was with Moorside near Oldham in 1882 and from there he was in continuous demand 'as one of the finest professionals of his time'.[12] Hall had seven seasons with Accrington, 1897-1903, and Todmorden, who lost ten of their 14 matches against Accrington in this period, had first-hand experience of his ability. His batting prowess was apparent in 1897 when Todmorden declared at 204 for 9, only for Accrington, led by Hall's unbeaten 87, to knock off the runs in the remaining hour and three quarters.

Hall also took 5 wickets in an innings 7 times in those fourteen matches, and it was for his idiosyncratic bowling that he was most prized. Saul Wade, a former Yorkshire all-rounder who played alongside Hall at Accrington during a long career as both professional and amateur in the Lancashire League, wondered 'how a bowler with his arm so low could bowl anybody out'. But Hall varied his pace, moved the ball both ways and had a faster ball that 'kicked up at you. His slow leg break tempted you to run out and drive him, and if you missed the ball you were stumped'. Descriptions vary as to whether Hall cut or spun the ball, and it is difficult to know as the distinction between the two styles only began to be made in 1907. As he had such a low arm, it seems likely that his quicker ball was a cutter to extract the lift and movement described, whilst his slower balls could well have been spun.

When Accrington beat Todmorden at Centre Vale in 1902 the local paper reported:

> Hall's deliveries were of such questionable character that 'the gods' ... began to shout 'No-ball'.

'The gods' were spectators who patronised the cheapest threepenny seats on the National School side of the ground, behind the bowler's arm. In the same edition 'Chit Chat' claimed:

> Walter Hall's bowling is proverbially doubtful not only in regard to the position of his arm in delivery but on account of a trick he has of dragging his foot over the crease.

No doubt these criticisms ceased in 1906 and 07 when 'Owd Walter' was at Todmorden. Hall quickly established himself 'a great favourite by the improvement...wrought in the team by his coaching', and the crowd enjoyed some fabulous matches in his first season. Church professional Huddleston, who received 'a flattering reception' on his return to Centre Vale, reduced Todmorden to 35 for 8 in reply to the visitors' 80 all out, but Hall (31 not out) and Walter Leslie Greenwood (13 not out, including the winning boundary) inched Todmorden home...

> ...the excitement of the spectators knew no bounds, and they rushed on the field...and carried Greenwood to the pavilion.[13]

Seven days later, chasing just 32 against Bacup, Todmorden collapsed to 15 for 7 before recovering to a two-wicket victory. When Hall took 10 for 46 against Haslingden on 8 June - still the only occasion that a Todmorden bowler has taken all ten wickets in an innings - Todmorden were top of the table, a position maintained until the end of the month thanks to two century first-wicket partnerships by Shackleton and Ratcliff, a reliable if short-lived opening pair. Unfortunately, an all too familiar slump in the second half of the season saw the team finish fourth[14]

Despite eleven abandonments in Hall's two seasons at Todmorden, he took 178 wickets at an average of 8.78, including five or more wickets in an innings twenty times. He was neatly summed up by the *Sunday Chronicle*'s Cricket Cameo, in parody of a Gilbert and Sullivan song:

A never-grow-old young man
A 'That's-how-they're-bowled', young man
A fresh every summer
To teach the new comer
A true Hall-marked gold young man!

The team fell to a familiar lower mid-table position, eighth equal with Accrington in 1907, and the main topic of conversation was once again the weather and its effect on finances. Of Todmorden's first eight home matches, only three progressed as far as the second innings. On 29 June the rain was so persistent that visitors Nelson left their cricket bags at the railway station; four of their team (including the captain) left to start their holidays before the match had been called off. To Nelson's embarrassment, at 4.50pm the umpires announced that play would commence in twenty minutes. Bags were hurriedly collected and Nelson eventually took the field at 5.50 with seven men, Todmorden declining to supply sub-fielders. Todmorden scored 78 for 1 wicket before further rain ended play.

By mid-July gate money totalled just £55. Other clubs were also in dire straits, Rishton, whose gates totalled just £40, resorting to house-to-house collections.

Not for the first time, Todmorden pinned their hopes on the season's most attractive home fixture, Burnley. Thankfully the day was fine. A special excursion train left Burnley's Manchester Road station and a gate of £55 3s 10d more than doubled the season's takings. With admission of 4d on the National School side, 6d for the rest of the ground and 3d extra for the pavilion enclosure, the gate plus members represented a crowd of over 3000. That Burnley won by one wicket chasing Todmorden's 116 all out was probably secondary for the committee.

Walter Greenwood, who hit 56, received a collection of £7 9s, the equivalent of several week's wages - a contemporary advert for weavers offered £1 5s to £1 15s per week. Unfortunately, this princely sum went to Walter's head and the following evening he and team-mate Walter Sutcliffe were arrested in Whalley for being drunk and disorderly. Subsequently convicted and fined by the Clitheroe County Bench, they were further punished when the committee dropped them to the 2nd XI.[15]

The last of Todmorden's long-serving players from their pre-league days was approaching the end of his career and the testimonial for John Crabtree was a highlight of 1908. He chose the visit of Colne on 6 June, against whom he had hit 112 not out three weeks earlier, his fourth and last century for the club, the first being 106 against Bolton in 1889. Crabtree began his career with the local Lydgate club, joined Todmorden in 1885 and, apart from three years as a club professional, 1893-95, served unbroken as a player, captain and later club chairman until 1927. Captain for over a decade, his shrewd field placing and bowling changes were frequently praised and invaluable to the transitional and inexperienced Todmorden team after the turn of the century. In 1898 he was selected for the Lancashire League XVI against Lancashire and represented the county in a non first-class match at Lord's.

Long-serving vice-president John Lord, writing in the *Todmorden Advertiser*, commented on his gentlemanly conduct, sense of fair play, his work for the club as administrator and in preparation of the ground, and how, because the club had been

Crabtree's Testimonial 1908.
L-R Row 2: W Storah, E Crabtree (Lgue rep), JW Widdup (treas), A Marshall,
F Foster (pro), EF Priestley (sec), W Law,
Row 1: W Sutcliffe, EB Shackleton, WL Greenwood, JW Crabtree, Walt Greenwood,
H Hudson, J Ratcliff.

in debt for years, he had paid his own expenses and taken neither talent nor prize money.

Gate receipts of £31 2s, boosted by ticket sales and donations to over £140, were testimony to the universal popularity of 'JW'. Reminiscent of the old days, the crowd was entertained by the Todmorden Brass Band, resplendent in new uniforms. Crabtree was presented with a cheque for £100, an illuminated address signed by members of the committee, an enlarged framed photograph of the team, an eighteen carat gold watch and chain and a double case of cutlery. The gifts were on view during the week at Mills & Co's shop on County Bridge opposite the Town Hall, attracting hundreds of viewers. This hugely successful testimonial celebrated the man as well as his cricket.

Crabtree was a fine example of the intelligent leadership and continuity necessary to the well-being of any club, only retiring as chairman in 1927 because of failing health.

The club was in contention for the title half way through the 1908 season, but won only one and lost five of the last thirteen matches to finish sixth, falling away badly after a mauling by Ramsbottom at Centre Vale in July. The visitors declared on 289 for 4, which remained the highest total conceded by Todmorden in a League match until 1999. Professional Emmott Robinson's 181 not out is still the highest individual score against Todmorden. 'Centre Vale…emphasised its claim to be the best scoring pitch in the league,' commented the *Hebden Bridge Times and Calder Vale Gazette*,[16] overlooking the stark contrast with the corresponding match three seasons earlier when Ramsbottom had been bowled out for 19, still the lowest total made against Todmorden in a League match.

Todmorden's professional in 1908, Frank Foster of Elland, who had been with Walsden in 1907, had a satisfactory season, but was criticised for not carrying all before him. Half a dozen other pros had fewer wickets but, as the *Todmorden Advertiser* noted in its review:

> ...these are not looked upon as tip-top men; but it is always as well to bear in mind that in order to attract a tip-top man a tip-top price is needed. Twas ever thus - ever since the deplorable system of paying a man several week's wages for an afternoon's play came into vogue.

John Lord commented that if Todmorden had a Cook, referring to Burnley's pace-bowling professional Billy Cook, they would have won the League but not all could afford tip-top bowlers like Burnley, Nelson and Colne.

Meanwhile, Todmorden continued to field a strong second team which won the junior cup for a fourth time in 1908. The 2nd XI competition had been re-organised in 1907. Clubs now arranged their own fixtures, playing a minimum of eight other clubs, with the championship decided on a percentage of points gained. At the 1908 presentation a proud Edward Crabtree claimed that 'Every lad in the Todmorden team was a native of Todmorden. And it would indeed

Emmott Robinson, Ramsbottom pro 1908-13; Yorkshire debut aged 36 in 1919; played until 1931.

be a model league if every club could say that'. At this time the Lancashire League's qualification rule was that players had to be born within two miles of the boundary of the district of the club, or to have resided or to have had a bona fide place of business or employment within this limit for not less than 12 months.

Isolated at the south-eastern end of the League, Todmorden had no real Derby matches to attract large gates, Bacup and Burnley being the most profitable. The only sure source of income was from members' subscriptions and the aim during this period was to achieve £200 per year from them, which represented about 400 members. 10s for ordinary membership was about 40% of the weekly wage, in real terms far more than membership costs today. Yet the only benefits were net practice and voting power, as there were no other social activities at the club. Indeed, it was possible to watch a full season's matches by paying less than half the price of ordinary membership at the gate.

Following meagre gate receipts in 1907 of just £161, the lowest for 20 years, the club was bailed out by an increase in members' subscriptions and a donation of £20 from Mrs Sarah Fielden of Centre Vale, but remained over £66 in the red. Despite the overdraft, the club spent £50 addressing the poor drainage highlighted by the wet summer and was delighted to receive a further £100 from Mrs Fielden prior to the 1908 season, virtually clearing their debts. The widow of the club's founder, Samuel, Mrs Fielden had, since her husband's death in 1889, kept a maternal eye on the club and effectively acted as its financial safety net:

> most generous in her donations...her valuable help on each occasion most opportune.[17]

On Monday 4 July 1910, as practice was in full swing, news was brought to the field that Mrs Fielden had died. Practice stopped immediately. The committee passed a

Sarah Fielden, widow of Samuel,
Centre Vale.

resolution of sympathy for her son, the club president John Ashton Fielden, and decided to close the ground until after the funeral. Aged ninety, Sarah was the last of the Fieldens to regard Centre Vale as her home. John Ashton considered Todmorden damp, dirty and dull; he no longer had any interest in the place but how would he dispose of his parent's home, the Centre Vale estate, which included the cricket ground?

By coincidence, John Crabtree's 26-season first team career ended at this time. The senior figure at the club, he had spoken effusively of the Fielden family on many occasions, reminding the audience at his testimonial in 1908 that 'they played practically on a private estate under the most glorious conditions'. The club anxiously awaited news of the sale. *The Fieldens of Todmorden* states:

> ...it was a curious transaction since for whatever reason the estate was not offered to the Corporation of Todmorden, but advertised in the Manchester press. Todmorden's Mayor, Edward Lord, saw the advertisement and approached Fielden's solicitors; a quick deal was made, to which no conditions were attached, at a price of £10 000, in effect an act of charity.[18]

Legally the estate belonged to Edward Lord personally but the town bought it from him and at the beginning of the 1911 season the local paper commented on:

> ...an intense feeling of relief that the future of the club is assured as far as the ground is concerned by the acquisition of the estate by the Corporation.

The Club's annual rent was increased from £7 10s to £20 but 'the removal of certain restrictions and greater security of tenure will more than compensate'. More specifically, the club could now admit boys under sixteen years as members and spectators, although initially the age for members was only dropped to fifteen. 3rd XI matches could be played on the ground as could the Tuesday afternoon matches of the Todmorden Tradesmen, in the Rochdale Tradesmen's League.

The pre-season match against Walsden in April 1911 was the first to which boys were admitted. At half price, 150 boys paid a total £1 5s 6d (mostly 2d each). Membership was still exclusively male and ladies continued to be admitted free.

The rest of the Centre Vale estate was to become a public park and it was necessary to erect a boundary between it and the cricket field. Prior to this, the cricket field had simply been an extension of Centre Vale meadow with no physical boundary. The Corporation granted the club part of this meadow to enlarge the field and plans were made to turf about six hundred square yards and to plant a privet hedge along the Centre Vale boundary. As the club was already overdrawn at the bank by £21 no one was sure how these improvements would be funded, but as the club felt for the first time to be its own master, an atmosphere of optimism prevailed.

An application to the Parks' Committee for a further extension to the ground resulted in a grant of the hillside beyond the pavilion from the end of the church wall to the Park End plantation. Thus the cricket field took on most of its present size and shape.

John Ashton Fielden resigned as president of the club with the sale of Centre Vale and would not reconsider his decision, so the committee approached his cousin EB Fielden, who had inherited Dobroyd Castle on the death of his uncle, John Fielden, in 1893. The committee reported: 'We are glad to say that he consented, so that the long connection between the club and the Fielden family will thus remain unbroken'.[19] EB Fielden never lived at Dobroyd permanently but visited regularly and retained the presidency until his death in 1942.

Passive and helpless throughout the land sales, the club's future at Centre Vale was briefly but entirely reliant on the considerable goodwill it had engendered in the community as a focus of local interest, in contributing to a sense of civic pride, and in advertising and representing the town's name in rival industrial centres. Without this goodwill, which earned the crucial support of the corporation, would the club have survived the uncertainty that followed the death of Sarah Fielden?

The ground secured, a Fielden reassuringly as figurehead and enjoying greater autonomy than ever before, the club looked to a settled and prosperous future, little knowing that a crisis of much greater magnitude lay just around the corner.

Edward B Fielden, TCC President 1911-42.

Chapter 3

Distant Guns

The week before Mrs Fielden's death, club officials 'openly boasted they have engaged one of the best and most promising professionals in England, one whose name is almost a household word'.[1] Within a week he was revealed to be 35 year-old George Cooper Gill who had played for Somerset, then his native Leicestershire from 1897 to 1906, and latterly for Staffordshire. Signed at £6 6s per week, a large amount for the club, he was a right-arm fast-medium bowler and, according to the *Todmorden Advertiser*, 'a slogger'. He moved to Todmorden with his wife and family. Popular with players and spectators and a sportsman both on and off the field, he showed himself to be the very best type of professional cricketer, assiduously coaching the youngsters.

An early season defeat to eventual champions Nelson put Todmorden's prospects in perspective. The visitor's professional Albert Hallam, who had taken over 1000 wickets for Nottinghamshire, took seven wickets in nine balls, including five in one over as Todmorden were bowled out for 46 to begin a run of six consecutive defeats. The team recovered to finish eighth and Gill was re-signed.

1912 began with a promising 132 run victory over East Lancashire, but news of this was submerged by comprehensive coverage about the sinking of the *Titanic* in the local press, which reported far more national and international news than it does today. The win was a precursor for a more successful season as the team moved up to fifth. Gill improved his wicket tally from 61 in 1911 to 86 in 1912, reinforcing the maxim that having a professional strike bowler is the surest way to success in the Lancashire League.

George Gill, TCC pro 1911-12.

Despite the excellence of Gill and Ned Stansfield with the ball, the team was let down by inconsistent batting and abysmal fielding. At the 1912 AGM an exasperated Edward Crabtree advised the batsmen to 'do nothing rash till they had either got ten runs or played for half an hour'. They had 'too many batsmen who were capable of getting runs when they were not wanted and too few who were capable of getting them when they were wanted'.[2]

The bar had been raised, both in batting technique and in the approach to building an innings, over the previous two seasons by Accrington professional Charles Llewellyn, the best batsman the Lancashire League had ever seen and its first international star. At 34 years of age, the left-handed Llewellyn was close to his peak, and had already played ten of his 15 test matches for South Africa. On his first innings for Accrington in 1911, the

Northern Daily Telegraph reported:

> This was something afresh in Lancashire League cricket. Every stroke was made with the ease and confidence of an artist with the bat. The ball was nearly always skilfully placed and kept low.[3]

Llewellyn's remaining five test matches were played in the Triangular Series between England, Australia and South Africa in 1912, and interspersed with appearances for Accrington. In the First Test Match against England at Lord's, Llewellyn hit 75 in the second innings, but came down to earth three days later against Todmorden when he 'fell victim to a trap laid for him by the wicketkeeper and Stansfield'. Chasing Todmorden's paltry 93 all out, Llewellyn was quickly into his stride, advancing to drive Ned Stansfield twice out of the Accrington ground. Todmorden's wily amateurs sensed his over-confidence and the left-arm spinner, 'responded promptly to signals which were given him from behind the wickets...bowling a ball wide of the sticks; Llewellyn stepped out to hit it but the ball eluded the bat', and Harry Hudson completed a 'smart stumping'. It was the key moment of the afternoon, opening the door for Gill and Stansfield, who bowled Accrington out for 52.

CB Llewellyn, Accrington
pro 1911-15, 1921-25.

Todmorden proved to be Llewellyn's bogey team and, although scoring 6276 runs for Accrington and leading them to two League titles, his top score against Todmorden in twenty matches from 1911-15 and 1921-25 was just 38. Perhaps Todmorden saw too little of Llewellyn to learn much from this master batsman.

Despite Edward Crabtree's frustrations at the team's batting, the 1912 season had been quite successful and Todmorden had a final bank balance of £27. A gift of £30 from Todmorden Amateur Players, the local dramatic society, offset the cost of the previous winter's ground improvements. Without the restrictions of the Fielden regime, further ground development was planned, the secretary minuting:

November 22, 1912
> Every cricket ground in the Lancashire League with the exception of our own, has an erection known as 'The Tea Pavilion' and it is the desire of the Committee...that a suitable building shall be constructed on the ground...in which our home or visiting spectators and players may partake of tea, coffee, cocoa, sandwiches, cakes etc.

February 8, 1913
> That the site for the tea pavilion be fixed for the corner of the field near to Centre Vale Lodge.

March 12, 1913
> ...the outbuildings to be of Accrington Red Brick instead of wood.

March 31, 1913
> The secretary to write to all Lancashire League clubs asking for particulars of Lady Members and asking if they are allowed all the benefits of Male Members.

April 18, 1913
>   That ladies be admitted members of the club

May 5, 1913
>   The Club now boasts 49 Lady Members. Tea pavilion to be opened at the match against
>   Burnley on May 24.

May 12, 1913
>   The committee tender their sincere thanks to the ladies for their generous offer to
>   undertake the duties necessary for the working of The Tea Pavilion.

Todmorden's tardiness in providing tea and coffee is clear from an article in the *Todmorden and District News* as far back as April 1902, questioning the assumption that 'the only requisite is of intoxicating character or...fizzy mineral water'. Burnley and Nelson had both supplied tea and coffee by 1902, the latter at the request of the local magistrates. 'Who will make the move at Todmorden?' Mr Needham of the Queen Hotel, who had the catering franchise, offered tea, coffee and sandwiches as a new feature at Centre Vale in 1903, but there was nothing permanent for another ten years.

As was usual for large projects, a committee was established to raise the necessary finance, estimated at £150. Who should they approach for donations? Many local organisations were pillars of both community and nonconformity, valuing sobriety. It is no coincidence that the fund received an early donation of £3 19s 4½d from the recently disbanded Lumbutts Cricket Club, connected with Lumbutts Methodist Chapel.[4] The Temperance movement, with its attendant 'Band of Hope' groups at all the chapels, was very strong at this time and the cricket club's astute fund-raising committee approached Todmorden's Band of Hope Union, which could hardly fail to encourage a tea pavilion on a ground that for decades had boasted an ale tent. The request yielded a donation of £15.

Seeking other likely wealthy subscribers, the committee perused the 'Burgess List' of those entitled to vote - a right dependent on income and property as there was no universal suffrage in 1912. Two hundred and fifty circulars were distributed asking for financial support and promising to build a tea pavilion that would be functional and 'in harmony with the beautiful surroundings of the ground'. Further funds were raised by a concert and a scheme for selling bricks. Supplemented by £5 from the club president, the amount received or promised by March 1913 was £145 19s 6d and local builder Jabez Greenwood's tender of £160 was accepted.

Lady members, an unavoidable necessity, were to pay 2s 6d, twenty five percent of an ordinary membership. This admitted them to the ground and pavilion enclosure on match days. Ladies who were not members were still admitted free to all parts of the ground except the enclosure, where they would pay 3d. In practical terms, lady members were being asked to pay 2s 6d for the dubious privilege of working in the tea pavilion. That they came forward in such numbers says much for the kudos of being associated with the club. Indeed, the committee was able to open a second refreshments outlet, a wooden hut for the third class spectators on the National School side, so that they could access tea and coffee without paying a transfer fee to the new red brick tea pavilion in the second class part of the ground.

The anomaly of having lady members whilst lady spectators were admitted free continued until June 1915 when a 3d charge came into force for the match against Rawtenstall, sixty ladies paying a total of 15s.

The final cost of buildings, furnishings and crockery was £224 12s 1d; donations of £172 9s 6d and a profit on teas of £20 left a debt of £29 2s 8d on the venture. To help

Red Brick Tea Tent, basically the same as when built in 1913, minus the clock turret.

defray this, an end of season match in aid of the 'Tea Tent Fund' was organised between the 1st XI and the 'Next XVI'. Enterprisingly, the match was advertised on the screens of the town's Hippodrome and Olympia theatres.

The kitchen area of the tea pavilion was extended before the 1914 season at a further cost of £44 17s 6d, whist drives, donations and profits on the teas eventually clearing all debts on the building. Still in use today, the 'Red Brick Tea Pavilion' is testimony to the drive and resourcefulness of the committee, but its conception and initial organisation provide an acute social comment on the attitudes to women and their place in society at the time.

It is doubtful that 1913's high profile suffragettes Emily Pankhurst, who was imprisoned for setting fire to Lloyd George's private residence, or Emily Davison, who lost her life under the hooves of the King's horse in the Epsom Derby, would have approved. If women had not been needed by the club, how long would it have been before their admittance as members? At national level, would women have received the vote in 1918, albeit at the age of 30, if they had not proved themselves capable of 'men's work' in manufacturing and agriculture during the First World War?

The team, which the new lady members might glimpse between queuing customers, was given a higher local profile by the writings in 1912 of Old Hand, clearly an ex-player. He took to task the players individually and the committee collectively in a series of open letters to the *Todmorden Advertiser*. Each week a player had his attributes praised, his faults criticised and suggestions made for his improvement. Although only one opinion, they provide interesting pen portraits of the main players at the end of the Edwardian age.

Captain Harry Hudson is praised for his wicket keeping but advised to concentrate more on his batting and to be more imaginative with the batting order.

Professional George Gill is congratulated on his bowling, particularly in cultivating a shorter run, and on his professional demeanour but advised to be more patient at the start of his innings - not easy for 'a slogger'.

Walter Leslie Greenwood, a 'good old warhorse', is praised for his efforts over many years and for being 'always merry and bright'. His ball which pitches on the leg stick and moves to the off 'should get him many more wickets...but why has he never concentrated on his batting and is it a certain lack of patience which prevents his success as a captain?' - a somewhat damning verdict on the previous two seasons when Walter Leslie was in charge. Nevertheless, 'may your shadow never grow less, or those 'tall stories' of yours less piquant and may your cricketing career be a long way from finished'.

Edward B Shackleton, the club's leading amateur batsman, is taken to task for recently forsaking his natural method where 'every stroke was marked by the stylishness of a Spooner' and instead trying to clear the boundaries; 'it was never your style. Give it up; return once more to your patient waiting for the right ball to hit, then hit as you used to do - all along the ground and out of reach of the fieldsmen'. Shackleton's strength was not hitting hard off the front foot, but in playing the ball very late so that he could adjust to any movement and he was notable for his late cutting.

Albert Marshall is greeted as the best all-rounder in the team and one of the best Todmorden has produced, but he had taken too long to build up his reputation - 'You did not flash like a meteor across the gaze of the Todmorden committee'. Perhaps this was because of weaknesses which Old Hand proceeded to catalogue: 'Marshall's fielding is not as smart as it might be and he might benefit by taking a longer run when bowling. When batting he would be a terror to every bowler in the league, as seen in his recent century at Enfield, if he was not such a poor starter. He should also improve his running between the wickets.' A minor plus was his off drive, singled out as 'one of your best strokes of which you have not a very extensive repertoire'.

William Law, another all-rounder, is commended as a 'sightboard shifter', a by-product of his usual fielding positions at third man and long on. His fielding is nevertheless graceful and his catching 'never quite bad enough to merit general condemnation which is sometimes extended to the team as a whole'. His batting is 'delightful to watch', although he is 'hardly the stylist of the team'.

> He's little but he's wise
> He's a terror for his size

This is Old Hand's view of Eddie Hargreaves, the team's bits and pieces player who could bowl a bit, keep wicket when needed, play some useful innings and was alert in the field. As one who was 'never beaten until licked' he needed only to add a little patience to rank as 'one of the best little men' to appear in Lancashire League cricket.

Edwin Stansfield, hailed as a young bowler of more promise than any Old Hand has ever seen in the League, is advised not to spin the ball too much because, as any first class batter will testify, it is the ball which breaks just a few inches, sufficient to beat the bat which gets his wicket.

Alfred Ormerod, who had made his first team debut with Todmorden in 1893, moved to Walsden in 1896 and returned in 1911, is gently chided for a lack of understanding when running with 'Teddy' Shackleton. This seems a little harsh as Shackleton had, in the previous month, run himself out in both matches against Accrington and both himself and Ormerod out against Colne. Ormerod is praised for his late and square cuts and his pushes past cover, but he seems to be ' getting rather slow as time goes by'. Advancing years are offered as the reason why he had not bowled at Todmorden although he did so at Walsden and he is enjoined to 'keep your end up' for another season or two. His return to Walsden during 1913 coincided with Johnny Ratcliff coming back to Todmorden from Bedford.

Committees universally invite criticism and Old Hand regards the cricket club committee as fair game:

> to the Aristocrats of the Greensward
> I cannot address you as 'Dear Everybody' – it would be presumptuous on my part, your exclusiveness being such, that, though individually every member of the committee is known to me, collectively I know you not, and I am never likely to make your acquaintance. All the spectators on the Centre Vale ground speak of you, if not with bated breath, at least with a sense of awe due to a body whose deliberations are secret and whose decisions are unknown until one of your number 'leaks'.

Committees it seems never change. At this time the club was signing a new professional for 1913 and Old Hand comments that officially no one outside the committee knows who he will be but:

> ...not a single enthusiast in the town has any doubt as to the new man, his age, cricket antecedents and all his records.

With rumours that the new man was the great SF Barnes quickly squashed, Old Hand advises the committee to take the public a little more into its confidence as 'the keenness of league cricket growing as it is every year makes the problem of the "new man" more and more acute'. He argues that the club belongs to the town, in which it is part of the social fabric; its performance matters and through its committee it has a responsibility to the wider community. That Old Hand's open letters were written in such detail, published in the paper and, presumably, widely read emphasises this.

The 'Aristocrats of the Greensward', as Old Hand described the committee, were by no means the elite of the town. Amongst the eleven members were two schoolmasters, a cotton manufacturer, a cotton weaver, a plumber, a rope maker, a railway surveyor, a tin-plate worker and an iron turner, including one current player and four former players. Many of them had been and would continue to be committee members for several years.

Old Hand is keen that the club looks to the future and 'now that the interdict on young members has been removed and the boys given a practice net', there must be someone there to train and coach them. The Lancashire League's strict amateur registration rules meant that amateur players could not be brought in from elsewhere. This necessitated the development of local talent, particularly at clubs which could not afford to pay for a 'top' professional to compensate for the team's shortcomings.

In August 1912 Old Hand penned a letter to 'New Pro - The Unknown, to let you know what you are coming to'. He warned him that he must show form in the first match or two:

> ...to ingratiate yourself with the 'fourpenny side' as we designate the crowd who congregate 'neath the shade of the old National School. But...the 'aristocrats' who sit on the windy side [by Centre Vale Park] and the 'autocrats' who sit and grumble in front of the pavilion, 'can't abide bad play either'.

It seems the pro was on a hiding to nothing. He is advised that he is joining:

> 10/11 of a rattling good team...if you can hit like the kick of a horse, bowl like Tom Richardson and field like a Jessop, you'll do, and we have been on the lookout for such a priceless treasure for years.

In another dig at the committee he says that expectations are so high that 'some souls are almost expecting a celestial visitation' and 'we are all looking forward to the long deferred announcement'.

Yours truly
G. Wilson

George Wilson, TCC pro 1913-14.

This came the following week when George Alfred Wilson signed for 1913. Born in 1877, the right-hander had played for Worcestershire from 1899 to 1906, taking 732 wickets as a fast round-arm bowler and scoring 2238 runs as a hard-hitting batsman.[5] Nelson's professional in 1908 and 09, he had previous experience of the Lancashire League.

Wilson's introduction to Todmorden was delayed. The first three matches were completely washed out and only three of the first ten were unaffected by rain. The League made the unusual decision to replay two of the abandoned matches in midweek. Todmorden's home match against East Lancashire was rescheduled for Monday 4 August, the committee distributing 1000 handbills to advertise it at the previous Saturday's home match. The away match at Accrington was played on Wednesday 9 July, which coincided with King George V's visit to the area, and Todmorden celebrated with a resounding six wicket victory. Shackleton scored 77 not out on his way to heading the League's batting aggregates with 574 runs at an impressive average of 41, an achievement which earned him an inscribed gold medal presented by the club.

To support the new top class professional, long overdue practice was organised for 6.30pm every Friday specifically to address Todmorden's legendary fielding, described at various times in the press as 'ludicrous', 'slovenly', 'miserable', 'disgusting', 'wretched', 'abysmal' and 'unworthy of a Lancashire League club'. Walter Leslie Greenwood conjured up an incentive fund by means of collections at matches to reward players according to fielding points gained, and 1913 saw the fielding improve and the reputation, if not the legend, dispelled.

Wilson galvanised the team and was a match-winner. At Rawtenstall, for example, with Todmorden defending a barely adequate 139 all out, he 'bowled throughout at terrific pace, spread-eagling the wickets like matchwood',[6] to take 7 for 22 and rout the home side for 61, of which future Lancashire batsman Alfred W Pewtress top-scored with 17. Wilson spearheaded the bowling with 107 wickets, ably supported by Ned Stansfield with 46, and also contributed 464 runs towards Todmorden's best season in the League, third with 32 points, behind East Lancashire (35) and Burnley (41).

Before the end of June terms had been negotiated with Wilson for 1914. Ever careful with money, the club agreed a fee of £7 per week, to include assisting the groundsman with weekly mowing during the season, 2s 6d to be deducted if a substitute was engaged to mow instead.

The club now also had a third method of transport to away matches. In 1907 Todmorden had become only the second town in the country after Eastbourne to introduce the motor bus, largely because it was one of the few industrial centres that did not have a tram service. Initially scorned for its noise, pollution and unreliability, the motor bus had become a feasible option by 1913, but sometimes the players had

Todmorden Bus 1913, supplanted the wagonette for team transport.

to wait until late in the week before learning their mode of travel and consequent departure time. For the trip to Rawtenstall it was 11.30am by wagonette or 12.30pm by motor bus. The train remained the most convenient mode for several destinations up the Burnley valley.

In contrast to this modernisation, the home match against Ramsbottom echoed cricket of the 19th century. The Todmorden batsmen were primed for the patience required against the 'seductive flight' of the visitors' record-holding amateur spin bowler, Billy Fenwick, but were caught unprepared when their captain, Jack Redfern, resorted to bowling irresistible, mesmeric underhand lobs.

> The balls are pitched very high and are evidently intended to drop straight down on the bails. It is almost impossible to play them - the batsman has to try to hook them over his shoulder. To meet this the field is laid out with four men at deep leg and two or three others in on the leg side.

George Wilson and William Law, making rapid progress towards Ramsbottom's 191 all out, were stopped in their tracks. In Redfern's first over Wilson was caught at deep backward square leg near the scorebox for 33. Centre Vale resounded with 'a great outcry against this unsportsmanlike proceeding' and Todmorden's incensed captain, Harry Hudson, was about to protest but, partnership broken, Redfern immediately took himself off. Todmorden held out on 143 for 8 so 'the match was drawn or there would have been difficulty in restraining some of the more unruly spirits'. This was the closest Todmorden came to the crowd disturbances which blighted the League in 1913. These were 'often precipitated by a blatant disregard by players to be bound by an umpire's decision', a growing number of batsmen appealing to opposing captains to overturn adjudications. Then, as today, ill-feeling amongst both players and spectators could often be traced to poor umpiring decisions. Church, dissatisfied with the quality of the officials, proposed a fitness test for umpires on knowledge of the laws, eyesight and hearing, but this was overturned at a League meeting 11 votes to 3.[7]

Todmorden's season ended with an emphatic double over Enfield, the match at Centre Vale illustrating the breakneck speed of some of the cricket. Starting at 2.00pm, Todmorden were all out for 190 by 3.50, Wilson contributing 72 in less than 45 minutes. The professional then passed 100 wickets for the season in taking 5 for 41, and Enfield were bowled out for 91 by 5.15. Johnny Ratcliff's fluent 109 not out steered Todmorden to 200 for 9 in the return at Enfield, before Wilson's four wickets in five balls finished off the home side (140 all out) and the season in style.

Success was in the air; the tea pavilion was a going concern; a popular professional had been re-signed and was backed by some talented amateurs; there was a surplus, albeit small, in the bank; 1914 was eagerly anticipated.

The committee ordered 475 members' cards, a 20% increase, plus 100 cards for lady members. Miss Sutcliffe of Lower Laithe, whose family owned Stansfield Corn Mill, gave half a dozen garden seats to the club. Others followed suit and there were thirty-six new ground seats by May 1914. Enjoying a healthy bank balance, the club added over seventy of similar pattern over the next two years to provide some of the best seating in the League by April 1916.

The committee introduced talent money for amateur bowlers who took five wickets in a match, putting them on a par with their batting colleagues who had for years been rewarded for scoring fifty runs. Bowlers were no longer merely 'the trundlers'.

The local sporting scene was enlivened by successes in rugby and football. Todmorden's northern union side defeated Elland in the semi-final of the Halifax Rugby Union Football League Cup, played at Sandholme about a mile from the town centre between Halifax Road and the River Calder. Burnley, back from their 1-0 victory over Liverpool at Crystal Palace, paraded the FA Cup before huge crowds, taking in several Lancashire League grounds, and in Todmorden there were special cheers for Billy Nesbitt who started his career with Portsmouth Rovers before professional football provided an escape route from the mill.

Todmorden's 1914 season opened with six consecutive victories, none sweeter than that over Nelson at Centre Vale. Nelson took control of the match, reducing Todmorden from 78 for 4 to 104 all out, and racing to 50 in 44 minutes. At 66 for 4 the visitors were still favourites when Wilson (6 for 35) and Stansfield (4 for 19) demolished the last six wickets without addition. Amid scenes of tremendous enthusiasm, the pair left the ground suffering 'well meant but distinctly uncomfortable attentions at the hands and shoulders of the crowd'.

Riding high with nine victories and only one defeat from the first 13 matches, the club distributed 2000 handbills in Burnley and arranged for a special train to run Burnley's supporters to the clash at Centre Vale on 20 June. The largest crowd for many years produced gate receipts of £62 12s 8d, but it was Burnley's professional Billy Cook who rose to the occasion. Bowling at terrific speed he took all ten Todmorden wickets for 36 runs, nine of them clean bowled, as Todmorden were dismissed for 52 to lose by 86 runs. At the end of the match the crowd 'rushed on', according Cook a 'great ovation', and Todmorden captain Harry Hudson presented him with the match ball.[8]

Ned Stansfield had already taken 57 wickets in the season and, 'as a compliment' to him, a collection was held raising £8 13s 3d. He went on to set a new club record of 81 wickets for which he received a nine carat gold medal and a silver ornament surmounted by a cricket ball. His handful of appearances for Yorkshire 2nd XI came at this time and included a friendly against minor counties side Staffordshire and his Todmorden colleague Wilson.

Between late June and early August, Wilson played seven midweek Minor County Championship matches for Staffordshire, six of which were won and one abandoned. He shared new ball duties with SF Barnes and future Todmorden professional Bertie Morgan, who was professional at Ramsbottom in 1914. This trio were devastating, bowling the opposition out for under 100 in eleven innings out of thirteen. The Minor Counties title was disputed but *Wisden* records Staffordshire as the champions. Wilson's 43 wickets at around 5 runs each made a key contribution and give some perspective to the quality of Lancashire League cricket at this time, where his 94 wickets for Todmorden cost double that at 10.02.

Todmorden's search for a professional for 1915 began in May when Wilson and the team were carrying all before them. Perhaps Wilson's impending absences from his midweek duties assisting the groundsman (as stipulated in his contract) were the reason. The net was widely cast and included approaches to former Yorkshire and England all-rounder Schofield Haigh, South African Aubrey Faulkner, a batsman and leg break/googly bowler who played 25 test matches, and fast medium bowler George Geary of Leicestershire. Patrick Morfee, a Kent fast bowler proing in Fifeshire was considered until Todmorden learned of his current earnings. In June Todmorden received a letter from Ambrose Williams, a twenty-six year-old right-arm fast bowler who had been signed by Yorkshire and was professional at Barnsley, offering his services for £7 per week. By early July Todmorden had knocked this down to £6 10s and signed him.

In 1914 the town was enjoying a wonderful summer. Across from the cricket ground, the Weavers' Institute, symbolic of the strength of the local Weavers' Union, was completed at a cost of £3000 and opened in May. Centre Vale Park saw the opening of the bandstand in June and, in July, the third Annual Show of the newly re-formed Agricultural Society. On 1 August Todmorden enjoyed a terrific nine wicket victory over title rivals Colne to consolidate their position at the top of the Lancashire League.

But a dark shadow was falling across this local prosperity. Rumblings amongst the European states had become ominous; Germany declared war on France and, in order to invade, marched through Belgium. Britain had guaranteed Belgium neutrality and, on Tuesday 4 August, declared war on Germany. On Friday 7 August local territorials from the 6th Battalion Lancashire Fusiliers marched from the Drill Hall on Dalton Street through Todmorden to their headquarters at Rochdale. By 14 August 150 horses from Halifax, Hebden Bridge and Todmorden were mustered in Fielden Square awaiting branding and shoeing at the forge.

The previous Saturday, Todmorden lost the leadership of the Lancashire League. Their match at Haslingden was abandoned whilst Accrington, their closest rivals, won, replacing Todmorden as League leaders. Accrington won their next four matches and Todmorden could not catch them. Nevertheless, as runners-up in both 1st and 2nd XI competitions, and £105 in credit, Todmorden had enjoyed the most successful of their 18 seasons in the Lancashire League.

But the war overshadowed everything. Sensitive to looming hardship, the club reduced admission prices for the last month of the season and organised a match with Walsden which, although spoilt by weather, raised £5 in aid of the local distress fund.

During August, amongst the usual Saturday night crowd which filled the streets, the European crisis and its consequences displaced the cricket team's prospects as the major topic of conversation. Would the cotton trade suffer from shortages of raw materials and lack of buyers? There was panic buying from the shops. Aeroplanes over

Local Fusiliers, August 1914, turning from Dalton St into Stansfield Rd
en route to Rochdale HQ.

Walsden, soon after midnight, startled the residents. The Mayor announced the appointment of an Emergency Committee which would be as 'representative in character as possible'.

Some mills closed. The Fieldens promised to keep their mills running as far as possible but stressed the importance, for those receiving a weekly wage, 'not to spend more than can be avoided until matters clear up'. They also announced that workers joining the regular forces would receive £10. James Duckworth, a regional grocery retail chain, paid any employees who joined the forces four weeks' full wages and guaranteed them their job when they returned. Any who were married continued on half pay for the duration of their service, whilst special arrangements were made for single men with dependents.

Many young men needed no incentive to go to war. They anticipated adventure and an escape from industrial drudgery. This naivety was dispelled locally when, in November, the first war casualties were admitted to Sam and Sarah Fielden's former residence, the mansion in Centre Vale Park, which now served as a hospital for convalescent soldiers and sailors. The war was not going to 'be over by Christmas', but no one yet realised how long the conflict would last nor how terrible it would become.

The effects of the war had begun to bite before the end of the 1914 cricket season. The locality was divided into six relief districts and by mid-September volunteers were providing meals at schools for over 500 needy children, the majority requiring breakfast, lunch and tea.

The final match of 1914 saw Todmorden bowl bottom-club Lowerhouse out for 75, with one batsman, Brown, retiring hurt after a Wilson express hit him on the 'bare knuckles'! Todmorden replied with 271 for 6 and hoped to reach the League record

Centre Vale Hospital 1915

score of 311 until Lowerhouse, understandably, declined to continue and stumps were drawn at 5.40pm. It was a memorable day for Clarence Lee who hit 55, his maiden half century for the club.

Clarence Lee worked on the staff at the *Todmorden Advertiser* and had a more comfortable life than most, but like many young men responded to Kitchener's call for unquestioning loyalty to king and country. His story, pieced together through correspondence to the newspaper via his family, is the war in microcosm.

In June 1915, training with the 8th Devon Regiment at Aldershot, he wrote to the club asking for a bat and ball. The club gladly obliged, as it did to many such requests from its troops. In July he was enjoying his cricket and, invited to play for the battalion, was complimented by the officers, including the Colonel, on the quality of his play.

> On each occasion we had tea with the officers on the lawn. It was fine. We play on a splendid ground and it is just A1. I never felt better and never had a better time.

By August 1915 he was at Loos in France:

> You will perhaps be surprised to hear I have been in the trenches. I am, in fact, writing this letter whilst in my dug-out. We are only in for 48 hours, and are being sent just to get used to the trenches and the noise of the guns…The Germans are about 450 yards away from us and they don't forget to let us know about it. Whilst I am writing, shells are passing over our heads, but we are quite safe in our dug-outs. By the way, the trench we are in is an old German one. It is about 7 feet high and stacked with sand bags all round…so it is not so bad in the trenches as one might think.

He moved forward for a spell in the 'firing line'

> …numerous shells and bullets passed over our heads, and I replied by firing a few shots…

before being relieved from duty.

> …After a struggle coming through the communication trenches we are now back in billets - an old building attached to a farmhouse. We have straw to sleep on, so shall not be at all bad.

On 23 September he wrote a field postcard, received on Sunday 26 September, stating that he was quite well. After that letters and parcels sent out to him were returned marked 'Casualty' or 'Wounded location uncertain'. A Todmorden man in the same regiment was wounded at Loos on Saturday 25 September and reported that, after his injury, he had seen Private Lee in the front firing line and he was all right but at the cricket club's sombre AGM in November, it was reported that:

> ...4 members have been killed in active service and it is hoped that C Lee will eventually be traced and that he will be returned to his family.

One of the four fatalities was the son of Edward Crabtree. A newspaper report of the AGM was read by a Todmorden man in the Royal Field Artillery, who wrote in:

> I see in the paper that C Lee is missing. When we were going into action with the guns on 25th September there was a battery in front of us. One of the guns slipped into a trench and our battery had to wait for half an hour before we could go forward. While we were waiting I had a look at some of the infantry men that lay dead around. I gazed at a young man that just resembled Clarence Lee. It went through me like a flash of lightning that it was him I saw laid there. He was about 20 yards out of the trench and looked as if he had been killed in a charge. He had a bullet wound through the back of his ear...I knew him as well as I knew anybody.

The antiquated strategy of charging the enemy was suicidal against modern artillery, but it took numerous massacres before the generals adopted the more attritional tactics now associated with trench warfare. It was too late for Clarence Lee. By the time Private Lee's family received the postcard he wrote on 23 September, he had been killed. Todmorden Cricket Club commissioned a photograph of Clarence Lee to be hung in the pavilion, but its whereabouts are unknown.

Clarence Lee and Johnny Ratcliff, who had returned to Bedford, were the only players from 1914 not to play in the 1915 season, which only went ahead after much deliberation. The 2nd XI competition was suspended to curtail expenses, which left Centre Vale available for the 3rd XI's home matches in the still functioning Todmorden and District League.

In the Lancashire League minutes for 1915, players' expenses, to compensate for loss of earnings on match days, were set at 2s 6d for those leaving work between 11 and 12, 1s 6d between 12 and 1, and 1s between 1 and 2 o'clock. Todmorden economised by negotiating a one third reduction from professional Williams's £6 10s weekly salary, and reducing the membership cards - now a patriotic khaki colour - to the size of the smaller ladies' cards. All who joined the forces were to have slips bearing 'On Military Service Honorary Member' stuck in their cards. In moves which led to younger boys becoming members, several on active service asked that their membership be transferred to their sons, most of whom were under fifteen years of age - hitherto the minimum age for membership. Servicemen in uniform were admitted free to matches.

For the first time, there was no tender for the right to sell refreshments at matches, so there was no ale tent. The franchise to sell pies was not taken up and the responsibility passed on to the ladies' committee. The club, reflecting financial uncertainty, proposed to the League:

> ...that any agreement entered into with a professional during the season, shall contain some clause whereby such agreement shall become void in the event of the war continuing.

Whilst Accrington went through the season unbeaten and retained the title,

Todmorden slumped to second bottom. The bowlers did their bit. Williams took 82 wickets, Stansfield 61 and Walter Leslie Greenwood 23, including 6 for 33 at Rishton in the final match, to become the second bowler after Jonas Clegg senior to pass 500 wickets for the club. The batsmen, however, did not perform well and no one reached 300 runs.

Two matches in particular demonstrated the team's strengths and failings. At Haslingden, the batsmen collapsed to 67 all out, but Williams and Stansfield dismissed Haslingden for the same total. Against Burnley at Centre Vale the two star bowlers again came to the rescue in another tie, both sides totalling 63. Despite such a close finish between these fiercest of rivals, played before a good gate considering the absence of cheap rail travel, the local reporter 'missed the usual fratching that has been a feature of these matches'.

People were subdued, their minds elsewhere, their priorities changed to cope with home front demands and austerity - winning a cricket match was secondary to winning the war. Cricketing opponents were also comrades in the greater cause, putting sport in its true perspective - greatly enhanced as a diversion and escape, greatly diminished in terms of who won.

The highlight of 1915 was an end-of-season Derby against Walsden to support the Centre Vale Military Hospital, both sides augmented by guest professionals. Four Yorkshire players agreed to play for just their rail fares, Victor Widdup of the Queen Hotel liaising with them and providing hospitality. Thus, on Monday 6 September, Wilfred Rhodes and Percy Holmes led the Todmorden batting against a Walsden attack spearheaded by George Hirst and Alonzo Drake. Walsden were bowled out in the final over of a well-contested match, the county players providing 'an example of keenness and alertness especially when batting'. Rhodes, who hit 93, gave over half of his £8 18s 9d collection to the hospital fund, enabling the club to hand over a total of £74. Alonzo Drake, who had done the double of 1000 runs and 100 wickets for Yorkshire in 1913, had tried to enlist for the army but was rejected on health grounds. He had heart problems and played his wartime cricket for Bingley and Eccleshill in the Bradford League believing that he did not have long to live. He was right. In February 1919 he died of a heart attack at the age of 34.[9]

The war situation worsened and in 1916, for the first time, conscription was introduced. The Lancashire League's honorary secretary from 1900-35, William Barlow of Ramsbottom, had difficulty fulfilling his duties because a staff shortage demanded additional hours at his insurance office.[10] The League continued to run, but without professionals, and the two-mile amateur qualification rules were held in abeyance so that anyone wishing to play as an amateur could be considered.

The use of German Zeppelin Airships as bombers brought the war close to home for the first time. At the start of March the public was told that a lowering of gas pressure and electricity current, causing lights to dim, was warning of a raid. The following week Walsden Cricket Club minuted 'That we insure Pavilion, Tea Room and Bowling Green Pavilion against damage by air raid'. On at least four occasions the town was blacked out after a Zeppelin warning and on the night of 26 September 1916 the much feared hum of a Zeppelin engine approached the town. The commander had crossed the east coast towards Sheffield but, it is believed, missed his bearings for Manchester. He located the railway line at Todmorden and followed it, flying close to the Walsden ground. Locals heard two explosions in the distance, but official reports state that the craft followed the line to Bury and Bolton, both of which it bombed, before returning east over the Yorkshire Moors and crossing the coast at Whitby.

Whilst the town feared destruction by German bombs, the cricket club was wary of the British government's new entertainment tax which applied to all forms of sport. Since leasing the ground from the borough in 1911, the club had learnt that independence brings responsibilities; added to the usual rent were rates and insurance, but at least these were local. The new tax was unwelcome interference from central government and, although accepted as a wartime necessity, it was treated with hostility.

Todmorden always conducted its affairs with fierce independence, and this was reflected by the decisions of the cricket club. Rather than deter spectators by increasing admission prices to include the tax, the committee left admission unchanged but took a collection around the ground. If the amount collected was insufficient to cover the 1d per head tax, the club made up the difference. The scheme was advertised in the town, emphasising that the tax collections were voluntary.

By April 1916 there were over 70 club members serving in the forces, including several players, but Walter Storah had returned from professional duties at Walsden and, in harness with Ned Stansfield, had a field day in the now all-amateur league. With players away fighting, the lack of depth in some teams provided rich lower-order pickings for Todmorden's two expert left-arm spinners. Storah set a new club record of 91 wickets, including 4 in 4 balls against East Lancashire, and he took 5 or more wickets on twelve occasions. When he completed 50 wickets in mid-July the committee held a collection for him at the match against Ramsbottom, stating '…on this occasion the war tax will not be charged'.

Todmorden lost fewer players than most and with Edward Shackleton setting a new club batting record of 721 runs, including two centuries, the club were in contention for the title until late August, when three defeats consigned them to fourth place behind Accrington, who won their third consecutive championship.

The club was now heavily involved with the local war charities, especially the Military Hospital. When the Hare spinning mill, now renamed 'Mons' after the first major battle of the war, had a flag day the club hosted a charity match, 'Spinners' versus 'Rest of the Mill', helping to raise £120. Another match, 'Centre Vale Soldiers' versus 'A Todmorden XI' saw old players Johnny Horsfall, Jonas Clegg junior and John Crabtree don their whites again to raise £50 towards 'cigarettes and other comforts' for the soldiers. Jonas scored 104 before retiring, proving that even at 55 years of age, he could still hit the ball very hard.

On Tuesday 5 September Todmorden played Walsden in a second celebrity match. George Hirst and the England football and cricket international, Jack Sharp, played for Todmorden, whilst Walsden were supplemented by Wilfred Rhodes, JT Tyldesley of Lancashire and the Warwickshire fast bowler Frank Field. The match was drawn, Shackleton enhancing his reputation with an innings of 47, mainly from the bowling of Rhodes and Field. Receipts of £50 included £7 from the auctioning of a donkey.

The committee was unable to fulfil a pre-season promise to donate any profit to the local war funds as, for the first time in several seasons, the club made a loss. The £10 deficit was blamed entirely on having to make good the much-loathed entertainment tax. The club continued to support the town to the end of the war. Charity matches of lower profile raised a further £160 and land behind the pavilion was offered for use as allotments to members, with no charge except the cost of ploughing. By March 1918 twenty allotments had been created and let out, assisting a national campaign launched to counteract a food shortage exacerbated by the sinking of merchant ships by German submarines.

Reacting to the ever-worsening situation, the League voted 11 to 3 (Accrington, Bacup and Church) to suspend League cricket in 1917. Clubs were allowed to arrange friendly matches so long as the title 'Lancashire League' was not used and Todmorden

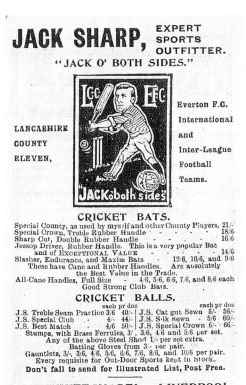

Jack Sharp, cricketer, Lancashire 1899-1925;
3 Tests in 1909: also soccer, outside-right,
Aston Villa; Everton; England.

JT Tyldesley, played for
Lancashire 1895-1923;
also 31 Test matches.

George Hirst and Wilfred Rhodes,
two Yorkshire immortals.

Frank Field, played for Warwickshire
1897-1920.

Allotment Workers WWI, group from Cornholme Methodist Church.

played a dozen against Burnley, Lowerhouse, Milnrow, Rochdale and Walsden. Even though there was little cricket to watch, the committee exhorted members to remain faithful and pay their subscriptions, which were reduced to 5s for ordinary members and 2s for ladies.

The Ladies' Committee raised money to help the families of 13 playing members serving in the forces. News from the front hung like a cloud over the town and in September 1917, the *Todmorden Advertiser* commented:

> With the suspension of the league tournament and with public attention concentrated on the grim business of war and its many grave problems, the game seems to have had no attraction even for those left at home.

The League remained suspended in 1918. Desperate for numbers, the government passed a new Military Service Act which extended conscription. In January 1916 only unmarried men aged between 18 and 41 had been conscripted, but by May 1917 married men were included and time-expired ones had their service extended. Those previously rejected were to be re-examined as were the Home Service Territorial men previously discharged as disabled or with ill-health. The Military Service Acts (4 and 5) early in 1918 further widened conscription to include men between 17 and 55 years of age, exemptions for protected occupations could be quashed and the two months' period of grace between call-up and joining the forces withdrawn. Released or exchanged prisoners of war were no longer exempt and time-expired soldiers could be recalled.[11] Unsurprisingly, Todmorden had difficulty in raising a team and cancelled any matches which had been arranged.

With the Lancashire League suspended, three of Todmorden's cricketers sought competition elsewhere. In 1917 EB Shackleton, Walter Storah and Wilfred Greenwood joined the Bradford League club Bankfoot, which still plays next door to Bradford's rugby league amphitheatre at Odsal Top. As just about the only major league still functioning, professionals from the counties and the leagues, including several familiar to the Lancashire League, flooded into it. With the likes of Jack Hobbs, Frank Woolley and George Gunn amongst them, most Bradford League teams were close to county standard. In the opinion of future Todmorden professional Fred Root, who played for Bowling Old Lane:

> Keighley…would have beaten almost any county team. It was the highest standard of club cricket the country has ever seen.[12]

Only Shackleton stayed on for the 1918 season, when Bankfoot were involved in the most remarkable Priestley Cup final of the Bradford League's illustrious history. Bankfoot were third from bottom of the league and their opponents, Saltaire, whose professional SF Barnes inspired them to successive titles in 1917 and 1918, were firm favourites. The 13,500 spectators crammed into Bradford Park Avenue anticipated a shock result when Saltaire were bowled out for 99. Shackleton and his opening partner Wilf Payton, who scored over 22,000 runs for Nottinghamshire between 1905 and 1931, set about reducing the arrears before the effects of the roller wore off. They added 20 in ten minutes, but the odds swung Saltaire's way when Payton was run out - a not uncommon fate for Shackleton's partners.

The Todmorden man could only stand and stare as Barnes (8 for 50, including a hat-trick) ran through his team mates, reducing Bankfoot to 41 for 7, 62 for 8 and 78 for 9. Excitement mounted as the last wicket pair added 20. Shackleton struck a powerful straight drive which seemed destined for the boundary and the winning runs, only to strike the stumps at the bowler's end and cannon away for a single to tie the scores. Shackleton's valiant partner was bowled next ball and the match was tied, Shackleton unbeaten on 47 out of Bankfoot's 99 all out. The *Bradford Telegraph and Argus* reported:

> Shackleton who had to hold his end up against twenty one overs sent down by Barnes, some of them when the wicket was at its worst, gave no real chance in his 47 and his innings was played when his side had their backs to the wall - just the circumstances that appeal to a Yorkshire crowd.

The replay at Bowling Old Lane two days later brought the total attendance to 24,500, but underdogs usually get only one chance of an upset and Bankfoot's opportunity had gone. Shackleton top-scored again with 29 of his team's 89 all out, Barnes taking 5 for 43 and his opening partner, Yorkshire's Herbert Sedgwick, 4 for 34, but Saltaire won by 7 wickets.

To score runs twice against one of the best bowlers of all time, in bowler-friendly conditions and in the most highly charged and competitive circumstances to be found anywhere in the country at the time, speaks volumes for Shackleton's temperament and technique. He was one of the very best amateur batsmen of his or any other generation.[13]

With no club matches on Centre Vale in 1918, the committee promoted a cricket competition amongst the elementary schools, using the old Calder Valley League Cup as the trophy. To facilitate this, the club purchased four lads' bats, three pairs of leg guards and one pair of stumping gloves suitable for boys with an average age of twelve, and three youths' match balls. All the schools responded, some of the smaller ones combining, to form a league of seven teams. The pitch was twenty yards long, otherwise MCC rules applied.

Centre Vale staged all 25 matches and the competition was a great success. The final match, league winners 'Roomfield' versus 'The Rest', attracted a gate of £21 9s 3d, which, at 3d per head equates to a crowd of 1717, amongst them the secretary of

Burnley CC who came along to study the competition.

The committee were very enthusiastic about this venture but, without the war and suspension of senior cricket would youngsters have been as welcome to use the ground? Having 'opened the gates', what would the club's attitude be when peace returned?

The AGM for 1918 was held on Wednesday 6 November, five days before the end of hostilities. The formalities in the committee's report - that 273 members and 100 ladies had paid subscriptions, that the club had survived the war with £131 in the bank even though it had helped to raise almost £500 for the war effort - were all positive, but seem inconsequential beside the simple statement:

> We await with eagerness the fulfilment of our present hope of the imminence of peace.

124 members, 25% of the male membership, had joined the forces. Many were traumatised for life, condemned to re-live the atrocities they had witnessed. Several had been wounded. Twelve, including Clarence Lee, had made the supreme sacrifice.

Chapter 4

Post-War Explosion

On 23 October 1918 the Todmorden Cricket Committee resolved:

> ...in the opinion of this meeting the time has arrived to make preparations to recommence Lancashire League Cricket!

Other League clubs shared this view and arrangements went ahead for 1919, albeit with caution about expenditure, as public reaction in the aftermath of the war was uncertain. Although Todmorden was financially sound, some clubs were in a fragile state, none more than Burnley. Turf Moor was in a state of disrepair, interest was low, members had been lost and the club only avoided losing its ground by becoming a Public Limited Company. It was decided that professionals should be optional for 1919 and that a bonus of ten points - the equivalent of 5 wins - should be awarded to any club playing without one. In the event, only Bacup fielded an all amateur team.

Todmorden began the search for a professional by placing advertisements in *The Sporting Chronicle*, *Staffordshire Sentinel* and a Gloucestershire paper. Letters were sent to Ambrose Williams, the 1915 professional, and to Lancashire pace-bowler James Tyldesley. John Alexander 'Jack' Cuffe of Worcestershire was approached and required £8 per week, talent money for scoring 50, collections for scoring 50 at home, 15s for taking 6 wickets in a match and £1 for more than 6 wickets. Driving the hardest bargain, Todmorden obtained his signature for £7 10s per week and Cuffe became Todmorden's first full-time overseas professional.

Born in Toowomba, Queensland, on 26 June 1880, Cuffe had played against AE Stoddart's 1898 England tourists in an up-country match, impressing Ranjitsinhji with his ability to move the ball both ways on a matting wicket. Cuffe moved to Sydney and played briefly for New South Wales before emigrating to England in 1903. A right-hand batsman and slow-medium left-arm bowler, his first-class career produced 7476 runs at 22.35 and 738 wickets at 25.47, predominantly from his 215 matches for Worcestershire between 1903 and 1914, which included the 'double' of 1000 runs and 100 wickets in 1911.[1]

The make-up of Cuffe's Todmorden colleagues was uncertain. The return of the forces from abroad took time and at least four regular players had not been demobilised at the start of the season. Edwin Stansfield had signed as professional for Halifax and wicketkeeper Harry Hudson was unavailable. Anticipating a player shortage, the Lancashire League delayed its 2nd XI competition until 1920, encouraging clubs to arrange a limited number of friendly matches instead, which Todmorden did. The 3rd XI was resurrected in the Todmorden and District League.

Early in the season teams were rarely at full-strength - Todmorden, for example, used 26 different first team players in 1919 and, as in 1916, bowlers were able to exploit some weak lower-order batting. The season opened with a spectacular win at Rishton. Todmorden, having been bowled out for 72, skittled Rishton for 30, Cuffe taking 3 for 20 and Walter Leslie Greenwood 7 for 9.

Three weeks later at Centre Vale, Haslingden were bowled out for 27, Cuffe 4 for 18 and Walter Leslie 4 for 3, Todmorden winning by 6 wickets. It was Todmorden's turn to suffer at Church on Wednesday 25 June when they collapsed to 16 for 9 and were bowled out for 28 in fifty minutes by a new and unknown bowler, James Winyard, who took 7 for 9.

Bowling variations of left-arm fast, medium and 'slow-breaks' from a short run, Winyard burst onto the Lancashire League with 29 wickets in four matches, including all ten against Accrington, and remains one of the League's great mysteries. Stationed at Whalley Military Hospital after being wounded and gassed, he was rumoured to be an England bowler under an assumed name. Rishton and Ramsbottom, both routed by Winyard, complained successfully that Whalley was not within Church's two-mile qualification limit and the League fined Church £20 and deducted the four points they had gained against these opponents. However, understandably sympathetic to Church's arguments about Winyard's war service and appreciative of his ability, they allowed him to play the rest of the season when, strangely, his effectiveness waned. Ramsbottom professional, Smith, recognised Winyard as a pre-war club professional at Forfar and Cuffe had also encountered him before, but kept his own counsel on the matter. Winyard, who left the area at the end of the season, considered that the war justified his playing as an amateur. He would not have encountered a League with amateur qualification rules as excellent and stringent as those in the Lancashire League and was probably unaware of the furore he would cause.[2]

Nelson won their first nine matches in 1919 and held a narrow lead over eventual champions East Lancashire when they came to Todmorden on 16 August. By this time there was an air of near normality about the cricket. Thousands travelled by train, many others cycled from Nelson and the gate of £78 19s 10d was a new record for Centre Vale. The crowd, packed to overflowing, was treated to a thrilling match. Shackleton (79) and Cuffe (54) shared a second wicket stand of 139 in Todmorden's 185 all out, the highest total Nelson had conceded all season. Left with two hours to play, both sides pushed hard for victory but time ran out with Nelson 176 for 8 and the match was drawn.

With such gates, and membership increasing to 582, including 125 ladies and 60 boys, nervousness about re-starting the Lancashire League had proved unfounded. As people re-established their individual and collective lives, crowds flooded to the matches, reinforcing the extent to which the local cricket clubs were integral to their communities.

If League cricket was one symbol of the return to normality, the townsfolk were determined to enjoy the first year of peace in other ways too. The four local railway stations took 5888 bookings for the wakes week holidays, mainly to Blackpool, Liverpool, North Wales, Scarborough, Bridlington, Morecambe and London.

A post-war boom had enabled cotton workers to achieve better pay and conditions. A strike by the spinners earned a reduction in hours from 55½ to 48 per week with an increase of 30% on the 'standard piece price list rate of wages' and an equivalent increase for all other workers in the industry. Once agreed the 48 hour week was fixed for eighteen months and the new rates of pay for at least nine months until April 1920.

Financially sound, Todmorden could afford to spend more on a professional, but did a team which had finished eighth in 1919 merit this? Edward Shackleton, who carried his bat through the innings for 62 not out in a one-wicket defeat at East Lancashire, and hit 518 runs in the season, was one of the League's best batsmen. His best amateur support came from the emerging Arthur Stephenson with 323 runs. Small and slightly built, Stephenson was a brilliant fieldsman and a determined and resolute batsman. Strong on the off-drive and late cut, he was most effective at wearing down opening bowlers with extreme patience and powerful concentration. He made his debut in 1908 but by 1919 had not played for six years owing to accidental injury. He batted solidly for the 1st XI until 1934 and, in his final season, became the second player after Shackleton to score 5000 Lancashire League runs for the club.

Walter Leslie Greenwood with 57 wickets and Cuffe with 83 bowled more than 720 overs between them. The successful professional also contributed 462 runs and in July agreed to re-engagement on the same terms for 1920, only to change his mind and ask for a further pound per week. The club declined and Cuffe's time at Todmorden was over. He played several seasons as a professional in the Bolton area in the 1920s and returned to the Lancashire League at Lowerhouse in 1923 and 24.

Cuffe was also the first Australian to play professional football in England. He made his debut for Glossop in the second of the Football League's two divisions in 1905, helped them to the quarter final of the FA Cup in 1909, and played until World War I, the club's final season in the league. Sadly, like many sportsmen, and particularly cricketers, he

Arthur Stephenson, a stubborn opening batsman 1908-34.

struggled to cope with retirement and, twelve days after accepting the post of cricket coach at Repton in May 1931, his lifeless body was found in the River Trent at Burton. The coroner's verdict was suicide by drowning. He was 50 years old.

Todmorden's extensive search for Cuffe's replacement began with another approach to Ambrose Williams, now at Dewsbury, and to Frank Field, the former Warwickshire fast bowler who had played in the 1916 Hospital Match at Todmorden. Perhaps fortified by the late-season gate against Nelson, they became more ambitious and enquired about three future England players, Leicestershire's George Geary, Gloucestershire's slow left-armer Charlie Parker, and the Hampshire all-rounder Alex Kennedy.

In mid-October Todmorden signed Pat Morfee, Nelson's professional of 1919. The club was at pains to explain that Nelson had given their consent, and with Edward Crabtree overseeing affairs Todmorden's diligence and propriety could be guaranteed. In 1906 it was Crabtree along with the Haslingden CC League representative who proposed the rule that no club could approach another club's professional before 1 July. This was approved and remains virtually unchanged over a century later.[3] Morfee's fee was £12 per week - over £3 more than Cuffe had demanded, signalling a clear intention to challenge for honours. Geary, whose test career was still four years away, became Nelson's professional, an exciting capture and a sign that Lancashire League clubs were beginning to entice players of increasing quality away from county cricket.

Morfee's signing proved to be a stroke of genius. At the annual meeting thanks were expressed to Robert Fielden for his assistance in the negotiations and for travelling the country at his own expense to meet with potential professionals. A bachelor from the Cloughfoot area of Bacup Road, he was a vice-president of the club for many years, hardly ever missed a committee meeting and worked tirelessly behind the scenes. By

1925 he had attended every home and away match for 25 years.

From every aspect Todmorden viewed the 1920 season with enthusiasm. The surviving pre-war players were fully available, Walter Storah had returned from Walsden, and Morfee was seen as the catalyst who would lead and inspire the team.

In addition to League matches, a full knockout cup was organised for 1920. Inspired by three regional competitions arranged between some Lancashire League teams from 1917 to 1919, the new competition was the brainchild of Edward Crabtree. The first round ties were to be a set of League fixtures, followed by a straight knockout competition. The trophy, donated by Haslingden's League representative, Alderman Tom Worsley JP CC, and used for the Burnley area regional competition in 1919, was the Worsley Cup.[4]

The new competition would help finances at a time when costs were spiralling. At Todmorden the groundman's wages had risen from £2 10s to £3 10s per week in twelve months, and match balls costing 9s each in March were 14s each by May. Players' expenses to compensate loss of earnings were also adjusted to reflect post-war inflation. By 1921 at Todmorden players received, for away matches 5s on Saturday and 10s on a weekday, and for home matches nothing on Saturday but 7s 6d on a weekday and 5s on a holiday.

The League fixed a new minimum admission price of 6d, inclusive of tax, and Todmorden raised its prices in proportion by about 50% to 8d for the school side and 1s for the rest of the ground, with an extra 3d for the pavilion enclosure. These were substantial increases but by keeping members' subscriptions at 10s 6d, with vice-presidents £1 1s, becoming a member was, for the first time, the cheapest way of seeing every match and also allowed entrance to the ground at any time. The upshot was that membership doubled and, because of lack of accommodation, a limit was put on boy members.

Hoping to fuel enthusiasm, the committee displayed team sheets at several shops and clubs in Todmorden and Hebden Bridge, but the first three matches of 1920 were abandoned and Todmorden did not take to the field until 8 May when they entertained Rawtenstall in the first match to double as both League and Worsley Cup fixture. The ground was in a deplorable condition but, with a result essential, play began at 3.50pm. Todmorden were all out for 52 but Storah (5 for 20) and Morfee (4 for 20) saw them home by nine runs, bowling Rawtenstall out for 43.

Todmorden staged another recovery in the second round at home to Bacup on Tuesday 25 May. Collapsing to 61 for 5, they were reliant on the lower order for a decent total. Harry Hudson, batting at number ten, top scored with 44 not out and added 55 for the last wicket with Walter Leslie Greenwood as Todmorden posted 221 all out. Morfee then routed Bacup for 39, taking 9 for 26 to earn a £10 collection. When he took a hat-trick four days later as defending champions East Lancashire were bowled out for 70, Todmorden's season really took off. Crowds came to enjoy Morfee's 'expresses' confident that he would take wickets and, if lucky, they would see a stump broken or a bail flying to the boundary.

With Todmorden top of the League, the club's treasurer was all smiles, especially on 11 June when a special train brought 1500 supporters from second-placed Nelson to see the contest against their ex-professional. A crowd of 4500 paid £182 1s 4d, more than double Todmorden's previous best gate, and to the home spectators' delight, Morfee (6 for 43), aided by Storah, bowled Nelson out for 88, George Geary causing 'much amusement by his fruitless efforts to hit Storah's puzzling deliveries'. Geary (4 for 44) made early inroads after tea, but Shackleton held firm with a stubborn 28 as Todmorden won by 5 wickets.

Walter Leslie Greenwood, the last playing link with the club's Central Lancashire League days, was granted a benefit in 1920. Joining as a batsman in 1894 from the Calder Valley League side Todmorden Church, he had scored over 2000 runs but it was his medium-pace bowling that thrived and his 678 Lancashire League wickets remain the most by a Todmorden amateur. He served on the committee from 1901 and throughout the war. To the role of treasurer he added that of secretary in 1917 and collector in 1918. He personified the 'good clubman'.

Walter Leslie's benefit was celebrated with victory over Ramsbottom. Stephenson nurdled a typically obdurate 33 not out to carry his bat as Todmorden recovered from 46 for 6 to 106 all out. Storah (6 for 21) then teased Ramsbottom out for 66. The beneficiary was supported by a gate of almost £100. The Todmorden Brass Band processed from the Town Hall to the field and entertained during the tea interval. As Walter Leslie strode out to bat the band struck up *Auld Lang Syne*.

At Bacup on 13 July Morfee took 6 for 25, including another hat-trick and his hundredth wicket, and along with Walter Leslie (4 for 4) dismissed the home side for 45. Todmorden limped home by one wicket and the batting failed again two days later in the Worsley Cup semi-final. Former Todmorden professional Ambrose Williams took 8 for 25 as Todmorden were bowled out for 82. Morfee took early wickets, but former professional Ted Riley had his measure like no other. It was said that he could 'bat Morfee with a picking stick' - the wooden rod which helped to propel the shuttle across the loom - and he hit an unbeaten 62 as Haslingden won by 4 wickets.

Todmorden's fragile batting was now derailing their title challenge. The opposition only reached three figures five times all season, but four of these games were lost including two to Colne who finished third from bottom and a pivotal match to Haslingden on 7 August. It was 4 September before a Todmorden batsman hit a 50, Eddie Hargreaves scoring exactly that against Church. Walter Leslie took 6 for 5 to rout the visitors for 30 in just forty minutes but by then it was too late. In the last match Haslingden blocked out for the draw they needed to clinch the title, becoming the first

Todmorden 2nd XI 1920 Champions.
L-R Row 3: James Lord, Uriah Holland (umpires), T Marshall, Ratcliffe, A Barnes, ____, Sunderland, Sunderland,
Row 2: Ratcliffe, Wilf Greenwood, John Lord, William Law, Charles Helliwell, W Hartley, JW Sunderland,   Row 1: R Sutcliffe, GR Lord.

team in 26 League and Cup matches to prevent Morfee taking at least four wickets in an innings. Todmorden had missed their chance and had to settle for third place.

In other respects it had been a good season. The 2nd XI, with only one defeat in 18 matches, had won the junior championship for the fifth time - two more than any other club at this time. Donations had raised Walter Leslie's benefit to a club record £200, comparable to the salaries of most club professionals. Subscriptions had more than doubled and gate money was up from £346 in 1919 to £901 in 1920, from which the club begrudgingly paid £288 in entertainment tax. To accommodate the crowds 175 extra seats had been bought and more were planned for 1921.

Morfee had taken 131 League wickets and 144 in League and Cup, both still club records, and was offered a further three years' contract at £16 per week, an increase of 33.3%, plus the prospect of a job in the winter. This involved building a terrace from the pavilion towards Centre Vale Park, and the Town Council gave permission to cut down any trees necessary to clear an area 40 yards long and 16 feet wide. Four rows 40 yards long, four feet wide, with a seven-inch step between rows were completed for the opening match and the club proudly announced additional seating for 1000 spectators. People were keen to associate with the club's prosperity and membership soared to 1780 by the end of the season, a 300% increase in two years.

Practice facilities were stretched to the limit. Four nets were provided for practice each weekday, with two, one each for the 1st and 2nd XIs, reserved for Tuesdays and Thursdays. Throughout the week the ground was 'a scene of unusual enthusiasm and activity'.

In comparison with all the preparations, the 1921 season was an anti-climax. It began excitingly enough with a tied match against defending champions Haslingden, both sides 110 all out, followed by wins against Lowerhouse and East Lancashire. In May the *Athletic News* promoted Morfee, even at thirty-four years old, to follow Barnes straight from the Lancashire League into the England team to play Australia as a possible solution to the country's lack of fast bowlers. But Morfee had lost much of his potency, taking just 75 wickets, and a final position of eighth was a disappointing return for the investment in the professional.

Morfee's bowling, reputation and popularity took a severe battering at the hands of his nemesis Ted Riley in the second round of the Worsley Cup. Coming in at 134 for 5, Riley smashed 148 as Haslingden totalled 385 all out, a new League record score for League or Cup. The innings lasted 4¼ hours during which time Todmorden bowled 98.2 overs and Morfee took 3 for 100. Demoralised, Todmorden were bowled out for 124, and their defeat by 261 runs remains a club record.

Despite some good days, a section of the crowd turned on Morfee, accusing him of not trying, and it was not a complete surprise when, just before the final match, Morfee asked to be released from the last two years of his contract, citing health grounds related to the local climate. The committee consented; it seems both parties needed a fresh start. With record gate receipts of £939 and 1780 members, the highest in the League, the club could certainly afford their professional's salary, and Morfee's search for sunnier climes took him no further than Rochdale, where he was professional for the next four seasons.

Why the dramatic decline in Morfee's effectiveness? Some theorised that the back-breaking work of building the new terracing the previous winter had taken at least temporary toll on Morfee's body. Certainly, a much improved summer produced better batting pitches - Todmorden themselves topped 150 eight times in 1921, compared to just once in 1920. Morfee's age is also consistent with a reduction in pace, but at Rochdale he inspired an unrivalled three consecutive league and cup doubles and was described as bowling 'terrifyingly fast off a long run' until 1925 when a leg injury forced him to cut his pace to medium.

During the following winter, 1921-22, the committee connected the refreshment pavilion at the site of the current scorebox to the gas supply and made alterations to this and the tea pavilion as requested by the ladies' committee. They also laid two concrete practice pitches behind the horse's stable at the Centre Vale end and extended three tiers of the terrace from the main pavilion to the old refreshment pavilion, so that it ran virtually the length of the south west side from Centre Vale Park to the National School. The ground's capacity was, nevertheless, barely adequate and victims of this unprecedented popularity were the five shilling 12 to 15 year-old boy members whose 'war members' privileges' ceased at the end of the 1921 season and were not renewed. After this any boy under 15 years could become a member by a special resolution of the committee and paying a full member's fee, but the club could not 'accommodate all those a lower membership fee would bring in'.

Although not yet hitting the cricket club, the post-war boom was over. The town was still largely dependent on the cotton industry and by May 1921 over 7000 people in the borough were unemployed or on short time. The July wakes week saw far more settling for local day trips instead of holidays away. The town's bus receipts from Saturday 9 to Tuesday 12 July 1921 were £363 compared to £116 for the equivalent period in 1920. The 1921 census showed that Todmorden's population had fallen by 1615 since 1911, partly because of war casualties, but nevertheless a worrying trend for town and club.

Todmorden's most influential contribution to the Lancashire League began in 1921 when Edward Crabtree, who had been the club's League representative in first the Central Lancashire, then the Lancashire League since 1891, was elected League president. A special fund was opened to mark his service to the club and to hire the Town Hall for a special presentation evening which was held on Wednesday 22 February 1922. A packed audience, included representatives of the Lancashire and Central Lancashire Leagues, Lancashire County Cricket Club and local dignitaries, and Crabtree was presented with a fine oil painting in a massive gold frame and a silver cake stand, both suitably inscribed.

In thanking them, he commented that this was not the first time the club had honoured him. On his marriage they had bought him a dining-room clock, and to celebrate his twenty-one years on the committee a drawing-room clock. On this occasion his wife had chosen the painting, as left to the club he might have got another clock!

The evening, with songs and humorous recitals interspersing the formalities, was a huge success and a collection at the door, held at Crabtree's request, raised over £20 for the local distress fund. John Crabtree remarked that when approached about the evening, Edward expressed concern about 'the state of trade and the distress that exists in many homes, very likely among our own members. There must be no begging, no undue solicitation'. This was typical of the man. In 25 years as Lancashire League President he was always 'cool in debate', showing a 'willingness to look all round a question' with 'consideration always for the weaker club'.

The search for Morfee's successor was wide and initially ambitious. Discussions were held with George Geary, released by Nelson, George Hirst and Wilfred Rhodes. Contact was made with Middlesex's Jack Durston, who had opened the bowling for England against Australia at Lord's the previous summer, and future England all-rounder Ewart Astill of Leicestershire. Committee representatives travelled to London to see Hunter 'Stork' Hendry, the Australian all-rounder who had made his test debut against England in 1921, offering £400 plus expenses, but his terms could not be met. 39 year-old Jack Hobbs, recovering from illness which had curtailed his cricket in 1921, and his Surrey colleague, all-rounder Thomas Shepherd, were also approached.

Perhaps frustrated at so many rejections - perhaps acknowledging the economic downturn, Todmorden lowered their sights and outlay in signing William Sadler, a twenty-five year-old right-arm fast bowler from the Surrey ground staff, for a relatively modest £200. The season was a huge disappointment. With Shackleton approaching the end of his career, the batting was inadequate and Todmorden were dismissed for less than 100 ten times. A run of 17 matches without a win, the first eight of which were lost, kept the team rooted to the bottom of the table. Injury to Walter Storah was a huge blow and only Walter Leslie Greenwood, with career bests of 64 wickets in the season and 8 for 14 in the last match against Accrington, had a good season. Winning the last four matches, Todmorden hauled themselves off the bottom for the first time since May to finish equal twelfth with Accrington, but by then only the diehard supporters remained and gates were down by £420 on 1921.

A highlight of 1922 was 'the most extraordinary county cricket match that was ever played'.[5] It featured Walter Herbert Livsey, who was born into a Todmorden cricketing family in 1893 before moving to Surrey at an early age. A talented wicketkeeper, his path at Surrey was blocked by Herbert Strudwick, but he forged a career at Hampshire where he became valet to his county captain Lionel - later Lord - Tennyson, grandson of the famous Victorian poet. Livsey was Hampshire's first choice wicketkeeper from

EA McDonald played for Lancashire, Nelson and Bacup. Along with JM Gregory, part of Australia's legendary opening attack.

1914 to 1929 and went to South Africa with the MCC in 1922-23, but broke a finger early in the tour and did not play in a test match. For all his expertise behind the stumps, Livsey is best remembered for two batting performances, a tenth wicket stand of 192 against Worcestershire in 1921 - still a county record - and an innings of 110 not out, in a remarkable match at Edgbaston in June 1922. After bowling Warwickshire out for 223, Hampshire were dismissed for just 15 and, following on, were 274 for 8, a mere 66 ahead, when Livsey went out to bat. A further 247 were added for the last two wickets, raising the total to 521, before Warwickshire were bowled out for 158, leaving Hampshire winners by 155 runs.

In the same week as Livsey's fighting innings, Todmorden began their hunt for 1923's professional, pursuing among others the great Sussex seam-bowling all-rounder Maurice Tate, a year before he played the first of his 39 test matches. At the end of August Bertie Morgan was signed at a fee of £312, or £14 per week, paid at £4 per week from January and £8 10s per week during the season. This put Todmorden in the middle band of Lancashire League clubs in payments to professionals. Research by the League secretary in 1923 found that three clubs were paying £10 10s per week, one £12, two £14, three £16 and two more than £16.[6]

The possibility of fixing a maximum wage for professionals was being investigated, and this study, in its attention to detail and prudence about the affordability of professionals, carries all the hallmarks of new League president Edward Crabtree. It also came at a time when Nelson in particular was threatening to escalate the cost of professionals. In 1922 they had signed Australian fast bowler Ted McDonald who had demolished England with 27 wickets in the 1921 Ashes series, and Crabtree was not the only one concerned. Lord Hawke made strenuous objections as McDonald was using Nelson as a stepping-stone to achieve his two-year qualification to play for Lancashire. Hawke's concerns proved justified as McDonald inspired Lancashire to four county titles in five years to end a period of Yorkshire dominance. McDonald was less successful at Nelson who finished eighth, third and second in his three seasons there.

The advent of such high-class bowling professionals, made possible by the post-war boom in sport and the economy, contributed to the 1920s being comfortably the lowest scoring decade in the history of the Lancashire League, Todmorden's matches producing an average of just 12.75 runs per wicket*. By contrast, in county cricket bat was dominating ball and the MCC experimented with a new lbw law more in favour of the bowler in 1929 and a larger wicket, one inch higher and wider than previously, in 1931. The Lancashire League, usually keen to ally itself to the first class game, adopted neither change. Bowlers did not need further assistance on Lancashire League pitches. (*see Appendices page 357)

The lowest scoring years were in the first part of the decade, average runs per wicket falling to 9.45 in Morfee's prolific summer of 1920 and 10.95 in 1923. Another contributing factor was the reduction in manpower and in the amount of cricket played which saw less attention given to squares in 1917 and 18. After the end of the war it may have taken time to repair or replace damaged equipment, although the main rolling and cutting was still powered by horse. There were few, if any, effective covers in the league and with water still carried to the pitch in buckets, little incentive to provide them, as rainfall in the right amounts at the right time saved labour.

The poor quality of post-war pitches was accentuated by some wet summers. In 1923 Todmorden's matches saw teams dismissed for less than 100 on 23 occasions and exceed 100 only 13 times, despite the fact that professional Bertie Morgan had, at 37 years of age, lost some of his potency. A left-arm pace bowler who played briefly for Somerset, Morgan shared new ball duties with George Wilson and SF Barnes for Staffordshire. He came to Todmorden from Werneth in the Central Lancashire League where he had played since 1919, taking over 100 wickets in each of his first three seasons.[7] He took 75 wickets for Todmorden and was well supported by a fully recovered Storah who took 64, but with only six wins the team finished tenth.

Home supporters felt particularly short-changed as the only home win came against East Lancashire on the last day of the season. Membership declined to 1500 and gate money fell by a further £130, despite a crowd of 3000 for the Worsley Cup semi-final which was lost by just eight runs to League and Cup winners Bacup.

Morgan was signed by Rawtenstall in 1924, but injury denied him a full season. Following his injury he changed to bowling slow left-arm and played many years for Billingham in the North Yorks and South Durham League, finally retiring in 1941 aged 56. An affectionate article about his time in the north east headed 'Fiery Bert Morgan' recounts that his captain could neither bat nor bowl and was immobile in the field but held his place as the only man who could control Bert Morgan.[8]

The cold, wet weather did little for public health and in May 1923 the League received - and refused - a request from the Haslingden Town Clerk for the postponement of a match against Nelson because of a smallpox outbreak. Church's talented Australian Frank O'Keefe, paid the ultimate price. A sensational signing, he had first class career averages of 71 in batting and 19 in bowling and appeared set to be the next great Australian all-rounder. Like most overseas professionals, he did not go home during the English winter and, after a successful 1923 season, including 13 wickets in his two matches against Todmorden, he succumbed to illness which proved fatal in March 1924. His grave in Dill Hall Cemetery, Hyndburn, was visited by Australian touring teams until World War II.[9]

1923 marked the end of full time involvement for Todmorden's two record holders. Walter Leslie Greenwood left the district in the close season, resigning from the committee and severing his official connections with the club. Then, following Todmorden's poor early-season batting, the axe fell on Edward Shackleton, although his 55 runs in 7 innings was not significantly worse than most. Dropped for the first time in his 20 years at the club, he retired having scored almost 7000 Lancashire League runs, over 2500 more than anyone else for Todmorden. As a tribute, over a year later on 21 June 1924, Shackleton was invited to come back for a testimonial match against Ramsbottom and was made captain for the day, a rare moment of sentiment and nostalgia amid the usual pragmatism of Lancashire League cricket. Todmorden Old Brass Band played *Auld Lang Syne* as he walked out to bat and, still a man for the big occasion, he proceeded to score 51, enjoying a fourth wicket partnership of 128 with Robert Sutcliffe (82). A near-perfect day was almost capped with victory, but Ramsbottom survived to draw at 141 for 8 in reply to Todmorden's 183 for 8 declared. His testimonial raised £118 and at a presentation evening in King's Rooms opposite the cricket ground he received a cheque and an inscribed canteen of cutlery.

Encouraged by his success, Shackleton was persuaded to carry on and was selected for the next match at home to Nelson. Having started the season with five consecutive defeats, Todmorden were storming up the table in pursuit of Bacup and Nelson and had every chance of causing an upset when Nelson collapsed from 111 for 4 to 115 all out, although Shackleton had pulled a muscle and would only bat in an emergency.

Defending this unexpectedly low total, Nelson professional Ted McDonald and outstanding amateur leg-spin bowler Alf Pollard ripped through the Todmorden batting, reducing the home side to 85 for 8. Only Arthur Stephenson stood firm among the debris, McDonald's 'lightning deliveries' failing to dislodge the limpet-like opener. But with Shackleton invalided and Walter Storah - career batting average 6 - coming in higher than usual at number ten, the cause looked hopeless.

To add to the drama, it started to rain and McDonald, who had bowled unchanged, suddenly lost his 'sting'. It was the classic Lancashire League scenario; the international star, just short of the decisive breakthrough, was a spent force, chopped down to size not because the amateurs had dominated him but because they had made him work. Over-bowled, now hampered by a wet ball and footholes, he was at the mercy of the remaining batsmen. As the rain intensified, Stephenson adopted a more urgent and bold approach and Storah put bat to ball, scoring from the Australian almost at will. The tin boys of the rudimentary scoreboard could hardly keep up, clattering their metal numbers on and off the hooks. When Storah struck McDonald for the winning boundary, hats and caps were thrown aloft and the celebrations could be heard half a mile away. Stephenson, unbeaten on a flawless 57, and Storah, a career best 26, were cheered to the echo as the locals heralded a famous victory.

Amidst the celebrations, Shackleton, the next man in, removed his pads for the final time. The injury had convinced him it was time to go. This fabulous victory and a half century in his final innings the previous week were befitting ways to end a great amateur career.

Todmorden's professional in 1924 was Ernest Moss, a right-arm fast bowler who had played at Batley in the Yorkshire Council since 1920. Born at Mountain Ash in South Wales, he had played one match for Glamorgan in 1923.[10] The son of Sam Moss of legendary speed and doubtful action, his fee was £215, including £3 per week during the winter, modest for a Lancashire League professional but way above the wages of most of Todmorden's working population.

With employment still uncertain, the club allowed members to pay subscriptions in instalments of 1s. By June 1924 admission prices had been reduced, the school side from 8d to 6d and the main ground from 1s to 10d,

Ernest Moss (son of Sam),
TCC pro 1924-25.

the lowest that could be charged as they still included that bone of contention, the entertainment tax. Despite further falls in gate money, by £80, and subscriptions, by £130, the club broke even, retaining a balance of £250.

Todmorden's charge up the table in 1924 saw them finish third. Moss and Storah were well supported by the significant return of JW (Billy) Sunderland, a right-arm medium-fast bowler, who had moved to Walsden in 1920 and played as professional at Halifax in 1922. In another low scoring summer Todmorden dismissed the opposition for less than 100 ten times, so that it was often sufficient to accumulate runs stubbornly, a role to which Stephenson was admirably suited.

Around this time the base for cricket in Todmorden was arguably as strong as it has ever been. The elementary schools' competition, started and run by the club during the war, had continued under its own organisation and in 1922 Todmorden was admitted to the Lancashire Elementary Schools' Cricket Association. The first match at Centre Vale against Clitheroe was watched by a crowd of 900. All expenses were paid by the Todmorden club and Edward Crabtree provided tea for both teams.

The following year Todmorden Schools beat both Burnley and Clitheroe to become Northern Section winners of the county schoolboys' competition but lost in the final at home to Manchester. The trophy was the Hacking Cup, previously used for the Hyndburn area knockout competition during the war.

Clitheroe were vindicated in switching their first round tie to Todmorden in 1926 when over 2000 turned up on Monday 26 June to see Todmorden, 166 all out, win by 98 runs. Centre Vale was also selected for the county schoolboys' North v South match as their 'supporters are the most enthusiastic in the whole league and there are better gates at Centre Vale than anywhere in the county'. Captaining the North was Todmorden's brilliant schoolboy batsman William Halstead who scored 55 not out from 101 for 6 before the South were dismissed for 25. Halstead burst into the first team as a 17 year-old in 1929, scoring 388 runs at 35.27, the highest average by any

Stanley Heyhirst, exceptional young batsman, whose career was cut short by illness.

Todmorden player since the war. He was invited to attend a Yorkshire trial at Halifax under the eye of George Hirst and played regularly for Yorkshire 2nd XIs from 1930-34, scoring 86 on his debut against Lancashire 2nds at Old Trafford. Unfortunately for Todmorden his family relocated to the Bradford area after 1930. In 1931 he was groundsman and one of four professionals at Spen Victoria, from where he moved to Hunslet, and by 1935 he was head groundsman and professional at Dewsbury Savile.

In 1927 the town's schoolboys won the county cup, defeating Manchester by 127 runs to 58 in the final at Gorton, and were cheered as they drove home through the district displaying the Hacking Cup.

The next level for the schoolboys was open age cricket in the Todmorden and District League which still had most of its clubs closely connected with the local churches or chapels. It had a senior division of twelve clubs and had run a second division since 1922. Schoolboy cricket was now an additional step in the local pyramid structure. Every boy had access to cricket and the most promising could progress via the schools to the district league and on to the Todmorden or Walsden clubs. At Todmorden the first team results did not yet reflect this depth, but the seeds of future success were germinating.

The latest product of the district league was 17 year-old Stanley Heyhirst, who scored 349 runs in his first full season in the first team. He particularly impressed Tom Lancaster, the old Lancashire cricketer who was professional at Enfield from 1892-1901 and later an amateur there. In 1924 Lancaster was employed by the *Daily Dispatch* to hold club coaching evenings. Todmorden applied to join the scheme and after his session at Centre Vale, watched by over 500 spectators, Heyhirst was invited to play for Yorkshire Colts.

Heyhirst's ability was apparent in 1925 when Todmorden reached the Worsley Cup final for the first time. Played at Centre Vale over the first two Mondays in September, Todmorden were in deep trouble at 61 for 6 in reply to East Lancashire's 197 all out, when Heyhirst counter-attacked and threatened to take the game away from the visitors. Unfortunately the youngster ran out of partners and was stranded on 69 not out from Todmorden's total of 161.

1925 saw two more promising youngsters, diminutive left-hander Ernest Hargreaves and wicketkeeper Tommy Carrick, join Heyhirst in the team. With Sunderland, who scored 312 runs and took 41 wickets, becoming a real force, a strong nucleus was developing. Carrick learned

Ernest Hargreaves, left-hand batsman 1925-44, set a TCC record with 897 runs in 1937.

Tommy Carrick, superb wicketkeeper
1924-52, 433 victims for TCC, also
played for Walsden and Bacup.

Harry Hudson, TCC
wicketkeeper 1905-26.

a great deal in his two seasons in the second team under the experienced captaincy of William Law, whose first team career had spanned 1899 to 1920. An autocratic but fair and popular leader, Law laid the foundations for Todmorden's most successful era by helping the development of several high quality cricketers.

The emergence of Carrick marked the end of the Hudson dynasty behind the stumps, and Harry was granted a testimonial match against Colne. On a difficult and deteriorating pitch, Arthur Stephenson's defensive technique was again to the fore as he hit 61 not out in Todmorden's 135 all out, becoming the last Todmorden amateur to carry his bat through a completed innings for 71 years and the only one to do so twice. Moss (8 for 26) then skittled Colne for 32 and a near perfect day was completed when Harry Hudson was presented with a cheque for £160.

After a difficult first half to the season Todmorden recovered to finish seventh. The economical Moss had done all that was expected with the ball, but he was no batsman and, although the amateur batting had improved, the team needed more runs and impetus from the professional. Moss was released and signed by champions Ramsbottom for 1926. He did, though, continue to live in Todmorden and played occasionally for the club as an amateur in 1930 and 31.

Helped by their cup run, Todmorden had arrested the decline in membership and gates were up by £100. £154 had been spent on ground infrastructure, mainly improving the toilet facilities from tub to water closets. Nelson's enterprise in signing McDonald in 1922, followed by South African Jimmy Blanckenberg in 1925 had also continued to pay dividends for their club, and as the *Todmorden Advertiser* commented on 22 August 1924:

> One of the penalties of such a piece of enterprise as that which in 1922 startled the whole cricketing world is that it sets a standard. People who are accustomed to watch and listen to a Henry Irving will not sit down to a barnstormer.

The 1920s saw the beginnings of the age of commercial entertainment. By the end of the decade 25 million Britons were going to the cinema every week, the film industry influencing aspirations and fashions in everything from cars and interior design to clothes, hairstyles and cosmetics as mass production began to feed mass consumption in an accelerating cycle. The popular press built up sportspeople, particularly footballers and cricketers, as personalities whose increasingly familiar features were exploited in the sale of books, magazines, comics, games and cigarettes, the latter through free collectable cards.

Nelson's policy of speculating to accumulate by signing big name personalities was not only sound cricketing and financial sense, but reflected the commercial pattern of the times. In 1926 Todmorden followed suit by pursuing a professional of international rather than just county standing. Astill and Tate were again approached, as were test cricketers Tich Freeman, the Kent leg-spinner, and Nottinghamshire all-rounder John Gunn. Before the end of the season Todmorden had signed Bill Hitch, the Surrey and England pace-bowler, on a three year contract at £400 per year, the highest the club had ever paid.

Bill Hitch was born in May 1886 into a cricketing family at Radcliffe. When he was seven his family moved to Cambridgeshire where his father had secured work as professional and groundsman, before acquiring a similar post at Cheveley Park near Newmarket, home of millionaire sportsman Col. Harry McCalmont. By the age of twelve Bill was playing for the village and he recalled a visit to the Oval where:

> Tom Richardson's bowling impressed me very much…towering above the rest of the players and sending the ball down at terrific speed. Returning home, my one ambition was to be able to bowl really fast…

He came to Surrey's attention at the end of the 1904 season when a County XI captained by Tom Hayward came to play XVIII of Cambridgeshire. Hobbs and Hayward had put on a century for the first wicket when Bill was brought on to bowl. His fourth ball nipped back and uprooted Hayward's middle stump. Bill's 4 for 28 impressed and in May 1905 he received a telegram:

> Report at the Oval to-day for trial
> Alcock, Secretary Surrey County
> Cricket Club.

Lancashire, the county of his birth, gave Surrey permission to sign him and he received a three year contract, his debut against Hampshire at the Oval in 1907 occasioning one cockney spectator to comment:

> …it's hall haitches: Ayward, Ayes, Olland, Obbs and now Itch. Soon it'll be hall haitches.

It was the start of a wonderful county career which yielded 7643 runs, 1387 wickets and 230 catches, most as a brilliant and fearless short leg fieldsman. On one occasion Lancashire's Reggie Spooner played an on-drive:

> …off the meat of the bat and looking for the ball at the boundary, was astonished to hear Tom Hayward say: 'Well caught Billie. You're out sir.'

Hitch had taken the catch cleanly and put the ball in his pocket, displaying at once brilliant reactions and skill, speed of thought and a sense of humour.

He was awarded his cap in 1908 and, a lusty and entertaining lower-order hitter, scored his maiden century in 1911. He toured Australia twice, in 1911-12 and 1920-21, playing seven test matches with modest success. Between these tours he was invalided out of the Sportsman's Battalion of the 23rd Fusiliers, seriously ill. On recovering he worked in munitions, necessitating a move to Bradford where he joined many other county cricketers in the Bradford League.

By 1925, approaching forty, Surrey intimated that he would have to make room for a younger man. Although feeling that he had more to give, he accepted that his time was up and Todmorden's offer could not be ignored.[11]

It was Hitch's enthusiasm for the game that impressed John Crabtree, Todmorden's astute chairman, and at the club's 1925 AGM he expressed confidence that the new professional would be a source of strength, inspiration and encouragement to the players:

> Like a tiger on the watch, he never tired and would spend as many hours of the day with young cricketers as they would let him, which is most unusual in a professional today.

Hitch's appearance was eagerly awaited and when the ground opened for practice in early April 1926 a large number of spectators turned out to watch. One talking point was the new professional's eccentric run up which incorporated two hops so pronounced that, on the 1911/12 tour, the ebullient Melbourne crowd had greeted the first with a 'Hip', the second with another 'Hip' and the delivery of the ball with a prolonged 'Hurrah'.[12]

It was a month before the hops made their Centre Vale debut. Rain prevented Todmorden taking the field until the fourth home match, and that was abandoned with Accrington 77 for 2. This was the first of Todmorden's then traditional three home matches over Whitsuntide on Friday, Saturday and Trinity Monday. A win by seven wickets after bowling out Rawtenstall for 49, and another on the Monday when Lowerhouse were bowled out for 26, Hitch taking 6 for 5, convinced the fans that the

Bill Hitch c1928.

season would be a good one and their support was assured.

Four double-decker buses carried 250 supporters to Ramsbottom the week after Whitsuntide and many more travelled by private cars, motor cycles and push bikes. They were not disappointed as Todmorden bowled the defending champions out for 92 and won by eight wickets. Such was the volume of support that the homeward cavalcade through the Rossendale Valley 'caused quite a sensation'.

The arrival of opening batsman Jim Kershaw from Walsden complemented Todmorden's promising youngsters. He and 19 year-old Stanley Heyhirst, whose 101 not out against Colne was Todmorden's only century between 1921 and 1935, contributed 950 runs between them. With Sunderland and Hitch forming the best new ball partnership in the League, Todmorden lost only twice all season. By August the title was a two horse race with Rawtenstall, whose only defeat had been at Todmorden. Todmorden needed to win the return at Bacup Road on 28 August to stay in contention. Supporters from a fleet of Todmorden buses swelled the gate to £147. They were optimistic when solid batting enabled their team to declare at 166 for 6, but Rawtenstall were content to draw and batted out time on 87 for 5. Todmorden had to settle for second place, although there was a winner's medal in the Hitch family as Bill's brother Reg was an amateur at Rawtenstall.

Could Todmorden go one better in the Worsley Cup? The knockout competition had been reorganised in 1926 so that, instead of a set of League matches doubling as a first round match, there would be three regional sections comprising: Bacup, Haslingden, Ramsbottom and Rawtenstall from Rossendale; Accrington, Church, Enfield and Rishton from Hyndburn; and Burnley, Colne, Lowerhouse and Nelson from the Pendle area. Omitted from these, Todmorden and East Lancashire would play each other in the first round every season, the winner joining the three sectional winners in the semi-finals.

The system increased the number of Derby gates and avoided excessive travelling, thereby allowing early starts to first round matches which had to be played in midweek and to a finish. Exceptions to this were Todmorden and East Lancashire, respectively on

the south east and north west edges of the League, 18 miles apart, for whom it achieved exactly the opposite. Missing out on a share of three guaranteed Derby gates, and with the away team travelling further for one match than some clubs were travelling for their three, these two clubs were financially disadvantaged in all but one respect - they had a one in two rather than a one in four chance of reaching the semi-finals, giving them a much increased chance of honours. This system lasted from 1926 to 48, minus a seven year wartime suspension from 1940 to 46 and Todmorden and East Lancashire, two of the League's strongest teams for much of this period, took advantage, the winner of their tie reaching the final eleven times in these sixteen seasons.

Surrey players, Hayes, Hitch and Sandham. Sportsman's Battalion - Royal Fusiliers WW1.

Unable to start early, the Todmorden v East Lancashire tie was quite likely to take more than one day - and one journey - to complete and when the Worsley Cup came under scrutiny in 1929 Todmorden, despite some Cup success, voted to abolish the competition.

To increase the chance of games being completed in one day, the 1929 meeting introduced a rule which compelled the team batting first to suspend its innings at 130, unless they had lost 8 or more wickets. When the side batting second reached 130, the first side could choose to resume its innings or ask the side batting second to continue. This reduced the chance of a dominant team wasting time scoring superfluous runs, as had happened in challenge matches before the introduction of the declaration rule in 1889. This minimised the number of matches spilling over into extra days and the Todmorden v East Lancashire tie did so only once, in 1947.

Hitch's Action.

In 1926 Hitch's 6 for 40 gave Todmorden first blood in their annual contest with the Blackburn side as, defending a modest 100 all out, they dismissed East Lancashire for 79. The bowlers faced a greater challenge at Centre Vale in the semi-final, as Haslingden professional Frank Edwards took 8 for 29 to dismiss Todmorden for 52, of which Hitch made 26. Heads may have been down and hearts heavy but with Haslingden on 17 for 2, Sunderland did the hat-trick. Runs and wickets were cheered in equal measure by rival supporters. Haslingden's last pair came together at 39 for 9. Gradually the score crept to 51 and then:

> Lees lifted a ball to the furthest corner of the field and apparently all was over, when young Ernie Hargreaves was seen sprinting towards the portion of the field where the ball might be expected to drop and there he brought off one of the most amazing catches ever seen on any ground. At first the spectators could hardly think it possible that he could have held it, as he half fell in taking it and when it was realised that he had really caught it and that Todmorden had pulled the match off after all, the crowd went almost wild, broke across the field cheering wildly…Hitch ran up to Hargreaves, seized him and carried him shoulder high to the dressing room!

A special train and special buses took supporters to Nelson for the Worsley Cup final on Tuesday 31 August, confident that Todmorden would repeat their two comfortable League victories over the Seedhill club. It was not to be. Todmorden were bowled out for 121 and the dangerous South African Jimmy Blanckenberg, who had scored hardly a run in the League matches, led Nelson to an eight wicket victory with a brilliant 102 not out.

Nevertheless, the club was happy. Hitch had caught the imagination, the value for money of his high salary reflected in two runners-up trophies, the enthusiasm of the public and the bank balance. Presenting the prizes, Colonel Gledhill pronounced that Todmorden Cricket Club was not a narrow parochial club, but belonged to the town.

Tributes were paid to the retiring Walter Storah, whose opportunities were limited by the success of the opening attack in his final season. Only three bowlers have taken

Todmorden 1st XI 1926 at Nelson.
L-R Row 2: E Hargreaves, JW Sunderland, S Heyhirst, R Sutcliffe, J Kershaw, ____,
Row 1: JW Hitch, C Halliwell, A Marshall (c), A Stephenson, T Carrick.

more than his 586 wickets for Todmorden and none more than his 51 five-wicket hauls. Although he played in an era when conditions were more favourable to bowlers, he rates as one of the very best produced by the club. Storah's seasons as professional for Walsden took his career tally to over 1000 wickets and also explain why Todmorden did not grant him a testimonial, unlike amateurs who had given largely unbroken service to the club over many years.

1927 began almost as the previous season had ended. Defending a total of 88 all out at home to Haslingden, Hitch and Sunderland bowled Todmorden to a narrow three run victory. The two opening bowlers took 26 wickets over Whitsuntide in consecutive home victories against Church, Bacup and Accrington, three of 14 matches when the opposition was bowled out for less than 100, confirming Todmorden's title challenge.

By 6 August East Lancashire, who had earlier knocked Todmorden out of the Cup, topped the League, one point above Todmorden. Supporters, in three double-decker buses and a fleet of cars, were more anxious than usual on the trip to Ramsbottom as Hitch was injured. His replacement, 43 year-old former Kent medium pacer Henry Preston, was not in the same class and struggled to make an impression. Ramsbottom made a solid start but were bowled out for 71, succumbing to Sunderland (4 for 17) and Heyhirst who, starting to emerge as a bowler, took 4 for 9. Todmorden won by seven wickets and embarked on the journey home through the Rossendale Valley where East Lancashire had been playing at Bacup. Keen to know the result, supporters shouted from the bus windows, 'How's Bacup gone on?' and were delighted to hear 'Won', with one finger raised signalling a one run victory. Bowled out for 66, Bacup had bowled East Lancashire out for 65.

Todmorden 1st XI 1927 Champions.
L-R Row 4: D Wright, E Gregson, FS Howarth, B Akroyd,
Row 3: F Crabtree, J Jagger, A Sutcliffe, W Law, E Akroyd, W Marshall (groundsman),
Row 2: S Heyhirst, E Mitchell, J Kershaw, JW Hitch (pro), JW Sunderland,
C Helliwell, E Halliwell (scorer),
Row 1: A King (Hon Treasurer), JW Crabtree (Committee Chairman),
E Hargreaves, R Sutcliffe, A Stephenson, A Marshall (Captain), T Carrick,
Hiram Dawson, GE Howarth (Secretary), W Sutcliffe.

With Hitch restored to fitness, Todmorden extended their lead and travelled to East Lancashire's Alexandra Meadows ground for the season's penultimate match knowing that both East Lancashire and Haslingden needed to win to keep their title hopes alive the table read:

	Pld	Pts
Todmorden	24	36
East Lancs	24	33
Haslingden	24	33

Todmorden supporters, who filled six buses, a large number of cars and much of a train, were put at ease by an opening stand of 83 by Heyhirst and Kershaw, both of whom passed 50, laying the foundations for a healthy 187 for 7 declared. Sunderland and Hitch then reduced East Lancashire to 33 for 5, and although the home side drew the game at 141 for 9, Todmorden had maintained their lead. An anxious wait for Haslingden's result followed. News arrived - they had lost to Church by 7 wickets, and there was great rejoicing. At the 31st attempt, Todmorden were champions of the Lancashire League.

The final match at home to Colne was a formality. All thoughts were on the celebrations to follow and stumps were drawn an hour early at 6pm after Heyhirst's 57 had put Todmorden in a winning position. Both teams, their officials, League officials, old players, groundsman, scorer and bag carrier made their way across the road to King's Café for tea.

> Thousands of delighted hero worshippers had the intense gratification of seeing the proud captain of the team [Albert Marshall] march off the field holding on high the coveted emblem of the Todmorden eleven's superiority over the other clubs comprising the Lancashire League.

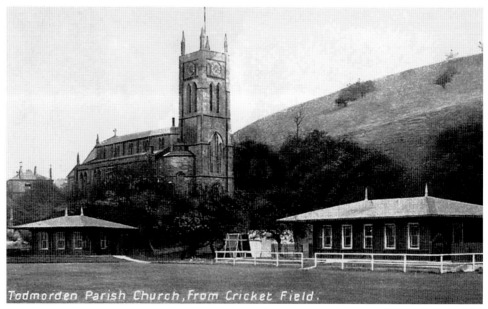

Todmorden Parish Church, from Cricket Field.

Centre Vale 1920.

There was a special word for Billy Sunderland. Hitch described him as 'the finest amateur bowler in the league' who in most overs 'conjured up one or two real snorters' and, presenting the cup, League president Edward Crabtree said:

> I have always had a personal interest in Sunderland because he was brought up in our weaving shed. I have known him ever since he was a little boy.

The Todmorden Old Brass Band, playing 'lively airs', led a procession from King's to the Town Hall. A platform had been erected outside the window of the council chamber from where the team was given a civic reception. The entire area between the Town Hall and White Hart Fold, St Mary's churchyard and the steps leading to the railway station was densely packed with onlookers. The team was then driven along the three valleys displaying the Lancashire League trophy, between footpaths lined with people, before returning to King's rooms for a social evening.

The world was a much bigger place in 1927 and to be top dog in your corner of it, the only corner accessible, recognisable and known to most local people, was something to celebrate.

Such success and publicity made the club a focus for local charities. They allowed flags to be sold at the gate in aid of the Mayor's Industrial Distress Fund, and acceded to an end-of-season request for help from the local Cancer Campaign Fund, organising a Tuesday evening match between past and present players. With the band in attendance, the event raised £40.

At the AGM John Crabtree announced his retirement from any official capacity at the club, ending forty years' service, the last sixteen as chairman. Although the club had made a loss on the year, he left it thriving in every other sense. The ground and support matched the playing strength which had secured the club's greatest achievement to date, the Lancashire League title. Crabtree's instinct about Bill Hitch had been spot on. The professional's excellent coaching and example had bound Todmorden into a formidable unit. At last the club had achieved the success it craved.

Chapter 5

The Constantine Factor

John Crabtree left the club in the hands of men with proven ability and familiar with its workings, providing a smooth transition and continuity. He was succeeded as chairman by Harold Sutcliffe, who had been secretary in 1913 and treasurer from 1920 to 24. Remaining in posts held since 1925 were secretary George Howarth and treasurer Alfred King, whose father Harry, a staunch supporter, owned the bakery, shop and adjoining rooms, across from the ground, that often hosted club presentations. These three men charted the club's affairs for the next thirty years.

Their first major project concerned the replacement of the players' pavilion which, although picturesque, provided only basic facilities. Rev A Aspin had broached the subject at every AGM since 1923. In 1927, supported by the eloquent Billy Sunderland, he persuaded the committee to act. They approached local architect JE Stott to provide a sketch and financial estimate for a replacement, and the council for planning permission. An appeal was made to the president, vice-presidents and local employers, but at the 1928 annual meeting it was reported that the financial response was insufficient and the club did not have the funds to pursue such a large undertaking.

Given the local economic climate this was not surprising:

> Unemployment was stubbornly high, and under-employment was endemic; a three or four day week; three looms running instead of four; and extended (unpaid) holiday stoppages. At Christmas 1928, for example, eighty percent of the firms extended the holiday break by up to eight days, and two months later many of the four-loom weavers had one loom idle.[1]

The club's 3rd XI became a victim of the financial situation. For some seasons the 3rd XI had played home friendly matches on Wednesday evenings, rather than expose its youngsters to the idiosyncratic surfaces of the local district league. In 1928 the 3rd XI team was discontinued so that Wednesday evenings could be used for a Workshop Knockout Competition. The idea and format were derived from workshop rugby competitions, which had helped bail the Todmorden and Hebden Bridge rugby teams out of financial difficulties two decades earlier, and the response was terrific. Fifty teams, a total of 550 players, entered, confirming both the popularity of cricket and the existence of fifty local firms able to field a cricket team. The committee was periodically criticised for not running a 3rd XI, but the schoolboys' competition and the Todmorden and District League fed a steady supply of players to Todmorden.

The organisation placed a burden on the committee, treasurer Alfred King complaining that he had to carry five and half hundredweights of copper coins to the bank, but the financial rewards made it worthwhile. Without the profit of £135 from this competition, the club would have made another loss, and they were not alone. The seemingly inevitable cycle of the free enterprise system had spun from boom to bust again. Money was scarce, Rawtenstall, champions in 1926, had lost almost 20% of their membership in two years, and eleven of the other thirteen Lancashire League clubs made a loss. As a token of assistance, Edward Crabtree's League committee cancelled clubs' subscriptions for the year.

Cartoon, Bacup v Todmorden 1930.

Among Todmorden's fine 1927 championship-winning team, 20 year-old Stanley Heyhirst was the jewel in the crown. In the previous three seasons he had played 21 matches for Yorkshire 2nd XI in the Minor Counties Championship, scoring 528 runs at 16.50 and taking 13 wickets at 17.92 in predominantly low-scoring matches. Inevitably he encountered some future stars, including team-mates Hedley Verity and Arthur Mitchell. His best innings was 49 at Worksop against a Nottinghamshire 2nd XI attack spearheaded by future 'bodyline' bowler Bill Voce. Heyhirst emerged as a bowler in 1926 and, after taking 3 for 22 against Northumberland at Jesmond, he took the new ball in the second innings, something he never did for Todmorden. Indeed, it was only after his success for the county that Todmorden started to use him as an occasional bowler, although his 18 wickets at an average of 10 in 1927 suggested there was more to come.[2]

Heyhirst was dropped by the county after scoring 54 runs in his first six innings of 1927, but he continued to impress at Todmorden, ending the championship season with half centuries in the last two matches. No one knew it, but they were the last two innings of his life. During the winter he was struck down by rheumatism from which he never recovered. Invalided for much of the rest of his life, he died in 1958, aged 50.

Without their leading run-scorer and partnership breaker, Todmorden found defending the title tougher than winning it. The opening match against Enfield set the tone, Todmorden declaring on 209 for 7 and Enfield defending stubbornly to draw on 104 for 9. Several clubs were happy to avoid defeat against the defending champions and, although unbeaten in the first half of the season, Todmorden were unable to force home their superiority. With 14 drawn matches, they had to settle for fourth place, twelve points behind champions Nelson, whose investments had finally yielded the League title.

Hitch's powers appeared to be waning, his 65 wickets significantly fewer than in previous seasons, and he was overshadowed by his opening partner Billy Sunderland, who took 95 League wickets and 102 altogether, which remain club records for an amateur. Both had done enough to earn contracts for 1929, Hitch accepting a lower salary from Todmorden of £325 and Sunderland signing as professional for Rawtenstall.

Billy Sunderland returned to play one more season for Todmorden in 1930 before leaving the area. He went on to serve as leader of Lancashire County Council and was elected as the Member of Parliament for Preston in Labour's landslide at the 1945 General Election, ousting Randolph Churchill, son of the outgoing Prime Minister. Sadly, after only four months in office, Sunderland died suddenly aged 49, whilst visiting a school near Whalley.

There was little optimism about Todmorden's prospects for 1929. Sunderland was, it was felt, irreplaceable, the loss of Heyhirst was still keenly felt and compounded by that of Jim Kershaw who, four matches into the season, left the district to take up work in Liverpool.

The Lancashire League, meanwhile, was world news, the *Sunday People* reporting:

> The effort to engage Learie Constantine, the best all round cricketer in the world to play for Nelson in the Lancashire League has been the outstanding sensation of the season.[3]

In *Slipless in Settle* (2010) Harry Pearson comments:

The Trinidadian's contract was said to be worth six hundred pounds a season plus bonuses and collections. In an era when the maximum wage was in force in football it was a salary that by common consent made Constantine Britain's highest-paid sportsman.

Nelson were gambling in taking their 'speculate to accumulate' policy regarding professionals to a new level. South African Jimmy Blanckenberg, their professional since 1925, was an excellent all-rounder but not the draw that his predecessor McDonald had been and, despite winning the League in 1928, Nelson were hit by the economic downturn and their balance sheet showed an overdraft of £2972. A sale of work raised £356 and a request to the community for contributions of one shilling a staggering £939, close to 19,000 shillings. But above all they needed people through the gate, and in Constantine they had hit the jackpot.

Constantine's reputation, established by spectacular displays on the West Indies' tour of England in 1928, primarily against the counties, captured the popular imagination far beyond the confines of the Lancashire League and crowds flocked to see him. Nelson's home gates for 1929 totalled £2452 - over £2000 more than any other club - and a profit of £1155 on the season brought their debt within manageable bounds.

As the 1972 *Wisden* describes in his obituary, Constantine was the complete cricketing package:

> Muscular but lithe, stocky but long armed, he bowled with a bounding run, a high, smooth action and considerable pace. His batting, which depended considerably upon eye, was sometimes unorthodox to the point of spontaneous invention: but on his day it was virtually impossible to bowl at him. In the deep he picked up while going like a sprinter and threw with explosive accuracy; close to the wicket he was fearless and quick; wherever he was posted he amazed everyone by his speed and certainty in making catches which seemed far beyond reach. His movement was so joyously fluid and…acrobatic that he might have been made of springs and rubber.[4]

Todmorden visited Nelson on May Bank Holiday Monday 1929 and were delighted when Constantine fell for just 18 to Ned Stansfield. The left-arm spinner, filling much of the void left by Sunderland, took 7 for 31 to bowl Nelson out for 114. The Nelson professional broke through early in Todmorden's reply, taking 4 for 37, and only the much improved Eddie Mitchell (30) showed any form with the bat as Todmorden were bowled out for 62, the fourth time in five matches they had failed to reach three figures. Constantine's magnetic presence attracted a gate of £270, and the *Todmorden Advertiser* of 24 May reported:

> …people were packed solid, the juniors overflowed onto the turf, all the wall tops were occupied and extra accommodation was found on top of the football stand, the spectators being willing to risk its collapse to have such an ideal vantage point.

The stand belonged to neighbouring Nelson Football Club, which played mainly in the 3rd Division North of the Football League from 1921 to 31, with one season in Division 2.

To the surprise of many, as the season progressed Hitch was able to galvanise the partially rebuilt Todmorden team. The batting particularly improved and Todmorden had climbed to second place when leaders Nelson came to Centre Vale on 29 June. *A Century of Bradford League Cricket* (2003) asserts that Centre Vale was one of Constantine's three favourite grounds in the world, along with Perth and Saltaire's Roberts Park.

The club made special arrangements and prayed for a fine day. Permission was obtained to use the boys' playing field on the adjoining park for 'the parking of motors'. Sixty extra posters were ordered, thirty each to display in Halifax and Rochdale. Canvas was erected on posts along the park side to prevent a free view of the match, extra police were requested to patrol the ground and additional seating was borrowed.

The day of the match dawned fair and special trains ran from Rochdale, Halifax and Nelson, the Nelson train requiring extra coaches. Although private transport was still largely confined to the wealthy, over ninety cars plus motor cycles and push bikes used Centre Vale Park. The gates opened at 12.30pm for the two o'clock start, 5822 spectators paid £245 16s 11d for admission and club members brought the attendance to 7000. Nothing like it has been seen at Centre Vale before or since. The previous largest gate, also against Nelson in Morfee's first season, 1920, was around 4500.

Batting first, Todmorden's in-form amateurs all contributed solidly. Young William Halstead scored fluently with some sublime cuts and pulls and even Constantine looked regretful when he deprived the youngster of the collection of a lifetime, bowling him off his pads for 48. Maintaining impressive pace through most of his 22 overs, Constantine concentrated on an off stump line and at times mid-on was his only fieldsman on the leg side, the majority being in the slips. He kept the batsmen at full stretch in taking 7 for 79, but was unable to prevent Todmorden setting a challenging declaration at 198 for 9.

The loss of two early wickets left Nelson's hopes resting on a big innings from their professional. Applauded to the middle, Constantine flicked his first ball through square leg for four and 'entirely dominated the game', hitting boundaries with 'apparently the slightest tap', including one clean over the pavilion which only counted four in those days. He had made 38 of Nelson's 72 for 2 when he was deceived by Stansfield and trapped lbw, Todmorden's celebrations betraying their relief. Todmorden pressed for victory, but it was not to be, and Nelson survived to draw on 133 for 8, the *Todmorden Advertiser* reporting:

> …throughout the match the West Indian was the cynosure of all eyes. He was always on the qui-vive.

Constantine at Lord's 1928

Despite this moral victory, made more impressive because Hitch had contributed so little, Todmorden could not keep pace with an inspired Nelson side in the second half of the season and the gap widened to five points. Nevertheless, second place represented an unexpectedly fine season for the club. Hitch, with 71 League wickets, had performed adequately, but at 43 years of age his time at the club was over. He had moulded Todmorden into a much more professional unit, particularly in fielding, and they had become accustomed to winning, legacies which would benefit the club through the next decade. His contributions at practice had been immense and he left for a winter coaching position in Ceylon (now Sri Lanka) with the best wishes of all, a job well done. He returned as a club professional in 1930, playing at Astley Bridge in the Bolton League, before taking up umpiring, officiating in four test matches. Later he moved to south Wales to coach Glamorgan and in his 50s took a position in a south Wales company, enthusiastically playing for their works' cricket team until the age of 60. Todmorden's total gate receipts in 1929 were £558 of which over 44% came from the Nelson match and in its Annual Report the committee wrote:

> We congratulate the officials of the Nelson club on an enterprise which has brought such a result to our club.

Not only to 'our club', but to every club in the League. 225,583 spectators had passed through the League's turnstiles in 1929, well over half to see Nelson and Constantine. A superstar undiluted by over exposure on television, the sight of Constantine in action thrilled thousands during his nine years in the Lancashire League - and for only 6d admission.

In 1933 the League presented Constantine with a cheque for £50 in appreciation of his abilities as a cricketer and his personal character on and off the field. Sportsmen's church services were popular at this time and, not surprisingly, Constantine was in demand. When Todmorden's Eastwood Congregational Chapel held one such in 1932, Constantine agreed to be the chairman, the speaker was 'Mr James, law student and friend of Constantine' and his subject was 'The Place of Sport in Modern Life'. He was CLR James, who was to become author of the acclaimed book *Beyond a Boundary*, and whilst living in Nelson with Constantine qualified to play and turned out for Nelson.

30 July 1933 saw a similar service at Christ Church when the vicar Rev M Patterson suggested that, in view of the important part played by cricket in the life of Todmorden, it would be a good idea to hold a 'Cricketer' Sunday. The club agreed, Todmorden's professional Fred Root offered to take part and the district league clubs were invited to attend.

The League was determined to keep Constantine. When Rochdale offered him £1100 to play for them in the CLL in 1935, it was agreed that at some point in the next three seasons at Nelson, Constantine would have a benefit and that the Lancashire League, through its clubs, would contribute £250 towards it. This was good business, concluded League chairman Edward Crabtree.

Bill Hitch, in his memoirs writes of Constantine:

> It was in 1923 when I first met Learie and of all the great cricketers I have played against I do not think that there is anyone that stands out so prominent in my mind as Learie Constantine. From his early days when he first made his visit to this country with the West Indian team...has there ever been so attractive and entertaining a personality? Learie's advent into the Lancashire League with Nelson must have been something the league clubs had longed for...Clubs who were on the verge of leaving the league owing to financial difficulties suddenly found themselves with a bank balance. Grounds were large enough to accommodate the huge crowds...to watch this wizard of the turf in

action. What a cricketer! What a personality! When batting, bowling, or fielding you were always getting something sensational. His tremendous hitting sent ball after ball soaring out of the largest grounds; his fast bowling with stumps flying in all directions; and his fielding, yes his fielding was brilliant and sometimes uncanny. A sudden spring, a dive, and a wonderful catch, a catapult return from the hardest of drives and the batsman winds his way to the pavilion, then a juggling act until the next batsman arrives, that was Learie Constantine. He was never happy unless he was on the field of play with one ambition, to entertain those who are keeping him and the game going.[5]

Less well publicised was Constantine's generous praise and encouragement for his Nelson colleagues and his patient coaching. As for his opinion of the Lancashire League:

…most of the players…are not in the least frightened by anyone's reputation, and will often start knocking the ball about the field in a way that would startle the Lord's or Oval crowd if it happened to the same bowler there.

And on the professional's role:

If he comes up against an equally good pro in the other team, an absolute battle of wits develops quite equal to anything seen in a Test Match - yes, and more exciting than that, because, in a sense these two are engaged in a personal duel…Never in my life have I played harder than in Lancashire.[6]

Any first class cricketer…whoever he may be or whatever he has done, who believes he can just walk into the league and proceed to be a success is making a great mistake.[7]

Such approval helped to establish the League's reputation worldwide.

Constantine was a force for good far beyond the cricketing boundary. A solicitor's clerk in Trinidad, part of his motivation in coming to England was to study law; his cricketing skills and charisma became a springboard for his fight against colour prejudice, as *Wisden* explains:

He made his mark in the only way a poor West Indian boy of his time could do, by playing cricket of ability and character. He went on to argue the rights of the coloured peoples with such an effect as only a man who had won public affection by games-playing could have done in the Britain of that period.[8]

Constantine was initially taken aback by some of the attitudes he encountered at Nelson and took time to come to terms with them. Many people in north east Lancashire had never seen a black man before and, as Derek Birley in *A Social History of English Cricket* explains:

…racism was not yet a major issue, more an ignorant assumption of white superiority.[9]

In Constantine's first season at Nelson, a man in the street asked:

Has ta' bin down t'coal 'ole, mister?

When this was translated, Constantine almost packed his bags, but was counselled by his wife, Norma:

Give them a chance to get used to us…They may grow to accept us, even to like us.[10]

Faced with such attitudes, Constantine, in the words of CLR James:

revolted against the revolting contrast between his first-class status as a cricketer and his third-class status as a man.[11]

Yet he did so by being himself, 'with a dignity firm but free of acrimony'.[12] The environment of Lancashire League cricket was conducive to breaking down barriers. The boundaries of social class, so clearly defined elsewhere in the game by the 'superior' status of amateurs, who could allegedly afford to play for nothing, over professionals who couldn't, were being eroded in northern club cricket long before the leagues were formed. The catalysts were the admiration of the professionals' superior ability and the emergence of a third class of cricketer, identified by David Edmundson in his history of the Lancashire League, *See the Conquering Hero*, as 'the working class amateur'. Working class amateurs predominated in the northern leagues because clubs emerged as part of their towns' civic identities, not as separate élitist organisations. As Fred Root observed on coming to Todmorden in 1933, active involvement at the club saw 'cotton manufacturers rub shoulders with their own weavers'.[13]

With cricket accessible to all and progress in the game based on ability rather than social class and connections, the northern leagues tapped into all available natural talent, giving them an edge over club cricket elsewhere and helping to establish the Lancashire League as the premier league in the country. This playing meritocracy was more in keeping with Constantine's principles of fairness than the aristocratic exclusiveness to be found elsewhere in English cricket.

> In league cricket ... players mix and are friendly. You do not find amateurs coming out of one exit and being called 'Mister' and the pros. creeping out elsewhere...nor do you find any colour bar. A cricketer is just a cricketer and nothing else.[14]

Constantine's high profile and league cricket's unique intimacy between professionals, amateurs, officials and supporters enabled him to express views and values which were sympathetically received.

> I don't think about black men or white men or yellow men; only about good men, indifferent men and bad men.[15]

One of Constantine's strategies was to display a disarming confidence in parodying prejudice when he encountered it, as in the story he told of a bus journey:

> The conductor asked me one shilling and threepence for the fare. I knew it should only be a shilling and I told him so. 'No' replied the conductor, 'you're wrong. It's one shilling and threepence.' So I turned to the white lady sitting next to me and asked: 'Do you know the fare?' She said 'Yes, you are quite right - it is one shilling.' So I smiled at the conductor and said 'Now do you believe me - now that you have got it in black and white'.[16]

Constantine won people over and changed the views of thousands about colour and race in north east Lancashire.

> Looking back on my cricketing days in the league I know that for every one insult there were ten thousand human expressions of warmth and friendship towards me. [17]

In 1937 when news leaked that Constantine and Nelson had agreed an amicable parting after nine seasons...

> ...I could not walk half a mile through the streets without being stopped literally hundreds of times by all sorts of people I didn't know...men, women and even youngsters begging me to stay.[18]

Emphasising the town's sense of loss, during the tea interval of the next match the

Nelson Old Prize Band rendered 'Abide With Me'. As Lancashire League historian Ron Freethy wrote in the *Lancashire Evening Telegraph*:

> Constantine…almost single handedly demolished the boundaries of colour prejudice…It was here [at Nelson] that Sir Learie Constantine proved that there should be no racism in sport and the Lancashire League was the first place he proved it.[19]

His fight included one of the landmark cases against colour prejudice when, in 1944, he won damages from The Imperial Hotel in London for 'failing to receive and lodge him'.[20]

In the wider context, prejudice against women was being slowly eroded by the time Constantine arrived at Nelson. In 1928 women over 21 received the right to vote on equal terms with men. In the textile industry, women machinists in the fustian trade earned more than the average wage for men, whilst weavers' wages, for the same number of looms, were low for both sexes.

But prejudice against race and colour had yet to be breached. Constantine's last five years in the Lancashire League coincided with the German 'Master Race' adopting policies based on racial ideology, communicating insidious, creeping propaganda against the Jews which escalated to their persecution and attempted extermination. Tellingly, Constantine described Lord Hawke's idea of 'dressing room harmony', with its formalised divisions between the amateur hierarchy and the professional under-class, as 'Hitlerian harmony'.[21]

Constantine was awarded the M.B.E. in 1945, knighted in 1962, made an honorary Master of the Bench in 1963 and created a life peer in 1969. In 1972 Trinidad posthumously awarded the Trinity Cross, the country's highest honour, to Baron Constantine of Maraval in Trinidad and of Nelson in the County Palatine of Lancaster.[22]

Constantine's father was Samuel Lebrun Constantine, a plantation foreman and cricketer, who toured England with the West Indies teams of 1900 and 1906. He scored the first century for a West Indian in England, against the Gentlemen of MCC at Lord's. Learie Constantine transcended many of the prejudices his father abhorred and fought. He was, in the words of Nelson supporter and journalist Noel Wild:

> …the man who came to us from a slave background and ended up in the House of Lords.[23]

Just over a month after the 1929 season ended, the Dow Jones Industrial Average lost 23% of its value in two days. The Wall Street Crash and the resulting Great Depression of the 1930s was the greatest financial crisis of the 20th century. In this climate Constantine, already viewed as the saviour of some cash-strapped clubs, if not the League, became indispensable. To capitalise fully on their investment, Nelson asked the League to permit pitches to be covered for 24 hours prior to matches.

In August 1929, Todmorden had signed the relatively unknown Herbert Haigh as professional for 1930. A Yorkshireman who had played for the county

Learie Constantine at Nelson.

2nd XI, Haigh had been professional with both Keighley and Low Moor in the Bradford League, and, spent the last five years with Huddersfield, heading the league's batting in 1925, 1926 and 1928. He bowled right-arm medium-pace and the locals were heartened when he scored 100 not out and took 8 for 29 for Huddersfield against Linthwaite shortly after Todmorden had signed him. Perhaps his greatest moment had been in the 1921 Priestley Cup Final played at Bradford Park Avenue when Keighley beat Saltaire, whose professional was SF Barnes. This match still claims the world record attendance for club cricket of 14,179. It was one of Barnes's rare failures. Haigh was the Keighley hero taking 5 for 34 as Saltaire were dismissed for 157 and hitting 70 not out as they eased to a 9 wicket win.

Earlier Todmorden had approached players of international class including Walter Hammond, Edward 'Nobby' Clark, South African fast bowling all-rounder, Derys Morkel and Alex S Kennedy, the Hampshire all-rounder, contacted via Walter H Livsey the Todmorden-born Hampshire wicketkeeper.

At the 1929 Annual Meeting, chairman Harold Sutcliffe commented on declining membership and gates at both county and club level. Haigh had been signed because 'Big names' wanted long engagements and in the current economic climate Todmorden could not afford the risk of signing 'big men at big prices for long terms'.

Nevertheless, Haigh's signing represented a shrewd assessment of the team's needs, coupled with what the club could afford as seen in August 1929. Billy Sunderland, returning after his professional stint with Rawtenstall, would spearhead the attack allied to Ned Stansfield's left-arm spin and the medium-pace of developing all-rounder Johnny Greenwood.

One of Todmorden's successes of 1929, Greenwood had contributed 337 runs and 35 wickets in his first full season. However, when praising Greenwood's all round ability at the Annual Meeting, the chairman added 'I hope he will stay with us'. 'Hear! Hear!' responded the meeting. Relations between Todmorden and Nelson were about to take a turn for the worse.

A few weeks later a postcard was received from the League secretary informing of Greenwood's application for a transfer to the Nelson club. All was legal and above board. Johnny had worked at Wilson's Bobbin Works in Cornholme near Todmorden, but a Nelson textile manufacturer, Moorby, a keen supporter of Nelson CC, bought a newsagent's shop which he then rented to Johnny. After running the shop for twelve months Johnny had built up a business qualification for Nelson, whilst still playing for Todmorden.

Todmorden replied that they understood and accepted that this came under rule 24 where a player was qualified for more than one club. The situation became a 'cause célèbre' which demonstrated the keen partisan support for each League club and how anything which smacked of sharp practice was denounced. His new qualification acquired, Johnny Greenwood played for Nelson from 1930 to 1952, apart from two years (1935 and 36) when he was professional with Farnworth in the Bolton League.

Herbert Haigh, TCC pro 1930

In 1933 Ernest Hargreaves, then Todmorden's leading amateur batsman, also requested a transfer to Nelson. Todmorden objected, and perhaps with the Greenwood furore still ripe, the League rejected his application. Nelson allowed Hargreaves to practise with them whilst still playing for Todmorden which suggests that the diminutive left-hander was working in Nelson. The *Todmorden and District News*,[21] referring to the newly formed ladies' team, commented:

> and someday maybe lady cricketers from Todmorden will be turning out with Nelson, whose power of attraction seems so magnetic.

Somewhat ironically, Johnny Greenwood returned to his original trade in bobbin manufacture after World War II, but even in his years as committeeman and chairman at Nelson he heard, quite unjustly, as he walked around the Lancashire League grounds references to 'shamateur'. As recently as 1998, a Nelson supporter, who in the 1930s had lived only a few doors away from Johnny Greenwood's shop where he spent his Saturday pence, brought a friend to visit Centre Vale. Todmorden were playing Nelson with opposing professionals Vasbert Drakes and Roger Harper. The friend had been apprised of the Lancashire League

Young Johnny Greenwood.

culture - including the Johnny Greenwood episode. Their pleasure in Nelson's victory was topped by hearing an elderly sage pontificate, 'Tha can't trust Nelson. Tha never wants to forget Johnny Greenwood'.

Johnny Greenwood with photo of Constantine.

Chapter 6

Ladies' Cricket

A Todmorden Cricket Club minute dated 20 October 1924 states:

> Letter re - information of Ladies' Cricket League lie on the table.

Following this inaction by the committee, it would be almost a decade before the introduction of a Todmorden Ladies' team. Nor is there evidence in the 1920s of the ladies' league, suggesting similar ambivalence at other clubs. Women's cricket was, nevertheless, slowly gaining momentum in the slipstream of major breakthroughs by women's rights movements, albeit as a new opportunity for sport and social recreation rather than political expression.

Ladies had played a form of cricket as early as the 1300s and their first recorded match was played in 1745 at Gosden Common near Guildford[1], but it was in the last years of the 19th century when formal women's matches began to be played in any number, as women asserted greater independence.

The most visible evidence of this independence came in cycling, made possible by the inventions of gears and pneumatic tyres in the 1880s. Women in great numbers abandoned the impractical bustle and corset for 'cycling bloomers', accelerating the change to shorter, more practical skirts. The degree to which bloomers affronted contemporary standards of decency can be gauged against the FA rule which stipulated that footballers' shorts had to cover their knees and which was only relaxed in 1904.[2]

Women's football also kicked on in this period. The first recorded women's match in Britain was played at Inverness in 1888, and the first in England was in 1895, the latter by the British Ladies Football Club which was founded by the splendidly named Nettie Honeyball.[3] Exhibition matches by this club inspired others and in spring 1895 there was a women's match at Turf Moor.[4]

The first women's cricket club, the White Heather Club, was established at Nun Appleton near Tadcaster in 1887, and in 1890 'The Original English Lady Cricketers' toured England, attracting a crowd of 15,000 for their first game in Liverpool.[5] James Lillywhite's *Cricket Annual* concluded that:

> As an exercise, cricket is probably not so severe as lawn tennis, and is certainly not so dangerous as hunting or skating...if, therefore, the outcome...is to induce ladies more generally to play cricket, we shall consider that a good result has been attained.

This team spread the word for two seasons until their manager absconded with their funds, but they nevertheless helped to inspire matches such as that played between two women's teams at Walsden CC in 1893. The *Todmorden Advertiser* was, however, not encouraging.

> Whether those of the feminine gender are as fit to indulge in the good old English pastime as men I do not care to argue, but... they seem to think they are as a match was played...between members of the petticoat club.

In Yorkshire, Brighouse had a women's team in 1898,[6] and cricket was played at prestigious girls' boarding schools in the early 20th century, but it was in the 1920s, after women had proved themselves more than capable of 'men's work' during World War I, that a significant number of women's cricket teams began to appear. Football had led the way, with factory-based women's sides playing many charity matches during and after the war. The most famous and successful of these teams was 'The Dick Kerr's Ladies' from Preston, whose match against St Helens Ladies in 1920 attracted 53,000 to Goodison Park.[7]

Shaken by this threat to their previously male preserve, the FA banned women from playing on its grounds in 1921 with the accompanying statement 'the game is quite unsuitable for females and ought not to be encouraged'. This ban lasted until 1971.[8] Meanwhile, whilst women's cricket never scaled football's heights of popularity, it moved ahead in organisation with the formation of the Women's Cricket Association (WCA) in 1926.

The WCA was the brainchild of enthusiastic ladies following a cricket holiday at Malvern.[9] In September 1931, the *Todmorden Advertiser* carried a report of the WCA's fifth annual 'All Women's Cricket Week' held near Malvern, and its influence in the formation of women's cricket clubs of which there were now 60 or 70, with many girls' schools affiliated. Based in the south of England, the WCA ran the game along the lines of men's club cricket in the south, where there were few leagues and most clubs played a circuit of 'club matches'. Many of the larger employers, as well as the established clubs, were fielding women's teams. Martin Bishop in *Bats, Balls and Biscuits* reports that in Berkshire, women's teams from the Huntley and Palmer Biscuit Factory (Reading), Berberry's (Reading), CW Horlicks (Slough) and Aspro (Slough) were regular opponents.[10]

The organisation of women's cricket in the north also reflected the men's game with the rapid formation of leagues. The Dearne Valley women's cricket league, based around Doncaster, was founded in 1927, Keighley Ladies Cricket Competition began in 1930, and the 1930s also saw a district league in Leeds and another of 16 teams in two divisions in Bradford. Brighouse was another hotbed. Encouraged by Brighouse CC, local women cricketers attracted crowds of up to 2000 and reports of their matches progressed from the *Brighouse Echo*'s novelty news items to serious sports' analysis during 1931. The Yorkshire Women's Cricket Federation (WCF) was established that summer, and by 1932 had founded the Yorkshire WCF Intercity and Town League whose clubs comprised: Bingley, Bradford, Brighouse, Dewsbury, Halifax, Holme Valley, Horbury, Huddersfield, Keighley, Liversedge and Sowerby Bridge, plus Littleborough from Lancashire.[11]

The Todmorden committee received a letter from the Yorkshire WCF in August 1932 but again took no action. However, a county federation was about to be formed closer to home. Inspired by their Yorkshire experience, but perhaps desiring more local competition, Littleborough formed the Lancashire WCF and provided its president in Mrs EK Taylor.

In January 1933 Todmorden secretary George Howarth attended a meeting of the Lancashire WCF at Rochdale but, following his report, it was resolved not to join:

> but in view of the increasing interest in Ladies' Cricket to give notice in the local paper that [the club is] willing to provide facilities for any ladies who are agreeable and desirous of taking up this sport.

Interested ladies were invited, via a notice in the *Todmorden Advertiser*, to attend a meeting at the Town Hall on 27 February 1933. Such was the response that on 6 March the club resolved to form a Ladies' Cricket Section and to join the Lancashire WCF.

By April, Todmorden had enrolled about 60 lady playing members, as had Burnley, Crompton and Milnrow.

Two committeemen were appointed as club representatives on the Lancashire WCF and the wives of four others were lady vice-presidents. Former first eleven batsman Johnny Ratcliff was asked to coach the lady members and Chairman Harold Sutcliffe agreed to arrange refreshments for the ladies' teams. A selection committee was appointed from the men on the cricket club committee, and the ground was made available for ladies' matches on Friday evenings. About 30 ladies attended practice nets and by June there was a notice stating:

> The Ladies' net on Thursday is reserved for the published team and reserves.

The club, already indebted to the ladies for manning the tearoom and fund raising, now had everything in place for the ladies' cricket team. There is no doubt that the ladies' cricket was being organised and run by men of the committee, but the ladies chose their uniform, a navy gym slip over a white shirt blouse with black stockings and white sweater, which met with the approval of the local press.

Following two early-season Friday evening scratch matches to assess the talent, the first ever ladies' team to represent the club was selected: M Gouke (captain), N Jackson, A Sunderland, I Greenough, F Law, W Leeming, A Copping, B Whiteside, M Richards, D Shuttleworth; reserves I Whitham, M Fiddling and P Clarkson.

They would play in a Lancashire WCF of eight teams: five from Central Lancashire League clubs, Crompton, Heywood, Littleborough, Milnrow and Rochdale; two from Lancashire League clubs Burnley and Todmorden; plus Facit, based at Whitworth between Bacup and Rochdale. The league season comprised 14 matches of between 25 and 30 overs per side, the exact number of overs determined, as youth matches continue to be, by the evening light. The points system replicated those of the

TCC Ladies' Team at Littleborough c1934.
Row 3: Eveline Greenwood (centre), Mrs Widdup (chaperone) (far right)
Row 2: Bessie Whiteside (2nd left)   Row 1: Nellie Jackson (left)

Lancashire and Central Lancashire Leagues, two for a win and one for a draw.

Like most ladies' teams, the Todmorden players were mainly young and single - just one, Mrs Whitham, was married - and team photographs include the formidable-looking Mrs Widdup, the team chaperon.

Todmorden Ladies made a handsome start at Rochdale, bowling the home side out for 13 to win by 40 runs, and had the measure of all their opponents except undefeated champions Littleborough, whose two seasons' experience in the Yorkshire WCF gave them a decisive edge.

Second in the league with ten victories from their fourteen matches, plus wins in two friendly matches against Lowerhouse, the season was a success. Batting technique and runs were at a premium. Miss Sunderland topped the bowling averages with 76 wickets at a staggering 3.42 each, whilst Nellie Jackson, Todmorden's star player, topped the batting averages with 184 runs at just 12.27. Jackson was selected to play in the end of season match for the Rest of the League against the Champions at Centre Vale, but Littleborough won easily, totalling 51 and dismissing The Rest for 23.

Reviewing the season, the *Todmorden Advertiser* was positive and supportive:

> This was their first season, many had not played before. Batting was variable 100 was only achieved once. Misses Jackson, Long, Law and Whiteside are promising. Miss Gouke, skipper, has often pulled the game round when things were going badly. The strength was in the bowling Misses Sunderland and Jackson were outstanding. Littleborough was the only side to score 100 against Todmorden. Todmorden had the best attack in the league. Fielding was good, with a high level of accuracy in catching, Miss Leeming, short-leg, Miss Jackson, point, and Miss Law, stumper, were outstanding.
>
> For a 1st year's club the girls have done exceedingly well. A thousand pities if an institution which has brought pleasure to so many spectators (and incidentally, profit to the club) should be disbanded, with a year's experience they will no doubt improve next season and become strong challengers to Littleborough.

With admission charges of 2d for adults and 1d for children, and half of one home gate set aside for Lancashire WCF finances, the team's £21 profit represented considerable support over their seven home games. Ominously, at Todmorden's 1933 AGM, the team's contribution to club funds took precedence over their playing success:

> A very interesting experiment has been attempted during the season in the innovation of a ladies' team resulting in addition to our income of £21, and the interest taken in their play [has] been the means of substantially adding to our membership.

The club had, nevertheless, paid the fares of four players to attend a Lancashire WCF trial match at Burnley, from which a team to play the first roses match against the Yorkshire WCF was selected. Nellie Jackson must have been inked in before the trial, for she neither batted nor bowled but was selected alongside four Littleborough players, two from Milnrow and one each from four other clubs, for the match at Rochdale on 23 June.

The *Todmorden Advertiser* reports good-humoured banter from two bus-loads of Yorkshire supporters, armed with rattles, who cheered their more experienced team to victory. Jackson took one for eight with the ball to help restrict Yorkshire to 90 all out, but made a duck as Lancashire struggled to 61 for 8 in reply.

A return match at Bradford in July was played for the Hannah Drake Trophy, named after the president of the Yorkshire WCF. Todmorden was represented by wicketkeeper F Law and W Holland, whilst one of the club's Lancashire League umpires, Uriah Holland, officiated. In a 28 overs match, Brighouse's Mona Greenwood put the match

The Social Side.

On the social side the affair went off in A1 style. On arrival at Blackpool on Wednesday, the party adjourned to the Winter Gardens for luncheon, at which both counties sat down together. After the conclusion of the day's play tea was served in the cricket pavilion by the Blackpool C.C., and Wednesday night was spent in "go-as-you-please" fashion, with the Tower, Winter Gardens and the Palace each finding its devotees. Afterwards the Yorkshire party stayed at the Doric Hotel, whilst the Red Rose party stayed at the Red Court, at Harrowside.

On Thursday morning "up early and out" was the Lancashire girls' motto, a long walk before breakfast being indulged in. It was amusing to see the girls make their raid on the first news-stand, and there was plenty of fun when the efforts of the press photographers of the previous day were seen.

The forenoon of Thursday was free, walking, visiting friends, and in one or two instances, practice on the ground, being the order of the day. We met at our hotel at 11.30 p.m., and were taken to the Winter Gardens for a civic luncheon. The Mayor and Mayoress of Blackpool (Councillor and Mrs. C. E. Tatham) were present, as was the Cotton Queen of England, Miss Gladys Wood, of Manchester. Officials of the English Women's Cricket Federation were present, and Coun. Hannah Drake, of Bradford (the donor of the "Hannah Drake" Trophy) was noticeable among a gathering of distinguished personalities in the realm of women's cricket. Mr. S. Whittaker presented the Lancashire players to the Mayor and Mayoress, whilst Mr. Joy, of Bradford, performed a similar duty for Yorkshire.

On our return to Stanley Park we had the honour of presentation to the Cotton Queen, whose gracious manner during the ceremony caused favourable comment amongst the spectators. Press photographers were very busy, in fact, I have never seen so many at a cricket match before. After the game, Miss M. M. Greenwood (captain of Yorkshire), received the trophy from the Cotton Queen, who, in a well worded and neatly delivered speech urged her hearers to use Lancashire goods at every opportunity, thus helping to alleviate the sufferings of the County. She also expressed her enjoyment of the afternoon's sport, and said that she hoped to see the Red Rose do better in future.

The rival captains made short responses, and the proceedings ended with a comprehensive vote of thanks, moved by Mr. W. Joy, secretary of the E.W.C.F., and seconded by Mr. Oddie, of the committee of the same organisation. This motion included every one who had helped in the game in any way, particular reference being made to Mr. Fred Berry, the energetic secretary of the Blackpool Cricket Club.

After tea had been served in the cricket pavilion, we returned to our bus, starting our journey home just after 7 p.m. We arrived at Todmorden at 9.15 p.m., after a function that will live long in the memories of those who were privileged to be there.

beyond Lancashire, hitting 106 not out in 70 minutes as Yorkshire totalled 163 for 4, Lancashire replying with 78 for 4. By 1937 Mona Greenwood was playing for England against Australia, at Blackpool and the Oval, scoring a total of 36 runs in 3 innings.[12]

Early in April 1934, Todmorden's enthusiastic ladies were 'already practising on the concrete pitch'. Facit's withdrawal left a season of 12 matches, of which Todmorden won 7 and lost 5 to finish equal third with Rochdale, behind champions Littleborough, who beat rapidly improving Burnley in a play-off at Turf Moor before a crowd of over 3000.

Nellie Jackson, fourth in the league's batting averages (285 runs at 25.9, including Todmorden's first half century) and third in the bowling (43 wickets at 6.7), had improved to become the outstanding all-rounder in the county. She was in the Lancashire team that beat Yorkshire for the first time, and with one win each from the scheduled roses matches, a decider was arranged at Stanley Park, Blackpool.

The match attracted 4000 spectators over the two days and was an unqualified social and sporting success. Uriah Holland again officiated and Jackson opened the Lancashire innings, but made just 17 and 3 as Lancashire, 69 and 82 all out, were comprehensively beaten, Yorkshire totalling 145 all out and 10 without loss. From gate receipts of nearly £75, the profit, after deductions for publicity, transport, accommodation and entertainment tax, was just £1 4s 8d, half of which went to Blackpool.

A surplus of £8 11s 8d on the Todmorden Ladies' matches, more than 50% down on 1933, suggested that 'the novelty may be wearing off'. Littleborough Ladies, by comparison, had made £120 over the previous three

Report of visit to Blackpool for Lancashire v Yorkshire WCF match. (TA 24-08-1934)

seasons. Comments at Todmorden's AGM suggested that the ladies' team was on annual probation rather than a permanent fixture.

Distant from the southern-based England Women's Cricket Association, the Lancashire and Yorkshire federations were now established and confident enough to join forces in what appears to be a rival organisation. On Tuesday 19 February 1935 they met at the most logical place, the county border at Todmorden, to found the ambitiously-named English Women's Cricket Federation.

The *Todmorden Advertiser* reported:

> The First Annual Meeting of the English Women's Cricket Federation, the founders of which were the Lancashire and Yorkshire Federations, was held at the Golden Lion Hotel, Todmorden on Tuesday night. Nearly 20 delegates were present representing clubs in each county.

Misses N Sandiford and N Jackson (TCC) open for Lancashire at Blackpool in August 1934.

As well as the formalities of creating a Board of Management of three representatives from each county and setting an annual 5s affiliation fee, the financial and social benefits of a ladies' team were recommended to clubs which had yet to form one.

The following week the Todmorden committee decided 'to join the Ladies' Cricket Federation' for 1935 in which Todmorden again finished third, despite winning only 5 and losing 7 of their 12 matches. With improved technique, batsmen were making fewer mistakes and more runs were being scored. In 1935 Todmorden Ladies scored over two runs per wicket more than they had in 1933, but conceded over 4 runs per wicket more to opposing teams.

Despite the formation of the new Federation, the women's game had reached a plateau of 15 clubs, 8 in Yorkshire and 7 in Lancashire. At a 1935 meeting, held in the Plummet Line Hotel, Halifax, President Mr Bowden of Littleborough, remarked on:

> many who did not think of women's cricket as they in the Federation knew it to be. The only way of proving its worth was to get people to see good games such as they had in the county matches. In that way they had made some impression.

At Todmorden's AGM in November, money was again an issue: 'There is a question over continuing with Ladies' matches as profit is down from £8 11s 8d to £6 2s 9d'. It was April before the committee resolved to enter a team in the WCF for 1936. Castleton Moor also entered increasing the number of matches to 14, of which Todmorden won 6, drew 1 and lost 7 to finish 5th. Nellie Jackson again topped the batting and bowling averages, but lacked support with the bat. Littleborough won their third title and, at the presentation Todmorden's A Fielden commented:

> what he wanted was that Todmorden should have a chance of winning the cup. The team had some very good bowlers but like others a dearth of all-round excellence. They

should train players to be all-rounders. Some men did not think cricket was a game for girls but he had seen them play some good cricket. Their fielding had been good and that often won the match when batting had failed.

Lancashire WCF Final Table 1936

	P	W	L	D	Pts
Littleborough	14	11	1	2	24
Burnley	14	10	3	1	21
Rochdale	14	7	5	2	16
Crompton	14	7	6	1	15
Todmorden	14	6	7	1	13
Milnrow	14	5	8	1	11
Heywood	14	3	8	3	9
Castleton Moor	14	0	11	3	3

On 6 November 1936 the AGM of the English Women's Cricket Federation was again held in Todmorden, this time at the White Hart. Although financially sound, the Federation still had only 16 clubs and a gentleman from Oldham promised to provide a trophy for a knockout cup competition to stir up more enthusiasm among other clubs.

To provide more quality cricket and increase funds, it was decided (provided the counties agreed) to have five instead of three county matches; the revenue from two to each county and from the fifth to the Federation.

Despite the improvement in playing standards, interest was stagnating. Coverage in the *Todmorden Advertiser*, which had reported ladies cricket in the same depth as other matches in 1933, had diminished, and the newspaper now adopted a patronising and sceptical tone.

TCC Ladies' Team c 1936.
Row 2: ____, ____, ____, Fred Root, ____, ____, Nellie Jackson, Mrs Widdup (chaperon),
Row 1: Irene Greenough, Bessy Whiteside, Marion Gouke, ____, ____.

In domestic life women for the most part are respected as 'bosses' but not so in the case of the Cricket Federation. This organisation is almost completely managed by men as indicated by the fact that the annual meeting was attended by twelve men and only five women.

When one of our representatives asked one of the lady wielders of willow why she preferred cricket to tennis and other pastimes the reply was:

'It's good exercise and strenuous. We played cricket as school girls and now we are following it up...it appeals to us more than any other summer game. It is such a thrill to knock up fifty and if you are a bowler, it is nice to see wickets falling down.'

Another lady with economy in mind - and perhaps the cost of the next permanent wave - exclaimed that cricket was cheaper.

Perhaps the reporter had captured the prevailing mood of Todmorden's all-male committee, which on 11 January 1937 decided:

No Ladies' Team 1937 - resign from Lancashire WCF.

The club would not risk the ladies' team running at a loss, even though the Ladies' Committee had, and did, use its resources to bail the club out of financial difficulty and fund essential equipment from time to time.

Nellie Jackson and Miss M Long played for Burnley in 1937, helping them to an undefeated season and their first title. Jackson also continued to play for Lancashire, team-mates at club and county level with Elizabeth Alexandra 'Betty' Snowball, described in *Wisden* as 'the outstanding wicketkeeper of her generation...always immaculate in turnout, and neat and tidy in technique, although enthusiasm added a flourish to efficiency'. Learie Constantine, in his book *Cricket in the Sun*, remembered coaching her:

> One of the pleasant memories of Nelson that I recall was coaching Betty Snowball, of Burnley, a member of the British Women's Cricket team that toured Australia. She was a wicket-keeper and a fine bat, and one of the quickest learners I ever taught.

Combining intelligence, dedication and an abundance of natural ability - she was also a squash and lacrosse international - Snowball took 'aggressive inspiration' from Constantine. His coaching helped her into the England cricket team and she played in the first ever women's test match at Brisbane in 1934. Opening the batting, she made 15 and 18 not out in addition to her wicketkeeping, as England won by seven wickets.

She formed a strong opening partnership with powerful Scot, Myrtle MacLagen, and in the second test at Sydney added 149 with her for the first wicket, hitting 71 before MacLagen went on to record the first women's test century to set up an eight-wicket victory. Snowball added a further 83 not out in the third test at Melbourne which was drawn, England winning the series 2-0. She then rounded her tour off with 189 against New Zealand at Christchurch. This is still the highest score by an England woman in a test match, and remained the world record score until 1986.[13]

Australia's women toured England for the first time in 1937, and Snowball helped England to draw the series with innings of 72 at Northampton and 99 at the Oval, where Yorkshire's Mona Greenwood scored 23. Snowball was denied a second tour of Australia in 1939-40 by the outbreak of war, but returned there in 1948-49. She played in all three tests at Adelaide, Sydney and Melbourne, but with limited success as Australia won the series 1-0, ending her international career at the age of 41. In her ten test matches Snowball scored 613 runs at an average of 40.86 and contributed 13 catches and 8 stumpings. She died in 1988, aged 80.

It cost Betty Snowball £80 to go on the 1934-35 tour, and two players missed the trip for financial reasons. Snowball was one of seven teachers in the party, most of whom were in white collar, professional jobs and, like most women club cricketers, single, without household responsibilities, children to care for or post-childbirth health problems to contend with.

The England players had to fund their own trips until 1998, when the Women's Cricket Association merged with the ECB. It took until the last decade of the 20th century before Betty Snowball's generation were widely perceived and valued as pioneers.[14]

The status of women players and the development of the game was undermined by the notion that playing cricket wasn't really something women should be doing, a prejudice both reflected and drip-fed by some male reporters. *The Times*, for example, commented on the 1934 England team's departure:

> It does not seem nice to think that they are future mothers charged with the responsibility of setting an example of gentleness, refinement and restraint to the next generation.

Such comments were discouraging to existing players and clubs, and to the further development of the game.

Since the 1930s Todmorden CC has fielded occasional ladies' teams which have played one or two friendly matches, usually against Walsden. Pat Hartley, sister of first eleven opening bowler Mike Hartley, was outstanding in victories against Walsden Ladies in the 1970s. In 1987 Todmorden played Walsden home and away with 12 year-old Alison Parker in the team. Like Pat Hartley and a number of the Todmorden players of the 1930s, Alison was from cricketing stock. Her father, Derek, played for Lancashire 2nd XI before pro'ing for 12 years in the Northern, Central Lancashire and Lancashire leagues, and her brothers, Stuart and Duncan, both played age-group cricket for Lancashire, and represented Todmorden's 1st XI.

Alison became the first girl to play regularly, on merit, for Todmorden's U13s team, but there were no local opportunities for her to progress further.

More recently, Evie Priestley has played for Todmorden and Lancashire U11s, the latest in a cricketing dynasty. Evie's father Stuart was 1st XI captain and a prolific batsman; brother Freddie has played for Lancashire U15s; her grandfather, Brian Whittaker, was a skilful swing bowler; her great grandmother, Eveline Greenwood, played in the 1930s ladies' team; her mother, Sarah, played in the 1980s ladies' team, works in the tea pavilion and also keeps the main pavilion sparkling; and Evie's grandmother, Elizabeth (Betty) Whittaker, has been membership secretary and helped out at the club over many years.

Where will Evie play as she gets older? Nationally, the ECB's coaching programmes have allowed many girls to sample cricket and more clubs are including girls in their youth teams, but there are still relatively few women's teams, and the coverage is geographically patchy. The nearest team to Todmorden is Burnley and Padiham

Alison Parker, the first girl to play regularly on merit with the TCC Colts U13s team.

Ladies, who play in the five-team Lancashire Women's Cricket League against teams from Bolton, Preston and the Fylde coast. There is more women's cricket played in Yorkshire, but the nearest teams are 20 miles away in Bradford and Huddersfield. Given the will, manpower and availability of the ground, the provision of a women's cricket team remains a gap that could be still filled by Todmorden Cricket Club.

Until then, the 1930s will remain the high-water mark for women's cricket in the town and, indeed, the region. Any long-term ambitions the England Women's Cricket Federation had to run the national game ran aground on their failure to expand. By 1937 the organisation was less ambitiously titled the Northern WCF and within a year or two it had been absorbed into the England Women's Cricket Association.[15]

By 1939 the flame of women's cricket was dimming across the region. The outbreak of war all but extinguished it.

Evie Priestley in her Lancashire U11 kit.

Chapter 7

See the Conquering Heroes 1930 to 1939

1930-39 was the League's most glamorous decade so far. Several clubs followed Nelson's lead in signing colonial pros including Amar Singh and Lala Armarnath from India, George Headley, Edwin St Hill and 'Manny' Martindale from the West Indies, Arthur Richardson and Sid Hird from Australia and Bill Merritt from New Zealand, whilst Ted McDonald returned to the League after his career with Lancashire. Yet, this enterprise was in contrast to the economic conditions under which people lived.

Predominantly a cotton town, Todmorden, along with others, suffered from industrial unrest, continuing from the General Strike of 1926 and the collapse of the American Stock Market (Wall Street Crash) in 1929.

Kenny Barnes, who first played at Rawtenstall in 1939, was born in 1925 and grew up during the 1930s. He recalls:

> 'Dad, like so many others was made redundant from his employment at the shoe factory in Bacup and mum had her wages severely curtailed, being reduced from four looms to one.'
> His father had to regularly collect three signatures from factories to verify there was no work, in order for him to collect dole money. As he wasn't allowed to keep using the same signatures he would have to walk to Bury, Rochdale and other towns to get different names to satisfy the Government paymasters…Many's the time Ken's mother would be given the remains of a meat joint (used by her sister's family over the weekend) and that had to sustain the family for another few days. Left overs and bread and dripping were often the order of the day.[1]

These conditions would be replicated in many homes at this time. In 1935, a meeting of Todmorden Trade and Labour Council heard of one mill where men in full time employment (and so unable to apply for Poor Law Relief) were earning just £1 4s 0d per week, 8s per week less than the unemployed received from the Employment Exchange. The following year the employers rejected an application by the Operative Weavers' Amalgamation for a wage increase of 3s 0d in the £ and a minimum wage of £1 10s 0d. In 1938 Jack Tout, the local weavers' secretary, stated that 'trade locally had not been so bad since the collapse of 1931'.

The textile trade suffered not only from unemployment but under-employment, whereby a weaver would be running fewer than a full set of looms. Thus the available work was shared and the employer kept his skilled workers on reduced wages. In Todmorden unemployment fluctuated throughout the decade. It was over 4,000 in January 1931, rarely fell below 1,000 and for most of 1938 exceeded 2,000 - these would not include the under-employed. In 1939 the Cotton Conciliation Board in Manchester decided that an adult cotton weaver's fall-back wage would be two-thirds of an individual's earnings (averaged over four full weeks' production), with a maximum of 33s and a minimum of 25s for weavers normally running four looms.

It was against this industrial and economic backdrop that the Lancashire League played its cricket during the 1930s. For 7d one could focus on success against the opposition and be partisan amidst the camaraderie, equality and banter of fellow supporters, briefly escaping the hardships of work or unemployment.

1931 was not the best time for Todmorden CC to fall foul of central government over non-payment of income tax. Having over the years reluctantly come to terms with entertainment tax, a dim view was taken of more interference. The chairman admitted:

> Previous to this year the club had never any idea that the profits were liable to income tax but it has been discovered that this was the case.

The amount was small but the principle rankled - especially when tax was demanded retrospectively for each season from 1921! However, as the tax only applied to profits on gate receipts and not on members' subscriptions, the club, hoping to circumvent the tax, stressed again the benefits of membership. This produced an enlightened change at the AGM. Since 1921 the club's only involvement with boys had been to provide practice facilities twice a week for the local schoolboys' teams. Anyone under sixteen years old could only be a member by special consent of the committee and payment of the full adult fee. Now, boys under sixteen could become members for a fee of 5s; 69 boys joined in the first year, one of whom was ten year-old Richard Horsfall, later to play for Essex.

Always on good terms with the local authority, the club readily agreed to release land behind the pavilion for use as allotments for the unemployed in 1933. These allotments, last cultivated during and just after World War I, were soon back in use.

In 1932 the League suggested the creation of 'Supporters' Clubs' to help raise money given 'the present financial position'. Todmorden responded in 1934 with the formation of a Ladies' Social Committee to organise fund-raising events. Whist drives, dances and a Christmas draw yielded £70 in the first year. When the workshop competition took place, it also helped to avert financial crises, raising £83 in 1932 and £100 in 1934, seasons which still made a combined loss of £154. In 1935 the chairman announced that the club's cash resources were exhausted, a position it had not seen for over 25 years.

The Ladies' Social Committee raised a further £87 in 1935/36 and £90 in 1936/37, when the men also organised functions raising £25. By 1938 the Ladies' Committee was able to buy the club a motor mower and a Supporters' Club was formed with the aim of funding a new scorebox.

The Co-operative Society Education Committee assisted the club in January 1938 by engaging the great Yorkshire and England opening batsman Herbert Sutcliffe to give a lantern lecture entitled 'International Cricket Reminiscences' at the Town Hall. About 1000 attended and the Co-op donated the £5 11s profit to the club.

Efforts to increase the Todmorden membership led, in 1939, to the club mounting a campaign in Hebden Bridge including hiring a room there, where those interested could become members. The chairman said that a year's membership was 'the best ten bobsworth in town'.

Despite an increase in fund-raising initiatives, most Lancashire League clubs made a loss in most seasons. At Todmorden membership had fallen from 1900 in 1920 to around 1100 by 1930 and subscriptions continued to decline steadily year-on-year, from £622 in 1927 to £445 in 1938. There was little money to spare in the households of the working class. The club minute books for this period show some being members intermittently, most likely when they could afford the fee at the start of the season. At the 1932 AGM, the chairman acknowledged that 'times were hard and not all could afford ten shillings'. Surprisingly, membership across the League increased from 8,785 in 1930 to 11,839 in 1936 before dropping slightly by the end of the decade.

Total Lancashire League crowds were consistently over 250,000 in the first part of the decade, peaking at 297,000 in 1933, but had dropped to 206,000 by 1938. Todmorden's gate receipts show fluctuations, up one year and down the next. As the depression hit hard in 1932, a larger proportion of the crowd sat on the school side of Centre Vale where admission was 7d compared to 1s for the Burnley Road and Park sides. As ever, gates were also affected by the team's performance and the weather, not least when Constantine was playing. In 1937, Todmorden ruefully reflected that rain had spoiled the home fixture against Nelson for the third successive year. A reduction of £1400 in total gate receipts for the League in 1938 was attributed by Edward Crabtree to very bad weather and the loss of Constantine to the Central Lancashire League.

Todmorden's anxiety to protect its gate receipts was clear when Todmorden Town Council created a path running behind the cricket field from Centre Vale Park to the town centre during the winter of 1933-34. Fearing that this would allow a free view, the cricket club asked for it to be closed on match days during hours of play and the council agreed.

Todmorden began 1930 brightly with wins against Accrington and Church, Herbert Haigh proving to be a solid batsman and useful bowler. A tight rain-affected draw at Haslingden was overshadowed by the sudden death during the match of Todmorden scorer Ernest Halliwell. Ernest had played from 1884 to 1897 and scored for the next thirty-three years. As his father was a player in 1850, a family connection spanning eighty years had come to an end.

Four matches into the season the playing strength was weakened when Ned Stansfield, having rejected other offers, became professional at Kearsley in the Bolton League. The press commented:

> Kearsley's was too tempting especially when industrial conditions are none too rosy and he could not refuse it.

The void was filled in mid-season by the transfer from Littleborough of left-arm amateur spinner Harold Haigh. A solid performance from professional Haigh helped the team to come third in the League. A lasting impression of the season was seventeen drawn matches, eight of them curtailed by the weather. Only two matches were lost, Nelson inflicting the only home defeat when Johnny Greenwood 'rubbed it in' by taking 5 for 24 as Todmorden were bowled out for 85.

The town's schoolboys continued to perform well, beating Rochdale, Bacup and Nelson on their way to the final against Manchester at Centre Vale, where they were outplayed, 129 runs to 31. Constantine, who had agreed to umpire this match, found he could not do so and sent a written apology which was posted at the entrance to the ground. The schoolboys were again finalists in 1933, losing by 12 runs to North Manchester. Todmorden's enthusiasm for schoolboy cricket was recognized in 1930 when Centre Vale hosted the Roses schoolboys' match, which Yorkshire won.

At the 1930 AGM the committee surprisingly offered no comment about professional Herbert Haigh's contribution to a successful season, but were pressed from the floor as to his salary. When the treasurer disclosed that it was £250, a voice opined 'He was deserving of more'.

Todmorden's 1931 professional, Edward W (Nobby) Clark, the Northants and England fast left-arm bowler, on the platform to present the prizes, could be in little doubt that his performances would be under the closest scrutiny! The chairman commented encouragingly that all successful seasons had been inspired by a fast-bowling professional - the members wanted 'one of those fellows who could knock the furniture back!' Former chairman JW Crabtree had, over the years, also proclaimed the virtues of extreme speed in the belief that very few Lancashire League batsmen could deal with a fast bowler who 'bumped a little'.

Clark, in response, gave a simple portrait of himself. Born near Peterborough, his first cricket was with his Sunday School team. Later, as an engineering apprentice in Bradford, his manager introduced him to Bankfoot in the Bradford League. His success there led to his playing for his native county Northants and 'now I am here'.

He made his county debut as a nineteen year-old in 1922, toured the West Indies with Tennyson's team in 1927/8, and played his first test against South Africa at the Oval in 1929. According to his *Wisden* obituary:

> A row with Northamptonshire, whom he left temporarily for league cricket, spoiled his chances of playing against the Australians in 1930.[2]

Todmorden seized their chance, agreed a salary of £400 for the twenty-week season, and felt that they had made a coup. He did not disappoint them. A truly fast bowler with a classic high action, red hair and a temperament to match, Clark took 80 wickets at an average of 7.8 runs per wicket. The

EW Clark

team maintained its third position in the League and reached the Worsley Cup Final, only to succumb to Constantine's Nelson, a gate of £205 softening the blow. This was despite soft wickets that blunted Clark's pace - 1931 was, even by Lancashire League standards, a wet season, twelve matches being either totally or partially abandoned.

Additionally Clark had come to an unsettled team. Young William Halstead had moved with his family into Yorkshire. JW Sunderland left the district on his appointment as secretary of Great Harwood Weavers' Association and transferred his cricket allegiance to Church. Ned Stansfield returned from Kearsley, replaced as professional there by Todmorden's Roy Whitham but, influenced by Stansfield's return, Harold Haigh left the club. So the bowling was light and Stansfield with 41 League wickets was the only amateur to take more than 12.

Clark was no batter, his total runs for the season being 23. As *Wisden* says:

> His cricket began and ended with his bowling, neither batting nor fielding did he regard as any business of his.[3]

Potential batting problems were, however, solved when John Crowther and Billy Scott transferred from Walsden. Scott, a compact batsman, had scored 3587 runs for Walsden since his debut as a sixteen year-old in 1916 and Crowther (nine years his junior) 1183 runs since his debut at a similar age in 1925. Their move to Todmorden followed the retirement from first team cricket of Scott's father Frank, who had played for Walsden 1st XI from 1892 until 1930. With over 6000 runs and 966 wickets he was Walsden's 'Mr Cricket'. Indeed, the road next to the ground is named Scott Street after him. It is understandable that Billy would not leave Walsden whilst his father was still playing. Runs did not flow at Todmorden in 1931, Scott with 348 runs and

Billy Scott; he and John Crowther formed a formidable opening partnership.

Crowther with 342 easily topping the averages, but with Clark bowling so economically the opposition only exceeded 100 five times.

By comparison, 1932 was a disappointing season, the final position of eleventh being the worst for a decade. Better weather and covered wickets helped Clark, who took 93 League wickets at 8.77, but he had little amateur assistance. Roy Whitham and Ned Stansfield took 50 wickets between them but were less economical than expected and no other bowler took more than 8. Hargreaves, Scott and Crowther led the batting supported by veteran skipper Arthur Stephenson, Bob Sutcliffe and Eddie Mitchell, but disenchantment showed when more players than usual missed matches during the holiday period, leaving a much weakened side.

Northants, missing Clark, paid Todmorden £6 per match to release him for some mid-week county matches. To maintain a good standard of practice Frank Dutnall, the Burnley player and ex-professional, was engaged to bowl and coach on Tuesdays and Thursdays when Clark was away. Failure to agree a further two-year contract with Clark led to a search for a new professional, letters being written to Maurice Tate of Sussex, and George Macauley of Yorkshire.

Clark returned to Northants and resumed not only his county but his test career, playing against the West Indies at the Oval and Old Trafford in 1933, where he shared the new ball with future Todmorden professional Macauley. Played in the aftermath of the previous winter's infamous 'Bodyline' tour, the issue of short-pitched bowling reared its head again when Constantine and Martindale subjected Douglas Jardine to a bumper barrage at Old Trafford, and the uncompromising England captain instructed Clark to return fire. Clark obeyed, but the establishment was fearful of further controversy and, despite taking six wickets in the match including 4 for 99 in 40 overs in the first innings, Clark was dropped for the next test. He returned to tour India under Jardine in 1933/4 and played the last of his 8 tests against Australia at the Oval in 1934. By 1938 Clark was professional with Darlington in the North Yorks and South Durham League but in 1946 he returned to Northamptonshire for a final fling and for a few overs was still as fast as anyone in England.[4]

In retirement Clark became 'mine host' at a pub in St Ives, Huntingdonshire, where the walls were:

John Crowther
(*Sunday Graphic* 1935)

lined with the pictures of some of Nobby's victims. Batsmen are shown in various agonizing postures grasping some part of their anatomy recently struck by a very hard cricket ball. You could be in the outpatients department of any big hospital.

In 1948 he was persuaded to turn out for Cambridgeshire of the minor counties. His first match was against Bedfordshire at Luton, for whom the ex-Surrey and England fast bowler Alf Gover had agreed to play. Cambridgeshire batted on a rough, lively surface but Nobby, batting at number 11, had faith in the fast bowlers' union and trusted Gover to pitch the ball well up to him. When the first ball reared up and flicked his right ear lobe, Nobby hurled his bat to the ground and stormed off warning the amused fielders:

> You are laughing now but I will fix you one by one.

By the time the Bedfordshire opening batsmen appeared, Nobby had already marked out his run ready to strike. The first ball, delivered with all his might, hit the batsman on the left ear felling him. Sympathetic fielders rushed to him failing to notice Nobby prostrate at the other end. Forgetting his age, he had put too much effort into the delivery and pulled several muscles. Probably uniquely, the opening bowler and opening batsman were simultaneously carried from the field.[5]

In the early 1960s when the Lancashire League batsmen were facing onslaughts from West Indians Roy Gilchrist, Wes Hall and Chester Watson, John Crowther, one of Clark's amateur colleagues at Todmorden, was convinced that in his opening spell Nobby Clark was as fast as any of them. Many years later Neville Cardus wrote:

> Root and Clark were among many of the new ball bowlers of the 1930s who would make nearly every seamer of 1968 seem mild and self effacing.[6]

In mid-August 1932 Fred Root of Worcestershire was announced as Todmorden professional for 1933. Aged 43, Root came to Todmorden at the end of his county career but with many years of cricket left in him. His initial one year contract extended to five, covering half of the club's most successful decade. Root was born in 1890 at Somercotes, Derbyshire and soon afterwards his father became groundsman at Leicestershire County Cricket Club. By 1909 Fred was playing for Leicestershire Club and Ground, top scoring with 79 out of 130 against Derbyshire Club and Ground. Despite this performance, Fred was overlooked for the 1st XI in favour of a young amateur and he accepted an offer to join Derbyshire for 1910.[7]

During World War I, serving as a dispatch rider in France, Fred was shot in the chest and invalided to St Luke's Hospital, Bradford, where the medical officer said he would never play cricket again. Confounding the specialists, Fred joined a galaxy of stars in the Bradford League, playing two wartime seasons for Bowling Old Lane. He moved to Dudley in the Birmingham League and by 1921 had qualified to play for Worcestershire. A run-of-the-mill 31 year-old fast medium bowler, he had modest success - 8 wickets in 1921 and 41 in 1922. During the winter of 1922/3 he worked at developing leg-theory, not the first to do so, but he quickly became its best exponent. Perfecting in-swing with a new or old ball, Fred bowled with immaculate control to five fieldsmen in close catching positions on the leg side and took an incredible 165 wickets in 1923. Fred explained:

> The in-swinger well bowled, does its work late.[8]

It was said that:

Sometimes the wretched batsman had to play a ball which started in the direction of outside the off stump and finished in fine leg's hands, at other times the swing was only an inch or two from a ball which looked as though it was going to do exactly the same. Then there was the ever-present menace of the one that straightened or even came back a little, and all this was done to an immaculate length and with a variation of pace from medium to medium-fast.[9]

Leg-theory is sometimes confused with 'Bodyline' but, whilst bowled on a similar line, leg-theory employs a much fuller length. Nevertheless, Root's success was influential in making leg-side line and field placings the vogue and was a precursor to Jardine's ruthless intimidatory 'Bodyline' tactics.

From 1923 to 1932 Fred took 1411 wickets for Worcestershire. He toured the West Indies in 1925/6 and played three tests against Australia in 1926. A respectable batsman, he did the double in 1928 and had career figures of 8089 runs at 15.37 per innings and 1512 wickets at 21.11 runs each.[10] This considerable cricketer came to Todmorden for a salary of £320 for the twenty-week season, which was £20 more than his final salary as Worcestershire's leading bowler for a full county season. Root describes his introduction to Todmorden in graphic terms:

> I arrived in the small border town to take up my duties at four o'clock one dreary April afternoon. I had travelled one hundred and fifty miles, and was looking forward to a meal and a rest, but the chairman, who met me at the station, took me directly to the cricket ground and I had surprise number one.
>
> Cricket was in full swing and as many people were on the ground to cast their critical eyes over my doings at the nets as would have been reckoned a good county match 'gate' at Worcestershire.[11]

Root's Action

In presenting the club prizes in 1932, Walter Leslie Greenwood commented that in Swinton, where he lived, the Lancashire League was criticized as a 'cup hunting business', in which matches were fought too keenly. Walter's opinion was that any cricket not keen, strenuous and fair was not worth playing and that high class professionals brought fresh knowledge to a club. Practically all the amateurs in county and international cricket were products of the public schools and universities which employed high class professionals as coaches, Hirst at Eton, Rhodes at Harrow, and if it was good enough for them, it was good enough for lads in the Lancashire leagues. Such a man was Fred Root who, by the end of his first season at Todmorden was:

Root's Leg-Trap

most pleased with the willingness shown by the older players to take tips when I have given them a word of advice.

For Root's bowling to be successful he needed fieldsmen who could take his catches in the difficult leg-trap positions, where the ball is seen late. Todmorden had such fieldsmen, especially Eddie Mitchell, John Crowther, Billy Scott and Harold Dawson. In Root's five years as professional these players took 189 catches; Mitchell 67, Crowther 36 (in three seasons, as he was professional at Darwen in 1936 and Millom in 1937), Dawson 48 and Scott 38, the majority of these being from Root's bowling. Equally important was Root's wicketkeeper and in Tommy Carrick Todmorden had a gem. Root had nothing but praise for Carrick:

> who kept to my bowling as well as any 'keeper' I have bowled to. [He was] the best wicketkeeper in the league and the most enthusiastic player with whom I have ever played.[12]

Diminutive he may have been but Carrick behind the stumps was an inspiration to the team. He was rarely silent and had, Root says:

> the wicketkeeper's disease in regard to appealing…when we were playing Nelson he squeaked 'How's that?' for lbw when Constantine was batting against me. 'Connie', with the agility which only he possesses, leaped round like greased lightning, leered at Carrick and howled 'NOT OUT'.
> The little wicketkeeper was really scared. When he got to my end he said, 'Freddie, he's "feared" me, I don't fancy appealing any more. I thought he was going to bite me'.
> 'He won't hurt you', I replied. 'It's only his excessive keenness'.
> Two or three balls later Carrick appealed again and 'Connie' went through the same performance. My words had made Carrick bolder and, assuming the air of outraged dignity and pointing to the umpire, he faced the West Indian like a pugilist and said to him, 'Thee shirrup. I'm not asking thee I'm asking t'umpire.'[13]

1933 began well; Todmorden's win at Haslingden (153 for 6 declared to 135 all out) was their first win at Bent Gate since 1916. Rain spoilt the first home match against Enfield who scored 169 for 5 declared. Newton, their Yorkshire professional, scored 77 and to counter Root's leg-theory 'eventually altered his stance so as to suit a bowler who might have been bowling from square-leg'. A week later the rain came to Todmorden's aid after Colne had bowled them out at Centre Vale for 44, causing a local wag to suggest to the would-be vendor of League handbooks that 'it was funeral cards he should be selling'.

This inauspicious start persuaded the committee to write to Harold Larwood 'respecting a professional engagement', but nothing more is recorded about this. Root, always economical and often penetrative, led an improvement and within a month had been signed for another year at £330, a £10 increase.

At the halfway stage the team had registered six victories and two defeats but the latter were comprehensive - bundled out for 57 at Nelson (Constantine 8 for 18) and 79 at Bacup (Ted McDonald 9 for 28). Honour was restored by defeating Nelson at Centre Vale by 144 to 116 in front of the season's best gate of £127. The second half of the season began with two wins firstly against Accrington and then Rawtenstall, who were bowled out for 34, Roy Whitham taking a hat-trick at which, predictably, 'Carrick threw his hat in the air exultingly'. Not even Rawtenstall's 60 year-old professional SF Barnes, in his last season in the Lancashire League, could dismiss Todmorden for 34 and the match was won by nine wickets. The next few matches yielded three draws and one defeat, causing the chairman to interview captain Bob Sutcliffe 'with a view to getting better results'. Whatever was said worked. Results improved and Todmorden were tying with Nelson at the top of the League with three matches to play.

Bob Sutcliffe

East Lancashire were comfortably beaten by six wickets at Alexandra Meadows but in the season's last home match Haslingden (88 for 7) clung on for a draw in reply to Todmorden's 153 for 9 declared. As Nelson won both their fixtures Todmorden were one point adrift with one to play. Nelson, playing away to bottom of the League Enfield, had only to win to be champions for the fifth time in six years. Todmorden, resigned to coming second, bowled Church out for 74, whilst neighbouring Enfield scored 121. Todmorden knocked off the runs quickly, but prolonged the game until the Enfield result was known. News that Nelson were 90 for 5 did not lighten Todmorden's hearts, but when this became 107 all out, they could hardly believe it. How high Carrick threw his hat or whether it ever came down again is not recorded.

Captain Bob Sutcliffe entertained the team and club officials to dinner at the Thorn Hotel Burnley, before they travelled home by open-topped motor coach, driving slowly to great acclaim from Portsmouth down the valley to the Town Hall. There, a huge crowd was waiting and a civic reception was given by the Mayor, Mayoress and Town Council. The motor

1933 League Champions: Root (centre) flanked by Edward Crabtree (League President) and Bob Sutcliffe (captain), in trilbies are Scott, Crowther and Hargreaves, behind Scott is Alfred King (treasurer).

tour continued down Halifax and Rochdale Roads before returning to the Town Hall for supper.

The success was built, not only on Root's all round ability - 467 runs and 106 League wickets at 9.83 runs per wicket - but on the way the team responded to his experience and enthusiasm. The amateur batting led by Scott 518 runs, Crowther 459, Stephenson 365, Hargreaves 353 and Walter Sutcliffe 287 performed well but the crucial amateur contribution was Roy Whitham's 60 League wickets. Commenting on the Lancashire League Root wrote:

> Never have I played in any sort of cricket that provides greater thrills than the Lancashire League. Crowds are large and the knowledge of the people who make up these crowds is exceptional...The standard of cricket is high, the amateurs comparing with many county players, and the professionals among the best in the world...matches are thrilling, short, snappy, and mostly decisive. Drawn games are looked upon with extreme displeasure...under such conditions the old lackadaisical methods of county cricket appear appalling.

On the members and supporters he commented:

> They would rather miss joining the Co-op than the cricket club, and when bad times make money scarce, they make sacrifices to enable them to pay their annual subscriptions...they do anything in their power to assist the club. They will be very annoyed if not included in the roller XI...and I have seen men do as much voluntary work on Lancashire League grounds in a week as a paid groundsman in county cricket does in a fortnight...the rafters of the Hare and Hounds or the Shannon and Chesapeake ring to the laughter of good natured arguments. Exaggerations abound, about, for example 'Jonah Clegg hit a ball over two hundred yards, and it dropped in yon shelter in the Park and that were o'er forty years ago.' It was barely relevant that the shelter was only 10 years old.
>
> Cotton manufacturers rub shoulders with their own weavers...Every member of the committee takes his job as seriously as an MP...There are no such things as class and creed when the committee is in session. Players will rush out of the mill, drop off their

THE 1933 TEAM
Back Row: E. Gregson (scorer), E. Mitchell, B. Ashworth, F. Root (professional), W. Sutcliffe,
R. Whitham, G. Howarth (secretary)
Front Row: E. Stansfield, H. Dawson, E. Hargreaves, A. Stephenson, R. Sutcliffe (captain),
T. Carrick, J. Crowther, W. Scott

clogs, don cricket boots, and practice seriously and enjoyably until darkness blots out
the nets. No social distinction - one common effort for one common weal.[14]

1933's success was not repeated in 1934, Todmorden sliding to mid-table, and,
although in subsequent years a higher position was maintained, no-one again
challenged Nelson's supremacy until Constantine left the club after the 1937 season.

The 1934 slump was due to batting collapses that cost four of the first five matches
and a lack of amateur bowling to support Root. Whitham (22 wickets) could not repeat
his 1933 performance; Sutcliffe (34 wickets) and Crowther (27 wickets) manfully
plugged the gap and, in total, the amateur bowling took 98 wickets, exactly matching
Root's haul. The difference was the economy rate; Root's wicket's cost 8.77 runs apiece
whilst the next best was Crowther at 16.85. The batting recovered from its early-season
debacles and only three more matches were lost but, on improved pitches in a dry
summer, twelve were drawn as Todmorden struggled to bowl out the opposition. Bob
Sutcliffe resigned as captain in June and Arthur Stephenson took over in his last season.
Stevenson was also awarded a testimonial match against East Lancashire which, despite
a chill day, raised £70.

Root remained at Todmorden for another three seasons, although he was only signed
on a year-to-year basis, probably because financial uncertainty brought a reluctance to
enter into longer-term contracts.

1935 saw Todmorden bounce back in both League and Cup. Root had his most
successful season with the ball, taking 117 League wickets including five or more
wickets on thirteen occasions and an incredible 21 wickets for 77 runs in the Worsley
Cup. He was ably supported with the ball by Will Raby whose 39 League wickets were
taken at the economical average of 12.15. Ernest Hargreaves broke the club amateur

batting record with 740 League runs plus 157 runs in the Worsley Cup as the club secured the knockout trophy without being threatened. In the final at Accrington on Wednesday 29 August, the Todmorden innings was suspended at 133 for 3 (Hargreaves 60, Crowther 31, Scott 24 not out) before Accrington were bowled out for 78 (Root 8 for 32). Todmorden Mayor, Col Gledhill, expressed the town's gratitude to the club, saying:

> The efforts of the team to uphold the dignity of the town were appreciated.

With two matches left Todmorden were in a position to win the League as well but three days after the Cup final Accrington took their revenge - winning by four wickets after bowling Todmorden out for 100. Todmorden were second, one point behind Nelson, who owing to Constantine's knee injury had signed Nobby Clark as professional for the last few matches. The significance of league cricket and of the Lancashire League in particular is shown by the *Sunday Graphic and Sunday News'* full page photographic record of Todmorden's final match at home to Ramsbottom. Unfortunately, replying to Ramsbottom's 236 for 6 declared, Todmorden were bowled out for 56. Nelson won at Rawtenstall and Ramsbottom overtook Todmorden who finished third.

The loss of John Crowther to his professional post at Darwen was keenly felt in 1936. The batting fell apart as a run of six defeats in eight matches, which included a first-round Worsley Cup defeat, consigned Todmorden to a mid-table finish. The bowling, however, received a boost when Alec Smith from Old Town was invited to attend early-season nets at Centre Vale. By early June he was in the first team and ended the season with 39 wickets, including 8 for 18 against Rishton. Fred Root was impressed with Alec and wrote:

> ...as proof that 'nip' can be learned, I quote the instance of a young bowler I coached at Todmorden last season [1936]. His name is Alec Smith and, if given the opportunity, this young man will be heard of in first class cricket in the near future. He came to me direct from a junior club, very raw but with a will to learn and succeed. Almost at once he saw the idea, (of high arm, effort at release and full follow through) and developed almost over-night into a really good bowler. From the very first time he was included in the (Todmorden) Lancashire League XI he got good batsmen out. Had he been qualified for Lancashire I have the word of Harry Makepiece he would have been engaged on the staff at Old Trafford. But he was born in Yorkshire.[15]

1937 was to be Root's last at Todmorden and the decision to release him provoked strong letters to the *Todmorden Advertiser*. One threatened to call a special meeting if a straight answer was not forthcoming:

> the best pro in the league, who had spent hours and hours on the ground assisting to improve conditions and prepare wickets, had been lost.

Root was quickly snapped up by Lowerhouse in early June and Todmorden received letters from three clubs in the League expressing pleasure that he would still be a professional in the League.

Root's positive relationship with the players was evident on a lively pitch at Rishton. Ben Ashworth, a middle order batsman - and rather stern 2nd XI captain after World War II - was batting with Root against some awkward, lifting deliveries from Rishton's fast-bowling professional, Bobby Rae. Ashworth was not getting quite behind the line and Root, at the non-striker's end, demonstrated how to do it. When a run brought Root to face Rae he fared no better and Ashworth, after watching a few balls, walked

Todmorden v Ramsbottom. (*Sunday Graphic* 1935)

Spectators at Centre Vale. (*Sunday Graphic* 1935)

down the wicket said laconically, 'Aye Fred, Ah see how tha means!'

1937 was Root's best all-round season, with over 800 runs and 92 wickets in League and Cup, including hat-tricks against both Bacup and Colne. Alec Smith played little, owing to injury, but Will Raby (53 wickets) and Ernest Hargreaves (808 runs) both excelled. Fourth in the League, five points behind champions Nelson, was respectable and the season was crowned by winning the Worsley Cup. In the final at Centre Vale, over two days in August, Todmorden scored 379 (Root 133, Sutcliffe 85, Hargreaves 72) and bowled Rishton out for 170.

His enduring quality confirmed, Root left for Lowerhouse as the most popular and successful professional in Todmorden's history, an assertion which remains true over 70 years later. Eddie Mitchell, the keystone of Root's leg-trap also left as his work took him and his family to Huddersfield.

Another player to move on, in less happy circumstances was wicketkeeper Tommy Carrick. Praised for his keeping by all of Todmorden's experienced bowling professionals, Carrick lost the gloves to Kenneth Fiddling from Hebden Bridge in June 1937. Fiddling was a better batsman and later kept wicket for Yorkshire and Northamptonshire. Carrick played for Walsden in 1938 and Bacup, where he was living, in 1939. Returning to Todmorden in 1946 he was automatic choice until his retirement in 1952. In 1949 he was granted a testimonial which raised over £279, a tribute to both his cricketing skill and popularity. Carrick's passion for cricket was life-long. On moving to live in Cornholme, he often played cricket with local children on spare land above Brookfield Terrace and after retiring he umpired in the Lancashire League and for Todmorden's junior teams over many years. Proud of his ability and achievements as a wicketkeeper, even in his nineties, the events of 1937 roused strong emotions:

> Fiddling was a better batter than me [and then, with a steely look and a grip of the arm] but he weren't a better keeper.

The 1930s is regarded as one of the League's most glamorous decades. In 1930 the League allowed clubs to cover their wickets from the day before the match. Todmorden could cover part of the pitch in 1931 and invested £111 to cover the whole pitch for 1932. The covers were made by a local firm, George Whitehead & Sons, where the club's chairman Harold Sutcliffe was managing director.

The introduction of artificial fertilizers and generally decent weather further assisted the batsmen and Todmorden's average runs per wicket rose from 13.63 in the 1920s to 17.75 in the 30s. In his annual report for 1937, the League secretary commented 'another season with no bowler taking 100 wickets'.[16]

With wickets harder to obtain there was an increasing number of drawn matches. To encourage positive play the League increased the number of points for a win from two to three in 1936, whilst a draw was still worth

Kenneth Fiddling in his Yorkshire cap and blazer

Fiddling Stumping (Northants 1947-53)

one. The Bradford League, also experiencing a glut of draws, implemented an identical points increase in the same season.

The Lancashire League adopted three more changes in 1939. The number of balls in an over was increased from six to eight, aiming to save time between overs so that more deliveries could be bowled. Scorers tabulated runs scored from the seventh and eighth balls to help evaluate the influence of the longer over.[17]

The League also introduced the larger wicket, used in the first class game eight years earlier, and the 1937 lbw rule. This meant a batsman could be lbw to a ball pitching outside the off stump, providing it would have hit the wickets and he was in front of them when it hit him. Under the old rule the ball had to pitch in line with the wickets to gain an lbw decision.

Despite purchasing covers, Todmorden, along with other clubs, could not afford to modernise facilities or replace all their equipment as they would have wished. In 1936 the Education Department built a new Open Air School at Stile, making the old wooden structure below the railway on Ferney Lee redundant. The council offered this free to the cricket club for use as a pavilion but the club could not afford the cost of dismantling, moving and re-erecting it. The old pavilion of 1864 remained in use until 1959.

Ground equipment was basic. A lawn mower was purchased in 1929, presumably for cutting the square and practice pitches, but each year a motor mower for the outfield had to be borrowed from the adjoining park, the golf club or a club member. Prices for rollers and mowers were sought, but the club could not afford to buy a machine until 1938. Seating accommodation was gradually increased in piecemeal fashion. Second-hand forms were bought on the closure of Old Royd Methodist Chapel in 1930 and on the replacement of the old Olympia Cinema in 1931. From 1933 to 35 three rows of planks on concrete pedestals, costing £29, were added along the school side.

The covers indicated how keen Todmorden was to get games underway. On Friday 12 August 1938 a deluge left Todmorden's Centre Vale ground standing in water. The following day was Nelson's visit with their professional Lala Amarnath. It was literally all hands to the pump as the fire brigade worked for three hours to remove the water. On Saturday morning sacks of sawdust were spread on the wettest parts and the game was played. Although it was a draw, a £76 gate saw some exciting cricket as Todmorden, batting first, scored 219 for 7 in 49.4 overs, declaring at 4.11pm. Nelson replied with 106 for 5 in 69 overs. Almost 120 (8 ball) overs were bowled in five hours!

The game typified the attitude of Todmorden's ebullient captain Walter Sutcliffe. His aim batting first was to score quickly and declare early, leaving as much time as possible to bowl out the opposition. In this match he scored 50 in 21 minutes, going on to make 74 in his big hitting style, in partnership with Harold Dawson (73 not out). Edward Crabtree likened him to a 'Young Jonas' a reference to Jonas Clegg junior, Todmorden's legendary big hitter. A successful all-rounder, Sutcliffe used himself

PORTABLE WICKET COVER
MAKERS: GEORGE WHITEHEAD & SONS LTD., TODMORDEN

PORTABLE WICKET COVER
MAKERS: GEORGE WHITEHEAD & SONS LTD., TODMORDEN

wherever the game demanded and was always positive. In a career truncated by the war he took over 160 wickets and scored over 3000 runs.

At the 1938 AGM the League president Edward Crabtree declared that the League:

> had become more of a social amenity as was proved by the fact that 25% to 35% of attendances at matches were of ladies. [He believed that] The grounds served as good a purpose as parks and similar things on which the ratepayers' money was spent. Cricket clubs were undoubtedly centres of social service for the whole community.

At Todmorden, the club remained, in the words of Councillor Johnny Whittaker:

> an integral part of the town, like the Town Hall or the Co-operative Society.

Unsurprisingly after Root's success, Todmorden looked for a well-known English county player to follow him. Arthur Wellard was approached when Somerset played at Old Trafford and Frank Woolley of Kent, having replied to the club's initial advances, was offered £320 for the 20 week season. Harold Larwood was seen at Old Trafford, club chairman Harold Sutcliffe being authorised to offer up to £450 per season for no longer than a two year contract. Morris Nichols was pursued when Essex played at Headingley, before Todmorden signed the highly respected ex-Yorkshire bowler, George Macauley for £300.

Macauley, had been professional at Ebbw Vale in Monmouthshire in 1937. In his 16 seasons at Yorkshire, he took 1773 wickets at an impressive average of 17. He took 100 wickets in a season ten times and played for England on eight occasions. Herbert Sutcliffe wrote:

> Macauley also has been and still is one of the game's finest medium paced off-spin bowlers.
> He is a militant type of bowler and all the better for that, but he is quite harmless. Meet him off the field and you will soon discover what a charming fellow he can be and what a sharp pointed wit he has.
> Macauley jealously guards every run until the pitch realises its promise, then he sets his leg-trap and the batsman who scores against him has to be either at the top of his form or desperately lucky.[18]

Against South Africa at Cape Town in 1922-3 he became only the fourth bowler to take a wicket with his first ball in Test cricket. EM Wellings writing in *Wisden Cricket Monthly* recalls:

> Time was when bowlers of emphatic pace made good use of spin...I clearly remember being struck above the heart and almost bowled over by an off-break of similar speed (to Alec Bedser) from George Macauley.[19]

Macauley was never afraid to speak his mind. When Brian Sellers, captaining Yorkshire for the first time in 1932 as deputy for Frank Greenwood, put the opposition in to bat, Macauley quizzed him about his decision. Sellers replied that his father had advised him to put them in:

> 'Then tell your father to bloody well come and bowl them out!' exploded Macauley.[20]

Macauley, with 146 runs all season, was never going to score many runs but the amateurs compensated magnificently. The loss of Ernest Hargreaves to Littleborough was offset by the return of the stylish John Crowther. Crowther and the pugnacious Dawson were both close to their peaks and topped 600 runs. With a solid opener in Billy Scott and a free-scoring middle order of captain Walter Sutcliffe, Ben Ashworth, Ken Fiddling and 17 year-old Richard Horsfall, the batting had balance and depth. Horsfall had made his first team debut in 1936 and the following year Root wrote of him:

> Todmorden has a lad sixteen years old, who has already stood the trial of Constantine and Martindale in the Lancashire League. For three years he has been the best boy batsman in Lancashire.[21]

Whilst Horsfall's county career lay ahead, Fiddling's began in 1938 and he occasionally missed Todmorden's matches to deputise for Yorkshire wicketkeeper Arthur Wood when Wood was away on Ashes duty for England.

Macauley's medium-pace off-spin was economical on good pitches and devastating on wet ones. He took 95 wickets at under 10 runs each and conceded less than two runs per eight-ball over. With Alec Smith taking 72 wickets at 12 runs each and conceding just over two an over at the other end, the League can rarely have seen a more cussed and miserly opening attack. Crowther's inviting leg-spin and googlies were a perfect foil for this pair and he took 46, often game-changing, wickets.

This talented team was in contention for honours all season but with one match to play Todmorden were fourth on 41 points, two behind joint leaders East Lancs, Haslingden and Nelson. With 3 points for a win only a freak sequence of results could give Todmorden any hope of League honours and the Worsley Cup Final against Ramsbottom was their main priority.

The odds on any honours at all were extremely long at the tea interval of the Cup final, when Todmorden had been bowled out for 73 by Ramsbottom's Australian spin-bowling professional, Sid Hird (7 for 35). But few could exploit a helpful pitch like Macauley who, in his finest hour for the club, took 9 for 10 as Ramsbottom were dimissed for 47.

There was a more remarkable twist on 3 September, the last day of the League season. Rain appeared to have scuppered Todmorden's slim

George Macauley, Yorkshire 1920-35; 8 Tests; took 1837 wickets in his career.

hopes as their match at Rishton was delayed until 3.15pm. However, Rishton were skittled for 83 and Todmorden took just 44 minutes to knock off the runs before it rained again. Meanwhile, the match between Haslingden and Nelson had been abandoned and East Lancs, chasing Burnley's 131 all out, were 94 for 5 in reply when rain prevented further play. There were now four teams at the top all with 44 points. Play-offs were hastily arranged, Todmorden beating Nelson at Centre Vale on Tuesday 6 September in front of a crowd of 4000. An excellent spell of 7 for 36 from Alec Smith saw Nelson dismissed for 72, and Todmorden cantered to an eight-wicket victory before batting on to 128 for 9.

In the other semi-final Haslingden beat East Lancs, so the stage was set for the championship final, a double innings match to be played at Turf Moor over the following Saturday and Monday between Haslingden and Todmorden.

Before a crowd of 6093 paying receipts of £303 14s 11d, Haslingden won the toss and chose to bat on a soft pitch. When Macauley had opener Holden caught behind by Ken Fiddling, Haslingden's West Indian professional, George Headley, one of crickets all-time great batsmen, came in at number three. Displaying some glorious square cuts and straight drives, he rattled to 50 out of 70 in 90 minutes. Alec Smith, returning for a second spell, bowled the obdurate Brierley for 14 and then captured the crucial wicket of Headley who fended a lifting delivery straight to the captain Walter Sutcliffe at leg slip, having scored 79 out of 116 for 4. Tea was taken at 145 for 5 but

Walter Sutcliffe, ebullient all-rounder
and captain.

George Headley, Lord's Test 1939.

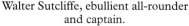

afterwards Haslingden collapsed, losing their last five wickets for 24 runs in half an hour. John Crowther's leg-breaks and googlies proved too much for the tail-end and his spell of 4 for 8 gave him final figures of 5 for 32, with Smith taking 3 for 56.

Crowther continued the good work when he opened the Todmorden innings, his excellent footwork and polished stroke play taking him to 50 out of 71 for 2. By the end of the first day Todmorden were in control of the match on 110 for 2, just 59 behind Haslingden, with the formidable pair Crowther and Dawson at the crease. Two days later Crowther and Dawson continued where they had left off, taking the score to 232 before Dawson was caught behind off Brierley for 89 to end a third wicket stand of 176. Crowther was finally out for 144, having batted for 3 hours 50 minutes and scored 14 boundaries. The players took tea at 321 for 6, after which aggressive batting against a tired attack propelled Todmorden to 411 all out. Bad light stopped play, with Haslingden on 15 for 0 and the match went into an unscheduled third day.

A long second wicket stand of 117 between Holden and Headley threatened to bat Haslingden back into the match. At 139 for 1 the deficit was just over 100 when Macauley bowled Holden for 60 on the stroke of tea. On the resumption Smith took the vital wicket of Headley for the second time in the match to spark another Haslingden batting collapse, the last eight wickets falling for 32 runs. Smith, 4 for 54, and Macauley, 4 for 29, were the destroyers as Haslingden slumped to 171 all out. Todmorden had won by an innings and 71 runs in the most famous match in the club's history.

Following presentations at Turf Moor, Todmorden arrived home in a motor coach parade, preceded by Todmorden Old Brass Band. Burnley Road was packed with people welcoming their conquering heroes. There was a civic reception and a speech

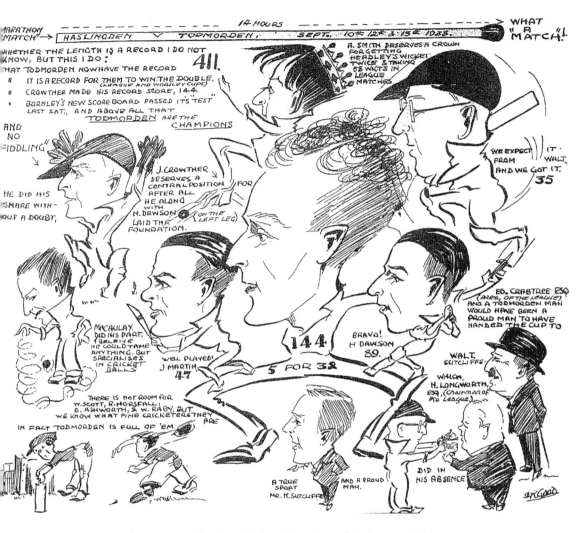

Cartoon, Haslingden v Todmorden, play-off for League 1938.

of congratulation by the Mayor at the Town Hall after which the team went on a further tour of the thronged streets.

The Supporters' Club organised a Victory Ball at the Town Hall on Friday 23 September, which also celebrated Todmorden Market Cricket Team's winning of the Central Lancashire Tuesday League. The Town Hall was once again packed for the club's presentation evening on Thursday 10 November. The Mayor and Mayoress and club president, eighty-two year-old Edward B Fielden, headed a list of civic and cricketing dignitaries who were entertained by the Todmorden Brass Band and several other local artistes.

Never again would the club's success be accorded such civic approbation. Yet alongside all the celebrations were ominous signs. 30,000 gas masks were to be delivered to Todmorden. A number of sites were selected, provisionally, for the digging of trenches and the siting of air raid shelters. Special arrangements in case of air raids were organised for school children, mill workers and workshop operatives.

Todmorden's double-winners, described as 'a great young team capable of challenging for the years to come', would find their chances of fulfilling this prediction guillotined by the outbreak of war.

Lancashire League Championship Play-off 'Final Tie' at Turf Moor
Saturday 10, Monday 12, Tuesday 13 September 1938
Haslingden v Todmorden

Haslingden

1st Innings			2nd Innings	
J Ashworth	st Fiddling b Crowther	14	c Crowther b Smith	11
H Holden	c Fiddling b Macauley	0	b Macauley	60
Headley	c Sutcliffe b Smith	79	c Fiddling b Smith	56
J Brierley	b Smith	14	lbw Smith	8
H Whittaker	c and b Crowther	31	c Dawson b Macauley	1
JH Cronshaw	lbw Smith	0	c Horsfall b Macauley	9
G Lees	b Crowther	5	c Fiddling b Smith	0
F Tattersall	not out	12	run out	7
WS Crawshaw	b Crowther	2	b Macauley	1
W Aldred	run out	1	not out	1
J Bonner	b Crowther	0	run out	0
Extras		11		17
Total	**all out**	**169**	**all out**	**171**

Fall of wickets

1-1; 2-51; 3-93; 4-116; 5-116;
6-145; 7-154; 8-158; 9-169; 10-169

Fall of wickets

1-22; 2-139; 3-145; 4-148; 5-150;
6-150; 7-167; 8-170; 9-171; 10-171

Bowling

	Ovrs	Mdns	Runs	Wkts	Ovrs	Mdns	Runs	Wkts
A Smith	27	10	56	3	29.4	5	54	4
Macauley	25	10	41	1	26	10	39	4
W Raby	10	2	29	0	11	2	17	0
J Crowther	13.2	3	32	5	13	1	34	0
W Sutcliffe					7	2	10	0

Todmorden
1st Innings

J Crowther	lbw Bonner	144
W Scott	b Crawshaw	6
R Horsfall	b Crawshaw	6
H Dawson	c Aldred b Brierley	89
W Sutcliffe	c Cronshaw b Bonner	35
B Ashworth	c Ashworth b Crawshaw	32
K Fiddling	hit wkt b Crawshaw	2
JW Martin	c Holden b Crawshaw	47
Macauley	lbw Crawshaw	2
W Raby	not out	14
A Smith	b Crawshaw	0
Extras		24
Total	**all out**	**411**

Bowling

	Ovrs	Mdns	Runs	Wkts
Headley	31	5	76	0
J Brierley	31	4	101	1
WS Crawshaw	31	3	126	7
J Bonner	13	0	75	2
JH Cronshaw	3	0	9	0

Fall of wickets

1-48; 2-56; 3-232; 4-294; 5-295;
6-318; 7-372; 8-379; 9-410; 10-411

Todmorden won by an innnings and 71 runs

Todmorden 1st XI 1938 Champions, League and Cup Double: Town Hall reception
with Civic Dignitaries, League and Club Officials;
players received grandmother clocks as momentoes.
L-R front: Mayor of Todmorden Percy Sutcliffe, Team Captain Walter Sutcliffe,
League President Edward Crabtree, Todmorden CC President EB Fielden.

Chapter 8

Calder Valley and Todmorden & District Cricket Leagues

The Calder Valley League was formed in 1891 to provide competitive cricket for existing teams representing, primarily, Sunday Schools, but also districts and mills around Todmorden and Hebden Bridge. Carried on a wave of sporting enthusiasm, most of these clubs were soon able to field a second team and in 1893 the Todmorden and District League was founded, comprising the 2nd XIs of eight Todmorden-based Calder Valley League Clubs plus one new club. In 1894 the Hebden Bridge clubs followed suit forming the Hebden Bridge and District League for their 2nd XIs. By 1896 there were 47 teams playing between Todmorden and Mytholmroyd.

Grounds were improvised on the most unlikely terrain, and this helps to explain why the 2nd teams played locally. With a number of venues on remote hilltop fields and most players working on Saturday mornings, transport and punctuality were problems. Cllr JJ Gledhill, speaking at the Hebden Bridge League cup presentation of 1909, recalled how he had helped to carry the team's tackle bag up the 'steeps' to Heptonstall, bowled for two or three hours, then carried the bag back down - which he described as 'Great Sport!'[1] Old Town's ground, Old Laith, at 1000 feet above sea level was even higher. A match there against Heptonstall Slack in 1955 was abandoned because of low cloud and fog!

In 1898, with an increase in the number of teams, the Calder Valley League was also regionalised into Todmorden and Hebden Bridge sections, with end of season play-offs between the top teams in each. Regionalisation was temporarily abandoned in 1901 when a 'free draw' was made to select section members. But with all four of the 1900 semi-finalists in Section A, and Section B having drawn hilltop grounds, it proved so unsatisfactory that it was never repeated. The travel required of the Section B teams (nicknamed 'the hill climbers') widened the rift between the two towns and in 1908 the Hebden Bridge teams broke away. Perceiving themselves as stronger than their Todmorden rivals at that time, they split from the Calder Valley League to expand the Hebden Bridge and District League into two divisions of ten clubs. The Todmorden clubs endeavoured to enrol more members and retained the name of Calder Valley League.

In 1910 the Calder Valley League had six chapel/church-based clubs, Bridge Street, Inchfield Bottom, Lumbutts, Roomfield, Unitarians and Todmorden Church, three secular clubs, Eastwood, Holme, and Todmorden CC 3rd XI plus Cloughfoot and Knowlwood which may have had connections with their respective Congregational and Methodist chapels. These eleven clubs gave the league its longest fixture list for some years. Eight of these clubs had 2nd XIs in the Todmorden and District League which, with Cross Stone and Cornholme 2nd XI, comprised ten clubs. Cornholme's 1st XI was in the Ribblesdale Junior League, which they won in 1910 for the fourth time in their first five years as members.

Fortunes fluctuated; by 1912 the Calder Valley League was reduced to eight clubs and, to increase the number of fixtures, the committee decided to present a set of caps to be played for in a knockout, the final to be played on Centre Vale. The winners of the league Todmorden Church played Eastwood, the winners of the 'caps' competition,

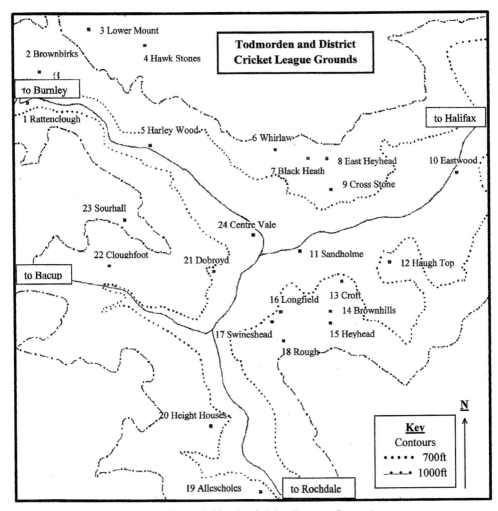

Todmorden and District Cricket League Grounds.

Todmorden and District Cricket League Teams and Grounds Where They Played

Team	Ground			Team	Ground		
Bridgeholme	9	10		Old Students	9		
Bridge Street		16		Patmos	6	14	
British Picker	16	11		Roomfield	11	18	
Charles Crabtree Ltd	15	21		Unitarians	17		
Cloughfoot	22			Wellington Road	7	8	12
Cornholme	1	2		York Street	15	16	
Cross Stone	9			**Grounds Not Known**			
Eastwood	10			Castle Street			
Excelsior	3			Knowlwood			
Harley Wood	5			Lydgate			
Inchfield Bottom	20			Mankinholes			
Knotts	3	4	23	Spiritualists			
Lanebottom	19			Todmorden White Rose			
Lumbutts	13	15		Walsden St Peters			
Old Royd	13			Walsden Wesleyans			

Key to Todmorden and District Cricket League Grounds.

Langfield hillside where local cricket teams played.

Cross Stone cricket field (centre), across the valley (right of pole) is Croft,
Old Royd's cricket field.

for the championship in late September also on Centre Vale, the scores being
Todmorden Church 26, Eastwood 69 for 8.

The following year, owing to a scarcity of clubs, the Calder Valley League disbanded.
Todmorden Church 1st XI joined the 1st Division of the Rochdale and District League,
Eastwood left for the Hebden Bridge League and the Todmorden and District League
was left with the rump of 7 clubs and had only attracted one more when the war caused
its suspension in 1915.

The following clubs revived the league in 1919: Todmorden 3rd XI, Todmorden
Church A and B teams, Unitarians, Wellington Road, Secondary School Old Students,
Bridge Street and Eastwood, comprising two Anglican, three nonconformist and three
secular teams. With the universal desire to return to normality, there was a resurgence

Roomfield Baptist Cricket Team c1905-10, pre-match on Langfield hillside.

Unitarian Church Cricket Team c1905-10, not in whites but smartly dressed.

Cornholme Cricket Team, 1910 champions of Ribblesdale Junior League.

Cornholme cricketers c1920 at Chatham meadow, Rattenclough, Portsmouth.

by 1920 to a total of eleven clubs. A knockout competition was organised where, after the first round, all matches were to be played on Centre Vale during June and July on mid-week nights, the Todmorden club donating the medals. The following year another three clubs enlisted causing the league to form two sections of seven. In addition a knockout competition amongst all 14 clubs was staged, the trophy being the former Calder Valley Cup which, since 1912 had been in the custody of the then president

```
┌─────────────────────────┐
│                         │
│    ‖‖‖‖‖‖‖‖‖‖‖‖          │
│                         │
│        ╳                │
│                         │
│   Excelsior  .          │
│                         │
│   Cricket Club,         │
│                         │
│    Member's Card,       │
│                         │
│     Season 1923.        │
│                         │
│    ‖‖‖‖‖‖‖‖‖‖            │
│                         │
│   W Heywood             │
│                         │
└─────────────────────────┘
   W. Cunliffe, Printer, Heptonstall.
```

List of Fixtures. First Eleven.				List of Fixtures. Second Eleven.		
Date	Name of Club	Grnd Rslt		Date	Name of Club	Grnd Rslt
April 14	Lydgate	H		April 21	Parish Church	H
,, 21	Walsden Wesleyans	A		,, 28		
,, 28	York Street	H		May 5	Dobroyd	H
May 5	Roomfield	A		,, 12		
,, 12	Oldroyd	H		,, 19	West End	H
,, 19	Mankinholes	A		,, 26	Unitarians	A
,, 26	Unitarians	H		June 2		
June 2	Patmos	H		,, 9	Dobroyd	A
,, 9	Parish Church	A		,, 16		
,, 16	Wellington Road	H		,, 23	Bridge Street	A
,, 23	Bridge Street	H		,, 30		
,, 30	Lydgate	A		July 7	Walsden Wesleyans	A
July 7	Walsden Wesleyans	H		,, 14		
,, 14	York Street	A		,, 21		
,, 21	Roomfield	H		,, 28	Walsden Wesleyans	H
,, 28	Oldroyd	A		Aug. 4	West End	A
Aug. 4	Mankinholes	H		,, 11	Unitarians	H
,, 11	Unitarians	A		,, 18	Bridge Street	H
,, 18	Patmos	A		,, 25	Parish Church	A
,, 25	Parish Church	H				
Sept. 1	Wellington Road	A				
,, 8	Bridge Street	A				

Excelsior CC Fixture List 1923, Todmorden and District League.

Edward Crabtree. The hillsides bristled with activity as pitches were fashioned from the most unpromising terrain.

The enthusiasm of these local cricketers is epitomised by one of the new 1921 clubs, 'Excelsior' formed from members of Shore and Vale Baptist churches in Cornholme. They acquired a ground at Mount, above Shore at a height of 1200 feet above sea level and, in order to prepare the pitch needed a roller, which was manhandled up the hill from the valley 600 feet below. Early in the season they played Inchfield Bottom Methodists on the latter's ground at Height Houses in Walsden, a mere 750 feet above sea level, and were bowled out for the Todmorden and District's lowest recorded score of 4. However, in the rarefied atmosphere at Mount they disposed of Todmorden Church, 32 to 29 in the first round of the cup, and, having scored 101, bowled out Inchfield Bottom for 39 in the next round. Revenge is sweet! Batting on these hillside tracks was something of a lottery, a score of 30 earning a collection, which argues that there were spectators. WJ Heywood made 34 not out for Excelsior in the victory over Inchfield Bottom; his collection totalled 3s 4d which bought his future wife a box of chocolates. In 1922, Irving Mitchell (Excelsior) won the Todmorden and District League batting prize, a medal plus free membership of Todmorden CC for one year, which he never took up, preferring to play with his pals.

The following season they won their section of the league and, although defeated by Wellington Road Baptists in the final, they had the satisfaction of playing on the Centre Vale ground. A contributor to the local paper wrote of these times:

> ...men played on the surrounding hills on wickets which at one end might add more than a cubit to the bowler's stature. We can still recall the feeling of inadequacy as we nervously awaited the bowler to top sky-line and tower menacingly above us before hurtling a vicious ball whose subsequent manoeuvres depended upon the contours of the ground. One watched in vain the bowler's grip, and the googly surprised no-one but the perpetrator.
>
> ...The man at point or cover had his difficulties. The ball knocked defensively in his direction would... rear...and smite one on the mouth or whistle past one's ear, if one was lucky...there were excursions during the week when gardening implements were distributed amongst the party and the hill climbed to the cricket field and renovations carried out. The roller was put on and the pitch prepared, but the outfield was beyond

Unitarian Church Cricket Team 1930s
L-R Row 2: ____, Harry Kershaw, George Brooks, ____, Joe Walton, Will Barker,
Row 1: Hiram Dawson, Albert Walmsley, John Nash, ____, Ernest Brooks, Will Greenwood.

cultivation. The coarse grass was left to the tender mercies of the half dozen stirks and strolling poultry.

Often it was the sheep who kept the grass down and these pitches were generally a bowler's paradise. When Excelsior's Tommy Stuttard topped the league's bowling in 1922 with 42 wickets for 87 runs at an average of 2.07 runs per wicket, no-one was surprised.

There was no concept of limited overs cricket. In the Calder Valley Cup Final on Wednesday evening of 15 June 1921, Wellington Road met Lydgate at Centre Vale. Wellington Road declared at 122 for 8 and had reduced Lydgate to 65 for 9 when time was up and the match deemed a draw. In the replay at Bridge Street Methodist's Longfield ground Lydgate replied to Wellington Road's 90 with 39 all out.

During the inter-war years the Todmorden and District League, fuelled by enthusiasm after World War I, was at its strongest. A glance at the fixture list for 1923 shows many clubs with 2nd XIs and the league with a strong community base. Of the twelve clubs, ten represent church or chapel and the remaining two, Mankinholes and Lydgate, are of well-defined local districts.

The Todmorden and District League, with its ten or eleven clubs, continued in its familiar pattern until the outbreak of World War II caused it to disband after the 1940 season.

As for quality of play the *Todmorden Herald* opined:

> It should not be regarded as...an exhibition of scientific cricket, but for downright earnestness and zeal, it was a treat.[2]

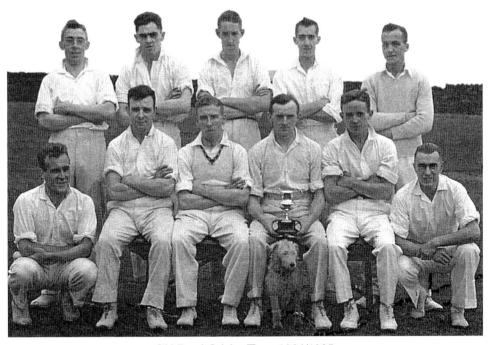

Old Royd Cricket Team 1934/1935.
L-R Row 2: ____, N Dawson, I Martin, W Sutcliffe, F Thorpe,
Row 1: T Hodgins, H Barker, R Parkinson, B Hollows (c), ____, N Brear. Mascot Trixie.

We have seen that low scores predominated. When JR Howarth hit 50 for Lumbutts in May 1900, it was the first half century in the history of a club which had been the first Calder Valley League champions in 1891. Poor pitches produced some truly extraordinary matches. Chasing Cloughfoot's 78 all out, Wellington Road's batting collapse induced pleadings from the local press:

> Come Wellington Road! This is beyond a joke! Ten of a total - six of them extras and four actual runs![3]

Another indication of the standard of play was an annual match, played from 1898 to 1904, between a Calder Valley League team, sometimes consisting of 16 players, and Todmorden 2nd XI which was particularly strong at this time. In 1899 Todmorden 2nd XI were Lancashire Junior League champions and had suffered just three defeats in six seasons. They enjoyed two comfortable victories over the Calder Valley League and one opponent commented, 'if we met a hundred times the Todmorden juniors would win every time. Such is the difference in style of play and general smartness of the two teams'.[4] [Smartness referred to slick fielding not apparel.]

Todmorden had the considerable advantage of choosing from the cream of the Calder Valley League players. This did not produce a particularly strong 1st team but provided a terrific depth of talent, hence the success at 2nd team level:

> A real deal of the credit of this almost unparalleled record is certainly due to the Calder Valley League, who have unearthed the players, and the Todmorden club have afterwards weeded them out and retained the best...at least a dozen of Todmorden's most promising cricketers at the present time have been brought to the front by means of the local junior competition. The tribute is well merited, as every member of

> Todmorden club is only too ready to admit, and it should act as an incentive to all the players still identified in the Calder Valley League.[5]

Most of Todmorden's leading cricketers of this era can be found playing in the local league at some stage, usually as youngsters. Occasionally established players used the Calder Valley League for early season practice, as when Jonas Clegg junior top-scored in Castle Street's opening game of 1897.[6] The most enthusiastic were able to extend their playing days once their Todmorden career was over, such as John Craven, who played into his fifties for Cross Lanes Chapel, Hebden Bridge.

Links with the Todmorden club were reinforced by the choice of league president, a post held by John Craven from 1891 to 1900. He was succeeded by Todmordian Jeremiah Crossley, a stalwart of Bridge Street United Methodist Free Church, one of the league's founder members. Crossley died in office at the age of 74 in 1907. The next president was Todmorden Cricket Club secretary and future Lancashire League president Edward Crabtree.

The Calder Valley League was keen to claim the moral high ground in terms of sporting conduct and president Crossley eulogised on the league's sporting standards when presenting the Calder Valley Cup to Mytholmroyd St Michael's in 1901:

> ...the Calder Valley League could claim exception from many of the charges of abuse which had been brought against other leagues...the rivalry had been good natured and friendly...there was no professionalism, and better still no over-professionalism in the guise of amateurism...the clubs had not gone about poaching other people's preserves...and...attached as much importance to the character of their players as much as to their ability as cricketers.[7]

Consistent with Crossley's claims, a rule was passed in April 1902 disallowing any player who had been paid in the previous twelve months from playing in the league. This was perhaps precipitated by the return in July 1901 of Walter Sutcliffe from a professional engagement at Barnoldswick to play for Todmorden Church. He took 7 for 14 in his first match, reducing St James's to 0 for 5 and 30 all out.[8]

It Just Isn't Cricket!

The league had difficulty in enforcing sporting conduct and the local press was eager to report any 'incidents'. Events at the 1902 cup semi-final provoked the headline 'A FIASCO! REGRETTABLE OCCURRENCE', which embarrassed both the president and the league. Playing at a neutral venue, Eastwood, Old Town were already in the mire at 8 for 4 in reply to Hebden Bridge Liberal Club's 134 all out when:

> F Greenwood skied a ball, ran for it and as he was passing close to the fielder under the catch shouted loudly in his ear. The fielder dropped the ball and, with the captain, appealed against Greenwood's act. They were successful for the batsman was given out...'wilfully obstructed'. A warm scene followed. The wickets were sent flying, the Old Town captain withdrew his men and refused to continue the game, and there was general tumult. Of course, the Liberals were given the game.[9]

Old Town again failed to finish a match in 1903. Heptonstall Slack 2nd XI declared at 93 for 4, after which 'a rather queer contretemps' saw Old Town 2nds refusing to bat. The match was awarded to Slack and the entire Old Town team was suspended for a fortnight 'for personal abuse of an umpire'. Heptonstall Slack 2nds were themselves in the dock in August 1904, when one of their players, WH Hollinrake, was suspended for the rest of the season for striking an umpire.[10]

Misdemeanours were not the sole preserve of the players, and the finger of suspicion pointed at the scorers after the Hebden Bridge League final of 1912. Salem Wesleyans had replied to Birchcliffe's 39 all out with 39 all out - according to Birchcliffe's scorebook - or 40 all out according to the Salem scorebook. The discrepancy was in the final over - which did little to dispel suspicions of sharp practice - and was scrutinised at the following Tuesday's league meeting:

> A blur in the Birchcliffe book...was thought to be intended for a one, which would make...each scorebook exactly alike, and the match was awarded to Salem.[11]

1912 had seen the introduction of a new rule in the Hebden Bridge League:

> The decision of the umpire shall be final (if in accordance with MCC Rules), and he shall be subject to no personal abuse or violence.

The vocabulary of the Heptonstall players elicited a letter to the club in July 1931 'with regard to certain of their players using abusive language'. It had little impact, the league issuing three separate punishments to individuals 'for using filthy language', plus a blanket warning to their 2nd XI.

Generally, in the local leagues, umpires' idiosyncrasies were accepted in good part. One earned himself the title of 'tea-time Tommy', it being recognised that after the tea interval any appeal with a hint of legitimacy was likely to be upheld. It may be apocryphal, but he is credited with dismissing two batsmen at once. One was caught off a skied ball and his partner was deemed 'run out' as he was out of his ground when the fielder who had caught the ball returned it to the wicket keeper who removed the bails and appealed - successfully!

Todmorden 3rd XI played its home fixtures at Centre Vale on mid-week evenings and, as the light deteriorated, the matches were, at times, concluded in semi-gloom. On one occasion as a new batsman came in the umpire, having difficulty in seeing a pitch length, walked down the wicket to give him his guard but had no hesitation in upholding an appeal for lbw a few balls later.

Not everyone could play cricket on Saturdays and tradesmen's teams had been playing matches for some years on Tuesday afternoons, half day closing for many shops. On 14 September 1898 nine town tradesmen's teams met at the Fleece Hotel, Rochdale, and formed the Rochdale and District Tuesday Cricket League. Todmorden Tradesmen won the league in 1900 and were runners-up in 1899, 1901 and 1902, despite playing against much larger towns.[12] Later they moved to the Rossendale Tuesday League and in 1938 won the Central Lancashire Tuesday League for the third successive year. By 1948 they were in the North East Lancashire Tuesday League.

World War II and Beyond

Towards the end of the 1930s, teams from the Hebden Bridge League began to gravitate towards leagues in Halifax, of which the Halifax League (originally the Halifax Parish League, formed in 1914), and the Halifax Association (formed in 1923), had emerged as the most durable from the remnants of the Halifax and District League (1894 to 1922) and the Halifax Amateur League (1892 to 1922).

The pattern of earlier failed leagues was threatening the Hebden Bridge League when World War II intervened. A surge of post-war interest saw the Hebden Bridge League reform in 1947 and advertisements for new clubs attracted several teams including the 1st and 2nd XIs of Mytholmroyd Methodists and Todmorden 3rd XI. The league table of 1949 indicates the quality of Todmorden's pitch compared with

Lumbutts Methodist CC 1947 champions of Hebden Bridge and District League.
L-R Row 3: V Sutcliffe, W Sutcliffe, E Whiteley, N Law, C Glass, D Webster,
WH Bentley, H Shackleton,
Row 2: S Hollows, V Webster, A Webster, A Law, W Greenwood,
Row 1: A Greenwood.

others in the league as Todmorden featured in all of the six draws that season.

<u>Hebden Bridge and District Cricket League Final Table 1949</u>

	Pld	W	D	L	Pts
Old Town 'A'	22	20	1	1	41
Birchcliffe 'A'	22	18	1	3	37
Hebden Bridge Salem	22	16	1	5	33
Heptonstall Slack 'A'	22	16	0	6	32
Heptonstall Slack 'B'	22	11	1	10	23
Todmorden 3rd XI	22	8	6	8	22
Lumbutts Methodist	22	9	1	12	19
Old Town 'B'	22	9	1	12	19
Mytholmroyd Parish Church	22	8	0	14	16
Mytholmroyd Methodist 2nd XI *	22	5	0	17	8
Birchcliffe 'B'	22	3	0	19	6
Friendly Methodists	22	3	0	19	6

*Mytholmroyd Methodists 2nd XI deducted 2 points for breach of rules

An attempt to revive the Todmorden and District League at a meeting called by pre-war secretary William Albert Bentley in October 1946 failed to gain enough support. It was not until three years later that his persistence bore fruit and the league recommenced in 1950 with six teams: British Picker Company, Cross Stone, C Crabtree and S & A Barkers, Knotts, Todmorden 3rd XI and Walsden 3rd XI. In contrast with the pre-war league none had any church or chapel connections. The league continued for ten years, disbanding in 1960. No transport was laid on for Todmorden 3rd XI, even during the 1949 season in the Hebden Bridge League. Playing at Heptonstall meant a bus to Mytholm, then hauling the tackle bag (bats, pads, balls etc) up the steep woodland path to the small but beautifully manicured ground at Popples. Fixtures against Birchcliffe and Old Town also entailed long uphill treks.

In the Todmorden and District League, where all the grounds were reached by walking, it was one thing carrying the equipment prior to playing but volunteers were scarce for the return journey. The fixture against Knotts, who played at Sourhall, involved a steep climb up the hill behind Centre Vale followed by a long walk along the road to the ground. During this fixture in 1950 the 1st XI were playing Bacup at Centre Vale. Bacup's pro was George Headley, the 'Black Bradman' who was standing in one season for Everton Weekes. The third teamers wanted to see him and got the chance when the Sourhall match finished early. Unsurprisingly, there were no bag carriers. The bag was left under a wall and retrieved later by taxi; the club was not pleased. From 1954 Todmorden had difficulty persuading its 3rd XI to play on the hillside pitches and for the league's last six seasons all its fixtures, home and away, were played at Centre Vale. Todmorden 3rd XI were the last winners of the Calder Valley Cup, which is still in the custody of Todmorden Cricket Club.

For a few years from 1948 a successful mid-week evening works cricket league was organised at Todmorden or Walsden. Teams from as many as eighteen mills and engineering works were grouped in four mini-leagues, the winners of each playing off in semi-finals and a final. This was the last flowering of a form of cricket which had been popular long before the war, attracting many spectators and creating fierce rivalry, especially where a team with one or two regular league players was beaten by a team of non-descripts. As the cotton industry contracted from the 1950s, it became increasingly difficult to field works' teams.

The Hebden Bridge League sustained two divisions until 1954 when an alarming haemorrhaging of clubs caused a reduction to one. Some clubs disbanded, others transferred to the Halifax leagues. The league was sinking fast. In 1955 when double winners Bridgeholme followed Hebden Bridge Salem, Mytholmroyd Methodists and Luddenden Foot St Mary's in jumping ship to the Halifax leagues, all of the Hebden Bridge League's first division champions since 1950 had left.

When the Bradford section of the Yorkshire Council's 2nd XI competition disbanded, the second teams of Halifax, Illingworth St Mary's and Sowerby Bridge joined the Hebden Bridge League in 1956. However, despite the best efforts of committed administrators, the end was nigh. In 1957 Old Town were awarded a walkover when Heptonstall Slack 'failed to field seven men' and both Sowerby Bridge and Halifax received walks-overs against the Halifax-based Royal Army Pay Corps.

Yet there was no hint that the league's last ball had been bowled at the annual dinner on 18 October. West Indies' opening batsman and Enfield professional, Conrad Hunte, presented the prizes for what league president Dr AH Clegg described as 'quite a good season'. League secretary Richard Farthing reported 'a possibility of one or two new teams joining for next season' and financially the clubs were sound.

Over the next two months the picture changed dramatically. By the AGM on 3 December Halifax, Illingworth and Sowerby Bridge had resigned, returning to the Yorkshire Council, which had re-formed its second team league. Birchcliffe, increasingly struggling to raise a team, announced they would not be competing in 1958 and, suddenly, the Hebden Bridge League was reduced to three clubs – Heptonstall Slack, Old Town and the Royal Army Pay Corps, the latter possessing no ground. As a final throw of the dice the meeting was adjourned so that the Todmorden League could be approached for the second time in four years with regard to an amalgamation. The Todmorden League, which itself had only six teams, offered membership to any new teams but wished to retain its identity and would not amalgamate. This policy of independence was insular and short-sighted. The Todmorden League acquired no new teams and within two years was also defunct.

Old Town were willing to support the Hebden Bridge League, but needed competitive cricket at their wonderful new Boston Hill ground, opened in 1957, and had gained provisional acceptance into the Halifax Association as a safety net. Realistically, the Hebden Bridge League could not stand in their way and Richard Farthing minuted: 'Owing to there being only Heptonstall Slack remaining, the league be disbanded.' The Hebden Bridge League, founded in 1894, folded on 30th December 1957. 'There are few men in the district who, at one time or another, have not turned out with one...of the teams in the league,' mourned the *Hebden Bridge Times*. Within a fortnight both Heptonstall Slack and Old Town were formally admitted to the Halifax Association.[13]

The legacy of the Hebden Bridge League lives on in the surviving clubs who cut their teeth there. These include Heptonstall Slack, one of the founder members of the Calder Valley League in 1891. In 1973 they moved from their Popples ground, which was common land frequently damaged by cattle, and settled to play at Spring Hall in Halifax, changing their name to Moorside.

There was one further meeting of the Hebden Bridge League committee in December 1971. The league's assets, its five trophies, had been held at the local council offices pending the unlikely event of the league being re-formed. In distributing its trophies, the league committee confirmed that there would be no second coming for the Hebden Bridge League.

Only two teams that played in both the Todmorden and District and Hebden Bridge leagues survive today (2010). They are Todmorden Cricket Club's 3rd XI and Bridgeholme Cricket Club.

The Bridgeholme Story

The formation of Bridgeholme Cricket Club owes much to the local Workshop League competitions run variously at both the Todmorden and Walsden cricket clubs. Walsden had run such tournaments as early as 1904, copying the idea from the local rugby and football clubs, which had run highly lucrative competitions for factory teams since the 1880s.

In 1950, two teams in Walsden's workshop league, Moss Brothers, Bridgeroyd Mills and JJ Tatham Ltd, Nanholme Mills, joined forces to form one club. The name 'Bridgeholme' was invented by combining 'Bridgeroyd' and 'Nanholme'. Prime mover in the amalgamation was Percy Sowden, manager of Bridgeroyd Mills, and he found a willing ally in Mr R Tatham of Nanholme Mills. Both were descended from cricketing families. JJ Tatham was a vice-president at Eastwood Cricket Club in 1900 and Percy Sowden's father, John, was a formidable bowler in the early days of the Hebden Bridge League.

Percy Sowden was extraordinarily active in local life. A man of outstanding general knowledge and administrative abilities he died in office as chairman of: the Hebden Bridge Master Dyers' Association, the Calder Divisional Education Executive, the

County Libraries Committee, the Heptonstall Exhibitions Foundation and the Governors of Calder High School. He was a member of the Hebden Bridge and District Technical Education Committee and the Elementary Education Committee. As chairman of the West Riding Education Committee, Percy had a high profile in education beyond Todmorden's boundaries and commanded a respect which brought influence.

He was also a JP and, from 1943, chairman of the Todmorden Juvenile Court. Among many other offices, he was president of the Hebden Bridge branch of the Old Age Pensioners' Association, president of the Hebden Bridge Lawn Tennis League and founder member and trustee of the Hebden Bridge Literary and Scientific Society. In addition, he was an active member of the Labour Party, a keen participant in amateur dramatics at the Co-operative Hall and Little Theatre and preached regularly at Nazebottom Baptist Church.

When he died in 1955, aged 73, the Reverend WS Davies paid this tribute before a packed Nazebottom congregation:

> Percy Sowden was a great citizen. One could hardly enter any realm of public life without encountering Percival Sowden. One could not think of a man in the community whose interests were so varied or who, when engaged in any activity, did so with such thoroughness and efficiency…the youth of the district have lost a great friend.

The Sowden Trophy, presented to the Hebden Bridge League as a Division 2 Championship trophy by Mrs Percival Sowden in 1952, was donated to Bridgeholme when the league disposed of its assets in 1971 and since then has been presented to the club's player of the year. Initially at Bridgeholme, all players had to be employees at one of the two mills, but this rule was soon relaxed. Despite having no ground, Bridgeholme were accepted into the Todmorden and District League in 1951, playing all their matches away from home. The club's first match was at Cross Stone on 12 May 1951, where they bowled the home side out for 19 and won by 7 wickets. Bridgeholme enjoyed a successful first season, finishing equal second in the six-team league behind another work's team, British Picker.

In 1952, Bridgeholme entered Division 2 of the Hebden Bridge League renting a ground at Cross Stone. The pitch was deadly. In ten completed home matches, the opposition were bowled out for 26 or fewer eight times, as Bridgeholme won both promotion to Division 1 and the knockout cup.

Meanwhile, work progressed apace on land leased from the Station House Hotel at Eastwood, adjacent to the old Eastwood Cricket Club ground, now scrubland. Nestled between the A646 road and the River Calder, there is hardly room for a cricket ground. Indeed, the Calder is so close that one visiting player, unfamiliar with the terrain, leapt the four-foot boundary embankment to retrieve the ball and plummeted ten feet into the water!

Drainage, levelling and laying of the square were priorities and banking on the road side was dug out to widen the playing area. The ground was opened on 19 May 1953, a fortnight before the Coronation of Queen Elizabeth II, and the club expanded operations by entering a second team in Division 2 of the Hebden Bridge League for 1953. This increased depth of talent helped the first team to the 1953 league and cup double, a feat they repeated in 1955. Impoverished by the lack of decent opposition, Bridgeholme followed other leading clubs joining Division 2 of the Halifax and District League for 1956. Further ground improvements enabled the club to enter the Halifax Parish Cup, to which they had been refused entrance in 1954.

After a difficult start, the club found its feet and were promoted to Division 1 as

Bridgeholme CC, 1957 champions of Halifax League Division II.
L-R Row 2: R Greenwood, S Graham, N Whittaker, A Leeder, A Martin, E Travis, J Whitehead,
Row 1: N Sowden (president), G Ashworth, W Davies, J Sutcliffe, S Hollows, ____.

champions in 1957. The former Essex and Glamorgan batsman Richard Horsfall, the only first class cricketer to play for the club did so briefly, before returning to Todmorden, where he had played in the Lancashire League double winning side of 1938. A less auspicious but more effective signing was that of future Todmorden and Hebden Bridge bowler - and future Mayor of Todmorden - Stanley Hollows. Hollows, with 44 wickets, supported by Jack Horsfall with 39, spearheaded a highly effective bowling attack.

Bridgeholme has proved remarkably resilient, having had to work its way up more than once from the 3rd Division of the Halifax Association into the Halifax League. Here they have competed in the 2nd Division since 2000. Following a lottery grant the club has erected a fine new pavilion, which not only provides post-match hospitality but serves as a community centre for the Eastwood area.

The progress at Bridgeholme owes much to the dedication of Keith Hudson, who was brought up just two doors away from the ground, and Peter Brennend. This has won both of them the Ron Wild Trophy, awarded annually by the *Todmorden News* for outstanding services to local sport. Peter Brennend first played for Bridgeholme in 1960 and still turned out for the second team well beyond his 70th birthday. 'You could not wish to meet a nicer bloke,' said Hudson. 'He seems to be friends with just about everybody in Tod. The number of funerals he attends is legendary!'

Hudson's workload includes chairing committee and selection meetings, overseeing correspondence and the weekly and annual tasks to maintain the square and the pitches. Often, he is working on the ground whilst his team mates are knocking up and he sometimes opens the batting on a pitch he was rolling only ten minutes earlier. Occasionally this lack of mental and physical preparation contributes to an early dismissal, but he has still accumulated around 500 runs per season on a pretty regular basis since the early 1990s. It concerns Hudson that the club is run by just a handful of loyal members and would be healthier with the load spread more widely. Lacking the depth of support and infrastructure of larger clubs, Bridgeholme are, like their predecessors in the Todmorden and Hebden Bridge leagues, vulnerable to losing key personnel. But they are also unimpeded by the bureaucratic safeguards of larger organisations and able to make and implement decisions quickly and efficiently.

As Hudson explains, there are pros and cons to being Todmorden's third cricket club, behind Todmorden and Walsden.

> If we develop a player who becomes particularly good, we're going to lose them, probably as an amateur to Todmorden or Walsden, although some have been offered money to play in Halifax. On the other hand, we are still developing our youth set up and have been grateful to acquire players from the Todmorden and Walsden junior teams. Not everybody wants to play at a club where, if you play well enough, you can end up in the first team playing against an international fast bowler. We know our place but we're a friendly club. We may not be the best cricketers around but we can play the game as sportingly as anyone else.'

Established over half a century ago in a decade when similar clubs were going to the wall and the local leagues were being disbanded, Bridgeholme continues to fulfil the need for an all amateur club in Todmorden. In 2010 successful links were forged between Bridgeholme and Todmorden whereby some of Todmorden's U17s played for Bridgeholme 2nd X1 and Bridgeholme had the use of Todmorden's practice facilities. Although Bridgeholme is long-since independent of its industrial parents, Percy Sowden would be proud that his brainchild lives on.

Chapter 9

Football: 'Round' or 'Oval'

Playing football in Todmorden has always been a test of determination versus the environment. The steep-sided narrow valleys which cradle the town offer few flat areas where football fields can be sited. Thus, during the past century, many clubs have taken to the hills to find a suitable field. Some of these clubs were short-lived, as initial enthusiasm waned under the need to support and administer a club on a bleak hillside when the weather was even bleaker and the team unsuccessful. In 1921 the local press wrote:

> Conditions were far from the best again last Saturday and all local games were played in the fog on hard grounds and towards the end in a snowstorm. Players not actively engaged were stiff in the bleakness of the afternoon and on the whole the best football was out of the question.

A team failing to complete its fixtures was not uncommon. The clubs with the few valley bottom fields, whilst having easier access for both players and supporters, had problems with drainage, reports often including the word 'quagmire'.

Typical was the rugby match played in 1901 on the Holme field (where Mons Mill stood, now the site of Hare Court and Asquith House). Under the headline 'Sowerby Bridge beat Todmorden at Water Polo' the local paper describes the weather as so boisterous and wet that the canvas, which shielded the roadside of the ground against non-paying spectators, could only be partially erected. The ground, a quagmire, had a miniature lake at one end - 'the venue for hostilities' - where the frequent duckings of players 'caused endless amusement...Sowerby splashed about as adept polo players and inevitably came through with the leather'. In reply 'Todmorden went in pure and simple for rough tactics and the visitors were mauled about to some tune'. They would 'collar an opponent in the Lake District' whereupon two or three pounced on him and when they had finished 'he was either half drowned or choked with mud...only the most intimate of the players' friends could recognise them'. It was a 'welcome relief for both spectators and players alike when the referee called time'.[1]

Rattenclough, the home of Portsmouth Rovers FC, was little better. The match against Hebden Bridge in November 1906 taking place 'upon an enclosure altogether unfit for football – a puddle bed'.

> The Portsmouth men have not lost a match for a long time, and little wonder for the setting in which they themselves have won prominence visiting teams are altogether at a loss...it could not be entertained that they continue to use this ground if there were a better one in the vicinity. Situated down in the bottom of the narrow valley, it is a fine receptacle for the plentiful moisture which finds its way from the adjoining hillsides, and the game provided a series of mud baths.[2]

The field at Eastwood, next to the present Bridgeholme Cricket Club, is described as 'a first class swamp'. The 'playing area seems too small for 22 men but the home side know how to play on it' and 'the goal line at the end nearest the dressing room is down a dip and the referee cannot see it unless he's near'.[3]

Walsden United AFC at Bellholme, 1923 winners of the Rochdale Amateur League's
Hardman Cup, 'Century' Shield Competition and joint winners,
with rivals White Rose, of the League.

The Sandholme ground, although low-lying and abutting the canal near the
gasworks, was seldom unused and was taken by Todmorden Association Football Club,
when the Holme was lost to them in 1907 for the building of Hare Mill (renamed
'Mons' after the World War I battle). Sandholme was ready in time for them to be
accepted into the Rochdale and District League in 1908, but the best that could be said
was that it was in 'fairly good condition'.[4]

Possession of a valley bottom ground did not always bring security. In 1930 Walsden
United resigned from the West Lancashire League after four years because its ground
at Bellholme (now the home of Todmorden Borough) was not well situated, gates were
poor and nothing more central could be found. In 1931 they joined the Halifax District
League.

Maintaining a steady, continuous pattern of football locally was never achieved.
Clubs and leagues formed, disbanded and re-formed; clubs changed leagues according
to their playing strengths and ambitions and yet football has formed a vital part of the
local sporting scene for over 130 years.

In 1897, Todmorden was predominantly a rugby town but the sport was in turmoil.
For some years there had been differences between those who wished to maintain the
traditional, strictly amateur, status of rugby union and those, who, with the
introduction of leagues, wished to legalise payments to players. At a meeting in 1895
at Huddersfield all 12 clubs from the Yorkshire Senior Competition and 8 from the
Lancashire Club Championship broke away from the Rugby Football Union. They
formed the Northern Rugby Football Union and instantly agreed broken-time
payments of 6s 0d per day to players who took time off work to play with their clubs.[5]

The 1896/97 season found Todmorden in the Yorkshire No3 B Group competition, still the traditional rugby union. Their rivals Hebden Bridge won the group and, watched by a crowd of 2000, beat A Group winners Bingley by 3 points to nil at Sowerby Bridge, to become 3rd Division Champions. Todmorden in mid-table won 9 of their 11 victories at home, mainly owing to the availability of players, which suggests that those working on Saturday mornings were unable to play in some away matches.[6]

Before the start of the next season, Todmorden decided to join the Northern Rugby Football Union Lancashire Section No3 competition, where they gauged they would meet stiffer opposition than in the Yorkshire Rugby Union competition, which was suffering other defections to the Northern Rugby Football Union. Todmorden also reckoned on having friendly matches with some of the well known Yorkshire clubs' A teams such as Halifax, Wakefield Trinity and Bradford.[7]

The opening match against Leigh Shamrocks was won by 3 points to nil in front of a large crowd, despite Todmorden CC playing against Burnley for the 2nd XI Championship just down the road at Centre Vale.[8] Meanwhile players, hearing of payments higher than their own made by other clubs, became dissatisfied and a strike was threatened.[9]

Additional to their league commitments, they decided to compete in the Rochdale and District Charity Cup competition which extended its cup area to include the Walsden St Peter's and Todmorden teams. These two teams met at Todmorden in the first round, attracting the biggest gate of the season. Todmorden won 17 points to 3 but were defeated in the semi-final by Rochdale Hornets A team.[10]

The report of April 1898 on Ossett versus Hebden Bridge in the Yorkshire Challenge Cup Final provides interesting statistics for the teams. The tallest player on each side was exactly 6ft, whilst 18 of the other players were 5ft 9ins or less. The heaviest player was 13st 3lbs and the average weight of a player for each pack was not much over 12st. The average player was of smaller physique than today.[11]

After only one season, Todmorden left the Lancashire competition when, at a meeting of the Yorkshire Northern Union at Bradford, in May 1898, chaired by Todmorden's Mr J Knowles, it was decided to form a No2 competition with two groups East and West. Todmorden joined the West. Two months later the Northern Union adopted professionalism officially. It was accepted that 'remuneration over and above travelling expenses has been practised more or less secretly for a long while'.[12]

Todmorden reorganised its team, signing several from Hebden Bridge, who were still traditional rugby union adherents, and JW Mitchell, who transferred back to Todmorden from Halifax. The season began well, the second defeat coming only in January 1899, away to Birstall, who had 'a reputation for winning at all hazards at home and visitors have begun to dread their rough tactics when fair play fails'.[13]

Todmorden won the Western Division and agreed to the play-off against Hull, the Eastern Division winners, at the Kingston Rovers' ground. This was clearly the better ground and would attract a larger gate, which it did, £128 12s 10d. Todmorden's share of £37 17s 9d was some compensation for a 36 point defeat.[14]

Having gone down the road of paying players, Todmorden was always going to struggle to balance the books and at the July 1899 AGM a deficit of £50 was revealed. Players' wages had cost £82 and Mr Knowles announced:

> We are at present soliciting donations from the public and my committee hope all followers of the game will respond liberally to the call and thereby reduce the debt which at present threatens the extinction of the club.[15]

The club continued and at the first practice of the new season over 1000 turned up

Todmorden RUFC at the Holme, 16 September 1899,
left of centre on the ball is JW Mitchell.

to watch. In late November, the match against Hebden Bridge, who had joined the
Northern Union, attracted a crowd of over 6000. A special train was run from Hebden
Bridge; the ordinary trains were full; the roads were lined with walkers; the Todmorden
Brass Band turned out and the Mayor, Alderman Ormerod JP, who had brought rugby
to Todmorden in 1878, kicked off each half. Todmorden won by 9 points (3 tries) to 2
points (1 goal).[16]

Financial pressures continued to plague the club. Players were asked to agree to
payment being withheld for the next two away games and to give their services at the
next home match. At this game members would be asked to pay for admission as non-
members did. Matters eased when John E Barker transferred to Bradford for which
Todmorden received a 'consideration' and later, in recognition of his services, Bradford,
Yorkshire Champions, brought a team (free of cost) to play Todmorden on Good
Friday 1900, attracting a crowd of over 2000.[17]

As the end of the season approached with no honours at stake and only a few fixtures
left:

> Arrangements were made to consider the matches off, as loss [financial] must inevitably
> come from playing them, seeing that all interest in football has now gone.

These matches were counted as draws and Todmorden finished 4th in the competition.
The club's liabilities still topped £100, including a £31 loss from running a Social Club
- formed to raise money. Moves were made to wind up the club by circulating an offer to
its creditors of 6d in the £.[18] However, another season was embarked upon, again in the
Western Section of the Yorkshire Northern Union No2 competition.

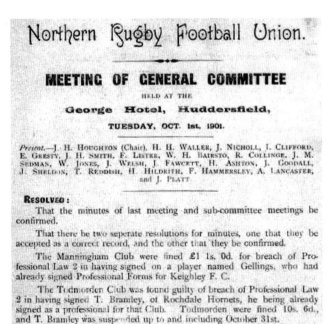

Northern Rugby Football Union.

MEETING OF GENERAL COMMITTEE

HELD AT THE

George Hotel, Huddersfield,

TUESDAY, OCT. 1st, 1901.

Present.—J. H. HOUGHTON (Chair), H. H. WALLER, J. NICHOLL, I. CLIFFORD, E. GRESTY, J. H. SMITH, F. LISTER, W. H. BAIRSTO, R. COLLINGE, J. M. SEDMAN, W. JONES, J. WELSH, J. FAWCETT, H. ASHTON, J. GOODALL, J. SHELDON, T. REDDISH, H. HILDRITH, F. HAMMERSLEY, A. LANCASTER, and J. PLATT.

RESOLVED:

That the minutes of last meeting and sub-committee meetings be confirmed.

That there be two separate resolutions for minutes, one that they be accepted as a correct record, and the other that they be confirmed.

The Manningham Club were fined £1 1s. 0d. for breach of Professional Law 2 in having signed on a player named Gellings, who had already signed Professional Forms for Keighley F. C.

The Todmorden Club was found guilty of breach of Professional Law 2 in having signed T. Bramley, of Rochdale Hornets, he being already signed as a professional for that Club. Todmorden were fined 10s. 6d., and T. Bramley was suspended up to and including October 31st.

Northern Rugby Football Union, 1901
extract of minutes relating to Todmorden.

The team suffered its ninth consecutive defeat, 15 points to 12, at Shipley in early January. The club was now entirely dependent on local lads and was attempting to pull itself together by means of amateurism. Other clubs in the competition were also in financial difficulties. Both Birstall and Luddenden Foot had resigned, whilst Hebden Bridge started a 1200 shilling scheme with door to door collections to clear a £60 debt (20s=£1).

In March 1901 Todmorden started a workshop competition which attracted 22 entries. It proved so popular that the entry fees and gate money cleared the debt and the semi-final attracted a bigger gate than the Lancashire League match on Centre Vale between Todmorden and Ramsbottom. Moss Brothers, fustian manufacturers of Eastwood, were the winners. They toured the town in a wagonette and in May played Todmorden's prospective team for the new season, all proceeds from the match going to the local hospital fund.[19]

For the 1901/02 season the club joined the Yorkshire A competition which included the 2nd teams of clubs such as Bradford, Batley, Hull, Halifax and Huddersfield. Todmorden had 5 local players with 1st class experience; Arthur Howarth (Rochdale Hornets), John E Barker and Bob Sutcliffe (Bradford), Alf Greenwood and JW Mitchell (Halifax). They realised that merely turning up to play on Saturday was not good enough and, led by Barker and Mitchell, began systematic mid-week training.[20]

A successful season found Todmorden's footballer/cricketers being singled out in a win against Batley:

> Ratcliffe...dodged the opposing halves by feigning to pass and then with only the full back to face he threw the ball to Law who was attending him and the two cricketers scored for Todmorden in the football field as they have often done in the cricket as well. Law took the place and passed an easy shot.[21]

Beaten in the Rochdale Charity Cup Final by Rochdale Hornets A, the team had an unsatisfactory encounter with Halifax A in the Halifax Charity Cup Final played on Calder Holmes at Hebden Bridge before a crowd of 5000, over 800 coming on a special train from Todmorden.

Halifax were favourites, having strengthened their team with as many 1st team players as were eligible. They won the toss and played with the strong wind behind them. Todmorden's Bob Sutcliffe was sent off but the game ended with no score. Todmorden refused to play extra time unless Bob Sutcliffe was allowed to come back on. The competition committee ordered the replay to be held at Sowerby Bridge on the following Monday. Todmorden protested that they could not play before Saturday as

Todmorden NRUFC at Sandholme, 1913-14

four players were badly hurt and most would not be able to get off work on Monday. The committee's decision was irrevocable and if they did not like it they must scratch, which Todmorden did - declaring they had been shabbily treated by the Charity Committee.

They communicated their decision to the secretary on the Monday by which time 3000 had turned up at Sowerby Bridge to be told there was no match. Todmorden had been offered £5 by the Charity Committee to cover any broken time payments for players who would have had to get off work. There was a feeling that there was more to Todmorden's attitude than met the eye. They were informed that Todmorden had forfeited the right to any medals and at a special meeting on the Wednesday called by the Charity Committee, Todmorden's representative Mr Collinge was uneasy and said that, for the sake of the charities who benefited from the competition, he was anxious that Todmorden should have raised a team of some kind.[22]

At the Todmorden AGM before the start of the next season a decision to reduce the players' wages to 3s 6d for a win and 2s 6d for a defeat caused trouble. Many players refused to sign on at the reduced rates, several of the committee members resigned, and a special meeting was called to consider disbanding the club. It was decided to carry on but the season was not a happy one. When Hebden Bridge was defeated 9 points to 2 in December, it was reported that the match did not arouse as much interest as usual:

> Undoubtedly Rugby Football is on the wane in the district, possibly because both clubs are deteriorating in class but the fact remains that the Socker [sic] game has taken firm hold of the young generation. Thus it is that a good many people predict that it will ultimately oust Rugby![23]

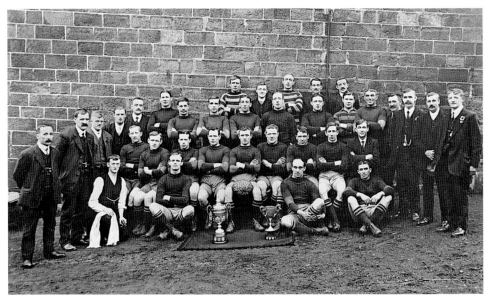

Todmorden Rugby FC 1914 at their headquarters the Shannon and Chesapeake Inn,
having won the Halifax and District League Championship and the Bradford and District Cup.

Following the AGM in July 1903 and after the players had agreed to give their
services free even though the club's debt was only £4, it proved impossible to form a
committee with officials who could work together, and by a small majority the club
was disbanded.

The sale of effects raised £10 6s 0d of which £6 was shared amongst the officials,
who had forgone their wages, and the rest was used as a nucleus to provide a
testimonial for the veteran player JW Mitchell (who was also a wicketkeeper for
Todmorden Cricket Club). At a special smoking concert held at the White Hart in
February 1904 Mr Mitchell was presented with 'a splendid marble timepiece with
bronze figures, and a gold mounted umbrella in recognition of his thirteen years
connection with the Todmorden club as an official and playing member'. He also
received an 'equestrian figure and a purse of gold'.[24]

It is clear that, when the rugby world split over the question of payments to players
- even though initially it was only 'broken-time payment' for time off work - it was the
beginning of the end for small clubs like Todmorden and Hebden Bridge. Attempts
were made to open up and add speed to the game by allowing teams of 12 or 13 players
instead of 15 and by discontinuing the practice of holding a scrum after every tackle
but in the end the question of money was crucial. This was even more so with the
increasing popularity of the association game or 'socker'.

Hebden Bridge, with whom Todmorden had always been keen rivals, continued with
its rugby team until 1907 when, with a debt of almost £60, it suspended operations
until the deficit was cleared.[25] Thus neither town had a rugby team until Hebden Bridge
reformed in 1910, entering the Halifax and District League. This may have stirred the
dormant rugby fans in Todmorden as, in July 1911, a meeting at the Hare and Hounds
declared that 'Todmorden had been without a town club for sufficiently long time to
realise the want of it'.

Within a month a field at Rough, near Swineshead in Langfield, had been secured
- an attempt to use part of the newly acquired Centre Vale Estate was ruled out by the
Council. The first meeting of the two old rivals in the Halifax Charity Cup, on

Hebden's ground at Nell Carr on the Wadsworth hillside, ended in a draw, 3 points each, but Hebden won the replay at Rough by 15 points to nil.[26] The end of the 1912/13 season saw Hebden Bridge 4th and Todmorden 5th in the 10 team Halifax League.

The following season Todmorden were pleased to obtain the Sandholme field in place of their inconvenient hillside home. Hebden Bridge had also left the hilltop and agreed to share Mytholmroyd AFC's valley bottom ground. Here the clash of the rivals was graced by local dignitary WA Simpson Hinchcliffe, who kicked off the match, which Todmorden won 13 points to 6. Todmorden's season continued to blossom. They beat Rastrick by 7 points to 2 at Thrum Hall, in front of a crowd of 2600, to take the Halifax and District Championship and repeated their success by beating Stanningley by 10 points to nil in the Bradford and District Cup. Simpson Hinchcliffe formally presented both cups in front of a large gathering at Todmorden Town Hall. On this high note the season ended, the war intervening before competitive rugby could start again.[27]

The 'Socker' Scene

When Todmorden Rugby Club first folded in 1903, the Holme field became vacant and, as the prime local site, it was soon snapped up by Todmorden Central Association, who moved from their Sandholme ground. The local 'socker' [sic] stronghold was in the Burnley Valley where, during the 1890s Portsmouth Rovers, Vale Swifts, Harley Wood and later Cornholme Albion had teams in the Burnley and District League. In 1900 the Harley Wood club became Lydgate, who took a field at Sourhall behind the Dog and Partridge Inn, and entered the Halifax and District League, which they won in their first two seasons. They then transferred to the Rochdale and District League joining Todmorden Association, who were newly promoted from the 2nd Division.

Thus from the start of organised 'socker' in the district, the pattern of the premier teams joining leagues in Halifax, Rochdale, Burnley or even further afield was set and has continued to the present day.

The first local league, the Calder Valley Association, was formed for the 1901/02 season following a meeting at the Fielden Coffee Tavern (later the Conservative Club) on Thursday, 23 May. By 1903 it comprised 12 clubs: Eastwood, Springside, Todmorden United, Todmorden Association Reserves, Monument Mystics (named after John Fielden's statue then in Fielden Square), Shade, Walsden, Walsden United, Lydgate Reserves, Portsmouth Rovers, St Joseph's and Pudsey Rovers.[28] In contrast to the local cricket league, only one club, St Joseph's, had a church or chapel origin. The association game continued to grow in popularity with 'every town and village from Todmorden to Halifax represented' in the Halifax League. The local paper commented:

> With the old local rivalry brought to life again, one can easily anticipate the stirring scenes when the local clubs meet next season. It will be something like the old times when the local rugby clubs met.

In 1905, the Todmorden Association and Lydgate clubs amalgamated as Todmorden FC and joined the Halifax and District League. They stamped their mark by achieving the league and cup double. The league title was clinched on Monday, 16 April, at Mytholmroyd, when Todmorden came back from being 3-0 down to win 4-3. 'The game was of a keen character throughout and towards the close so much misdirected vigour was introduced into the play that three players were ordered off.' They met Hebden Bridge in the cup-final. Todmorden had not helped themselves by playing Portsmouth Rovers in a 'friendly' match on the day before the final, which required two replays, the second at Mytholmroyd where Todmorden won 4-0.[29]

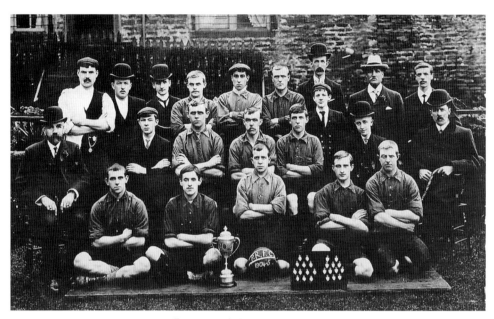

Portsmouth Rovers 1904-05

The following season, 1906/07, the Halifax and District League organised itself into four divisions each of 13 clubs. Todmorden, Portsmouth Rovers and Hebden Bridge were in the 1st Division, whilst the Calder Valley League joined as its 2nd Division. Signs that the game was still developing was the decision that all Halifax 1st and 2nd Division clubs must have good nets affixed (nets were first used for a North v South match in 1891) and comments, by the league president Mr Higginson, suggest that rugby tactics were still prevalent in 'socker'. He complained that referees allowed too much heavy charging and jumping, that the halves tended to stay behind the ball instead of helping the forwards in sustained attacks, that forwards tended to want to dribble the ball into goal instead of shooting when they had chance, and that going for the man instead of the ball should cease[30]

Portsmouth won the Halifax and District League in 1906/07 with Todmorden runners-up, Todmorden Reserves winning the Calder Valley Division. Portsmouth, feeling themselves ready for more challenging fixtures, joined the NE Lancashire Combination in 1907/08, into which Todmorden were provisionally accepted if they could find a field. Unfortunately they could not and had to suspend for a season, before securing their original ground at Sandholme, and in 1908/09 they joined the Rochdale and District League. Meanwhile Portsmouth Rovers had reached the final of the Lancashire Junior Challenge Shield in March 1908, only to be beaten by Skelmersdale United at Accrington Stanley's ground. Nevertheless the Rovers entered on a golden period. They won the NE Lancashire Combination for three successive years from 1908/09 to 1910/11.[31]

This success brought an invitation to join the Lancashire Combination 2nd Division which, at a special meeting in June 1911, Portsmouth Rovers unanimously accepted, although they realised that this promotion was challenging not only in a football sense but also financially. The club prefaced an appeal for funds by saying:

> We would like to point out that our team is composed entirely of local working lads, who receive no remuneration for their services and the fact of having won the NE

Portsmouth Rovers 1905-06, champions of: Calder Valley League; Calder Valley Cup;
Todmorden Borough Championship: in playing positions; goalkeeper and fullbacks, halfbacks,
forwards.
L-R Row 3: R Walker, JA Greenwood, T Sugden (c),
Row 2: Mr Joshua Lord (sec), L Bulcock, J Rhodes, H Sugden, Joseph Lord Esq (vice-pres),
Row 1: D Stott, CR Nesbitt, J Hobson, J Dawson, H Mason.

> Lancashire Football Combination for the last three years in succession, we think
> justifies our action in putting them in a higher class of football.

They assessed their expenses at around £4 for each away match and that they would
need to start the season with £50 to £60 in hand 'to be anything like guaranteed to
fulfil all our fixtures' and:

> in conclusion we beg to say that our club is worked on the cheapest possible lines as all
> the officials give their services voluntarily, in fact they are all subscribers.

In early 1911 Portsmouth's star player, Billy Nesbitt, signed for Hebden Bridge, who
were looking to move up a class by joining the Yorkshire Combination. Nesbitt's stay at
Hebden Bridge was short as he was signed by Burnley, for whom he made his first team
debut in February 1912. He was described as having great physical advantages, being
very deaf but as plucky as a lion, fast and clever with the ball and possessing a strong and
accurate shot. Re-signed by Burnley in 1912, he became a vital part of the first great
Burnley team, along with his Portsmouth Rovers' colleague, goalkeeper Jerry Dawson.
When Burnley won the FA Cup in 1914, they granted Portsmouth £15 and Hebden
Bridge £10 in recognition of Nesbitt's apprenticeship with them.[32]

On the more local scene things chopped and changed rapidly. In September 1908 a new
league was formed, which became the first Todmorden and District League. By the
following year it had two divisions with a total of 24 teams, some of them reserve teams

of 1st Division clubs. In August 1910 a Hebden Bridge and District League, also with two divisions was formed.[33] There does not seem to have been room for both of these leagues and by 1912/13 several Todmorden clubs were playing in the Hebden Bridge League.

The Todmorden Association Club suspended operations following the disbanding of the Rochdale and District League in 1909 and folded altogether in 1910, leaving its Sandholme ground vacant. In 1912 a determined move revived the town's team and, using Sandholme, Todmorden Borough entered its 1st team in the Halifax and District League and reserves in the Hebden Bridge League.

At the end of 1913/14 Portsmouth Rovers withdrew from the Lancashire Combination 2nd Division, where they had struggled to compete, and decided to join the all-amateur Blackburn League instead. However, when Hebden Bridge were accepted into the Lancashire Combination in their stead, Portsmouth had a change of heart, cancelled their decision to join the Blackburn League, and were re-elected to their former league. The chopping and changing which characterised the local leagues was soon to be put in perspective by the onset of World War I, although the Lancashire Combination played through the 1914/15 season before closing down for the duration of the war.[34]

The local response to the ending of the war was to get back to normal as soon as possible and, even though the Todmorden and District League had folded prior to 1914, it was up and running again in 1919. Cross Stone, Eastwood, Inchfield Bottom,

Lydgate, Secondary School Old Students, Patmos, Portsmouth Rovers Reserves, St Joseph's, Todmorden United, Todmorden Church, Unitarians, Walsden United, and York Street Wesleyans all joined, six of which had a church or chapel base. Portsmouth Rovers' 1st team along with Hebden Bridge joined the Halifax and District League.

Portsmouth had a successful season reaching the semi-final of the West Riding County Cup and went on to win the league. Although they lost to the old enemy Hebden Bridge in the final of the Halifax Charity Cup, watched by a crowd of 3000 at Luddenden Foot, they beat Stainland by 5 goals to 1 to win the Halifax Challenge Cup, again at Luddenden Foot. On arriving home they were greeted by the Cornholme Band (which had been parading the district during the afternoon) and were escorted to the club's headquarters at the Roebuck Inn to the inevitable *See the Conquering Hero Comes!*

As the post-war momentum

Jerry Dawson and Billy Nesbitt, goalkeeper and outside-right, for Portsmouth Rovers and Burnley. Nesbitt was in the FA Cup winning side of 1914 and both won Football League Championship medals in 1920/21.

Unitarian Church FC 1908-09

increased, the Todmorden and District League, in 1920/21, was able to form two divisions comprising 17 teams, which rose to 21 in the following year. In the Burnley Valley two new teams emerged, Cornholme YMCA in 1920/21 and the following year a team called simply Cornholme. The YMCA's base was the former Frostholme millowner's Oakleigh House (a social centre for its employees since 1902) and which, in 1920, became a branch of the YMCA as a memorial to World War I. The YMCA ground was at the bleak and well named Height Top, on the south side, above the Burnley Valley. In their first season they won both the Calder Valley Shield and Cup competitions. In the semi-final of the former, amidst considerable rivalry and a good crowd, the YMCA beat Portsmouth Rovers Reserves by 6 goals to 1 at Height Top on Good Friday morning. Unfortunately, Rovers' player Richard Crawshaw broke his leg

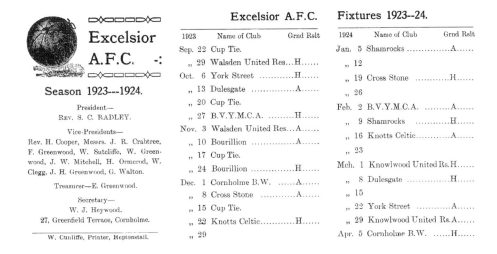

Excelsior FC Fixture List 1923-24 Todmorden and District League

Knowlwood United AFC 1923-24, their home ground was The Rough.
L-R Row 2: J Green, I Stansfield, R Barker, G Heap, H Fielden (c), A Dawson,
Row 1: I Mitchell, T Judson, L Crabtree, W Mitchell, W Fielden, W Gibson.

and, in pre-social security days, faced a hard time financially. However, the YMCA stepped in organising a benefit concert by local artistes at the Gem Cinema, which raised 'a handsome sum' to tide him over this period.

By 1923 the fragility of the local football scene was reappearing. In 1920/21 Portsmouth had joined the revived NE Lancashire Combination, where prospects were considered bright, but the Portsmouth Committee had to apologise when, owing to a delay in clearing their Rattenclough ground of hay, they had been handicapped in making arrangements for the coming season. They dispensed with the reserve team in 1923, probably as a cost cutting move. It was immediately replaced by a team formed by Wilson Bros' Bobbin Works, as part of the firm's general welfare scheme.

A proposed town team foundered for the want of a ground. The plan was to play on a hilltop ground in 1923/24, whilst the Town Council Health Committee made Woodhouse tip suitable to play on, but this was deferred until 1924/25 and in fact did not happen at that time.

The second half of the 1920s saw great changes in local football. Todmorden teams, capitalising on their three valleys and border location, were spoilt for choice! In search of a higher standard Hebden Bridge, Walsden United and Knowlwood joined Portsmouth Rovers in the NE Lancashire Combinaton, but none of them prospered. Hebden Bridge failed to complete the season and, following problems in the West Riding Cup in which they were also competing, disbanded. Walsden United transferred to the West Lancashire League in 1926, where Portsmouth Rovers joined them in 1927, having spent a year in the Padiham and District League. By 1926 Knowlwood were back in the Todmorden and District League, but not for long, as only five of the eleven clubs completed the 1927/28 season and the league disbanded, whereupon Lydgate joined the Bacup Amateur League.

Cornholme Bobbin Works AFC 1923-24,
they replaced Portsmouth Rovers Reserves which disbanded in 1923.

The big shock of the decade was the demise of Portsmouth Rovers. It was reported in May 1928:

> On Saturday concluded what appears likely to be their last season in the W Lancashire League, the increased support anticipated has not been forthcoming and the club is in straightened circumstances.

It hoped to raise enough money in the close season to be able to carry on but this did not happen and the club folded, selling its effects for £35 to Wilson Bros Bobbin Works, whose team took over the Rattenclough ground and entered the Padiham and District League:

> as practically all the local players who were connected with Portsmouth Rovers will be eligible for the new club prospects are very encouraging.[35]

In January 1924 when making a presentation, on behalf of Portsmouth Rovers's players and supporters, to their long serving secretary, Joshua (Jos) Lord, John Webster Greenwood recalled Rattenclough in the 1890s:

> There was a hill at the right wing top corner like a miniature grandstand and the river was many times higher than the ground. The dressing room was fairly warm being warmed by hot air at about four cow pressure. If you were short of room to strip, well you pushed a cow a little further over.
> Subscriptions were about 2d per week and anyone who got behind was left off the team.

Rugby Revival

In 1925 rugby was in the air. Having been without a local team since 1914, there were suddenly two. The Todmorden Club re-formed and was happy to share Eastwood's cricket field, next to the present Bridgeholme cricket ground. The Bourillion Club, also in the Eastwood area, decided to change from soccer to rugby and acquired a field at Haugh Tops. The two clubs joined both the Rochdale and the Halifax District Leagues.

Todmorden's liaison with Eastwood lasted for three seasons but they had to play the last two matches of 1927/28 on Centre Vale Park as Eastwood needed its ground for cricket. The 1928/29 season found them at Rough in Langfield, where they had played at times in the club's early days. It was no more convenient than it ever had been and they failed to complete the 1930/31 season, playing only 10 matches. Failing support was blamed; supporters were not prepared to face the arduous climb regularly to reach the ground. The club decided they would continue only if they could find an accessible field, hoping for one at Scaitcliffe, but they were unsuccessful and the club folded.

An attempt to rekindle interest in a Todmorden rugby club in the late 1950s only lasted a few years owing to lack of players, but one of the keen youngsters was Ray Dempsey who went on to play for Barrow. On his return in the early 1970s, he took up the cause of local rugby. In 1973 an advertisement in the *Todmorden Advertiser*, invited anyone interested in forming a rugby league team to a meeting at the Golden Lion. The initial response was disappointing but the few who turned up persevered and eventually had enough players to form a team. A ground was rented at Highfield, Cross Stone, previously used by Lydgate United. A strip was obtained from Whitehaven RLFC and during the 1973/74 season the team played only friendly matches. The club was based at Cross Stone's Bay Horse Inn and initially two tin baths in the car park were used for post-match ablutions. Later a site hut was obtained and a rudimentary bath with gas boilers for heating was installed. In 1974/75 they were admitted to the 3rd Division of the Pennine League. In a baptism of fire they were beaten 72-0 by Greetland but they soldiered on. Then ex-international MJ Price (Pontypool, Oldham, Rochdale Hornets and Salford, 14 caps for Wales, British Lions and Great Britain) came to coach them. Results improved and by the season's end they were able to defeat Greetland 13-9. Demoted to the newly formed Pennine League Division 4 in 1975/76, they continued

Todmorden Rugby Club 1974
L-R Row 2: Ray Dempsey, T Barlow, R Parkinson, Bob Greenwood, David Grant,
Stephen Grant, Terry Stretton, Barry Chapman, Halstead (ref), MJ Price,
Row 1: Alan Clayton, Adrian Wisneweski, Philip Shaw, Fred Crabtree, Trevor Mackriel,
Dougie Mansfield, Brian Coyne, David Heaton, Billy Collier.

to improve under player/coach Johnny Hammond, ex Rochdale and Oldham, and won the 4th Division title. The Rochdale Charity Cup was won the following season, when Saddleworth Rangers were defeated on Rochdale Hornet's ground, and the 3rd Division title was also clinched.

The end of the 1970s saw the team move from Cross Stone to Centre Vale Park, which was to be their home for the next 20 years. In 1999 Todmorden Rugby Club celebrated its Silver Jubilee, the season in which they reached the Halifax Cup Final. They won promotion to the 1st Division of the Pennine League after the 2002/03 season, but sadly, they were never to play in it as, during the summer of 2003, the club surprisingly folded. No-one was more dismayed than John McGrath, a player from 1983 and player/coach for the last five years. He had announced his retirement owing to family commitments and on his return from holiday received a phone

Neil Cowie played rugby for Todmorden, Rochdale Hornets, Wigan, Wales and Great Britain.

call from the *Halifax Courier* regarding the closure of the club. It transpired that a discussion amongst the players at a training session on Centre Vale Park resulted in the decision to wind up the club.

Since then, aspiring local rugby players have generally played at Littleborough. The Todmorden club's 29 year span is the longest that soccer and rugby have co-existed locally as, historically, Todmorden could never decide whether to be a soccer or rugby town. The club did, however, produce one of Todmorden's top sportsmen in Neil Cowie who played for Rochdale Hornets before joining Wigan in 1991. During his time there as prop-forward, he played 320 matches. He also won seven caps for Wales and three for Great Britain.

<u>Back to Soccer</u>

The Todmorden and District Football League re-formed for the 1931/32 season. The Bourillion Club (whose rugby days had ended) joined, making a total of 13 clubs, which had risen to 22 in two divisions by 1933 but two years later only 6 completed the season. Not until 1937 was it revived yet again but collapsed in 1939 and war intervened. Given the uncertain nature of the Todmorden and District League, it is not surprising that the better teams sought to play in other leagues but, this route entailed extra expense and in the depressed economic conditions of the late 1920s and early 1930s money was scarce. This was experienced most keenly when, in September 1930, Wilson Bros, who had been a major employer in Cornholme since long before the turn of the century, decided to close its Cornholme works, moving everything to the main centre at Garston, Liverpool. This was 'the biggest industrial blow ever experienced in Todmorden and in Cornholme in particular'. The firm's football team had to disband leaving its Padiham and District League programme unfinished.[36]

The major local teams of the 1930s were Springside, Bourillion and Walsden Central, who competed in the Rochdale Amateur League. A local Derby still attracted a good crowd and when, in October 1935, Bourillion White Star and Walsden Central (2nd and 3rd in the league) met at Sandholme, the Mayor and the Chairman of the Parks Committee were introduced to the teams and match officials. Miss Mary Midgley, well known local solo dancer and instructress, kicked off.

Two local players of the 1920s and 30s joined the professional game. One was goalkeeper Clifford Binns of Portsmouth Rovers, who played for Halifax Town then Blackburn Rovers and later Barnsley. The other, Clem Rigg, joined Nelson and then Newcastle United.

A meeting, in October 1940 at the Weavers' Institute, saw the Todmorden and District League re-form for the coming season with 10 clubs participating, 4 of which were army teams from troops based in the area. Grounds were shared: two army teams used Centre Vale Park and the other two Rattenclough at Portsmouth; Roomfield Old Boys and the Liberal Club played at Sandholme; Langfield Rangers and Ferney Lee United used Haugh Tops; whilst Portsmouth Rovers and the British Picker Company had the ground at Sourhall.

In mid-January, owing to army duties, the forces' teams had to cancel their fixtures. The remaining 6 clubs played out the season before disbanding, because of the war situation. Wartime football was left in the hands of youth teams. Todmorden Youth Centre and the Air Training Corps both competed in the Burnley Wartime League.

Todmorden's best known footballer of the immediate post-war years was JT (Jack) Connor. Born in 1919, he played his local football with Walsden Central and would most likely have begun his professional career with Rochdale if war had not intervened.

John Crowther introduces his team, Walsden Central FC, to the Mayor of Todmorden before the match against Bourillion White Star at Sandholme in October 1935.

Stationed at Carlisle, he signed for Ipswich Town in 1944 and guesting at Carlisle in the 1945/46 season he scored 30 goals. In December 1946 he left Ipswich for Carlisle where he played for two seasons before signing for Rochdale in 1948, where his career blossomed. He scored 42 goals in 88 matches, which aroused interest in several clubs, one of which was Stockport County. In April 1951 he signed for Bradford City but Stockport were persistent and signed him in October of the same year in rather unusual circumstances. Jack and his wife were in a Bradford cinema when a message flashed on the screen saying, 'Would Jack Connor, Bradford City's centre forward, please go to the foyer?' Fearing bad news, Jack was surprised to be met by Stockport's manager and chairman but signed on the spot for a fee of £2500. He was 32 but had five wonderful seasons at Stockport, scoring 140 league and cup goals in 217 games, including 17 hat-tricks. His last season in league football was with Crewe Alexandra in 1956/57. When he retired aged 38 he had scored 201 goals in 380 games. On his death in 1998, a Stockport team-mate, Eddie Moran told the *Stockport Express*:

> Jack was an out and out finisher, he was always in the right place at the right time and when he got into space he just hit it. And did he hit it! He would never tap the ball but even from two yards he would smash it.

Jack Connor's popularity at Stockport was emphasised when, in a millennium poll he was voted Stockport's player of the century. An all round sportsman he also played cricket as a wicketkeeper/batsman for Walsden, Todmorden and Stockport.

With the return of peace and as servicemen began to return home, the indefatigable Walter Southwell, who had been a major force in local football from the 1920s, called a meeting at the Weavers' Institute in July 1946 to re-start the Todmorden and District League, but was disappointed when only two of the clubs, which had expressed an interest, sent representatives.

The first local team off the mark was Walsden, joining the Rochdale and District Amateur League in 1946, to be followed in 1947 by Todmorden British Legion who, having no ground of their own, were in danger of being asked to resign from the league but were able to obtain use of Centre Vale Park. The Legion team included local cricketers, Harold Dawson, Frank Saul and Howard Wilkinson and attracted several hundred spectators to their matches, especially when they played league leaders Hamer

Jack Connor (no 9) scores for Stockport County at Edgeley Park.

Cornholme Methodians U16s in 1947
L-R Row 2: Donald Dean, Albert Norton, Jeffrey Rawsthorn, Neville Crossley,
Eddie Hargreaves, Peter Horsfall, Fred Crowther, Arthur Lord, Edwin Banks,
Row 1: Bernard Crowther, Stephen Crowther, Jack Gore, Gordon Crowther,
Frank Shirt, Terence Hanley, Reggie Norton (trainer).

United and beat them by 5 goals to 1.

In June 1947, Cornholme Methodians was formed by Cornholme Methodist
Church and entered the Burnley and District Sunday School League Junior Division.
It was a youth team with an age limit of 17 years but with two players aged 18 allowed.
The former Portsmouth Rovers' pitch was rented and enthusiasm was high. The
opening match, away to Padiham Green on Fenyfolds Field was a 3 all draw and, as a
reminder that it was local football:

> Three old ladies either oblivious to or ignoring the fact that a match was in progress,
> strolled across the pitch. The referee suspended play until the intruders got clear.

The first home match, against Burnley Lads' Club, was scheduled for Saturday, 18
October. On the previous day, at 1.30pm, an enormous river of mud thundered down
Ratten Clough, whose stream normally flowed under the Burnley Road and alongside
one end of the football field. The mud, some 30ft wide and 9ft high, resulting from
disturbance caused by open-cast coal mining on the moor above, pushed a lorry across
the road into the wall opposite turning it on its side. The river of mud stopped just
short of the pitch itself but the game was played the following day, although 'before the
match was over the players were over the ankles in water'. The mud was bulldozed
from the main path of the stream and spread over the playing area - ending its days as
a football field. The Methodians were able to rent Chatham Meadow, the next field to
Rattenclough, which in years past had been Cornholme's cricket field.[37]

Any stay at Chatham was short-lived. Within three months the team had taken a
field at Wittonstall End, Shore, high above the valley bottom and rather exposed, but
certainly drier than Rattenclough. By 1948 the Methodians were fielding three teams,
the ground at Shore being used by the reserves and juniors, whilst the seniors had use

Cornholme Methodians 1949-50, winners of the Burnley Sunday School Challenge Shield.
L-R Row 2: Rev A Hunt, Billy Coulton, Gordon Whitehead, Bob Simpson,
Lewis Blacka, Jack Nesbitt, Norman Stansfield, Will Greenwood (trainer),
Row 1: Wallace Pickles, Stanley Coulton, Wally Winter, Jimmy Collinge (c),
Eric Brennan, Roy Wadsworth, Dan Jackson.

of Centre Vale Park. In their most successful spell, 1949 to 50, they were winners of the Burnley SS League Challenge Shield, runners-up in the league and semi-finalists in the Burnley and District Hospital Cup. The following season saw them again runners-up in the league and winners of the cup, this time beating Whittlefield GT by 7 goals to nil at Turf Moor, supported by four coach loads of fans plus many who travelled by service bus.

Eventually, Walter Southwell's persistence paid off and, by May 1949, enough clubs showed interest for the Todmorden and District League to re-start. The 8 team league included two of the district's oldest clubs Lydgate and Knowlwood. Unfortunately, but predictably, it was short-lived lasting for only two seasons and has never revived.

In the early 1950s Todmorden had five teams in the Burnley and District Amateur Combination: Todmorden British Legion, United Services, Cornholme Methodians, Lydgate and Todmorden AFC.

Cornholme Methodians' last season was 1954/55 and Lydgate gained some of the players, including Todmorden cricketer Peter Brownbridge. Lydgate, Todmorden and Walsden continued as the leading local teams, Walsden in the Rochdale League, whilst by 1960 Lydgate and Todmorden had progressed to Division I of the Burnley League.

Lydgate were the dominant local team. They had won the Calder Valley Shield (a competition open to teams from the valley, who might play in various leagues) on seven consecutive occasions during the 1950s. They went on to win Burnley's Captain Grey Shield in 1957/58 in the final at Turf Moor.

Prior to this, in 1956, they were invited to participate in a Festival of Football held across Belgium and Northern France, a prestigious event normally confined to leading amateur clubs in SE England. For many local players it was their first trip abroad and, on the Thursday morning before Good Friday, the team left Todmorden with a civic send off. On Easter Sunday the tournament officials took the team from their base in

Cornholme Methodian supporters at Turf Moor
L-R Row 2: Jacqueline Marshall, Margaret Crowther, Jennifer Hulme, Kenneth Jacques,
Michael Wrench, Victor Crowther, Edward Lumby, Glennis Whittaker, Jean Brennan,
Peggy Jackson,
Row 1: Clive Bulcock, Jeffrey Pickles, Timothy Marshall, David Marshall, Rodney Tregellas.

Ostend to Waterloo, near Lille in northern France, where, after a civic reception, Lydgate beat Waterloo by 2 goals to 1:

> Lydgate were then treated royally to dinner, some of the party taking too much of a liking to the liberal offerings of Champagne and were overcome either by sleep or the urge to sing all the way back to Ostend.

Lydgate went on to win the Burnley Combination 1st Division in 1963/64 and 1965/66. Also in the 1960s, they organised the Sir John Cockcroft Shield competition, which was open to clubs within a 10 miles radius of Todmorden. Perhaps their crowning glory came in 1967/68 when, having joined the Halifax League, they performed the treble, winning the Halifax Premier League, Halifax Senior Cup and Halifax Challenge Cup. Add to this the Sir John Cockcroft Shield and their cups were overflowing. No-one was prouder then long serving secretary, Joe Rigby.

Todmorden AFC had also left the Burnley Combination to join the Halifax League. Still in the Burnley Combination were Lydgate's C and D teams. From the Lydgate team of the 1950s and 60s several players attracted the interest of professional clubs. Barrie Pickles signed amateur forms with Burnley for the 1955/56 season. Now, he recalls with affection the help given to him, a 17 year-old, by the Burnley coaches, ex-Welsh international inside right Billy Morris, and wing-half George Bray.

Terry Stansfield and Barry Sharphouse also had trials with Burnley. Terry Priestley

Lydgate United FC 1957 at Turf Moor, having won the Captain Grey Shield.
L-R Row 2: John Glover, Brian Howley, Arthur Glover, Donald Houghton,
Terry Stansfield, Steve Boam, John King, Jim Ramage,
Row 1: Barrie Pickles, David Baxter, Peter Brownbridge, Tony Ridout, Barry Sharphouse.

played with Halifax Town, whilst Ray Fielden emigrated to Australia, where he played professional soccer. Ian Mitchell went to Leeds United aged thirteen, playing with their youth side, Pudsey Juniors, and later transferred to Bolton Wanderers. The most recent Todmordian to have success at a high level in professional football is David Wilson. Following his success with the England Schools' team, several clubs were eager to sign him and Manchester United were successful. Starting as a junior in 1984, he made his 1st team debut in 1988. In 1991 he joined Bristol Rovers before embarking on a long career in Scandanavia. Playing for various clubs in Finland and Sweden, he played in several European Cup ties, prior to managing clubs in Sweden.

Nick Sutcliffe, Todmorden AFC, and Simon Barker of Lydgate, both qualified as referees in careers which lasted thirteen years. They each became Class I referees, running the line in the Central and Conference Leagues, refereeing in the NW Counties League and acting as fourth official in the Football League and Premiership. Also a cricketer Simon captained Todmorden 2nd XI for several years in the 1990s.

In 1969 Michael Endley joined the Lydgate Committee, where he became a lynchpin for the next 30 years, 22 of them as secretary. The problems of administering teams in two leagues led, in the 1970s, to Lydgate leaving the Burnley Combination to play all its teams in the Halifax League. As ever in Todmorden, finding pitches was a problem. Lydgate with four teams had Centre Vale Park for the A team and Walsden Recreation ground for the B team, whilst teams C and D used a field at Red Lees Road in Cliviger. The latter received this verdict from the *Todmorden Advertiser* in January 1966:

> Granted their pitch at Red Lees is no advert for good football with its awkward slope and thick clinging mud, it would have served ideally as an assault course for the army.

As the changing room was a communal hut with no lights or washing facilities, players made their way home often caked in mud. Even this pitch was better than

Barrie Pickles, Lydgate, in action at Centre Vale.

nothing and, when the land was taken for building in 1967, Lydgate searched for a replacement. The old Portsmouth Rovers' ground at Rattenclough was used briefly, until the field behind the Bay Horse public house at Cross Stone was pressed into service. The team changed in the inn and after the match washed themselves off in the stream which flows alongside the path down to the Bay Horse.

Lydgate tried their fortunes in the Rochdale League in 1980. They then had three teams in the Rochdale Alliance League and one in the Bacup Amateur League and eventually, the Corporation completed the ground at Woodhouse where the 3rd and 4th teams could play.

In an attempt to redress the shortage of sports' grounds in Todmorden a scheme was mooted in the mid 1970s to develop the land at Bellholme, along the Rochdale Valley and close to the borough boundary. It was planned to create two pitches, one for soccer, the other for rugby, with a cricket square between them and an athletics' track round the perimeter. To this end Todmorden and Walsden cricket clubs invested money intending that their 3rd teams would play there. Despite many setbacks, the Trust overseeing the scheme clung on tenaciously and finally brought it to fruition by the millennium - albeit without the cricket square or the athletics' track.

During the 1990s a move towards a 'town' team began to gather pace. It was born of an idea by Lydgate player, Darren (Daz) Widdup, when working on a joinery contract in Antarctica! Here he conceived the idea of Todmorden United and Lydgate merging to form a town team. On his return he took the idea to Nick Sutcliffe, who was coming to the end of his refereeing career and ready to become involved in local football. Together they were seen watching both teams. Lydgate's Dave Hatton and Steven Parker from Todmorden United became involved and the decision to merge the two teams after the 1998/99 season was taken.

Lydgate took the necessary formalities to close down the club, and Dave Hatton's clearance, from the Centre Vale pitch onto the cricket field, was the last kick for a club whose name went back to 1900. In the event Todmorden United did not complete the merger, so Lydgate re-formed themselves as Todmorden Borough for the 1999/2000 season. Happily Bellholme with two pitches and a clubhouse was ready for play and the

BURNLEY FOOTBALL CLUB
The Burnley Football & Athletic Co., Ltd

Telephone: 2052 Ground   Telephone: 4907 Chairman

TURF MOOR,
BURNLEY,
LANCS.

MANAGER : ALAN W. BROWN
TEL. 4818
SECRETARY   H. SMITH

10th. May, 1955

B. Pickles, Esq.,
71, Industrial Street,
TODMORDEN.

Dear Barrie,

        I am pleased to note that you
have signed an Amateur Form for us for Season
1955/56, and wish you every success.

        I will notify you as soon as
our Training Sessions start in order that you
can attend same as when it does not interfere
with your Schooling.

        Please find enclosed herewith
copy of Registration Form.

        With very best regards.

                Yours sincerely,
        p.p. BURNLEY FOOTBALL CLUB.

                Manager.

Letter to Barrie Pickles from Burnley FC.

Lydgate United 1967, winners of Halifax Premier League, Halifax Senior Cup, Halifax
Challenge Cup and John Cockcroft Shield.
L-R Row 2: Raymond Newell, Colin Hudson, Maurice Ormerod, David Gledhill,
Terry Stansfield, Jimmy Halley, Ken Hollows,
Row 1: Terry Priestley, Barrie Pickles, Tony Lyons, Barry Shackleton, Ray Fielden.

Lydgate celebratory ablutions

Bellholme Trust leased the complex to Todmorden Borough for a peppercorn rent of £1 per year. The club fielded five teams, two in the West Lancashire League, two in the Rochdale Alliance plus the Boro' Veterans.

Todmorden United folded in 2006, some of the players joining Todmorden's other teams: Jack's House in the Rochdale Online Alliance League; and Woodhouse United and Todmorden Wellington in the Rochdale Sunday League.

Ten years on and Todmorden Borough has three all-age teams, two in the West Lancashire League and the Boro' Veterans in the Rochdale Alliance Division 2 - Todmorden has a thriving town club with a well-appointed, modern base.

David Wilson, wearing his England Schoolboys' cap
and Calderdale Schools' sweater, receives an award
from Halifax's Bill Carter.

Todmorden AFC in the late 1960s.
L-R Row 2: Peter Brennend, Richard Costello, Barry Shackleton, Terry Mayers,
David Marshall, Chas Woodall,
Row 1: Barry Duffield, Gordon Lord, Donald Parfitt, Malcolm Beet, Kenneth Hanson.

Opening Match, 2000, at Bellholme

Chapter 10

Clubs and Competitions

The 20th Century saw a variety of recreational activities, some of which flourished while others were fleeting. The briefest were walking competitions.

<u>Walking Competitions</u>

Todmorden's terrain of high hills, falling steeply into deep valleys was perhaps too challenging for competitive walking. However, possibly inspired by publicity for a one-off 'walking match' between Lancashire and the Rest of England on 4 July 1903, there were half a dozen high profile races in the space of four weeks.

On 20 June 1903 thousands lined the streets to witness a circular race organised by Todmorden Cycling Club. The course from Todmorden via Littleborough, Blackstone Edge, Cragg Vale and Mytholmroyd, was too much for some of the 21 entrants, and 'a few of the stragglers…abandoned the task as hopeless and caught the train back from Mytholmroyd'. JW Greenwood did not get that far as he was disqualified for sprinting along Littleborough Flat. The event was, nevertheless, deemed a great success and was followed by races on consecutive Saturdays organised by Walsden Cricket Club, and a Walking Fête which attracted a crowd of 3000 to the Holme field. This event featured four concurrent races including a one mile ladies' race. Remarkedly, having built up such local interest, the craze had been played out.[1]

<u>Roller Skating</u>

A more commercially driven craze was roller skating. It had last swept the district in the 1880s and returned in 1909 when 212 companies were registered in twelve months across the north of England. In June of that year Todmorden Petty Sessions heard five applications, by private speculators, to play music at their rinks. A curious prerequisite was that the venues also had to be licensed for dancing.[2]

Three of them, the Co-operative Hall and Union Street rinks in Hebden Bridge, and the Phoenix Rooms (also the home of the Phoenix Miniature Rifle Club) at Millwood, Todmorden, were

OLYMPIA

Skating Rink, Burnley Road,

TODMORDEN.

OPEN DAILY.

Morning 10 to 12, Afternoon 2 to 5, Evening 7 to 10.

Orchestral Band in attendance.   Refreshments at Reasonable Charges.

Admission 6d., Skates 6d. Children under 14, Half-price.
Morning Session, 6d., including Skates.

12 ADMISSION TICKETS, 4/6.   12 ADMISSION & SKATE TICKETS, 9/-.

The Best Floor in East Lancashire.

Cloak Room & Lavatories provided.   Skate Fixing Free.

Professional Instructors in attendance. The Best of Everything.

PIANO SUPPLIED BY T. PARKER, YORK-STREET.

Roller Skating at the Olympia, August 1909

quickly passed. Safety concerns were expressed about skating 'into a fireplace where the ginger beer bottles were stored' at Castle Grove United Methodist Chapel, and skating down the unprotected open staircase at the Sobriety Hall. Only the Sobriety Hall was denied its music and dancing licence - although the skating, which was identified as the greater cause of danger, could continue.[3]

The most impressive of the local rinks was opened two months later. Speculators leased the bottom of the garden of Ridgefoot House on Burnley Road and constructed the Olympia Skating Rink, a corrugated iron building with a 102 by 54 feet maple floor, tea room, orchestra balcony, refreshment area and electric lighting. On the opening night, a fancy dress skating carnival attracted 600 skaters, plus a further 600 spectators, and many more were locked out. The speculators' lease closed with a similar event in December, by when the craze was on the wane.[4]

Knur and Spell

Knur and spell flourished across northern regions and especially in the Pennine area for many years, fuelled by betting, which was an integral part of its appeal. An account in the *London Morning Post* in November 1912 by ET Osbourne evokes the flavour and evolution of the game:

> In the days of my boyhood…in the hilly borderland between Lancashire and Yorkshire I often attended knur and spell matches. It was seldom merely a case of knur and spell. Barrels of home-made ale and baskets (also used for the transportation of carrier pigeons) full of 'belly-timber'…would be taken to the meeting place, and…invariably…some of the spectators waxed quarrelsome when too much liquor had aroused the Celt in them, and there would be improvised fights with the naked fists, and, worse still, puncing matches or kicking contests with brass toed clogs, all collectively known as 'gradely feighting' by the fortunate spectators.
>
> It is greatly feared that the fighting that followed rather than the knur and spell match was the real cause of the gathering together in these sky-high places, where policemen were emphatically not…for many miles around. On one occasion, the fat goose, the prize of victory, was nowhere to be found after the match and on that glorious day the knur and spell men themselves fought with their pommels or clubs.
>
> Today [1912] knur and spell matches are generally played decently and in order on enclosed grounds…There is probably more money in the game now for the highly-qualified expert, and yet I am very sure it is not nearly so popular as it was thirty of forty years ago, when many schoolboys living in the Pennine Region, of which Robin Hood's Rock on Blackstone Edge is the central point, possessed a rough and ready set of implements, a rude pommel, and a crude wooden trap to throw the ball up.
>
> Last time I tramped through that countryside, nowhere did I see schoolboys engaged in 'knur-laiking': wherever three or four were gathered together in a field they had a football and almost always, sad to say, a round football.

Requiring little in the way of equipment it was cheap and easy to organise. Whilst Todmorden was still developing as a valley-bottom town, there were still large open areas where knur and spell were played. The lower part of Halifax Road towards Stansfield Bridge was a popular venue, followed later by the Holme field adjacent to the Hare and Hounds Inn. The survival of knur and spell into the twentieth century was in part down to the substantial amounts of money involved in professional contests. As well as side betting on the outcome, stake money was raised by each player and his backers. A typical amount, £30 per side - about £2000 at today's values - was the stake for a match between Todmordians James Sutcliffe and John Crossley at the Hare and Hounds in July 1901.[5] This event was abandoned because one of the players contended that the Holme field was 'not of sufficient dimensions for the proper playing of the game'.

There were two basic types of knur and spell contest. The first was decided by the cumulative distance achieved over an agreed number of rises (hits), with units of distance measured in scores (20yds). One such contest involved Tom Greenwood of Todmorden and J Dean of Burnley over thirty rises at Halifax Racecourse in August 1897. Odds of 5:4 were laid on the favourite Dean, but despite striking nine score on four occasions to Greenwood's one, three 'clean misses' scuppered the Burnley man's chances. Greenwood's total was 223 scores (4460yds) to Dean's 213 scores (4260yds).

The second and, after the turn of the century, most popular type of match was 'longest knock', where the longest distance achieved in an agreed number of attempts won. This speeded up the event for spectators as it was not necessary to measure most of the hits, and it encouraged power rather than safe hitting, as misses were not costly. Greenwood struck the knur significantly further under these rules than he had at Halifax the previous year, beating A Marshall by 12½ score (250yds) to 10½ (210yds), before 500 spectators at the Hare and Hounds in October 1898.[6]

Occasional matches between enthusiastic amateurs were reported, but even then a stake was deemed necessary. At the Hare and Hounds in March 1905, Thomas Helliwell (Castle Street) beat James Barratt (Woodhouse) by 93 score to 86 over 20 rises 'for beef steak puddings...Helliwell, hearing of Barratt not being satisfied with his defeat, will play him again for either black puddings or white ones'.[7]

Hosting knur and spell matches was lucrative for local publicans. The Roebuck, Bird i' th' Hand, Shannon and Chesapeake, Shepherds Rest and Black Horse all staged occasional events but the Hare and Hounds remained the main venue until, with the

Knur and Spell, Heyhead c1920, Barker Halstead demonstrates.

building of Hare Mill in 1907 and the creation of the bowling green at the Hare and Hounds in 1908, the sport moved to the uplands. Then Mr Uttley, the enterprising landlord of the Rose and Crown, ran a tournament involving weekly heats, which lasted from early summer until autumn - developing these one-off windfalls into a season-long source of income. By 1912 he had so many entrants that the final was not played until October.[8]

Continuing its popularity after World War I, Haugh Top on the Mankinholes hillside was the venue when two locals, Barker Halstead and Wally Schofield, played a longest knock match over 20 rises, using a wooden knur, for a stake of £100. Halstead's longest knock of 12 score and 5yds (245yds) beat Schofield's by 7yds.

By the 1930s a series of handicap matches were held annually at Heyhead, below the Shepherds' Rest Inn on the Longfield hillside. Typical of these, the 1934 tournament began in July and the final heats, the 13th and 14th , were held on 11 August with the final on 8 September. These were closely contested; the scores for the longest knock with handicap included were:

W Schofield	10 score	14 yds	2 ft	1 inch
H Shut	10 score	14 yds	2 ft	0 inch
W Whitham	10 score	14 yds	0 ft	9 inch
Walker	10 score	9 yds	2 ft	7 inch

Todmorden veteran player Barker Halstead presented the prizes at a good old fashioned meal and concert held that evening at the Shepherds' Rest.

In 1940 a contest at Heyhead, using ½ ounce pot knurs and 4 feet spells, for the longest knock over 20 rises per contestant for a stake of £20, attracted 200 spectators. Although its popularity waned there are still those who remember, in the post-war years, Sunday morning 'billet' matches drawing large crowds to the Haugh Top venue where, no doubt, much betting took place.

The billet, a piece of wood, was balanced on the flat side near the end of an otherwise cylindrical long hitting stick. It was flicked into the air by the contestant and then hit as far as possible with the stick, the longest knock winning the day.

The fore-mentioned Mr Uttley of the Rose and Crown, having tasted success with his knur and spell contests, kept his regulars entertained by switching to another contemporary staple of the pubs and betting fraternity - pigeon shooting. The *Todmorden Herald* of 6 March 1901 provides a vivid description of the sport.

Pigeon Shooting

£25 stakes are handed over from each man to the referee, which suggests that we have come into a land of golden promise, and that stories of lack of work in the mills, and...pinching and scraping in the little house to 'give th'little uns a bit to ait,'...are myths. When money is scarce, so too, is indulgence in sport restricted, but when the looms are rattling from morn to night, and th'owd woman has been thought of first, the bread-winner is never short of a 'peaund' or two with which to support the local champion in a trial of skill.

We join the crowd of sportsmen on the high hills.

We witness the setting out of the traps and the marking out of the boundary line...we are disinclined to refuse the proffered flask which a square-jawed individual in drab coloured corduroys unearths from the depths of a capacious pocket which has too surely held many a grouse and rabbit, slaughtered perhaps not quite according to the cannons of shooting orthodoxy.

...the rivals decide by the spin of a coin who shall go to the mark first, and whilst the mixed and typical Yorkshire crowd behind the ropes indulge in the luxury of backing

Billet Match on Midgley recreation ground, Jack Horsfield is about to strike.

either the bird or the gun for a modest shilling, the referee superintends the loading of the guns...each shot must only contain one ounce of shot. Very solemnly...does the competitor fill up the little brass measure provided by the referee, and still more solemnly does the referee run a pencil flush over the edges of the cup to see that not one single pellet too many is contained therein.

The defeated competitor acknowledges...that he has been outshot, and his supporters bear their losses without murmur and clatter down the mountainside to seek the warmth of the inn fire, where, amid the fragrant-smelling steam of hot toddy, they see fifty golden sovereigns handed over to the winner, and pass the evening in shooting the match over again. Men who, believing with those in authority that pigeon-shooting is perhaps the fairest method by which the relative skill of two guns in shooting on the wing may be decided, have little sentimental objection to the sport.

Not everyone shared this view, as a letter to the same newspaper made clear.

Sir, - Will you allow me once more to lift up my voice...in indignant protest against the blackguardly pastime of pigeon-shooting which meets with such favour in this neighbourhood...In my opinion the sport is both cowardly and demoralising and exists simply and solely for betting purposes...The sport may not be illegal but betting most assuredly is and I cannot understand how it is the police never interfere. They must know when the matches are to take place, and if they attend they must see the betting, unless they close their eyes.[9]

An effective riposte highlighted class bias towards the grouse-shooting gentry.

...whatever may be said in condemnation of pigeon-shooting as cruel and degrading will apply with equal force to the sport of the gentry. To admire, or regard with complacency, or excuse the latter while denouncing the former as low and wicked and vulgar...[is] sheer cant and hypocrisy.[10]

Sometimes landlords organised competitions open to any number of entrants but it was the professional contests which attracted the biggest crowds. Over 1000 turned up to see two of the Calder Valley's best exponents, W Claydon of Warley and James (Jim at Knowle) Sutcliffe of Todmorden on 27 January 1906. The bookmakers went home happy as the match was drawn, each hitting five out of fifteen birds.[11]

The *Sporting Chronicle* facilitated fixture planning in a number of sports and Sam Wilson, local athlete and bookmaker, ran in several events organised through the newspaper in his twenty years career. Nearing the end in athletics, Wilson appeared in professional pigeon shooting in 1912. By 1914 he was proficient enough to shoot for a £25 stake before 500 spectators at Elland Cricket Club, beating W Wedgewood of Halifax by 6 hits out of 15, to 4. That night Wilson's winnings, plus property worth £100, were stolen from his Industrial Street home.

> Wilson returned with a considerable sum of money in his possession. The perpetrator of the theft must have been aware of this fact and made good use of his knowledge.[12]

Pigeon shooting was one of the more difficult sports for the enthusiastic amateur. Around the turn of the century a party of Todmorden amateurs arranged for a shoot at Longfield and ordered 30 pigeons from a dealer in Littleborough, who later wrote:

> Gentlemen, - I beg sincerely to thank you for your patronage, and to intimate that I shall be only too happy to supply you with any number of birds on future occasions of the kind. The whole of the 30 for which you paid me at the rate of eight pence per head returned home in safety, bringing with them moreover, a stray pigeon. My price to your party will henceforth be 1½d per head.

An even more hapless, if perhaps apocryphal, performance was reported of a Todmorden tradesman in the late nineteenth century.

> When the first bird was released from the trap, it showed its contempt for and defiance of the novice with the gun by perching on top of the receptacle from which it had just been turned. The man at the mark…immediately fired in the direction of the impudent feathered biped, but it merely hopped too and fro, head on one side, cooing softly…The gunner…'blazed away'; still the pigeon, far from being hurt, was not so much as scared.

PIGEON RACING.

NORTH-EAST LANCASHIRE FEDERATION OF FLYING CLUBS.—The Todmorden section of the above Federation had a race from Swindon on Monday last—distance 151 miles. 258 birds were sent by 33 competitors, and were liberated at 10 20 a.m. The following are the velocities (in yards per minute) recorded by the local birds which competed :—

Barstow and Barker	1161·42
F. Sutcliffe	1153·32
J. M. Firth	1136
B. Simpson	1128
Oldfield and Shawforth	1126
G. Evans	1114
Barstow and Barker	1103
M. Fielden	1092
Barstow and Barker	1000
E. Bancroft	1068

YOUNG BIRD AVERAGE.

Hoyle and Greenwood	1042
E. Bancroft	1024
Fielden Bros.	1016

Pigeon Racing 1908

Homing Pigeons 2010, almost a mile a minute for Phil's winner. Recording methods are remarkably similar in 1908.

HOMING

Almost a mile a minute for Phil's winner

TWELVE members of Todmorden Homing Society had 312 pigeons at Wolleston last Saturday.

Liberated into a light south west wind, the race was fast and easy.

First to clock was Phil Williams, his bird flying 84 miles in 89 minutes, just in front of Lee Brennan in second with Damien and Bill Fleming in third.

Phil also demonstrated a magentic attraction to money by winning the lucky minute!

Next week's race is from Wolleston.

Result: 1, P. Williams, 1669.45; 2, L. Brennan, 1663.07; 3, Fleming and Son, 1659.76; 4, Mr and Mrs Fisher, 1659.03; 5, Brennan in second, 1658.56; 6, L. Brennan, 1658.26; 7, Fleming and Son, 1657.96; 8, L. Brennan, 1656.76; 9, Winterbottom and Pomfret, 1654.83; 10, Cullinane and Son, 1605.42; 11, K. Thorp, 1604.16; 12, B. Sheard, 1572.06; 13, F. J. Hunter, 1505.38; 14, C. E. and C. W. Roberts, 1480.05; 15, Walker and Horsfall, 1364.40; 16, Mr and Mrs Gengler, 1083.37.

It stood still for a full minute, looking the unskilled amateur in the face…The weapon was reloaded, the callous bystanders urged the shooter to 'have another go' but the latter retorted…'No gentlemen, I will not shoot at a standing bird.'[13]

This, to us rather barbarous, sport died out after the First World War, although pigeons still feature in the local Homing Society. A more legitimate use of the gun was encouraged by the founding of the Calder Valley Rifle Club.

Calder Valley Rifle Club

The Calder Valley Rifle Club came into existence in response to a national campaign following the British army's experiences during the Boer War.

…thousands of young men volunteered for the South African War, many of whom had hardly handled a rifle before. A pitiful thing it was to let them go to face the Boers, every man of whom, from sixteen to sixty, knew how to shoot and take correct aim.[14]

Lord Roberts, who as Field Marshall Earl Roberts masterminded eventual victory over the Boers, spearheaded sustained propaganda throughout the decade, which mobilised both military and civilian forces to improve Britain's rifle-shooting skills.

I am convinced that it is a matter of the highest importance, not only to the regular army and the ancillary forces of the country, but to the Empire at large, that rifle shooting should be made a national pursuit, and skill with the rifle a national accomplishment, in the same manner that archery and skill with the long-bow were so considered in the olden days of England.[15]

Inspired by patriotism and an enthusiasm for shooting, several gentlemen of Hebden Bridge founded the Calder Valley Rifle Club on 25 October 1900. Unlike other towns Hebden Brudge did not have a volunteer force. Todmorden had its volunteer G Company Lancashire Fusiliers, who practised shooting at Facit, next to the railway line between Bacup and Whitworth. The new rifle club would not only fill a military void but provide a facility for civilians the length of the Calder Valley.

Land was leased on Lord Savile's Johnny House estate, high on Midgley Moor, above Old Town. The house was to be the club room and armoury, with the range on the hillside behind. 800 yards from the house, tons of earth were excavated to form a target area 16 feet deep, 40 feet long and 10 feet wide. 16 tons of sleepers banked the sides, and butts (shooting sites) were erected at intervals along the 800 yards back towards the house. Concern was expressed about a public footpath, which ran between the butts and targets but the inspectors passed the range as 'most excellent and perfectly safe', a red flag on the hill to the right of the targets deemed sufficient to warn of shooting in progress. The range was ready by July 1901 and after a few weeks' practice and tuition, there were 39 entrants to the club's first internal competition on 21 September.[16]

The range was recognised as one of the best in the country and, with a membership of 220 in March 1903, the club had quickly grown to be one of the biggest. However the membership fell to 150 by the following year, as initial interest waned, the weather on such exposed moorland being an unrelenting test, not only of skill but enthusiasm, resolve and fortitude. A match in April 1902 went ahead 'in spite of cyclonic weather which at that altitude took the form of a high storm of wind and snow…The snow was blowing in their faces as they took their sights at the target, but they persevered until 40 rounds had been delivered, when the markers refused to stay any longer'. The markers went on strike again in June of that year, a blizzard halting a match against the Todmorden Fusiliers.[17]

'Very serviceable shelters' were erected in 1905 at the 200 and 600 yard butts, which it was hoped would 'have an appreciable effect in improving membership'. A stove providing 'welcome refreshments on the spot' followed at the 600 yard mount. But the *Hebden Bridge Times and Calder Vale Gazette* cited other obstacles over which the club had little control:

> ...getting to that range means a long and arduous walk...the public generally speaking...have not tumbled to Lord Roberts's idea that it is the duty of every Englishman to learn how to shoot...[and most tellingly] the expense, week after week, is too great.[18]

At the annual presentation evening in November 1903, club president Handley Ashworth acknowledged that 'the cost is prohibitive to a very large section of the young men who wish to practise shooting' and desired the War Office to encourage the many new rifle clubs by providing cheaper ammunition.[19] There was a sincere desire to teach the masses and in Harry Ashton the club had a remarkable tutor. A natural with a rifle he had learned to shoot with the 7th West Yorkshire (Leeds) Rifles, which he joined in the 1870s, becoming their outstanding marksman before retiring with the rank of colour sergeant in 1890, when he moved to Hebden Bridge. Ashton won the first internal competition in 1901 and coached virtual novices into more than holding their own in annual matches against the military volunteers of Todmorden, Halifax, Brighouse, Huddersfield and Bradford.[20]

When, in September 1906, the War Office, dissatisfied with the progress of rifle-shooting nationally, ordered 3,000,000 rounds of ammunition to be distributed to clubs using the new miniature rifle, the Calder Valley Club reacted swiftly. Within a fortnight the Calder Valley Miniature Rifle Club was formed, with 'the object of providing instruction and practice...among the youth of the district, ultimately inducing them to use the bigger range at Johnny House'. Secretary and treasurer, Harry Ashton helped to secure a 33ft long room at Hebble End for the club's range, which was opened to members in late October. Rifle shooting was now a year-round sport.[21]

The National Society of Miniature Rifle Clubs was five years old, but under Ashton's tuition and captaincy the Calder Valley team was unbeaten in matches against more experienced clubs, including two against the impressive Todmorden Phoenix Club based at Millwood. This included former Todmorden cricketers Jonas Clegg junior and Johnny Horsfall. In March 1907 at Dean Clough Institute, Calder Valley won the Club Championship of Halifax and District, a feat they repeated in 1908.[22]

The authorities dropped the licence duty for guns used on affiliated clubs' premises and organised a national miniature rifle competition for 1908.[23] Receiving a bye in round one, Calder Valley was drawn against unlikely 2nd round opponents, Falkirk Congregational. The teams did not travel but shot on their own range. Six players had seven shots from seven yards under the supervision of an independent range officer and the score was wired to the opposition. Victories over teams from Falkirk, Sheffield, Doncaster and Carnforth saw the Calder Valley team in the last eight with finals to be held at Birmingham Town Hall on 16 May 1908. There they beat Trelau from South Wales before losing to eventual winners Birmingham Central in the semi-final. They received their bronze medals from the president of the society, Lord Roberts, who used his presentation speech to promote the Territorial Army, the latest initiative 'to try to get men to take an interest in the defence of their country'.[24] In February 1909 the *Hebden Bridge Times and Calder Vale Gazette* put the blame firmly at the door of sporting distractions:

> The recruitment is slow and it is not being taken up by our young men…Their games and amusements must be attended to…cricket and other games in the summer, football, billiards, hockey etc in the winter, and golf at all times - and no time is left for the deliberate cultivation of patriotic sentiments and habits…The National Service League has issued an appeal for a four months compulsory training of all youths between the ages of eighteen and twenty. This is signed by Lord Roberts, the Duke of Wellington, Lord Meath, Lord Milner, Lord Cortin and Lord Raglan.[25]

Their lordships were more encouraged by the progress in miniature rifle shooting, the number of clubs increasing from around 400 in 1906 to 5000 by January 1909. Despite greater competition, the Calder Valley men were again Northern Area champions and took their place on finals' day at the Temperance Hall, Birmingham, where they were beaten in the final by Edgbaston Hotel by a mere two points, the result being decided by the final shot of the match.[26]

In September 1909 England shot against South Africa in the first air-rifle shooting international. Each side had 60 shooters, the best 20 to count, of whom Calder Valley's AR Edwards (7th) and Harry Ashton (8th) contributed valuably to England's victory. The same pair scored again in victories over South Africa in 1910 and 1912, and a defeat in 1911.[27]

Despite the best efforts of organisers to ensure fair conduct, there were deep suspicions of cheating in postal matches. 1908 had seen a few cases in which 'the targets had been tampered with…the shot holes had not been made by air-rifle pellets'. In the 3rd round on their way to the finals of 1909, Calder Valley's accusations that Hull Central had cheated were justified but rather than contest the charges, Hull destroyed their targets.[28]

The Calder Valley Club retained a good reputation and won most of a series of 'postal' friendly matches against opponents as far afield as Winchester and Whitehaven. Lord Roberts was made an honorary vice-president of the club in 1911 but the sport, both indoors and out, was losing momentum. Only two teams entered the previously popular Halifax and District Cup in 1911. The summer repairs and improvements to the Johnny House range were unsuccessful in attracting greater numbers to long-range shooting. The Miniature Rifle Club was also losing members and, no longer able to afford a private clubroom, became affiliated to a public house, Harry Ashton reluctantly negotiating the use of a room at the Neptune Hotel.[29]

During World War II the Hebden Bridge Home Guard used Wood Top Delph as a firing range. This range was used after the war when the Wood Top Rifle Club was founded. Amongst its founders was a member of F & H Sutcliffe Ltd, makers of sectional buildings, who may have influenced their move to a long wooden building situated below the railway embankment near Fallingroyd. For many years the large white letters WOOD TOP RIFLE CLUB painted on the roof could be seen clearly. In the early 1960s the club relocated to a base at Jumble Hole, near Sandbed. Here rifle shooting took place indoors and pistol shooting outdoors. A further move took the Wood Top Rifle Club to Adamroyd Mill, Todmorden, where it remained until 2007 when the mill was scheduled for demolition, since when the club has remained dormant.

Shooting locally is now in the hands of three clay pigeon clubs: Todmorden Gun Club shoots at the Shepherds' Rest, Langfield; the Sportsman's Arms Gun Club has a range behind the inn (known also as Kebs) at the old Redmires Dam; and the Cloughhead Gun Club operates near the top of Bacup Road.

Todmorden Cycling Club

National movements also took a hold locally, the earliest being cycling which flourished for over 60 years. The Todmorden club attained its 50th birthday in 1943 but postponed its celebrations until 1947 when the war was over and members who had served in the forces could attend. A founder member from 1892, Mr R Stephenson, gave his recollections. He said that 14 cyclists accepted the invitation to meet at Stansfield's Temperance Hotel (on the site of today's Yorkshire Bank) and by the end of the first season there were 30 members; now (1947) there were over 100. They rode the 'safety bike' with solid rubber tyres but later their cycles had 'cushion' tyres and later 'pneumatic' ones. The first of these had a rubber air tube in a canvas bag, with the outer cover solutionised to the rim - it took two hours to mend a puncture. The roads were in a terrible condition; after leaving Portsmouth, the road became two ruts all the way to Burnley.

First Meeting held February 29th, 1892, at Stansfield's Temperance Hotel, Todmorden.

John Learoyd was voted to the chair.

Moved by John Greenwood and seconded by George Townsend : "That this meeting resolve itself into a Cyclists' Club to be known as the Todmorden Cycling Club."

"That an entrance fee of one shilling be charged each member, and the Annual Subscription not less than two shillings for each member."

All present (fourteen in number) gave in their names and paid their entrance fees :— J. Learoyd, J. Ridgeway, J. Greenwood, R. Stephenson, W. Mackriel, W. Midgley, J. W. Sutcliffe, J. H. Clewer, J. E. Mills, G. Townsend, J. Crossley, A. Taylor, John Knowles, F. Halstead.

And the following joined during the season 1892 :—W. H. Cockroft, Jos. Knowles, J. Bailey, T. H. Bancroft, G. Clayton, E. Ogden, C. Broadbent, A. Clarkson, H. Newell, J. Sunderland, H. H. Cunliffe, E. Lord, J. W. Fielden, T. R. Sparks, J. E. Stott, J. Robinson, W. Sutcliffe, A. Wood, W. Stott, A. West.

Todmorden Cycling Club, inaugural meeting.

The club never turned out without a bugler, who rode at the back and sounded his bugle if anyone 'came a cropper'. The roads were so dusty that the bugler, having all the dust thrown back at him, returned home looking like a miller.

The *Todmorden Herald* commented that competition brought the prices (of cycles) down by the mid-1890s and 'the working classes, finding the recreation healthy, inexpensive and enjoyable, entered into it with ardour'. By 1901 hundreds of bicycles could be seen on the streets of Todmorden in the course of a week, yet, despite their huge popularity, the sales of bicycles still reflected the local economic patterns. Cycle-maker Herman Edgar Barker, having traded profitably at his Millwood Phoenix Works from 1898 to 1903, went out of business in 1905 after 18 months depression in trade.[30]

The bicycle was one of the great liberators of women and from around 1893 there was an increase in the number of lady cyclists in the district. A further development in independence came in the summer of 1898 when long skirts were condemned by a resolution of the West Riding Association of Cyclists Touring Club, swayed by a letter from Viscountess Harberton which said:

> Skirts are easily disarranged by the wind and are a constant source of danger. Rapid motion, flying wheels, whirling machinery are but ill-adapted to the close contact of floating drapery.[31]

A Mrs Van Gelden concurred, adding support for the revolutionary and, to many, shocking garb now being displayed:

> ...in the North of England, especially in Yorkshire, the people claim above everything else to be practical...knickerbockers reduce the laundry bills![32]

Norris and Herman Barkers' Phoenix Mill cycle works, Millwood, 1902

Many were unprepared for this sudden shift. When a local farmer's wife was asked for directions by a 'beknickerbockered' lady cyclist, she concealed her in the porch 'out of sight of the men folk'. She then returned with an old skirt of her own, believing the cyclist had accidentally lost hers on the road.

A group of cyclists arriving at Hardcastle Crags in May 1898 were the object of abuse from some young men. The local reporter commented:

> The writer feels somewhat ashamed of the nasty reception which the Hebden Bridge youngsters gave to young women who wore the latest invention of female attire known as bloomers.[33]

Cycling elicited other reactions:

> Many who used to be found in Church every Sunday morning now spend their Sabbath leisure, at least on fine days in...country excursions...churches are being emptied through the cycle.

The cycling season ran from April to September. Sunday was the only full day away from work and clubs organised a full season of 'runs' for their members. The annual brass band contest at Belle Vue, Manchester, and Military Sunday Service which consistently attracted over 10,000 visitors to York, were favourites of both the Todmorden and Hebden Bridge clubs.[34]

The keenest cyclists remained undaunted by the weather as witnessed by the Todmorden club's visit to Blackpool, which began at midnight on Good Friday 1900. 'The wheelers started out with grim determination in their hearts and a howling wind in their teeth.' After several punctures, heavy rain drove the riders, 'now sorry they had come' to take shelter in a shed at Freckleton. They eventually reached

Cycling advertisement, 1907

Blackpool at 8am. Three hours in the resort was enough before another eight hours journey home: '…the return journey was run over slippery roads…the whole lot, considering the roads, weather and distance having had quite enough.'[35]

Local parades often featured an eclectic mix of cyclists in fancy dress, their machines decorated with ribbons, banners and flowers, either for entertainment or to promote a social, political, religious or commercial cause: for example in 1906, both the Todmorden Lifeboat Demonstration (which raised £324 that year) and the annual Littleborough Cycle Parade featured local church groups, temperance organisations, suffragettes and a motorbus.[36]

Given the state of the roads it seems amazing that cycling became so popular. Paved roads were rare. In Todmorden the paved section from the Town Hall along Rochdale Road to the canal bridge was known as 'Pavement'. If most roads were bad some were notoriously so, Sowerby Bridge being particularly dreaded by cyclists. 'I don't think the people there pay any rates', commented a Rochdale cyclist in 1910. Tuel Lane, then as now a main artery between Huddersfield and the Calder Valley, taxed even the strongest legs.[37]

Todmorden Cycling Club, c1905

I never heard of a cyclist riding up or down. If I did I should expect to hear that he was dead…you've got to climb down, hanging on to your cycle with both hands and digging your heels into every crevice. I quite believe the best way to go up Tuel Lane is by balloon.[38]

Todmorden presented other problems as highlighted by the *Hebden Bridge Times and Calder Vale Gazette*:

Todmorden people have a very peculiar fancy for promenading on the road and leaving the footpath almost vacant…Frequently on summer evenings, when the road is dry, Todmorden pedestrians can be seen walking leisurely about the town five or six abreast, and the warning ring of the cyclist is almost totally disregarded.[39]

Another local cyclist agreed:

Yes it's a most extraordinary thing, and what one never meets with in other towns. I was at Burnley…just as people were assembling at Turf Moor

Cyclist, c1910

in thousands for an important football match. The crowd was ten times that of Todmorden tonight, and yet they kept the footpath for the most part, and I had less difficulty threading through them than I had coming through Todmorden. It looks like pure cussedness, don't it?

With Centre Vale Park recently acquired by the council, the *Hebden Bridge Times and Calder Vale Gazette* in March 1911 surmised:

Who that has ridden a bicycle or driven a conveyance through the extraordinary crowd of Sunday evening paraders will not realise the value of the…Corporation…constructing a good road just inside the Park.[40]

Cyclists were subject to stringent 'lighting up' regulations. Unlike carters in charge of horses and wagons, the gas lamps of cyclists had to be lit by sunset, which was fine when everyone could agree the time of sunset. Confusion reigned at Halifax in August 1900, the local magistrates still operating on Greenwich Mean Time two years after the Court of Appeal had established that local sunset times took precedence. As sunset in Halifax is 19 minutes later than Greenwich in August, the defendant was reprieved, the local paper concluding, 'There is really no excuse for magisterial and police ignorance of the law'.[41]

Cycling provided an escape from the grime and tedium of the working week, married or courting couples often sharing a tandem. About 30 members of the Todmorden club would set out by 5am on summer Sunday mornings for such destinations as Stainforth, Pen-h-ghent, Walton-le-dale, Burton Leonard (via Harrogate and Ripley), Knaresborough, Ingleborough, Coniston Cold and so on. When youth hostels became

Todmorden cyclist
Arthur Gledhill

available in 1930, longer weekend runs became popular.

For keen bikers there were special challenges. In 1922 the club held its first 24 hour reliability ride. Nine members set off from Skew Bridge, Gauxholme, at 6.05pm on Saturday, 9 September, to cycle to Shrewsbury and back in 24 hours - a distance of 173½ miles. Despite minor incidents - a few punctures, an animal unseating a rider by leaping across the road in the darkness and a frisky dog causing two cyclists to collide, the whole group arrived back on Sunday at 5.50pm with 15 minutes to spare claiming, 'splendid weather, good roads' but admitting to a 'wee little tiredness'.

A cherished record was the 100 mile run which entailed cycling from Scaitcliffe to Gauxholme, back again then on to Lancaster and returning to Scaitcliffe. On 6 September 1939 (3 days after the declaration of war on Germany) Norman Young left Scaitcliffe at 3am and completed the run in 5 hours 26 minutes, beating the previous year's record by 5 minutes, and meeting other members setting off on their day's run to Glasson Dock.

Although competitions and races were suspended during the war, a full syllabus of 'runs' continued. In 1946 when competitions recommenced, Arthur Gledhill, despite spending time as a Japanese prisoner of war, repeated his 1939 success by winning the '25 mile Unpaced Handicap Cup'. A special event was held on 26 August 1945 at the end of the war: leaving the Town Hall at 10am, members cycled to Sabden Fold for a sports' day comprising a slow cycle race, three legged race, sack race, egg and spoon cycle race, long jump, flat race, tug-of-war, and culminating with a tyre bursting competition!

Weekly runs were not for the faint hearted. The *Todmorden Advertiser* reported on 5 August 1949:

> Leaving Todmorden for Appletreewick on Sunday morning the local Cycling Club rode via Nelson, Earby, Skipton over Eastby Brow, Barden Tower to the New Inn Appletreewick. Unfortunately the request for tea was greeted with a sickly smile and 'You'll have to have it outside' which with a howling wind and threatening rain did not meet with approval. So leaving instructions in chalk for any latecomers the club moved on to the Manor House at Burnsall.

The afternoon ride was through Thorpe, Cracoe and Heton to Gargrave for tea. 'Riding against the wind on the homeward journey the members had to be content with a slow speed arriving home about 8pm.'

Members' Cards listed not only the planned runs, but the yearly competition winners. The 1957 card shows no competitions in 1956 and indeed 1957 was the club's final active year. Younger members were not being recruited and, given the increase in traffic - especially at weekends, cycling was no longer the pleasure it had been. The club lay dormant until, on 24 February 1964, a meeting was called at which the club was wound up.

Scouts and Guides

The scouting movement founded by Baden Powell in 1909, followed a year later by the guides, spread rapidly throughout the country, not least locally, where troops were usually attached to one or other of the churches. During World War I, when Centre Vale mansion became a military hospital, it was recorded that 'the Boy Scouts also kept up their reputation for good works, coming each evening and helping in many ways'.[42] These scouts may have been part of the 1st Lydgate Troop which was flourishing in the 1920s when it won the Calder Valley Scouts' Shield.

By 1930 scout and guide troops thrived at Vale Baptist Church, under the enthusiasm of Rev Gates. Towards the end of the 1930s they moved up the road to St Michael's Church. The author, who joined the brownies in 1942 recalls:

> In brownies, meetings began by forming a circle and reciting the Brownie Law whilst saluting. This was followed by our lining up in patrols (Elves, Fairies, Pixies, Sprites) for inspection. Brown Owl would check for clean faces, hands and nails, that hair was tidy and shoes and badges polished. She would make sure we had five items in our pocket a pencil, paper, piece of string, safety pin and a clean handkerchief . We then went to corners for instruction. This included learning to make a cup of tea, setting a fire ready for lighting, making a telephone call and an emergency call, washing up properly, stitching a button on, making a bed and other guidance for helping at home. We also played team games and always finished in a circle with a sung prayer. For the war effort we knitted squares for blankets and collected paper and jam jars from local houses. These went down into a barn at Scaitcliffe Hall. On one occasion all the Todmorden brownie packs were invited to Scaitcliffe Hall. It rained and we sang songs and played indoor games. One competition was to dress a brownie using only newspaper and scissors.
>
> At the end of the war, I moved into the Swallow patrol of the guides and proudly wore a sheath knife on my belt. Here instruction was more challenging. We learnt how to tie and use different knots. First aid was taught by a St John Ambulance nurse. From Tongue Hill across the valley to Bonks we communicated using semaphore flags and

Lydgate Scouts, c1920, winners of the Calder Valley Scouts' Shield.

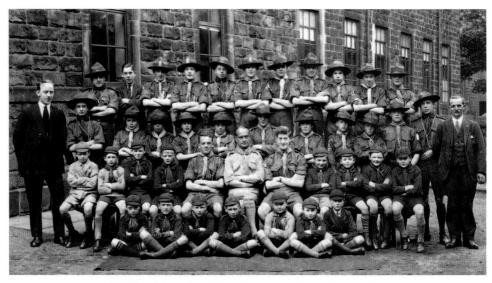

Vale Baptist Calder Valley Capt Scott Scout Troup 1930

Vale Baptist Guides and Brownies 1930

Morse code. In the summer we went tracking or stalking on the hills getting as far as Orchan Rocks. In a field above Cross Lee, local guide companies competed to cook the best meal. We collected wood, cut out sods, lit a camp fire and rigged up a tripod for dixies, eventually producing black sausage and speckled mash followed with burnt rice pudding. At least it was hot! Finally after clearing away, we replaced the sods, leaving the field in pristine condition - unlike the cooks!

Badges were awarded for successfully completing courses. My sister and her friend, Annie Sutcliffe, attempted the Campers' badge, sleeping overnight in a tent in the vicarage garden but, invaded by cats, they sped home. Brownies, guides, scouts and cubs always took part in parades and pageants; dressed as an Anglo-Saxon, I escaped the Vikings on Centre Vale Park in 1944.

The Girl Guides at St Michael's disbanded in the mid-1950s but the Boy Scouts continued under the leadership of Jack Jarman along with Keith Gavaghan, Philip Suthers and Leonard Barker. Jack recalls that shortly before 1960 the scouts severed connections with the church in order to open membership to all boys in the district. As the 7th Calder Valley troop they based themselves, firstly at Vale Baptist Church and then at the old Liberal/Labour Club, Rosebery Street. In search of a permanent base, they obtained a site next to the Frieldhurst Tavern, where, prior to going on their annual camp, the foundations for a hut had been completed. Camps were on a three year rota basis, Windermere, Scotland and Betws-y-Coed. On their return from Windermere, and much to their surprise, they found that a group of regulars from the Staff of Life Inn had erected the hut. About 1970, owing to declining numbers, the Harley Wood troop joined them. Following moves to Cornholme Methodist Church and then Cornholme School, they disbanded in the early 1980s.

Post war, there were certainly other troops of Scouts at: St Peter's, Walsden; Central Methodists; Castle Grove Methodists; and at Christ Church.

Pre-war Christ Church had a Church Lads' Brigade and Girls Friendly Society, then in 1945, Rev Black started the Scouts, which Harry Tootell took over in 1948 remaining as scout master until 1966. Under Harry's leadership the numbers increased to around 100. The Cubs were ably led for many years by Akela, Amy Holt. Harry was innovative in putting scouting activities to practical use, such as constructing bridges across streams and, when Dutch elm disease was prevalent, his scouts learned to fell diseased trees in Gorpley Wood.

The annual summer camps became legendary. Accompanied by his wife Joy and their growing family, the camps were their sole holiday. The first in 1948 was on a site near Sandsend, Whitby. Harry and Joy were unable to travel with the party, having to wait until their ironmonger's shop in Todmorden closed for the annual Wakes Week Holiday, not even closing at Saturday lunchtime. They travelled later that day by train and taxi to be pointed in the general direction of the camp by the taxi driver - 'It'll be over there somewhere'.

In 1954 a lorry, costing £35, was converted to carry the scout party of 29 plus equipment, for a fortnight's camp in Switzerland; by then the Wakes Week had become a fortnight. Scout John Hodgson, who later became scout master, sent reports to the local paper describing their adventures and in return, Waddingtons (newspaper proprietors) treated the party to a pie and pea supper in the National School. When travelling through France, John and Geoff Tizzer were answering a call of nature behind some trees where they came across a crater of live ammunition. Geoff was unhappy when told he could not keep a live mortar shell as a souvenir.

By Harry's last camp in 1966 they had graduated to owning a secondhand coach, bought from Hughes Bros near Leeds. It took them into Germany and back through Belgium with nothing worse than a puncture. On their return they called at Hughes Bros for a replacement tyre and, on seeing the coach filled to the eaves with scouts and equipment, the garage owner exclaimed 'You mean you've been to Germany and back in that! It used to belong to Bronte Coaches. It's never been further than Blackpool.'

John Hodgson, who was District Commissioner from 1979 to 86 and had over 30 years in scouting saw interest increase throughout the 1960s, followed by a decline starting in the 1970s which accelerated in the 1980s. He feels that horizons were widening for everyone, including teenagers, who became less willing to commit themselves to a regular group activity. Regardless of other interests, when the school leaving age was 15, at which time most started work, scouting, except for the keen ones took a lower priority. He hopes that experiences gained in scouting and guiding will help the boys and girls to become good, caring citizens who will put something back

Christ Church 20th Calder Valley Scouts embark for Switzerland 1954

into society, be confident, have a spirit of independence and be able to make good use of their time.

Currently there are both Guides and Brownies at Roomfield Baptist Church and two local Scout troops, which now include both boys and girls. The 26th Pennine Calder Valley Scouts meet each Thursday at the Central Methodist Church under the leadership of Dave Payne, scoutmaster since 1982. Slowly increasing in number, there are about 20 members, one third of them girls. They cater for Beavers, Cubs, Scouts and Explorer Scouts spanning the ages six to eighteen years. Acknowledging that interest can wane in the mid-teens, he organises a varied programme of activities including air rifle shooting on the local Gun Club's range behind Kebs, hiking, canoeing, rock climbing, go-carting, ice skating and archery in addition to the traditional Scout badge work. The 20th troop meets at Ferney Lee School but maintains connections with the Parish Church at monthly parade services. The facilities at Ferney Lee, especially the extensive grounds are ideal for Scouting activities such as camping. Tuesday evening sees over 70 Beavers, Cubs and Scouts there, whilst on Thursday a dozen Explorer Scouts plus the 6th Todmorden Rainbow and Brownie troop of 50 meet there. Apart from the 6th troop they comprise both boys and girls. One of the leaders, Rowena Goldthorpe re-enforces the aims of scouting as detailed previously by Harry Tootell, John Hodgson and David Payne. One highlight of the year is the Gang Show, which has been staged at the Hippodrome Theatre annually since 1965. The 2010 show in May saw 100 Scouts from across the age groups, virtually all from Todmorden, command the stage for four nights in a superb example of team work.

Still on Cue

By the early years of the 20th century, following their success in cricket and football, leagues became popular both regionally and locally. Some were contrived, such as the East Lancashire Waltzing League, encompassing Burnley, Colne, Padiham, Accrington and Clayton-le-Moors. The *Todmorden Herald* reported:

> Waltzing is the latest subject of the tournament system. The rules are that the teams (5 couples) waltz 40 yards on the outside of a mark and the team which legitimately waltzes the distance in the longest time counts the difference in seconds over its opponents as its points.[43]

Locally, billiards espoused the league format, the game having been popular for many years. When Dobroyd Castle was built in 1869, it had a billiard room.[44] The Todmorden Liberal Club opened its new rooms in Roomfield Buildings in 1876[45] and was soon playing billiard matches, which were on an 'ad hoc' basis between the political clubs.

The early years of the 20th century saw competitive tournaments begin. In November 1902 Todmorden Conservative Club was competing for the Sowerby Division Billiard Tournament Challenge Shield against other Conservative clubs in the Sowerby constituency, which stretched from Todmorden to Elland. This competition continued for several years.

In 1904 the Todmorden Border League was founded, comprising the Liberal clubs of Todmorden, Walsden and Cornholme plus Todmorden Conservative Club and the Todmorden Working Men's Club. By September 1905 it had changed its name to the Todmorden and District Orme Billiard League. 'Orme' was a famous billiard table maker who presented a shield to be won; an early form of sponsorship.[46]

In 1908 the Calder Valley Working Men's Billiard League was formed with nine teams from Todmorden to Hebden Bridge. It included one from the recently built Shore Working Men's Club, high above the Cornholme Valley, the hill presenting an additional challenge for visiting teams. In response to the popularity of billiards commercial halls were built. In 1911 the Black Cat Billiard Hall opened on Halifax Road, the premises later being part of John Bentley & Sons printers and now the site of Lidl supermarket. The Empire Billiard Hall on Rochdale Road occupied the top floor of the buildings now converted into apartments opposite the Conservative Club (recently closed and sold). Nearby was the Ceylon Billiard Hall, which took over the Post Office building when the Post Office moved to Todmorden Hall in 1924.[47]

When, in 1897, Todmorden Liberal Club moved from Roomfield Buildings to the Oddfellows Hall, it

Private Billiard Club, Todmorden, c1910

Wilson's Cornholme Bobbin Works Billiards Team,
1926 winners of Todmorden Orme Billiard League.
L-R Row 2: R Greenwood, F Dawson, JW Winder, A Pounder, A Ninnis,
H Earnshaw (works manager),
Row 1: R Hollinrake, J Knowles, JA Wilson, T Ackroyd, D Crowther.

furnished a billiard hall with three tables. Meanwhile, the Todmorden Weavers'
Association took over at Roomfield and before long was in the local billiard league. In
its turn this association moved into the newly built Weavers' Institute on Burnley Road
in 1914 with its fine billiard room in the basement.

The local league continued until World War II, the number of teams, all from clubs,
varying from six to nine. In the same period the Calder Valley League had around
eleven teams.

Billiards, at least competitively, did not survive the war. Snooker took over and by
1964 the Calder Valley Snooker League had twenty teams - albeit none from Todmorden,
which did not have a league. In the 1970s Todmorden British Legion played in the Calder
Valley League and by 1980 had been joined by Todmorden Conservative Club, which
entered four teams, three of them in Division 2. Currently the British Legion still plays
in the Calder Valley League, which has 35 teams in two divisions.

Locally 'pool' is now the popular game. Played on a small table, it can be found in
most public houses. The Todmorden league comprises about 25 teams in three
divisions.

Although the game has changed since billiards first became popular there are more
players cueing off than ever.

Todmorden Natural History Society

Todmorden Natural History Society is one of the oldest local organisations. Its roots
can be traced to the Todmorden Botanical Society, founded in 1852.[48] Re-formed more
than once, its members have walked the district, gone further afield on rambles

throughout the summer and attended a series of illustrated lectures during the winter. It currently attracts over 70 enthusiasts who follow the objects of the society 'To stimulate interest in Natural History and record observations of local nature'.

Natural History Society members studying local flora.

SUMMER SYLLABUS 2008

May 3rd	Clapham	Derek Jackson	9.35	Calder College for car share
May 10th	Colne including Canal	P & J Marshall	9.35	Calder College for car share
May 24th	The Ram,Cliviger to Burnley	E & L Fielden	10.10	Bus fr Todmorden
Jun 7th	Todmorden local walk	volunteer leader	10.00	Stansfield Rd CP
Jun 21st	Colden to Todmorden	G & V Barker	10.10	Bus to Jack Bridge fr Mytholm
Jul 5th	Greenfield (Binn Gn CP10.45)	Marolyn Colley	9.35	Calder College for car share
Jul 19th	Mytholmroyd to Heb Bridge	Charles Flynn	9.45	Mytholmroyd Rlway Station
Aug 2nd	Hebden Bridge	Miriam Adams	10.30	Hebden Bridge Marina
Aug 16th	Cromwell Bottom	P & J Marshall	9.20	Train fr Todm to Brighouse
Aug 30th	Brearley (leaving10.15)	Christine Newell	9.40	Bus fr Tod to Ellen Royd Rd
Sep 13th	Shore & Todmorden	Christine Newell	10.30	Stoney Royd Lane,Todmorden
Sep 27th	Jumble Hole	Gary Thomas	10.30	Jumble Hole Road
Oct 18th	Fungus Foray in the Crags	G & V Barker	9.55	Old Town bus fr Heb Br Rlway

Todmorden Natural History Society, summer syllabus 2008

Todmorden Photographic Society's first outing to Fountains Abbey, May 1907.
18 year-old Herbert Hardaker (extreme left) won the outing's photographic competition.

Todmorden Photographic Society

A single incident can have unexpected results as in the case of Todmorden Photographic Society. One of Todmorden's oldest mills, Lob Mill situated near Springside, Halifax Road, was redundant by 1906 and the mill chimney was to be dropped. The steeplejack, who would fell the chimney in September, offered a gold medal as a prize for the best picture of the chimney as it fell. This attracted photographers from a wide area and, locally, led to the formation of the Photographic Society.[49]

Sixty-four members enrolled in January 1907, when it opened its doors in a second floor room of Roomfield Buildings. A winter syllabus of lectures, demonstrations and competitions was arranged. In the summer, weekend rambles and excursions were planned, where wives joined in an otherwise male preoccupation. The first outing in May 1907 was to Fountains Abbey, where the competition for best photograph was won by 18 year-old Herbert Hardaker, on his way to becoming one of the town's most distinguished photographers.[50]

1910 saw the society move to a studio at Ridge, off Doghouse Road. It was a wooden hut previously occupied by a commercial photographer. Increasing membership necessitated a further move in 1924 to rooms above Wellington Road Co-op.[51] These had been reading rooms where the Co-op provided newspapers and journals, as it did at its branches throughout the district. The Photographic Society remained here for fifty years. Currently it meets in the community room in St Michael's Church, Cornholme, and having celebrated its centenary in 2007, is one of the town's oldest - and thriving - societies.

The annual exhibition, held over three days in the Town Hall, is very popular and demonstrates the wide range of subjects and techniques employed by the members; a far cry from the notice in the local paper on 16 January 1920 announcing a series of lectures by Mr Hardaker on 'The Camera and How to Use it' comprising developing, printing, enlarging and lantern slide making, which attracted about twenty students.

Photographic Society at Towneley Hall in 1954
L-R Row 2: Clara and Jack Lever, Fred Elliman, Bill Kerr, Robert Cunliffe, Arthur Barker,
Row 1: Peter Lever, Colin Lever, John Elliman, Rudy Holzapfel, Lynn Lever, Richard Holt,
____, Donald Simpson, Ann Barker.

Photographic Society at Gorpley, 2000
L-R John Crossley (seated), Roger Birch, Will Sutcliffe, Grace Anstess, Margaret Crowther,
Janet Wright, Jacqui and Roy Cordingley, Ian Wright, Douglas Wright (front), Geoff Boswell
(back), Peter Anstess, Frank Sharp.

Chapter 11

Public Recreation

When Todmorden became a borough in 1896 it had no public park or any obvious available site for one. The Ashenhurst hillside was considered, hence the name Park Road. Initially, a recreation ground was created west of Ferney Lee Road and south of the Railway (currently occupied by the residential home and Lower Ferney Lee bungalows). By May 1900 the *Todmorden Herald* noted, 'the new recreation ground at Ferney Lee is beginning to look ship shape'.[1] The higher part had a rockery, path, plants, shrubs, seats removed from outside the Town Hall, a fountain and by May 1901 was said to be looking good with 'beautiful grass' and 'adults have been keen to stop kids being a nuisance in it [the fountain]'.

Below this was the play area which was immediately popular. 'You would be surprised at the number who flock to play here on any fine evening. Mostly they play cricket - several sets of wickets can be pitched here without inconvenience to the lads engaged.' Naturally there were problems. Football was banned, because it was not intended that young fellows of 20 or so should monopolise the playground for football! It was however conceded that this was a temporary expedient. 'It will be withdrawn for winter.'[2]

Another difficulty was from:

> the constant use of the vilest and most abominable language by some of the young men and even small boys frequenting the playground, but this practice which has been far too prevalent in our streets must somehow be suppressed, otherwise old and self respecting persons, especially ladies, for whose enjoyment a portion of the enclosure is specially designed…will…be unable to use it.

Ferney Lee Park and Recreation Ground 1901

Young children's play area, Ferney Lee Park 1901

To keep order, one of the workmen employed in building the ground was 'retained as caretaker and his authority must be upheld'.[3]

The lowest part of the area was set out with swings for the younger children. There were no obvious facilities for girls in the planning of the main playing area. However, the playground was well used:

> the only objectionable feature…arises from the volumes of dense black smoke which, the wind having been easterly, blows along the valley from adjacent mills.[4]

No other development took place on the Ashenhurst site because the town acquired the Centre Vale Estate in 1910. The only conditions were that Centre Vale should never be used as either a cemetery or an infectious diseases hospital.[5] The estate comprised some 75 acres and when Mrs Greenwood of Glen View donated Ewood Wood and part of Buckley Wood, a further 13 acres were added. Designated Todmorden Centre Vale Park, the official opening was on Saturday, 30 March 1912 amidst a storm, which started as the civic procession left the Town Hall and ceased as soon as the ceremony was over. At this time the park was simply an open space for relaxation with no special facilities. The town end was allotted as a children's playing field, boys and girls being separated by a fence.

In recognition of increased interest, construction of two bowling greens began in May 1913, the local paper commenting:

> Here on the borders we are at infancy in the game of bowls. Get a bit into Yorkshire or a few miles into Lancashire and the game is not only much played but forms a very fruitful theme of conversation.[6]

The first greens in the district were in Walsden where the Hollins Inn opened its green in 1875, followed by one at Walsden Cricket Club in 1895, both still going strong. These were followed in 1899 by a green attached to the Roebuck Inn, Portsmouth, the team there entering the Burnley Bowling League that summer.[7] This green produced the district's first bowler of note when A Lord of Cornholme reached the 2nd round of the 51st annual Talbot Hotel tournament at Blackpool in September 1911. A fortnight later saw the inaugural Waterloo tournament for which the Talbot had set the blueprint.

Remarkably it was May 1908 before a green was opened in central Todmorden. This was a private venture adjacent to the Hare and Hounds Inn and, with no town club, the team was passed off as representing the town. Predictably, early matches against well established teams, including the first against the Akroydian Club from Halifax, were lost.[8] But the facility was impressive, well laid out with plenty of seating, and so popular and financially successful that some town councillors were keen to establish one on the limited area of the Ferney Lee Recreation Ground for 1909. Their recommendation was hotly opposed as it would rob the children of their playground.[9]

Todmorden played further matches in 1909, losing home and away to Hebden Bridge, but recording their first victory against Old Town at the Hare and Hounds. Amongst the early players were former Todmorden cricketers, Fred Blakey and Johnny Horsfall.[10] It is unclear whether the early greens in the district were crowned or flat but on 1 September 1909 the Hebden Bridge club, in its seventh year of existence, added a nine-inch crown to its green following a defeat on Elland's crowned green.[11]

Against a background of mounting frustration, work was suspended on the park bowling greens and the bandstand after just three months, as the Corporation prioritised its funds. This halt coincided with Portsmouth clinching the Burnley and District Bowling League championship in front of a rapturous crowd at the Roebuck.[12]

Work in the park restarted the following year, 1914. The bandstand was formally opened on Friday and Saturday, 26 and 27 June, when four concerts were given by the band of the First Life Guards to a total audience of over 16,500. The bandstand was modelled on that at Falinge Park in Rochdale. It was double boarded throughout to increase its resonance, whilst the roof was hollow and covered with felt.

The first of what would become four bowling greens was opened the following year on 11 June. The low-lying site had been raised by 3ft 6ins and a pavilion comprising bowl house, toilets and shelter, was erected. By the early 1920s there were four greens

Centre Vale Park, opening of the Bandstand, 26 and 27 June 1914

Centre Vale Park, opening of the first bowling green, 11 June 1915, by Mr JW Coombs, President of the British Crowned Bowling Association. Bowling is Robert Jackson, Mayor of Todmorden, with Alderman William Ormerod behind.

Walsden Bowling Club 1981 winners of Todmorden and District Bowling League Divisions 1, 2, and 3, plus the Dearden Cup.
L-R Row 3: Alan Hall, Billy Mutch, Mick Watson, Brian Horsfall, Keith Cryer, Brian Howley, Eric Wilson, Roy Connor,
Row 2: Jack Coupe, Colin Price, Kevin Hird, Russell Sutcliffe, Keith Rudman, Graham Hird, Garth Hall, Jesse Fielden, Geoff Helliwell,
Row 1: Mark Howley, Fred Jackson, Tom Lord, Howard Hughes, Jim Allonby, Arthur Crossley, John Sutcliffe, Bob Tyler.

Aerial View of Centre Vale Park, mid 1920s

in the park, which were the last to be built in the district. In 1923 came a proposal to form a Todmorden and District Bowling League. The idea was not to draw the clubs away from their current leagues, as most of the new matches would be played on mid-week nights or a club could run two teams. The clubs suggested for the new league were Roebuck, Walsden Cricket and Bowling, Hollins, Greenvale (Summit), Savile (Hebden Bridge), Todmorden Park and Hare and Hounds. The league commenced in 1924 and has continued ever since, although with many changes in membership.

The Hare and Hounds club did not survive World War II and its once spacious green is now a tarmacadamed car park. Some local clubs have always played in more than one league. In 1951 Portsmouth (Roebuck) were also in the Burnley and District League, whilst both Walsden and Todmorden Park competed in the Hebden Royd Amateur Bowling Association.

For many years the Todmorden Park Veterans were a powerful force in bowling circles. In September 2001 the green at Portsmouth closed, owing to a disagreement between the bowlers and the Roebuck Inn, but the Todmorden and District League continues. Its teams represent the Hare and Hounds, Rose and Crown and the Catholic Club all using the Centre Vale Park greens, plus the Hollins and Walsden clubs and also the Wardle, New Street and Hare Hill clubs from the Rochdale Valley. This gives a two-division league comprising 16 teams from 8 constituent clubs. When the two-division Veterans' League is included, the total rises to 37 teams from 14 clubs.

The next development on the park was for tennis. By 1921 there were three courts, on the land now occupied by the car park below the Sports Centre, these being the first public courts in the district. Until this time tennis had been an elitist sport, the only local club being Hollins Tennis Club formed in 1881 at the Hollins Inn, Walsden, and

Hollins Tennis Club 1904

Hollins Tennis Team 1953 winners of Hebden Bridge and District 'B' League Trophy.
L-R Row 2: Derek Crabtree, Jack Taylor, Harold Hirst, Donald Whitehead,
Row 1: Jennifer Ashworth, Sylvia Forbes, Dennis Forbes (c), Jenny Cockcroft,
Pat Greenwood.

Todmorden Park Tennis Team, 1952 Champions of Hebden Bridge and District Tennis League.
L-R Row 2: D Greenwood (treas), F Turner, J Lofthouse, DM Horsfall, G Varley, J Clayton,
E Hartley (sec),
Row 1: D Marshall, E Marshall, T Horsfall (c), B Barker, L Bastow.

playing on a levelled area above Henshaw Wood. Later, in 1890, the club moved to its present home at The Grove behind Stansfield Hall but retained its name Hollins.[13]

The local press records Hollins playing Southholme at Manchester in 1899 and 1900 and, in 1902, playing a representative party from Manchester, which included the North of England champion, the Manchester visitors winning by one match. In the same year the club beat Kirkheaton, Huddersfield, by 8 matches to 4 with 1 drawn.[14]

The park tennis courts were in response to a boom in interest following World War I. Courts were built in Cornholme adjoining and in connection with its churches, at Cornholme Methodist, Vale Baptist and the Parish Church. Also, on land usually used for poultry, a court was built next to Holyoake Terrace in Portsmouth, where most of its players lived. Todmorden Unitarian and Patmos Congregational churches built courts and two others were created at Sandholme.

Some of these clubs combined in 1921 to form the Calder Valley Tennis League, although not all joined because of lack of accommodation, which could result in loss of members if courts were devoted exclusively to league matches at weekends. The council's response was to construct a further six courts in the park, a project which also provided labour for the unemployed. The park soon had its own team and a pavilion was being built by the council.

The Calder Valley Lawn Tennis League final in 1923, between Cornholme Methodist Church (East Team) and the Park Tennis Club, was played on the Sandholme courts - admission to the ground not to be made through the gas works property! The popularity of tennis grew and another six courts were constructed on the park.

By the late 1930s competitive league tennis in Todmorden had contracted to the Hollins and Todmorden Park clubs. They competed in the Hebden Bridge and District Tennis League whose Riverdale Trophy competition in 1937 attracted 16 teams from 13 clubs.

Tennis on the park, as with all local sports, prospered in the post-war boom. Anyone wishing to book one of the 15 courts at the weekend had to be there by 2pm to avoid disappointment and the Todmorden Club's annual Tennis Tournament, as before the war, was extremely popular. However, by the mid 1960s interest was waning. The Todmorden Park club disbanded and the Hebden Bridge and District League soon followed.

Of the 15 courts on the park only three are left. A children's cycle track occupies the site of the six lower red shale courts and an all-weather sports area is where two of the six higher tarmacadam courts were sited. Todmorden Lawn Tennis Club (Hollins), competing in the Halifax and District League is the only local survivor of this once popular sport. It has an active youth section of about 40 members. During the winter months indoor coaching for youngsters (not necessarily members) takes place at Todmorden Sports' Centre and transfers after Easter to The Hollins. It is equally popular with both boys and girls. With only two courts at The Hollins and the three at Centre Vale being in too poor a state for match tennis, home matches in the Halifax League have to be played away. The club is in negotiation with Calderdale to sell its Hollins site and put the proceeds towards resurfacing the Centre Vale courts and adding a fourth.

After World War I, provision was made for children's play in the park. A circular paddling pool, built by ex-servicemen in the 1920s was followed in 1931 by a playground with swings, French swing, slide, climbing frame, 'tippling' bar, round-about, rocking horse and sandpit. In the area between the pool and playground, a boating pool was constructed in 1935. These were very popular but, given the combination of children and cold water with sparse toilet facilities, the planting of numerous rhododendron bushes can be seen as either fortuitous or far-sighted. During the 1960s the childrens' facilities were replaced by a new playground and paddling pool near the Gandy Bridge entrance to the park. Recently, as part of the flood alleviation scheme a new 'state of the art' playground has been created, again near to the Gandy Bridge entrance.

The final sporting facility on the park was the nine-hole miniature golf course on the rolling hill behind the tennis courts

The Paddling Pool, Centre Vale Park, built in the 1920s.

leading up to Ewood Hall. It was opened on Saturday, 30 July 1938, with an exhibition match between two prominent members of Todmorden Golf Club, RH (Bob) Fielden and R (Bob) Sutcliffe, the latter having been a popular hard-hitting batsman and former captain of Todmorden Cricket Club.[15]

Opening of Todmorden Golf Club at Rive Rocks 1905, after its transfer from Todmorden Edge

Todmorden Golf Club

Todmorden Golf Club was founded in 1895, with its links at Todmorden Edge and relocated to its present home across the valley at Rive Rocks in 1905. The challenging nine-hole course of 5874 yards is at a height of 925 feet above sea level and, although open to the elements, has panoramic views over the surrounding countryside.

It was for many years the domain of the business and professional members of the community. Gaining admittance was not easy. A prospective member required both a proposer and seconder from within the club and was then interviewed by club officials. If this was satisfactory the name was forwarded to a meeting of the club council, who publicised it to members. After one month the name was formally proposed at the council meeting, where fate was decided by secret ballot - five white balls and one black - if 'blackballed' the membership was rejected. Today a proposer and seconder are required along with three supporters and, of these five, three must be council members.

The secretary, Peter Eastwood, identifies the aftermath of World War II as the time when the rules relaxed slightly and the trail was blazed when he and his friend were admitted as members in 1949, whilst still at school. Given the club's situation at the top of a steep hill, he believes that owning a car is a necessity.

There are currently 180 members, including 25 ladies plus 10 juniors, drawn from Littleborough, Whitworth and Burnley as well as Todmorden. One lady member, the late Helen Gray is entered in the *Guinness Book of Records* for winning the Ladies' Championship on 32 consecutive occasions and a total of 38 times between 1951 and 1992.

A red letter day was 14 August 1962 when British Ryder Cup Captain Dai Rees and his colleague Bernard Hunt visited Rive Rocks and played an exhibition match with club members RH (Bob) Fielden and W Sutcliffe.

Opening of the Extension
to the Golf Club Premises
in 1933.

Visit to Todmorden Golf
club by Dai Rees, Ryder
Cup   Captain,   and
Bernard Hunt in August
1962.

Swimming

> In the matter of swimming baths, the Todmorden Union is far behind the age. There is
> not a single swimming bath in Todmorden or Hebden Bridge - none between Bacup,
> Burnley and Rochdale in Lancashire, and Sowerby Bridge in Yorkshire…when will this
> grave defect be remedied?

So questioned the *Hebden Bridge Times and Calder Vale Gazette* in April 1903.

For years local people had improvised their aquatic pleasures in the unsatisfactory environs of local dams and the Rochdale Canal. By the early 1900s drownings were almost a weekly occurrence and, although many were suicides, 'accidental drowning whilst bathing' was a common verdict of the local coroner.

Pressure on the local council was increased by reports of improved teaching methods

Swimmers in the Canal at Old Royd Lock, early 1900s

and results from other districts.

> The method of instructing children has evolved from an organised water scramble to
> an almost perfect science. The old idea of throwing a child in and leaving him/her to
> struggle out has been exploded.

In 1902 Leeds Board schools provided tuition for 9240 pupils, boys and girls, and
there were numerous flourishing ladies' clubs across West Yorkshire 'consisting chiefly
of girls who had been taught at school'.[16] By contrast, very few women in Todmorden
or Hebden Bridge could swim. Indeed, walking in the vicinity of bathing places could
be an ordeal. In July 1900 the *Todmorden Herald* arbitrated in a complaint from a lady
correspondent 'that what she and her party…had to encounter along the canal bank
from Sandholme was embarrassing to say the least'. The *Herald* could only advise:

> …any who wish to avoid the risk of coming suddenly upon a company of youths naked
> and unashamed will studiously turn their eyes from beholding the portion of the canal
> which runs near the gasworks, that having for many years been a favourite spot for a
> dip with lads in the locality who are not too fastidious as to the purity of the water.[17]

The canal and dams saw little swimming in 1903 'in consequence of the wretched
inclement weather', but in November the council ended a two-year investigation by
once again finding more urgent calls on the public purse:

> The public baths question has been once more shelved at Todmorden…No doubt the
> vast outlay in the sewerage works has something do with it.[18]

The situation was eased when a small pool, completed in September 1904 as part
of the new school at Shade, was made available to the public in June 1905. The first
week's figures were telling - the baths had been used by 443 men, 143 boys and 5
women.[19] Nevertheless, considering that few homes had a bathroom, this was
refreshing news.

The Shade pool was too small to stage the sort of galas enjoyed in most public baths. Sowerby Bridge, for example, where the baths were opened in 1879, enjoyed its 25th annual gala in 1904. Todmorden got a taste of what they were missing when Burnley Amateur Swimming Club held a gala before 700 spectators at Shoebroad Dam on the Longfield hillside in September 1909. The event included exhibitions by Maggie Scott of Burnley, a former Lancashire Ladies' champion, and the famous David Billington from Bacup, who had set the world record for 500 yards at Burnley baths in 1907.[20]

The nearest Yorkshire pool at Sowerby Bridge also produced a champion. In January 1912, at Batley baths, George Webster set a new world record completing the 400 yards backstroke in 6 minutes 38 seconds. He subsequently reduced this time by 20 seconds, at the gala which opened Brighouse baths in July 1913, and by a further second in beating Willie Lutznow of Magdeberg at the Hyde gala three months later. He added the 150 yards world record in his home pool in June 1912, but was unable to repeat his form a month later at the Stockholm Olympics where, handicapped by the shambolic preparation of the British team, he was eliminated in the semi-final. At 5 feet 5½ inches tall and 11 stones 9 pounds, the 26 year-old was powerfully built but the only backstroke race was, according to the *Athletic News*, 'not long enough for him…there is no-one in the wide world to beat him at the longer distance'.

In a heartfelt letter home Webster bemoaned, that whereas other countries were given several weeks to acclimatise, the British team had five days, which was just long enough for the swimmers unprepared for the extreme heat to acquire debilitating blisters in training.

> We stand no 'earthly' against the Yankees. They reign supreme. They trained six months for the event. Until the British Olympic Association start training swimmers, England will be behind. Training should be begun now for the Olympic Games at Berlin in 1916.[21]

In August 1913, Lords Grey, Harris, Rothschild, Strathcone, Westminster and Roberts adopted a strategy familiar to local sporting and musical organisations by launching a national subscription fund to secure 'adequate representation' at the Berlin Olympics.

> …the results of Stockholm were a shock to everyone who cares for sport in Great Britain…such results must never again occur…it would be better to withdraw entirely from the Olympic movement than to repeat our experience of Sweden…It is in our opinion a national duty to provide funds.

Their conviction, that sporting excellence contributes to national pride and morale, is well founded: it reflects the joy felt at local successes in places such as Todmorden and acknowledges the importance of sport to national well-being.[22]

Despite the general acceptance of the need for a public swimming baths in Todmorden, there was never the money, or perhaps the will, to achieve one. In 1936, detailed plans were drawn up for an open air pool in Centre Vale Park. The 120 feet by 50 feet pool with gas-fired heating, 32 dressing cabins, 384 lockers, toilets, showers, café and sunbathing area for 420 spectators was costed at £10,400 but not constructed and, as World War II intervened the plan was shelved.

In the 1930s, Tom Porter, a tackler at Joshua Smith's mill in Cornholme and a part-time swimming instructor, rented a disused dam belonging to the old Frieldhurst Mill at Vale and started a community swimming club for the locality. The reservoir at Rattenclough, Portsmouth, was another favourite with local swimmers as were the other dams in the district.

Swimming Gala, 1933, organised by Tom Porter at Law Mill Dam, Cornholme.
Swimmers L-R: Othello Ashworth, Dennis Fielden, Norman Stansfield, Walter Stuttard,
Harry Nuttall, Jean Eastwood, Roy Duffield, Violet Shaw, Doris Shaw, Kathleen Reader,
Heath Cote, Audrey Graham.

Swimmers at Portsmouth Reservoir 1930s

Many children learned to swim at the Shade pool and the weekly class visit to Shade
was quite an event. Two of the authors recall at the age of 10/11 years in the mid 1940s,
catching the bus to Todmorden from Carrfield, Portsmouth, with bus ticket provided,
then walking along Rochdale Road to Shade. After the swim and, funds allowing, they
bought a pie at Shade, before returning to school - all unaccompanied by any teacher
or adult.

In the post-war years those keen enough travelled to the nearest pool. A group from
Cornholme, went by bus each week to Bacup Baths on 'ladies' night. In summer
Gaddings Dam, Portsmouth reservoir and Hollingworth Lake were favourites. The

author recalls:

> We cycled to Portsmouth reservoir usually with a costume under a dress and returned similarly clad - but wet, occasionally, with parental consent, taking a towel and knickers. My father insisted on our learning to swim, as he would not have survived a 1917 World War I torpedo attack, which sank his ship off Alexandria, without the ability to swim to a raft.

The demand for a swimming pool reasserted itself. To publicise the need, John Slater of Todmorden Swimming Club (the club without a home) began a New Year's Day swim at Lee Dam, Lumbutts, in 1960. This has become so much a part of the town's annual events that it has continued and celebrated its 50th anniversary in 2009.

Taking the Plunge at Lee Dam, New Year 2010

The swimming club began fund raising. Its tenacity bore fruit and Todmorden Swimming Pool was ready for use in Centre Vale Park on 5 February 1973. The 25 metre pool was the climax of the Swimming Club's fourteen years of fund raising, which realised £14,000 towards the total cost of £90,000, Todmorden Council paying the rest. The pool's maximum depth was 10 feet and the minimum 3 feet. The entrance side was of red brick and the other sides of prefabricated aluminium and fibreglass. The bright green roof was a double skin of fibreglass for insulation.

The official opening was in May 1973 by which time the sauna and café were complete. It was not entirely coincidental that the pool opened less than a year before local government reorganisation, which saw Todmorden become part of Calderdale Municipal Borough Council.

The baths were not of a robust construction and in time water was lost through leakage and a replacement was needed. The town now boasts a modern sports centre, comprising a swimming pool with moveable floor, sauna, sports' hall, fitness centre, crèche and café.

The Todmorden Sports' Centre was opened in 2000 by ex-West Ham United and England footballer, Trevor Brooking, representing Sport England which provided most

Opening of the New Sports Facilities, Centre Vale Park, 1994.

of the funding. It caters for most ages and its excellent facilities attract customers from out of town. Here junior football coaching sessions are held on Thursdays and Saturdays in appropriate age groups. The football teams (run independently of the centre) cater for U7s to U16s, playing in the Halifax League and using the Centre Vale Park pitches.

The so-called 'Midnight League', which operates each Saturday from 7 to 9pm, was initially temporary but has proved so popular that it is now permanent. Catering for the 12 to 19 age group, it offers free use of the sports hall, gymnasium and all weather floodlit pitch, for a variety of activities; football, table tennis, two-wheeled skating, hockey, gymnastics and badminton. About 50 teenagers, of which around 30% are girls, attend each week. There is a good response from girls to tennis coaching after school on Tuesdays and the centre runs its own netball league comprising teams from within the centre for girls over 16 years. During school holidays coaching in football (most popular), golf on the pitch and putt course, tennis, junior gymnastics and snorkelling and diving in the pool are on offer.

Todmorden's New Leisure Centre, Centre Vale Park 2000.

The most popular girls' activity is swimming, which is well catered for. Lessons, which follow the Amateur Swimming Association teaching plan, are held for ages 5 to 15 years. Currently, under a 'Swimming for All' two year discretionary national scheme which began in April 2009, swimming is free for all under 17 years or over 60 years. By spring 2010 it had attracted over 3000 under 17s to the Todmorden pool. A 'Schools for 50 Pence' is an after school scheme which runs from Monday to Friday and includes junior gymnastic work and swimming sessions with instructors. Our 2009 survey of 14 year-olds shows that over 74% of boys and over 54% of girls go swimming. For girls this is not only the most popular, but for some their only, sporting activity.

Todmorden Swimming Club hires the pool three times per week for its members from 5 year-olds to adults. It runs its own galas both within the club and with other clubs.

Todmorden is very fortunate to have the bandstand, the multi-discipline sports' centre and other outdoor sporting facilities plus a large area for events, all within the beautiful setting of Centre Vale Park which, along with the adjoining cricket field, represents an outstanding recreational facility for the town.

Chapter 12

Music and Drama

At the turn of the 20th Century Todmorden, with a population of 26,348, was at its peak. Cotton and its ancillary trades provided the main employment, the working week being 55½ hours which included Saturday mornings. How did those who had been cooped up in the mill 5½ days elect to spend their precious freedom? It was said in 1897 by John Craven, solicitor, ex-cricketer, President of the Musical Society and well-regarded citizen, that there was:

> nothing that Todmorden had been distinguished for during the past quarter of a century more than cricket and music.[1]

and these twin pursuits continued strongly during the 20th Century.

Todmorden Musical Society had been in existence for nearly 60 years when, in 1914, it suspended operations because of the war. But members came together one last time at Christmas to perform the *Messiah*. The choir of 120 voices plus orchestra, with Todmorden's own Arthur Laycock as solo trumpet, gave a superb performance. It was the society's swansong.

Todmorden was not without a choir as, in 1906, the Todmorden Male Voice Choir had been formed under conductor Harold Lees. As well as performing locally, this was a serious competition choir which entered musical festivals throughout Lancashire, West Yorkshire and as far afield as the Isle of Man. By 1914 the choir had entered 36 competitions, always taking one of the top three places, and had twice won the prestigious Blackpool Festival.

TODMORDEN MUSICAL SOCIETY.
IN AID OF THE RELIEF FUNDS.

'The Messiah'

IN THE TOWN HALL,
TUESDAY, 22nd DECEMBER, 1914.
Principals—
Soprano—Miss HILDA NELSON.
Contralto—Miss GERTRUDE BROOKES.
Tenor—Mr. WILFRID ABOR.
Bass—Mr. FOWLER BURTON.
Solo Trumpet—Mr. ARTHUR LAYCOCK.
Conductor—Mr. F. GREENWOOD, Mus. Bac.
(Dunelm).
Admission—3s., 2s., 1s.   Doors open at 6-30.
To commence 7-15.   Tickets at Messrs. J. Bentley and Sons.
1056

Advert for the *Messiah* 1914

The choir continued throughout World War I and until 1933 when, owing to dwindling numbers which had halved since 1923, it agreed to disband. Conductor Harold Lees had retired the previous year, perhaps because of the waning interest. During its 27 years existence the choir, as well as giving many live concerts in the town, won 66 prizes at musical festivals, of which 31 were firsts.

The gap was short-lived; by mid-December Harold Lees attended a meeting which heralded the formation of a new choir with himself as conductor. Before the end of the year the Todmorden Orpheus Male Voice

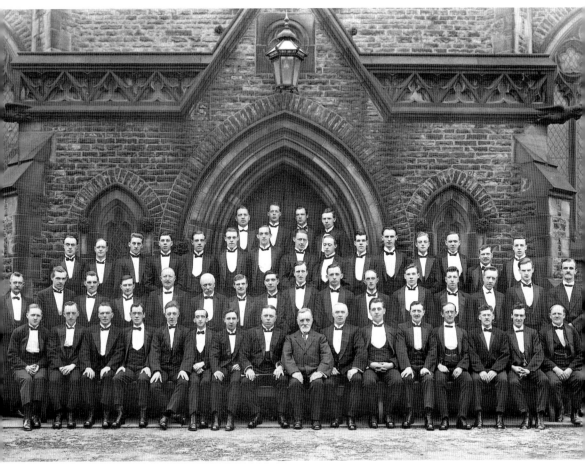

Todmorden Male Voice Choir 1923 at the Unitarian Church entrance,
the Conductor, Harold Lees, is seated centre-front.

Choir was founded. The choir emulated its predecessor by entering regional musical festivals such as Lytham, Hazel Grove, Keighley and, on Sunday 2 October 1938, they broadcast an evening concert on the BBC North Regional Programme from the Leeds studio.

In 1919 the Todmorden Glee and Madrigal Society came into being and in December 1920 joined with the orchestra to perform the *Messiah* in the Town Hall, fulfilling the role of the old Musical Society. The Glee and Madrigal Society became a competition choir. In October 1922 it won the 'B' Class Mixed Choir contest at the Blackpool Musical Festival. A fortnight earlier they had presented a Grand Subscription Concert at Todmorden Town Hall, featuring Sir Hamilton Harty and the Hallé Chamber Orchestra. For this concert a subscription of one guinea bought four first class or six second class seats, whilst 10s 6d (half a guinea) bought two first or three second class seats. A ballot for the order of booking these seats was held at the Police Room in the Town Hall, after which, booking was open to the general public with seats at 5s 3d, 3s 6d and the gallery at 2s 4d, all including tax. In November of that year the Society celebrated its eighth consecutive success by winning the Mixed Choir Class at Bacup Musical Festival.

On one special occasion in November 1935 the Glee and Madrigal Society, and

Todmorden Glee and Madrigal Society at Laneside 1922.

Todmorden Old Brass Band combined in 'An Evening of British Music'. Directed by the Glee and Madrigal Society's conductor, local musician and organist, John Crowther FRCO, the concert was chaired by Dr John de Ville Mather. The pianists were Mrs Lavena Wood and Miss Dorothy Pilling and there were no fewer than 17 local soloists. This concert demonstrated the depth and quality of local musical talent. Dorothy Kershaw (now 90) recalls her childhood and evenings at her terraced home in Cornholme, when her elder sister Alice, an accomplished pianist, and local renowned soloists Gladys Hesketh, Kathleen Proctor, Willie Crossley and Enoch Stanyer would rehearse for a forthcoming concert.

Neither the Orpheus Male Voice Choir nor the Glee and Madrigal Society, which celebrated its Silver Jubilee in 1944, survived World War II.

The Orchestral Scene

In August 1915 a small group of local musicians met to consider forming an orchestra to help fill the gap left by the demise of the Musical Society. By October, with 15 members, the Todmorden Orchestra came into being under the baton of Walter Mitchell. The membership fee was 1s 0d, plus a weekly subscription of 2d. The Brass Band Room, which was above King's bakehouse on Harley Street was booked for Sunday morning rehearsals.[2] Walter had already conducted the Knowlwood Orchestra for 20 years and it was from this that the Todmorden Orchestra was born.

Todmorden Orchestra has had an unbroken existence since its foundation and will celebrate its centenary in 2015. In a new venture in 1920 it held Popular Sunday Concerts at the Olympia (the old Olympia). After the first of these the *Todmorden Advertiser* reported:

> There was a crowded attendance, people standing in rows at the back, and lining the sides of the hall. It was not very long before the desolating fact was made apparent to

BLACKPOOL MUSICAL FESTIVAL

PROGRESS

Class 62.

MIXED VOICE CHOIRS "B" (Open)

FRANCEYS TROPHY.

First Prize

AWARDED TO

Todmorden Glee and Madrigal Society.

CONDUCTOR—Mr. J. CROWTHER.

OCTOBER,
1922.

G. W. Stansfield

Hon. Secretary.

President :
THE MAYOR (Coun. D. DICKINSON, J.P.)
Vice-Presidents :
Sir A. LINDSAY PARKINSON, J.P., M.P.
Alderman J. HEAP, J.P.
W. BATESON, A.C.A.
J. L. SMITH.
Councillor J. GAUNT (the President of the
Blackpool Chamber of Trade).
Chairman of Executive Committee :
Major LEONARD G. S. MOLLOY, D.S.O.,
M.A., M.D., J.P.
Vice-Chairman :
LIONEL H. FRANCEYS.
Hon. Treasurer :
CYRIL CHANTLER.
Assistant Treasurer :
T. E. BLAND.
Adjudicators :
Madame EDITH HANDS, A.R.A.M.
Madame C. GLEESON-WHITE, A.R.C.M.
Miss D. C. VINICOMBE.
FREDERIC AUSTIN   JOHN BRIDGE
H. PLUNKET GREENE.
HARVEY GRACE, F.R.C.O.   GRANVILLE HILL
CHARLES KELLY   ERNEST NEWMAN
WALTER S. NESBITT.
GEOFFREY SHAW, Mus. Bac., Cantab.
ED. SWINGLER   R. H. TERRY, Mus. Doc.
STEUART WILSON.
Hon. Director of Competitions :
Alderman J. COLLINS, J.P.
Asst. Hon. Director of Competitions :
Coun. T. P. FLETCHER.
General Secretary :
FRANK HOWARD.

Blackpool Musical Festival 1st Prize 1922

us, that owing to the unpardonable oversight on the part of the promoters, no seat had been reserved for our representative. We had therefore to take up a position against the rail on the port side.

Unsurprisingly the report on the concert was less than enthusiastic: it does not pay to alienate the press!

Arguably, Todmorden's most talented musician was Ben Horsfall, who joined the orchestra in the 1920s as a teenage violinist. He later studied at the Royal Manchester College of Music, played in the Hallé and BBC Northern orchestras and became one of the rare breed who, having achieved the degree of Doctorate in music, continued his orchestral playing for thirty years. He recalled his early days when Todmorden Orchestra rehearsed on Sunday mornings in the Sobriety Hall, also the headquarters of the Band of Hope Temperance Society. Any aura of temperance failed to influence the orchestra, rehearsals which began at 10.30 sharp ceased at 12.25 sharp, members hastening to the White Hart - which opened at 12.30.[3]

Horsfall took a taste of Todmorden with him to the BBC Northern Orchestra. As a youngster in the local orchestra he sat between Albert, the principal cellist, and Willie another teenage violinist. Willie regularly continued playing after the conductor had stopped the orchestra to repeat a section. In orchestral circles 'playing on' is regarded as a cardinal sin. Albert found this particularly irritating and relieved his frustration by lifting his cello and driving the spike into the floor. After one excruciating recital from Willie, Albert, having driven his spike in from a great height, leant across Horsfall and with gritted teeth said 'Na than Willie - tha sees th' advantage now i' choppin' orf wit'others'. After Horsfall related this to the BBC Northern Orchestra it had an immediate effect - when anyone committed the 'cardinal sin' someone piped up 'Na then, Willie!'[4]

Walter Mitchell's successor as conductor of the Todmorden Orchestra was Arthur

Todmorden Orchestra in front of Ewood Hall 1915-16.
L-R Rows 2,3: Ernest Playford, Harold Laycock, Wright Sutcliffe, Walter Warburton, Raymond Law,
Greenwood Shuttleworth, Jim Swindells, Jacob Maden, Fred Helliwell, Arnold Nuttall,
Herbert Greenwood, Will Lumb, Joe Woodhead, Wilfred Kingsbury, Jesse Stockwell, John Ackroyd.
Row 1: Charles Clegg, Sam Pavis, Tom Sutcliffe, John Wadsworth, Herbert Jackson,
Walter Mitchell (conductor), John Bentley, Barker Ackroyd, Elsie Mitchell, Harry Horsfall, Albert Starkie.

Greenwood until his resignation in 1926, when Fred Leach took over. Fred Leach had
trained as a violinist at the Royal Manchester College of Music and played with the
Hallé Orchestra. In 1919 he became conductor of the Rochdale Philharmonic
Orchestra and Choral Society and in 1928 he brought the Todmorden Orchestra to
Champness Hall, Rochdale, for a joint concert with the Rochdale Philharmonic. In
1930 he presented Elgar's *Dream of Gerontius* at Todmorden Town Hall with the
Todmorden Orchestra and Rochdale Philharmonic Choir. 1935 saw the orchestra
winning the *News Chronical* trophy for their playing of the slow movement from
Schubert's *Unfinished Symphony* at Blackpool Musical Festival, Ben Horsfall being the
leader of the orchestra.

At a presentation in 1951 to mark Fred Leach's twenty-five years as conductor, Dr
John de Ville Mather, as well as praising his abilities as musician and conductor, said,
'His greatest virtue is his charm of character and unfailing good temper'. Leach held
the position until his death in 1955, which occurred only six days after he had

Todmorden Orchestra, Ben Horsfall conductor, Owen Brannigan soloist

conducted an orchestral concert in Centre Vale Park. Viola player Vernon Foulds, who had studied conducting under Leach, took charge. In 1962, on Vernon Foulds's retirement, Ben Horsfall took the baton, to the great delight of the orchestra, and remained in control for the next twenty-two years. He was responsible for many first-rate concerts and, with his connections was able to bring friends from the BBC Northern, who invariably gave their services. On one occasion in December 1968 he engaged Maurice Murphy to play the solo trumpet in the *Messiah*. That night the BBC Northern's rehearsal in Manchester lasted until 9pm, whereupon, Maurice jumped into his car and made the journey to Todmorden in 30 minutes. The young student playing 2nd trumpet knew he had to deputise should Murphy not appear and, when the moment arrived, rose to accompany the bass soloist in the recitative *The Trumpet Shall Sound*. As it ended, Murphy, having rushed up the stairs, arrived on the platform and, without music, played the aria beautifully. Horsfall continued to conduct as though nothing untoward had happened: it was probably the only time that the recitative was played by one trumpeter and the aria by another.[5] Horsfall confided that he 'considered it his duty to assist the society for as long as he was physically capable' - and this he did.

Todmorden was the breeding ground for several professional musicians: horn players Frank Taylor (Hallé and BBC Northern Orchestras) and Jack Johnson (Liverpool Philarmonic and City of Birmingham Orchestras); violinist Thelma Maden (Mrs Jack Johnson) (City of Birmingham Orchestra); bassoonists Maurice Ashworth (Royal Liverpool Philarmonic) and Clarence Town (Hallé Orchestra); cellist Mary Hartley (Mrs Clay), who returned to support the local orchestra for many years; and of course trombonist Geoff Love, who went on to fame with his own orchestra having been given his first instrument by Dr John de Ville Mather.[6]

The musical highlights of the summer up to World War II were the Centre Vale Park annual concerts in aid of the Todmorden Sick Nursing Association and Hospital Fund which made donations to the Halifax and Manchester Hospitals. At these concerts, held in the afternoon and evening on a Sunday in August, the Male Voice Choir, Glee and Madrigal Society, Todmorden Orchestra and the brass bands of Cornholme (until its demise in 1929), Todmorden and Walsden all came together to perform.

Brass bands had been popular since the Todmorden Band formed in 1854, followed by Cornholme in 1863 and Walsden Temperance Band in 1890 (an off-shoot of an Inchfield Bottom Band). Todmorden Old Brass Band was particularly successful in the 1920s winning The Peoples' Challenge Shield at the National Brass Band Festival at Crystal Palace in 1921 and coming second in 1922.

Local bands were not the only ones to perform in the park; visiting bands also provided entertainment. These were organised regionally. In 1920 a meeting at Burnley of representatives from Burnley, Todmorden and Nelson, allocated bands to each other. Todmorden's programme comprised the band of the Life Guards on Whit Sunday, the Seaforth Highlanders on Sunday 13 and Tuesday 15 June, the Grenadier Guards on Sunday 8 August and the Scots Guards on Monday 23 August. All this cost no more than a walk into the park where band concerts have continued to the present day.

Churches and Chapels

The wealth of local musical talent in the first half of the 20th Century had as its base the local churches and chapels of which there were thirty-three in Todmorden, each with its choir master, organist and choir. Walter Mitchell became choir master at

York Street Methodist Choir 1922, at Roomfield House, having won the Band of Hope Shield.
L-R Row 3: Mr Egerton, George Crowther, Willie Greenwood, Sam Beaumont, Tom Bromley, Charlie Crowther, Willie Clay, Philip Stansfield, Willie Crossley, Walter ___, John Horsfall, Barker Beaumont.
Row 2: Mr Prime, Gertrude Barker, Edith Dawson, Annie Hartley, Florrie Stephenson, Hilda Stansfield, Alice Hudson, Amy Waddington, Annie Greaves, Ethel Eastwood, Doris Greaves, John Dawson.
Row 1: Edna Dawson, Evelyn Crowther, Alice Bromley, Doris Dawson, Vinnie Heyworth, Amy Waller, Tom Parker, Edmund Schofield, Mrs Ada Clewer, Gracie Marshall, Alice Dawson, Cissie Fielden, Nellie Prime, Maggie Eastwood.

Roomfield Baptist Church in 1916 and, during three years of World War I, he also conducted the choir at Lumbutts Methodist Church. He took over the choir at Bridge Street Methodist Church in 1922 and remained there for 22 years.

Many members of the town's musical societies would be found in their respective church or chapel choir each Sunday. They were brought up learning to read music and sing in harmony. For many, the highlight of the year was the Sunday School Anniversary, when each church or chapel choir might be augmented by singers from neighbouring places of worship. Thus the anthems sung at each of the three services, morning, afternoon and evening, with the pews full, would ring out and do justice to the day. These were not always deeply religious occasions but a once a year chance to show off each church or chapel at its best, not least by the size of the collections, which were tabulated in the local paper. The anniversary was also a day for reunions as those who had left the district returned to their mother church to remember past times and renew friendships.

A sobering recreational outlet provided by many chapels was the Band of Hope. This temperance movement founded in 1869 took a strong hold locally with annual processions and, for those affiliated to the Todmorden Band of Hope Union, an impressive joint gala day. Members were encouraged to 'sign the pledge' undertaking to abstain from intoxicating liquor. The regular meetings were also social occasions

1919 and 1920 figures are given for each school, and immediately below the denominational totals will be found the corresponding figure for 1914.

TODMORDEN AND DISTRICT.

	1919 £ s. d.	1920 £ s. d.
Church of England:		
Tot. Par. Church ...	100 0 0 ...	132 7 0
Cross Stone...	41 15 10 ...	53 13 0
Walsden...	40 0 0 ...	36 0 0
Harleywood	38 4 0 ...	52 0 0
St. Mary's	41 0 0 ...	64 0 2
St. Aidan's	16 0 0 ...	20 0 0
Cornholme... ...	52 10 0 ...	62 8 11
Totals (1914—£186) ...	£329 9 10 ...	420 9 1
Baptist:		
Shore	160 0 0 ...	205 2 11
Vale	116 0 0 ...	140 13 9
Lineholme... ...	103 0 0 ...	128 4 8
Lydgate...	88 0 0 ...	100 12 0
Roomfield	71 3 4½ ...	83 11 6
Wellington Road ...	58 8 8 ...	73 0 0
Nazebottom... ...	37 15 6 ...	50 4 7
Totals (1914—£334) ...	£634 7 6½ ...	781 9 5
Wesleyan:		
York Street	120 11 9 ...	140 1 9
Mankinholes	81 10 0 ...	85 0 0
Springside	69 15 0 ...	71 6 2
Walsden	47 0 0 ...	54 12 7
Shade	30 0 11½ ...	46 0 0
Lanebottom... ...	51 0 0 ...	60 15 0
Blackshawhead ...	57 0 0 ...	65 0 0
Totals (1914—£279) ...	£456 17 8½ ...	522 15 6
United Methodist:		
Bridge Street	76 1 9½ ...	102 2 8
Cornholme... ...	128 17 0 ...	159 10 0
Inchfield	80 0 0 ...	100 2 6
Lumbutts	45 10 0 ...	63 5 6
Castle Grove... ...	38 0 0 ...	63 0 1
Totals (1914—£232) ...	£368 8 9½ ...	488 0 9
Primitive Methodist:		
Knowlwood... ...	68 12 0 ...	93 0 0
Castle Street	50 0 0 ...	65 0 0
Bottoms	38 0 0 ...	47 10 0
Victoria Road	13 0 0 ...	16 1 8
Totals (1914—£96) ...	£169 12 0 ...	221 11 10
Congregational:		
Eastwood	60 0 0 ...	80 0 0
Patmos...	57 0 0 ...	83 0 0
Cloughfoot... ...	60 0 0 ...	87 8 0
Totals (1914—£124) ...	£177 0 0 ...	250 8 0
Unitarians (1914—£48)	74 1 8 ...	90 16 0
Oldroyd I.M. (1914—£21)	36 14 2½ ...	48 11 1

Sunday School Anniversary Collections 1919 and 1920.

The annual returns from societies were read, which showed that two societies had joined the union during the year—Patmos and the Spiritualists—the number of members of each society being as follows :—

	Present No.	Increase.	Decrease
B.W.T.A.	117	10	—
Roomfield	262	93	—
Castle-grove... ...	141	41	—
Lanebottom	163	4	—
Bridge-street	277	—	1
Myrtle Grove	145	—	2
Patmos	99	—	—
Spiritualists... ...	83	—	—
Springside	78	5	—
Vale	127	2	—
Harley Wood... ...	63	—	13
Unitarians	250	—	—
Inchfield-bottom..	275	—	1
Castle-street	183	—	—
Mankinholes	80	10	—
Cloughfoot	51	—	22
Knowlwood	258	—	221
Lumbutts	127	4	—
Oldroyd	125	3	—
Shade	78	4	—
Walsden Wesley.	20	—	—
Lineholme	120	—	60
Shore	150	—	7
Lydgate...	104	—	26
Sobriety Tent... ...	952	22	—

Cornholme, Wellington-road, and York street did not supply number of members

Annual Returns of Band of Hope Members 1908.

St Michael's Sunday School Procession, Cornholme, c1907

Band of Hope Procession, Halifax Road, c1914.

and in 1927 Cornholme Methodist Band of Hope performed the operetta *The Magic Key*. The annual galas and demonstrations continued until World War I but did not survive it. There were thirty local Bands of Hope in 1924 but these had dwindled by 1931 in line with the dwindling church and chapel congregations - some religious beliefs were undermined by the carnage of World War I.[7]

Todmorden Operatic and Dramatic Societies

One more group which, strangely enough, came into being at one of the darkest moments of World War I, was the Todmorden Amateur Operatic Society. The musical director was Harold Lees and the producer JW Helliwell, who had played leading roles in Cross Stone's productions of *Yeomen of the Guard* (1898) and the *Mikado* (1900) staged at the Town Hall.[8] For its first production *Yeomen of the Guard* was chosen and was performed at the Hippodrome Theatre for six nights in June 1917. The cast comprised some eighty performers, selected from all the choirs in the district, and the proceeds from the show were donated to the local Centre Vale Military Hospital.

After 1918 Harold Lees handed the baton to Walter Mitchell, who served as Musical Director of the Society for 12 years. He followed this with four years at Cross Stone Operatic Society, working alongside his friend JW Helliwell in an annual production of a Gilbert and Sullivan opera.

The Operatic Society was fortunate in having a purpose-built theatre in which to stage its shows. Built in 1908, the Hippodrome filled a need in Todmorden, which in the past had relied on travelling companies who erected their wooden theatres on Stansfield Road or the market ground. One such, the Gaiety Theatre, which had been on the market ground for about two years, relocated. Refurbished, it opened as the Theatre Royal on Halifax Road in 1895 on the site of the present Hippodrome. Unfortunately, its licence was not renewed in 1896 as it had originally been granted on condition that it moved to a different site; a wooden structure, it could not be regarded as permanent and additionally it had no sanitary arrangements.

The town was then without a venue for touring companies and in September 1898 the council decided to fit out the Town Hall as a theatre with the necessary scenery and effects. Travelling theatres still visited the town, including in 1905 Mr Walter Leybourne's New Empire Theatre whose opening play was *Weary Willie and Tired Tim*. Walter Leybourne had learnt his profession with his uncle George Leybourne, the original 'Champagne Charlie'.[9]

The town needed a permanent theatre. Richard Dewhirst, stationer, tobacconist, printer and proprietor of the *Todmorden Herald*, a rival to the *Todmorden Advertiser*, had his premises in Halifax Road next to where the Theatre Royal had been. Here he planned and built a theatre, the Todmorden Hippodrome, which opened on 5 October 1908.[10] When Dewhirst became bankrupt in 1911, the theatre came into the hands of the Hartley family of Nelson. It became an integral part of the town's activities, witnessing the era of music hall and silent films, the demise of the travelling theatre companies and the increasing dominance of the cinema via the 'talkies' and technicolor films.

The Hippodrome was also a venue for Todmorden's amateur dramatic societies, the first to grace the stage being the Shakespearean Society in 1909 with *The Merchant of Venice*. This society wound up in 1912 and was superseded by the Todmorden Amateur Players, who presented plays at the National School, the Unitarian Sunday School and the Hippodrome. These productions were always for the benefit of some cause, usually local, including Todmorden Co-op Fire Brigade, Todmorden Cricket Club, and the wartime charities Centre Vale Hospital, Todmorden and District Nursing League and the Blue Cross Fund for wounded horses.

Two Lancashire Lasses in London, the Hippodrome Theatre's opening show
on 5 October 1908.

Having been dormant during the latter war years, the Players revived in 1920 playing regularly at the Hippodrome until 1925 after which, from 1929 for financial reasons, plays were presented at the Co-op Hall, Dale Street, continuing there until the outbreak of World War II.

The Hippodrome had a rival when the Olympia converted from skating rink to picture palace in 1910 with a programme of silent films and live variety acts. One artist who appeared there in 1911 was 'Kidd Love The Renowned Coloured Vocalist and Dancer'. He married the girl who worked in the theatre box office, and their youngest child was Geoff Love. The local theatre scene was complete when, in 1915, the B.O.S. Cinema (proprietors Batty, Ogden and Spencer of Nelson) opened in Cornholme.

Amateur theatre was not the sole province of the Todmorden Players and the Operatic Society. Churches and chapels began to develop dramatic societies. These began in the Anglican churches. In 1907/8 Cornholme St Michael's gave *Luke the Labourer* or *The Lost Son,* Harley Wood *The Lady of Lyons* and *The Vicar of Wakefield* and Cross Stone *The Rivals.*

The Independent (Congregational) Chapel at Patmos was the first of the non-conformists to form a dramatic society,

Advertising card for a music hall act at the Hippodrome, April 1912.

Todmorden Shakespearean Society rehearse *Twelfth Night*.

performing *The Governor of Bergerac* and *Martin Chuzzlewit* in 1908.

Church and chapel based societies, both dramatic and musical, burgeoned after World War I. In 1933 when Todmorden Amateur Players proposed the formation of a Todmorden Theatre Guild 23 societies were circulated.

In March 1931, Cornholme Methodist Church Choir Operatic Society presented Edward German's comic opera *Merrie England* with full orchestra. It was a considered choice given that the village's major employer Wilson Bros, whose forebears had founded the church, had closed their bobbin works the previous year. The producer's introduction in the programme was poignant:

Cornholme Methodist Choir's production of *Merrie England* 1931.

Cornholme Combined Churches Drama Group's production of *The Thirteenth Chair* 1936.
L-R Row2: Peter Hodgins, Harry Dawson, Tom Stott, Jack Hopwood, Hilda Webster,
Ernest Barker, Frank Turner, Jack Houghton, Will Banks, Frank Sagar.
Row 1: Florence Nuttall, Annie Howard, Doris Irene Greenwood, Nellie Hammond,
Norah Blacka, Agnes Higgins.

The world of make-believe is a wonderful place, in its proper place, and was ever a
generation more in need of some such form of relaxation than the present? What more
fitting a medium than the Amateur Stage; where, given the inspiration of text and
music, an ordinary workaday individual can, for a brief time, live on another plane and
forget that tomorrow one must go about the business of earning one's daily bread, or,
more doleful still, seek the nearest office of the Ministry of Labour and sign in the space
indicated...

A glimpse at the productions staged in 1933 shows the amount of activity in the
town:

Todmorden Amateur Operatic Society	*The Quaker Girl*
Walsden Methodist	*The Pirates of Penzance*
Cross Stone	*The Gondoliers*
Unitarians	*The Grand Duchess*
Cornholme Methodist	*Veronique* and *The Case of Lady Camber*
Todmorden Parish Church	*My Lady Molly*
Todmorden Amateur Players with local branch The League of Nations	*Journey's End*
Unitarians	*Skin Game* and *Caste*
Lanebottom Methodist	*The Seal and Envelope*
Bridge Street Methodist	*Lord Richard in the Pantry*
Walsden Cricket and Bowling Club	*Sarah Ann Holds Fast*

Also, when owing to the disbanding of the Male Voice Choir and to the Glee and
Madrigal Society's crowded programme, there was no performance of the *Messiah*

scheduled for the Town Hall, James (Jim) Hindle with his Cornholme Methodist Choir and the Todmorden Orchestra stepped in to present the traditional oratorio. The local press gave a glowing report noting that:

> with the exception of two principals and the trumpeter everybody was of the home town.

The Clef Club

Not all local societies flourished. In September 1920 the inaugural meeting of the Clef Club held in the Unitarian schoolroom attracted a large attendance. Its aims - to study and experience music - were explained and membership soon reached 150, swelling to 270 by the second meeting held in Patmos schoolroom a fortnight later. The subject was 'Chamber Music' illustrated by pieces from classical composers played by local musicians on string, woodwind and brass instruments, the chairman being John Crowther. Local soprano Annis Studd sang two operatic arias (her test pieces at the recent Blackpool Festival) whilst Messrs EL Bentley and Ronald Cunliffe were the pianists. The club was not an isolated entity as visitors from the clubs of Nelson and Colne attended some meetings. However, by December 1924, in its fifth season, the club was winding up owing to decreasing membership.

Ronald Cunliffe's Boys' Choir

A major success story was Ronald Cunliffe's Boys' Choir. Born in 1899 Ronald Cunliffe was a piano teacher and, for a time, organist and choir master at Todmorden Parish Church. In 1922 he formed a boys' choir and introduced them to classical music. In September 1924 the choir performed Mozart's *The Magic Flute* for five nights at the Co-op Hall. The boys had learnt the opera during a summer camp on the hillside above Lumbutts. Sidney H Nicholson, organist at Westminster Abbey, came to see the

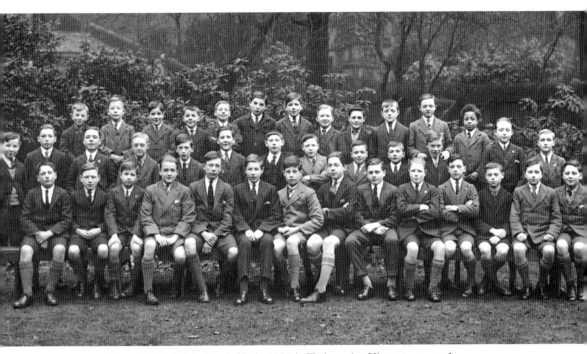

Ronald Cunliffe's Boys' Choir 1926 in Todmorden Vicarage grounds.

choir perform *The Golden Cockerel* in April 1925. He wrote in *The Times* that:

> The tone of the boys' voices was wholly delightful, the great feature of the singing being its naturalness and lack of apparent effort...The boys seem to be in tone with their work. The audience was not crowded nor was it demonstrative: evidently the good people of Todmorden have yet to realise what important things are going on in their midst.

At Manchester's Houldsworth Hall in September1925, the choir gave the first of three Tuesday midday concerts broadcast on the city's radio station, receiving critical acclaim. In the three weeks spanning Christmas and the New Year in 1925/6 the boys presented *The Magic Flute, The Golden Cockerel, Pagliacci* and *Susanna's Secret* in a total of 20 performances - despite Ronald Cunliffe's absence for part of the time, when he was recovering in hospital from an operation. Unfortunately for Todmorden, in 1927 Cunliffe accepted the post of music master at the Latymer School, Edmonton, London, and this marked the end of the choir. During his time Cunliffe had trained 150 boys, one of whom was Geoff Love, and presented 100 concerts at the Co-op Hall. In 1942 he took a full time post with the BBC but his life ended tragically when he was discovered gassed in his London home in 1944.[11]

The Co-op

The Co-operative Hall featured prominently in Todmorden's leisure activities as a venue for concerts, plays and dances but the Co-op itself had a positive impact. To celebrate Todmorden cricket team's winning the Lancashire League in 1927, the Co-op promoted a lecture by Neville Cardus, the *Manchester Guardian*'s cricket correspondent. Following this the Co-op President proclaimed:

> The Society is looking after the interests of members not only from the view of the 'divi' but from a social and educational standpoint.

Todmorden's professional JW Hitch chaired the meeting supported by his victorious team and admission was free.

From the beginning of the 20th Century the Education Department of the Co-op had organised concerts during the winter using chapel schoolrooms - all of which had a stage. In January 1902, the Reedyford Concert Party performed at the Congregational School, Eastwood, and a month later the Northern Opera Company appeared at a Soiree in Cornholme Methodist schoolroom. November of the same year found the Ambrose Concert Party at Springside Wesleyan schoolroom. Admission at 2d or 3d shows that these events were subsidised by the Co-op.

In February 1905 the Haydn Opera Singers were the performers at a Grand Concert in Lineholme Baptist Sunday School and in the same month at the Co-op's main Dale Street building, Ambulance Classes (First Aid) began, for females on Thursday evenings and males on Fridays. Drs JA Parker and JL Russell were the instructors.

Also in this month Mr Philip Snowden, parliamentary candidate for Blackburn, was engaged to give a lecture on 'John Ruskin - The Man and his Message' - admission free. Snowden became MP for Blackburn and Chancellor of the Exchequer in the first Labour government.

The Todmorden Co-op did not impinge on the Walsden valley where Bridge End and Walsden Co-operative Societies held sway. Bridge End held an annual treat for the children of members. On 12 June 1925 the schools in its area, Shade and Cloughfoot, were granted a day's holiday by the education authority and the children assembled at Shade School for 1.30pm. Each received a bag of sweets before processing up the hill to a field at Swineshead, lent by Tom Hollows. Here they enjoyed games, races and a Punch and Judy show, then went back to school for a bun and coffee. After refreshments they returned to the field for more activities, which were accompanied by Cornholme Brass Band from 6.30 to 9pm.

Co-operator's Day, a celebration of the Co-op and its ideals, was revived in 1927 after a lapse of 20 years. There was a Grand Procession of children followed by a Gala in Centre Vale Park. This was held annually until 1939 but did not survive World War II.

The Hebden Bridge Co-op Comrades Circle Dramatic Society performed the play *Nothing But The Truth* in 1925 at Cornholme Methodist schoolroom, and Lineholme Baptist schoolroom was the venue for the Futurists Concert Party in 1927. Gradually events were centred at either the Co-op Hall or the Town Hall. In November 1927 a free lecture, 'Eclipses and What we Learn from Them' by Rev Theodore R Phillips, President of the Royal Astronomical Society, was held at the Town Hall. Here in December 1931 the Co-op presented the Celebrated Crossland Moor Handbell Ringers, and the following week, the Oldham Industrial Co-operative Society Players gave *The Wreckers* at the Co-op Hall. In the previous month Hebden Bridge Players had performed *When Knights were Bold* and local communist councillor William (Billy) Holt lectured on 'The Co-operative Movement in the USSR'.

Perhaps building on the strength of Neville Cardus's visit in 1927 and the town's sporting interests, the Co-op engaged Fitzwilliam Wray, alias KUKLOS, the cycling correspondent of the *Daily News* to lecture at the Co-op Hall, and followed this with F Stacey Lintott, ADJUTANT of the *Daily Mail*, who spoke on 'The Place of Sport in our Daily Life'. The chairman for the latter was JW Sunderland, Todmorden's amateur pace bowler, who was also active in town affairs.

This pattern of concerts and lectures organised and subsidised by the Co-op Education Department continued throughout and beyond the war. 1943 saw the Co-op Education Department join with the National Union of Teachers Association, Todmorden Workers' Educational Association and the Society for Cultural Relations between the British Commonwealth and the USSR in a series of six public lectures at 3pm on consecutive Saturdays, the first in the Unitarian schoolroom and the rest in the National School.

Still under the Co-operative banner, the Elite Concert Party performed at Cornholme St Michael's Sunday School in 1949, admission 6d.

<u>Military Two-Step</u>

In a seemingly new venture, the Co-op Education Department held a Grand Dance at the Town Hall in September 1941, with music by the Havercake Hurricanes dance band of the Duke of Wellington's Regiment, admission 1s 6d. Saturday night dances had become popular between the wars and had been held regularly during World War I at the Weavers' Institute accompanied by small groups of musicians. However, the first local dance band was the Belvedere Dance Orchestra formed in 1922. It was immediately popular and applications for engagements were to be made to Hardaker Varley, 40 Adelaide Street. This band continued playing in Todmorden and further afield until 2005.

Another local dance orchestra which became almost legendary was Ellis Wood and his Astorians. Ellis Wood's first instrument was the violin, with which he earned an engagement at the Gem Cinema, Cornholme, where, with Edith Astin on piano, he accompanied the silent films. He then studied the saxophone and joined the Belvedere Dance Orchestra. Soon he formed his own orchestra, the Astorians, which built up a reputation at local dances and played occasionally between feature films at the Hippodrome.[12]

The Belvedere Orchestra c1922, Todmorden's early dance orchestra

The Astorians' favourite venue became the Co-op Hall. In August 1937 for admission of 1s 0d you could dance the evening away (7-11pm) and join the Foxtrot Competition, although owing to unforeseen circumstances the Milk Drinking Contest was postponed until Saturday, 6 November. Earlier that year the Astorians were engaged to appear at the Palace of Varieties at Nelson, billed as their 'first appearance on the legitimate stage'.

The Social and Economic Background

It is difficult to overstate the influence of the Co-op in the town's social and economic life during the first half of the 20th Century. By 1939 the Todmorden Society had a membership of 5833; the Bridge End Society had absorbed the Walsden Co-op in 1935/6 when between them they had about 1800 members. As most members represented a family, not just an individual, it can be seen that few of the townsfolk were untouched by the Co-op.[13]

All societies need administrators and few served more widely than Herbert Stevenson who, in the true non-conformist tradition, was on the Management Committee of the Co-operative Society, becoming president in 1947. He was secretary

of the Liberal Club for 17 years and also of the Royal Humility Lodge of the Oddfellows Friendly Society from 1926 and Grand Master in 1933. He had a lifelong association with the Unitarian Church as treasurer, Sunday School teacher, and choir member, and still found time for an active role in the town's musical life. Joining the Male Voice Choir in 1915, he served as secretary for seven years and was there at its disbandment in 1933. From its inception in 1919, Herbert was in the Glee and Madrigal Society and was secretary until 1934; he assisted in forming the National Association of Competitive Choirs in 1920, and served as secretary. For several years, three of them as secretary, he was in the Operatic Society. His working life was spent on the staff of Fielden Bros and on his death in 1948 at the age of 49 years, it was said:

Herbert Stevenson

He was a glutton for work, thoroughly reliable in word and deed and when he did a job he did it well.

Herbert Stevenson was typical of those who, whilst working full time, used their leisure in the service of the community.

The whole spectrum of leisure activities, whether emanating from church, chapel, Co-op, the council, musical societies, dramatic and operatic societies, cinemas, cricket, football, tennis, golf, bowls and cycling or from societies such as the Natural History and Photographic has to be seen against the social and economic conditions of the times. There was little in-home entertainment for the majority, other than card, domino and board games, songs round the piano or listening to a wind-up gramophone (for those who had one). Even the advent of radio was beyond most people's pockets.

In 1923 members of Cornholme's Wilson Bros Bobbin Works Club formed a Wireless Club, 300 members collecting £50 to buy a good instrument 'so they would be able to listen to concerts at London and other big centres'. In the early thirties and continuing beyond the war some households used the local relay system for their wireless reception. An entrepreneur would install a receiver and transmitter in his house or business premises and run wires to the homes of those who, for around 1s 0d per week, could then receive, via a speaker, the radio programmes he transmitted. WL Lumb, electricians of Halifax Road, and Lumb's on Patmos offered their customers a choice of the BBC Home or Light programmes, whilst John Pickles, who ran a similar scheme in Cornholme, offered no choice - only the one he selected to relay to them.

Many homes were without electricity and were lit by gas, but power for an independent radio could be supplied by an accumulator (a lead/acid system of producing a current of electricity) which had to be returned to the shop periodically for recharging.

Todmorden's low-wage cotton based economy was subject to depressions in trade, with periods of high unemployment or under employment which could mean working less than a full week or, in weaving, operating fewer than a full set of looms. Some families had mixed feelings about the annual 'wakes week' which was simply another spell of unemployment. Jack Tout, secretary of Todmorden Weavers' Association, told the Trades

Advertisement for Relay Wireless, December 1937

Union Congress in 1937:

> There must be hundreds and thousands of workers to whom the prospect of a holiday is one that fills them with feelings almost of horror.

Not until 1939 were the textile unions successful in achieving one week of paid holiday per year.[14]

There was little money to spend on leisure, especially if it meant travelling out of town. In fact, given Todmorden's configuration along three valleys, communities such as Walsden and Cornholme were virtually self-contained. Each had several churches, community centres as well as places of worship, and Co-op stores plus a full range of private shops and public houses. Cornholme had its own cinema and Walsden its league cricket club and both had all-age schools and children's playgrounds. Todmorden provided within its borders sufficient leisure activities for its inhabitants, especially given the freely accessible open countryside. For those who could afford it, there was a train on Saturdays in the 1930s which would convey you to Blackpool and back including entrance into the Tower Ballroom for 2s 6d.

War Intervenes

The onset of World War II created a watershed in the nation's life, as had World War I twenty-five years earlier. This time it was total war with conscription from the start, identity cards, rationing of food and fuel, blackout of street and house lights, distribution of gas masks, erection of air raid shelters - 18 locally, British Restaurants and, for relatively 'safe' places like Todmorden, an influx of evacuees. In the face of a common enemy community spirit intensified.

A national fund raising week, to help finance the war, was held annually. Donations, war savings certificates and proceeds from special events built up the fund. In 1941 War Weapons Week saw events like the Mill Workers' Promenade Concert. Each mill nominated its most popular singers 'including crooners' to sing at the Town Hall on 7 May. The town raised £400,341, well above its target. In Warships' Week 1942 Todmorden easily raised £210,000 the cost of the hull of a destroyer to be named HMS Vidette. Concerts were held at Bridge Street Methodist Chapel and the Town Hall, which was open daily from 2pm to 10pm with incidental music in the afternoons and a concert each evening. The town was delighted to learn in 1943 that HMS Vidette had sunk a U-boat with depth charges in the Atlantic.[15]

The target in 1943's Wings for Victory week was £200,000. The Burnley Valley Civil Defence services (Home Guard, Air Raid Wardens, Fire Watching personnel, Women's Voluntary Service and Auxiliary Fire Service) assisted the appeal by presenting a concert 'High Jinks Afloat' on 5 and 9 June in Cornholme Methodist schoolroom. On Sunday 6 June they organised a church parade, involving the valley's churches and chapels. Starting from Portsmouth it finished with a service at Lineholme Baptist Chapel. The next day a concert by the valley's Sunday Schools was held at Cornholme Methodists and on Tuesday 8 June Cornholme British Legion held a whist drive and dance in its hall at Portsmouth. The total collected in the town was £265,936.

The last of these special weeks was Salute the Soldier week in May 1944. Lady Louis Mountbatten visited Todmorden and the town's youth organisations performed a 'Pageant of British History' on the park golf course. The target of £200,000 was exceeded by £60,000.

With the town's young men serving in the forces and some of the women also on war work such as Land Army and munitions, the Civil Defence personnel organised events. They ensured that the *Messiah* was performed annually at the Town Hall with the

Choral Society (formed in 1938 with Jim Hindle as conductor) and Orchestra plus invited guests. The soloists included Janet Hamilton Smith, Kathleen Ferrier, Isobel Baillie, Martha Dyson, Robert Easton and trumpeter Harry Mortimer, all of them celebrated artistes. Proceeds went to the local war funds as did those from other events such as the Burnley Valley Civil Defence's pantomimes, *Mother Goose* 1943 and *Aladdin* in 1944. In 1943 Rochdale Civil Defence's concert at the Town Hall featured its own choir.

Popular Dance Bands

By January 1944, perhaps in anticipation of better times, Ellis Wood and his Astorians were at the Co-op Hall advertising 'Select Dances every Saturday - Admission 1s 6d, member of the forces 1s 0d'. A few months later the 'First Appearance for Dancing in Todmorden of Ellis Wood and his full Dance Orchestra' with 13 players was announced for a dance at the Town Hall. The Astorians were once again synonymous with the Co-op Hall where they held sway each Saturday night. It was the place to be and young people flocked there, so much so that it became known as the Astoria Ballroom rather than the Co-op Hall.

Throughout the 1950s dancing retained its popularity and local musical groups served such venues as the Conservative Club, the White Hart, Sobriety Hall and Weavers Institute. Talented local cornetist Colin Sutcliffe was, at the age of eighteen, solo cornet with the Todmorden Brass Band but later became devoted to dance and big band music. He recalls starting with the new Belvedere Band, which was formed from part of the old Belvedere and Albany Players. The residue of the old Belvedere became the Paramount Dance Orchestra. He says that the number of local musical groups was phenomenal for a town the size of Todmorden. In addition to the Astorians were groups such as the Mayfair, Wadsworth and Percy Dobson Trios, Eddie Clark and His Band, and the Tony Hall Quartet led by Ralph Marshall on vibes, Bill Birch on double base, and George Hatton pianist. Each group had its individual style and they catered for the many local venues. Colin ran the Belvedere, a survivor of the local groups, for almost forty years until 2005, playing at venues around East Lancashire and West Yorkshire.

Ellis Wood and the Astorians at the Co-op Hall

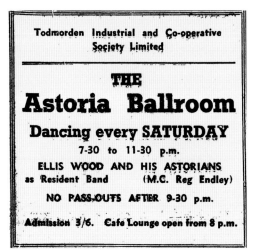

Advertisement for the Astoria Ballroom,
September 1956

Advertisement: Todmorden Co-operative
Hall, November 1963
(no longer the Astoria Ballroom)

He still plays with 'Sounds 18' the East Lancashire based band, keeping abreast of the changes in musical tastes.

However, fashions change. The Astorians' type of dance music lost its popularity and, by the early 60s, By-Land Productions were advertising 'Rock, Jive Twist and Twitch' every Saturday at Todmorden Co-op Hall, but this had a limited life and regular dancing ceased at the Co-op Hall after 1963. For a time the National School hall became a popular venue featuring the local group Logger and the Lumberjacks along with Dino and the Travellers, The Roadrunners or Phil Plant and the Planets. The market changed with the advent of discs and CDs, which are cheaper than paying a live band and have seen the demise of many local groups.

One of the Belvedere's regular venues was the Brighouse Ritz, which still maintains its Todmorden links through Ginger Taylor who, as resident Disc Jockey (DJ), has been spinning his Northern Soul discs there for over a dozen years.

John Raymond (Ginger) Taylor's story is remarkable. Born on Coronation Day 1953, he became interested in 'soul' music as a teenager, whetting his appetite at the Burnley Mecca. In 1970, he was asked to become DJ at Todmorden Stile Youth Club, where he teamed up with Eddie Antemes. When the club closed in 1971, they organised a Soul Night at Todmorden's Ukranian Club, which met at the Sobriety Hall, where Todmorden's teenagers packed the hall to capacity. When, in 1973, the Ukranian Club moved to the former Mons Mill offices, Ginger and Eddie moved with them. By this time they were playing at other venues in Burnley and Todmorden and their reputation spread, following an invitation to play at the Cleethorpe's Pier 'all-nighter'.

In the mid-1970s, Ginger and Eddie split up but Ginger carried on as a DJ. Following a break in the early 1980s to concentrate on his building and joinery business, he took up the Northern Soul trail again. Surviving a major illness in 1999, he is now in greater demand than ever, being resident DJ at numerous venues from Torquay to Brighouse, Whitby to Blackpool, Skegness to Prestatyn. Not only a national Northern Soul icon, Ginger makes annual visits to Gothenberg, Valencia, Ibiza, Rimini and Pisa - and still finds time to fit in as many local appearances as he can.

He knows the business inside out and can keep his audience happy and dancing. Tributes flow from his many fans, each echoing the presenter of Gloucester FM Radio, 'He is the best DJ on the Northern Soul scene, there is always a full house when Ginger is playing.'[16]

Library Lectures

Since 1931 the local council had sponsored Popular Library Lectures at the Town Hall on selected Tuesday evenings during the winter. Admittance was free and the programmes were varied. October 1931 saw a lantern lecture on the 'West Craven Highlands', whilst December offered a 'Grand Recital of Lancashire Dialect' by Messrs R Ben Brierley and Frank Milnes. Slide shows were popular and 1933 included 'On and Off the Beaten Track in Yugostan' and 'Morocco and the Empire of Sultans in Spain', each with 100 slides. 1945 saw 'The Glamour of Morocco' by Alex Keighley, President of the London Salon of Photography. These popular free events became a fortnightly feature of the winter leisure scene and continued through and beyond World War II. From 1942 these were augmented by concerts presented by the Choral Society, the Orchestra or the Brass Band. Concert versions of Edward German's *Tom Jones* and *Merrie England*, Bizet's *Carmen*, the Brass Band under Walter Mitchell in An Evening of Verdi's Operas or The Brass Band in Musical Comedy were there to be enjoyed and all free.

Post War Choice and Change

The urge to pick up the threads following the war's violent interruption was seen clearly in the churches and chapels where the dramatic and musical societies sprang back into life, as these productions from the spring of 1948 show:

Bottoms Methodist	*Wanted Mr Stuart & The Lady from Abroad*
Central Methodist	*Cinderella*
Central Methodist Dramatic Society	*Pink String and Sealing Wax*
Cornholme Methodist	*Ten Little Niggers*
Cornholme St Michael	*Night Must Fall*
Cross Stone Church	*The Capture of Spring & Meet the Family*
Eastwood Players	*Wasn't It Odd*
Knowlwood Dramatic Society	*A Fiddling Fantasy*
Springside Methodist	*Paying Guests*
Trinity Methodist	*The Devil a Saint*
Unitarians	*The Queen's Portrait*

This resurgence is also exemplified by the wealth of activities at St Paul's Church, Cross Stone. John Cockcroft, then a teenager, remembers the busy parochial life. Annual pantomimes were produced from 1947 to 54 which, following the four night run at Priestwell, toured to other churches and chapels in the town and Stansfield View Hospital. From the late 1940s to the mid-1960s the Dramatic Society performed at least one full length play each year. The Mothers' Union and Men's Club were very active, the latter having snooker tables, cards and table tennis to which teenagers were welcome until 9pm. A Sunday evening youth club, which ran until the mid-1960s, attracted many teenagers. The bell-ringing group, comprising both young and old, met weekly - nor was the church aspect dormant. The choir had a good mix of men, women, boys and girls capable of performing the *Messiah*. The Sunday School, held in the original school next to the church, had, until the early 1960s, about 120 members. When viewed from a distance, they appeared as so many ants climbing the hill on a Sunday afternoon. This renewed interest across the age groups was mirrored in most churches and chapels but, as John recalls, a decline set in during the 1960s.

In 1949 the Town Council initiated a winter series of Municipal Concerts, usually six in number, involving the Choral Society, the Orchestra and the Brass Band, often with visiting soloists. These were very popular for many years but in 1973 Ben Horsfall took the council's Civic Entertainment Committee to task. He accused them, over a period of six years, of insidiously phasing the local Brass Band, Orchestral and Choral Societies out of municipal entertainment. He claimed that activities sponsored by the Mid-Pennine Association for the Arts were taking over. In an episode which could have come straight from a piece by JB Priestley, he complained of being kept waiting for forty minutes when he had an appointment with the Entertainment Committee at which he was accused, during a dressing down by the chairman, of 'putting on highbrow stuff'. Ben objected that the orchestra had been allocated only one concert per year and its subsidy reduced.[17]

Ben had a strong case, although the Mid-Pennine Association brought some celebrated artistes to the town. Emlyn Williams gave a magical 'Evening with Dylan Thomas' which brought the poet unforgettably to life and Dame Edith Evans presented an evening of poetry at the Hippodrome, which had an amusing sideline. It was her custom to have a cup of bovril before her performance; she presented her cup complete with bovril but the theatre had no means of boiling water. However, caretaker, Leslie Forrester, came to the rescue returning shortly with the steaming drink, which Dame Edith gratefully consumed and made her entrance exclaiming 'lovely theatre'. Only later did it transpire that Leslie had bled the central heating system.

The 1973/74 winter season of concerts was the last before local government reorganisation saw the birth of Calderdale and the demise of Todmorden Borough Council - which decided to bow out with a bang. The Entertainments Committee organised six events at the Town Hall during the autumn but really went to town in the New Year. January saw the comedian Cyril Fletcher at the Town Hall, followed in February by Foden's Motor Works Band, and The Todmorden Orchestra with several noted guest players. The London Opera Centre presented Mozart's *Don Giovanni* at the Hippodrome. Then, not without some dissenting council voices, a cabaret night, with a licensed bar and informal seating at tables, was held at the Town Hall, with Alex Welsh and his Dixieland Band, Valentino and his four channel stereo electric accordion, Sheba a celebrated belly, tassel and snake dancer, plus Scottish comedian Chic Murray. Nothing like it had been seen at the Town Hall before and it was a sell-out. In March there was the film *What's Up Doc* and the Todmorden Old Brass Band with the Colne Orpheus Glee Union. The Public Library Committee's swansong was 'Gems From the Savoy Operas' by Burnley and District Gilbert and Sullivan Society. Rounding it all off was 'These You Have Loved', a concert with visiting instrumental and vocal artistes plus the Todmorden Brass Octet. This grand season of fifteen concerts, all heavily subsidised, was the reward for earlier thrift by the exiting Town Council.

The incoming Todmorden Town Council had nowhere near the financial resources of its predecessor but helped local organisations with small grants where it could. Currently it helps by reimbursing local societies, on at least one occasion each per year, for the considerable cost of hiring the Town Hall. Peter Conway of the Choral Society says, 'We regard the Council as our friend'.

The Brass Band Scene

In July 1949 Walsden Temperance Band requested that all instruments and uniforms be returned to the band room at Travis Holme and announced a special public meeting on Sunday 14 August - at which it was voted to disband. Having performed since 1890 this was a sad day for its remaining supporters. Thus Todmorden Old Brass Band was

Todmorden Brass Band at North View, Halifax Road, 1949

the sole surviving band in the borough. Its conductor Walter Mitchell was a remarkable musician to whom Todmorden owes an enormous debt. Born in 1874, he first played with Todmorden Old Brass Band with his father as conductor in 1888. On his father's death in 1892, Walter took over the baton. He also became conductor of Nazebottom Temperance Band to further his experience. In 1895 he left the Todmorden Band to concentrate on Nazebottom but, following his return to Todmorden in 1909, he had 42 years unbroken service, leading the band in many contests, winning major prizes at The Crystal Palace and Belle Vue.

He had studied harmony and counterpoint under Canon Lightfoot, Vicar of Cross Stone, and became an excellent arranger of music for choirs, brass bands and orchestras. He arranged over 160 hymn tunes for Nazebottom Band and even more at Todmorden. He was almost lost to the town in 1913, when he applied for the post of conductor with Hawick Town Band in Scotland. This was a paid position as the band was supported by the town's corporation. In the final choice between himself and H Brown (bandmaster of Black Dyke Band) Walter lost but his loss was Todmorden's gain and he continued working as a clothlooker at Sandbach's Mill, whilst pursuing his musical work as a voluntary hobby.

Given for the Library Committee at the Town Hall, Walter's lectures, enhanced by the Todmorden Band, attracted full houses of up to 900 people. In 1949 he was awarded the National Brass Band Club Certificate of Honorary Life Membership and he retired in 1951 after over 60 years of musical service to the town.

Twenty years on, trombonist Maurice Greenwood recalls telling Jack Dowling, a colleague at Mons Mill and a member of the Todmorden band, that he had always fancied playing a trombone. A few days later Jack said, 'Call at our house on your way

Mabel Wilson, Dr Ben Horsfall and Geoff Love receiving the Freedom of the Borough of Todmorden in 1985.

home, there's a trombone and tuition book waiting for you'. Six weeks later Maurice, who as a pianist could read music, was sitting next to George Mitchell rehearsing in the band room: this was in 1972.

Since then, with a break of a few years owing to pressure of work, Maurice has been a stalwart member. He remembers the commitment required for competitions, rehearsals on two nights per week plus at least half an hour at home on other nights 'to keep the lip in'. These contests found the band competing against some of the top bands from Yorkshire in their section and from the mid-1970s to 1980s, having come second or third in the Yorkshire Area Finals, the band twice played in National finals in London. He has fond memories of Geoff Love, who, every two years, returned to Todmorden, where he first learned music, to conduct the Todmorden Brass Band and Orchestra. A Friday night rehearsal was followed on Saturday and Sunday by concerts which filled the Town Hall. After the band concert on Sunday, there was a traditional 'pie and pea' supper at the nearby Queen Hotel.

In 1976 the band was invited to take part in ITV's 'This is your Life' TV programme featuring Geoff Love. On New Year's eve the band marched down the avenue towards Geoff's house with presenter Eamonn Andrews, although owing to ITV contractual restrictions only thirteen were allowed to play. Geoff answered the door and, ignoring

Todmorden Community Band performing on the Todmorden Station platform.

Andrews with his 'red book', turned to Maurice with 'Have you brought the 'pie and peas'?

Owing to unfortunate circumstances, Todmorden temporarily lost its brass band with all its assets including the band room in 2000. Maurice initiated a fight back, contacting former members of the band, one of whom placed an advertisement in the local paper calling a meeting for all former members. A committee was formed on 19 April 2001 and four weeks later Todmorden Community Band gave its first performance under David White, who is still its director. Years of determined effort have resulted in the return of most of the original assets including the Wellington Road Band Room, which has been refurbished. There are now three bands, a Beginners' Five Note Band, Intermediate Junior Band and Senior Band, all in popular demand.

The Hippodrome Theatre

At town level, the revival of drama after the war was spearheaded by the Children's Theatre, whose driving force was Mrs Beatrice Greenough. Its first public performance in the Central Methodist schoolroom was 'Four Plays for young People' in March 1945.[18] Then in 1951 came the Todmorden Amateur Players formed from the Regnal Amateur Dramatic Society and a group from Cornholme Methodist Amateur Dramatic Society. The Regnal Circle was a Christian men's group meeting at the Central Methodist Church, which formed a dramatic group, initially to raise money. Requiring women to complete the cast it was obliged to include them for its opening play in November 1949, JB Priestley's *They Came to a City*. Led by producer Hubert Town the society enjoyed success. *Chiltern Hundreds* was advertised as the play in 1951 at the Central Methodists and rehearsals were under way, when the church objected to certain 'expletives' used in the play and also to the drinking of sherry. This was the catalyst

Todmorden Operatic Society's production of *Annie* April 1985.
L-R Row 2: Hugh Farrington, Peter Durham, Renee McCabe, Andrew Lupton.
Row 1: Betty Sutcliffe, Sue Morris, Suzanne Proctor, Christine Harrison, Julia White.

which launched the formation of the Todmorden Amateur Players, who performed *Chiltern Hundreds* at the Hippodrome in September of that year. The four plays performed in that season attracted an audience of over 9000.[19]

A successful move was made in 1954 to revive the Todmorden Amateur Operatic Society, which had lapsed during the war and its first production *Magyar Melody* was staged at the Hippodrome in 1955, followed in 1956 by *Masquerade*.

The public had barely become accustomed to drama and musicals again when in June 1956 the Hippodrome theatre suddenly closed. The owners, Hartleys of Nelson, offered to lease it to the Operatic Society at a nominal rent of £250 per year, with the Society taking full responsibility for both internal and external repairs. Bravely the Society agreed and the theatre was saved for the town. In 1986 the Players and Operatic Society merged to become Todmorden Amateur Operatic and Dramatic Society (TAODS). The following year the Hartleys decided to sell off some of their properties including the Hippodrome which they offered to TAODS at a price of £26,000. TAODS agreed to buy it and it finally became theirs in 1990.[20]

Much hard work by many volunteers has seen the theatre refurbished and celebrating its Centenary in 2008. It is a vital part of Todmorden's leisure scene, being home, not only to the Society's music, drama and thriving youth section (with over 90 members), but to the scout and guide Gang Show, St Joseph's Church annual pantomime, performances by the West Yorkshire Savoyards and also to local dance schools for their shows.

Changes in lifestyle had brought about the closure of the Hippodrome as a cinema in 1956 and Cornholme's Gem Cinema closed the following year. The Olympia Cinema carried on but was clearly struggling. In 1960 it was leased from Hartleys by Star Cinemas who carried out some modernisation and on re-opening presented a continuous film programme from 5.30pm each evening Monday to Saturday. A public meeting was held at the Town Hall on 29 September on the subject of 'Sunday Cinema'. Over 400 people attended and Councillors Harry Wilson and Harold Cockcroft spoke in favour of Sunday cinemas, not through strongly held feelings but on the principle of freedom of choice. No-one spoke against and the vote was 390 to 12 in favour. There was still time for the statutory 100 objectors to force a poll of the electorate but it did not happen.

The Olympia showed its first Sunday film on 15 January 1961. Star Cinemas, following the popular trend and in an agreement with the Operatic Society and Todmorden Players, began the Hippodrome Bingo Club. This ran on Friday evenings at 7.30pm starting on 8 September 1961.

In August 1963 Bingo transferred to the Olympia on Wednesday and Thursday evenings with films shown during the rest of the week. By 1966 Bingo had claimed a third night and the following year the Star Bingo and Social Club met every evening and Sunday afternoons, the only films being for children at the Saturday afternoon matinee. The Olympia eventually closed and had been empty over 10 years before opening as Kwik Save Supermarket in 1982.

Demise of Cotton, Co-op and Chapel

We have noted how, immediately after the war, churches and chapels, mainly through their social activities, were still central to their communities. This did not last.

Todmorden had only eleven textile firms left by 1962 and this number had fallen to seven by 1969. Between 1953 and 64 Todmorden lost 20% of its jobs and the population continued to decline. In 1931 it had been 22,222 falling steadily to 19,000 by 1951, 17,428 in 1961, 15,140 in 1971, and 14,800 in 1981 but 1991 saw a slight

THE REMAINS OF ZION

Central Methodist Church

Lumbutts Methodist Church

St Joseph's Roman Catholic Church

St Mary Church of England

St Peter's Church of England,
Walsden

Roomfield Baptist Church

St Michael and All Angels
Church of England,
Cornholme

Vale Baptist Church, Cornholme

Christian Fellowship Church

Interior of Shore Baptist Church from the gallery 1970

rise to 14,941 and again to 15,168 in 2001.[21] This decline in industry and consequent decline in population, allied to the increasing secularisation of Sunday and a fall in religious observance, particularly by the younger generation, meant that the town's churches and chapels, nearly all built in the 19th Century, were maintained by dwindling bands of elderly supporters. Our survey of 125 senior citizens shows that when aged fourteen 49% of men and 62% of women engaged in worship, whereas of 111 students only 11% of boys and 4% of girls in the survey engaged in worship in 2009. No longer viable, most churches and chapels were demolished or converted to other uses in the last half of the 20th Century.

Non-Conformism is now represented by two Methodist, two Baptist and one Christian Fellowship congregations; in addition there are three Anglican churches and one Roman Catholic. As centres of worship and leisure activities, over twenty are no longer there. The closure of so many chapels and churches in a relatively short space of time may be dismissed as a sign of the times, but each closure involved decisions causing heartache for those involved. At what point does a dwindling band of worshippers, some of whom would be the second, third or even fourth generation of a family to attend, decide that maintaining the fabric is no longer possible? One congregation, thankfully, did not have that decision to make.

At Shore Baptist Chapel, the chapel itself had not been used for some years, services being held in the schoolroom. Suddenly during one evening in September 1985 the chapel roof collapsed and the rest of the building was declared unsafe for use. Various items of furniture and equipment such as the electric organ were moved out and the congregation decided to join with that at Vale Baptist in the valley. The time came for a final visit to be made by two members of the congregation. Entirely independently and from different parts of the building they each sensed a coldness and emptiness not felt before as though the 'spirit' had departed from the place where worship had been held for over 200 years.

As churches and chapels succumbed, another seemingly rock-like institution the Co-op was struggling. The Todmorden Society, with its prestigious Dale Street premises and fifteen branch stores stretching from Eastwood in the Halifax valley to Walk Mill in Cliviger, had catered for the basic needs of most people for longer than anyone could remember. However, cotton's decline, a falling population, the growth of supermarkets and a more affluent and mobile society, where people did more of their shopping out of town, adversely affected the Co-op's trading position. The 'divi' dwindled, branches closed, the Society contracted to Dale Street where, following a fire which damaged part of the premises, a small supermarket 'Krazy Kuts' was built. The 'divi' became trading stamps and finally disappeared. In 1995, and by then part of the Norwest Co-operative Ltd, Dale Street was abandoned and a new Co-op food supermarket with electrical store opened on the site of the former Albion Mill in Halifax Road. When this closed, the premises re-opened as Lidl supermarket in 2005 and no vestige of the Co-op remained in the town. For many years before this, the Co-op's influence on the town's social, cultural and leisure activities had ceased.

Leisure patterns have continued to change. Horizons have been widened as travel has become more affordable. Conversely, the home is becoming a leisure centre with the development of high definition television, increasingly sophisticated computers and access to the Internet. There are however, still some constants. The Choral Society

Todmorden Industrial and Co-operative Society's World War I Memorial Stone now in the Garden of Remembrance, showing the various departments.

performs its season of concerts as does the Orchestra, both groups joining for the Christmas performance of the *Messiah*. Following his appointment as head of Castle Hill Primary School in 1968, Jack Bednall, who had been conductor of Rochdale Male Voice Choir, joined Todmorden Choral Society as its director in 1972, a position he held for 28 years until his untimely death in March 2000. He was at the heart of Todmorden's musical life and at the time of his death was rehearsing his favourite oratorio *Elijah*. Rehearsals continued under Anthony Brannick and the performance went ahead on Palm Sunday 16 April 2000 (under guest conductor Darius Battiwalla). As a tribute to Jack Bednall it was outstanding. A knowledgeable member of the audience commented:

> A concert of such quality was beyond belief in a place the size of Todmorden since this was undoubtedly the finest performance of *Elijah* I have heard anywhere.

Todmorden Choral Society and Orchestra under the Directorship of Jack Bednall in 1986.

Chapter 13

Wartime Challenges 1939 to 1945

The 1939 cricket season was played against a background of impending war. Under Hitler, Germany had annexed Austria and, at Munich in September 1938, was allowed to take the German speaking part of Czechoslovakia, the Sudetenland. In March 1939 the Germans occupied, without opposition, the rest of Czechoslovakia.

For Todmorden the season was unremarkable apart from the new scorebox, which was officially opened at the first match against Rawtenstall and funded by the 350-strong Supporters' Club. Leslie Forrester, the scoreboard operator since 1926, had his pay doubled to 2s 0d per match, an acknowledgement that working the new board, with its additional information, was a more arduous task.

Knocked out of the Worsley Cup by East Lancashire in the first round, Todmorden finished a respectable fifth in the league. Only five matches were lost but only seven were won and fourteen were drawn. Indeed 38% of all league matches were drawn, many of them rain-affected.

Opening of new Scorebox with Supporters' Club members.
L-R Row 3: J Hirst, E Duffield, A Sutcliffe, JJ Claxton, E Butterworth,
Row 2: E Ormerod, E Hirst, J Ratcliffe, J Crowther, C Saul, J Rowland,
Row 1: W Stuttard, E Hargreaves, W Sutcliffe, WA Bentley.

In September Hitler invaded Poland and Britain along with France was at war with Germany. In October, the land behind the pavilion was again cultivated for allotments with club members having preference. In December Todmorden's pro for the last two seasons George Macauley was informed that 'owing to the state of war' his contract for 1940 was cancelled. Instead, Macauley turned out for Farsley in the Bradford League before joining the RAF. The following December, whilst stationed at Lerwick in the Shetland Isles, he contracted pneumonia and died. He was never robust; JM Kilburn, quoted in Derek Hodgson's *History of Yorkshire County Cricket Club*, wrote of him:

> the passion in his bowling supplied fuel for his most dramatic performances and gave
> him strength to endure when a rather frail physique was obviously hard-pressed.[1]

Throughout 1939 preparation for war had become increasingly apparent in Todmorden. Air Raid Wardens underwent training, especially on anti-gas courses. Advertisements for the formation of a Todmorden Battery of the 58th Anti-Tank Regiment encouraged fitters, motor mechanics and drivers to volunteer at the Town Hall Recruitment Office. The regiment held a demonstration, with guns, on the park in May. In early June all men aged 20 to 21 had to register for military service at the Employment Exchange, where they could state their preference for naval, air force or army service. A 'blackout' was instituted after dark; street lights were extinguished and prosecution could follow if light showed from buildings. Only necessary journeys by cars were to be made between sunset and sunrise with lights obscured by at least two thicknesses of newspaper; bumper bars and running boards had to be painted white. Owing to the blackout, winter meetings of the Lancashire League were held only when there was a full moon. Petrol rationing began on 23 September and on 21 October men aged 21 to 22 had to register for service.

Some volunteered, maybe in search of excitement or to escape from an unappealing job and each would have a story to tell. One such was Terry Halstead:

> I joined the RAF aged 18 at Padgate in January 1941 going to Blackpool a few weeks later for six weeks 'square bashing' and PT on Bloomfield Road football ground or the promenade (most of the time covered in frozen sea-water). This was followed by nine to ten months at Squires Gate training on aero engines and air screws, accommodation being in various boarding houses.
>
> My first posting was to the East Coast (even colder than Blackpool). The aerodrome was subject to occasional strafing and bombing, the main target being Hull. Who would have thought that the many schoolboy battles and accidents, resulting in a twisted and blocked nose, would have seen my removal from a draft to the Far East in 1942, to have an operation? The medical officer had read my medical records from Dr Bayley in 'civvy street'. The operation, though not pleasant, saved me from being a Japanese prisoner of war or even death.
>
> Most of my war was then spent in Yorkshire working on Halifax bombers, mainly changing, maintaining or modifying engines, often going on routine training or test flights (the pilot's insurance policy) but emerging from the many incidents and accidents relatively unscathed.
>
> The latter part of the war I spent in South Wales. The pressure was off and I was allowed to go to Cardiff Technical College three nights a week and on day release for twelve months to study plumbing (thinking that it might come in useful). It became my occupation for the rest of my working life - and beyond - firstly in Hebden Bridge and then with Woodhead's in Todmorden.
>
> I remember how, as a boy member, I practised in the cricket nets on Centre Vale, and at weekends watched some of the great professionals, especially Constantine and of course Fred Root bowling to his effective and deadly 'leg-trap'. One lasting memory is

of half a dozen 'old chaps' on the school side checking and comparing their pocket watches when the church clock struck the hour - a sort of competition which they never quite solved - the time continually changing.

In addition to housework and gardening, Terry at 87 years, still serves as reader at St Mary Church, is a full-time bell ringer, a member of the choir and also sings with the Todmorden Choral Society.

Robert Duffield did go to the Far East and left his diary (now with his son, Ian) from which the following is written. Robert (Bob) joined the Territorial Army in March 1939 and went to a camp at Bridlington. On his return to Priestwell School in September he and his compatriots were embodied into the army and marched to Halifax. After various postings on coastal and airport defense, his regiment sailed, in October 1941, from Gourock in Scotland to Durban en route for the Middle East. But, there was a sudden change - they sailed at high speed without escort to Singapore, which was under attack from the Japanese. Singapore capitulated in February 1942 and Bob was amongst those rounded up by the Japanese to be used in working parties.

There was little food, beatings on the slightest pretext and the prisoners had to salute or bow to all Japanese soldiers. In June 1942, having contracted both malaria and dysentery, Bob was moved to Changi hospital, where he was put with those expected to die but pulled through with encouragement from a Todmorden pal, Jimmy Colclough.

Later he was moved 1800 miles by train into Siam, where tradesmen were set to work in an engineering workshop making parts for locomotives. The daily walk to work was accompanied by *Colonel Bogey* played by the POW band - accordion, guitar and trumpet. Bob recounts:

> One night we were numbering off, the Japs, unable to count in threes, we had a blank file. The lads numbered 1-10 then Jack, Queen, King, no bid. The Japs went mad and beat us all; made us line up in fives whilst they drew in the dust to add up.

Bob relates that by late 1942:

> there was a railway being built along a planned route which had previously been surveyed and abandoned by the British engineers in 1936. This was the Burma railway built by POWs.
> We were selling all we could pinch; we stole the inner linings of tents to make shorts and G strings as by now, we had no clothes, boots or anything as they had all rotted. We had no meat for weeks...Pte. Stapleton [a professional poacher]...taking some hairs from ...[a] horse's tail...picked one of the fattest horses and tied [it] round one of its fetlocks...it [became] lame so the Japs shot it and it ended up in our cookhouse...the Japs had a morbid fear of...anything [that] died through disease or being crippled.

On another occasion they were given some 'ailing' pigs:

> The pigs were ill due to us keeping them in the sun and swinging them round by the back legs until they were dizzy.
> [Here at] Nong Pladuk, we paraded every night...whilst the dead were taken out to the cemetery; at first two or three a day; then as parties of sick came back from up the [railway] line it got to be as many as ten. This camp had now some 7,000 men. Water was short, food was poor and the conditions were terrible...I must say that but for the marvellous Doctors, Surgeons and our Siamese benefactor, Boon Pong, the death rate would have been far higher. Operations were done with primitive tackle most of it made by POWs from hacksaw blades and the like...Morphine and anaesthetics were smuggled into the camp...supplied by Boon Pong and paid for by Promissary Notes

until after the war, when he was paid in full and awarded the George Cross.

In 1943 Bob was made a steam engine driver pulling Jubilee trucks onto an embankment.

> It did not get me any better treatment…our health went steadily worse. Dysentry, ulcers, malaria, eye complaints, mental disorders and malnutrition were common.

By trading items stolen from the camp with the Thai villagers they were able to eke out the meagre food supply:

> …snake, lizards, pork, little white grubs and fried rice.
> Water had always been a problem; we were down to 4 pints of drinking water per day and one bucket of dirty paddy water between six men for washing.

In November 1943 they were moved to Kaoring Camp, well equipped with workshops and near the River Kwai Bridge. 'Another party arrived from farther up the line. Amongst these was Leslie Whittaker and some other Tod lads, who had come to load ballast for the line.' When the others left for Singapore Leslie stayed behind in hospital with Black Water Fever. (Leslie married Eveline Greenwood, a lady cricketer, and their son was Brian Whittaker one of Todmorden's best amateur cricketers.)

By December 1943 Bob states, 'I realised that I had either ridden on or driven steam locos from Singapore to Mandalay'. However, in April 1944 the bridge was bombed and the POWs built a replacement wooden bridge alongside in one month.

On 15 August 1945 one of the Thais in the workshop said, 'War finish. You go home'. Two days later all the camp was paraded in front of the commandant and a high ranking officer and told, 'Now war finish. All people friends'.

> There was a deathly silence until it finally sank in. Then as one mind but with a single thought we rushed at them but they were off. Before the guards could mount the machine guns however, we were there. We grabbed the guns and men and threw them in the ditch and went after the officers.

The journey home was long. Boils, suffered because of the new rich diet, turned to carbuncles and Bob also had bouts of malaria and dysentery. 'I was given massive doses of penicillin and quinine.' Eventually on 13 October 1945 'I was pronounced almost A1 weighing 7st 4lbs. And as weak as a kitten'.

Bob in a post script says the railway on which he had worked was sold to the Thai Government for £875, 000.

> Eventually the proceeds of the sale were split up. My share was made in two payments one of £50 and one of £25, for three and a half years of misery and privation.[2]

Meanwhile, back in Todmorden food ration books had been issued and customers had registered with their chosen retailers by January 1940. The weekly rations per adult were: butter 4ozs, bacon 4ozs and sugar 12ozs. Meat rationing was introduced the following month.

The local cricket leagues had played out the 1939 season unhindered but how would they respond to wartime restrictions? The North-East Lancashire Tuesday League, to which Todmorden Market Team had transferred, did not operate in 1940; the Todmorden and District League disbanded after 1940; and inter-town schoolboys' cricket ceased after 1939. The Lancashire and Central Lancashire leagues both decided to play without professionals in 1940, but there the similarity ended. The Central

Peter Greenwood

Richard Horsfall

Lancashire League waived qualification rules; whilst being all amateur it became open to all comers including former professionals. The Lancashire League retained its traditionally strict rules; amateurs had to be born or to have resided or worked for twelve months within the district of the club, defined as within two miles of the local government boundary. Ex-professionals could play as amateurs if they had a birth qualification for a club, and the league looked favourably on those with a residential qualification who applied.

As in World War I, Todmorden gave free membership to all members serving in the armed forces. All other members of the armed forces in uniform would be admitted to matches for 3d. Membership cards included a note exhorting members to maintain their membership during the war despite the league being all amateur. With no 2nd XI cricket, the 3rd XI was able to play its Todmorden and District League matches on Saturdays when the 1st XI was away. Thus in 1940 there was cricket at Centre Vale on most Saturdays.

As players were called into the forces, youngsters were given their chance to perform and 1940 saw fifteen year-old future first-class cricketers Peter Greenwood and Derek Shackleton, a member at Todmorden since 1936, make their 1st XI debuts. Ken Fiddling, now on Yorkshire's books, had moved to the Bradford League, but with Richard Horsfall and Harold Dawson still around, four of Todmorden's post-war county cricketers were in the same team. Greenwood took 25 wickets, whilst Shackleton played purely as a batsman. The following season Shackleton scored nearly 400 runs and Greenwood almost 250 in addition to taking 39 wickets. By 1942 both were accomplished all-rounders, Shackleton leading the batting with 388 runs, including 113 not out against Burnley, plus 20 wickets and Greenwood scored 360 runs plus 44 wickets. The war had allowed these two cricketers opportunities that, given the strength of Todmorden's pre-war team, they would probably not otherwise have enjoyed. A season as a goalkeeper on the books of Burnley Football Club in 1942/43 confirmed Shackleton's natural ball-playing talent.

By 1943 Shackleton and Greenwood were conscripted into the forces.[3] Shackleton was assigned to the non-combative pioneer corps because of rapidly deteriorating sight

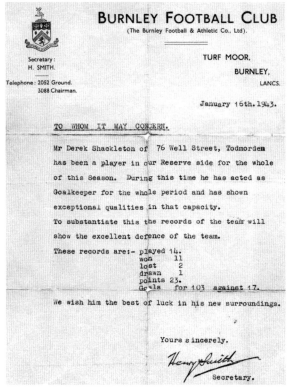

Letter regarding Derek Shackleton from Burnley FC

in his left eye. Amazingly, he was able to keep this secret from both his employers and opponents in county cricket for over twenty years.[4]

The League made changes as it became obvious that the war would be prolonged. In 1941 no mid-week matches were played and the programme was reduced to twenty-two Saturday matches. Todmorden did not play Church and Ramsbottom at home nor Enfield and Rishton away in that season. The following year the birth and residential distance qualification was extended from two to five miles and, acknowledging that players were becoming scarcer, the League resolved that 'any club having difficulty raising a team may borrow a player belonging to any other Lancashire League club (consent being necessary) but only when both teams were engaged in League matches on the same day'. There was no suggestion that even under wartime conditions the League should become open.

Todmorden faced another problem when, in 1942, the local bus department cancelled the contract for buses to away matches owing to scarcity of petrol. Todmorden, situated on the Yorkshire border of the League, had more travelling than the other Lancashire League clubs. New travel plans had to be made for each away match. Burnley could be reached direct using the service bus; for Church and Accrington it was the bus to Burnley from where a taxi was hired; Rishton, which at that time had a nearby station, could be reached by train, changing at Rose Grove. The train also took the team to Blackburn where taxis completed the journey to Alexandra Meadows; Rawtenstall with no easy links by train or bus meant taxis direct from Todmorden. The club was fortunate that committee member Frank Sunderland owned a local taxi firm.

With no 2nd XI cricket and the District League disbanded there was the prospect, in 1941, of a barren Centre Vale apart from the eleven 1st XI home matches. Not so! Cricket was integral to the town's life and an obvious way to maintain spirits, encourage comradeship and escape briefly from the grim realities of war. The lead was given in 1940 when the police played the special constables in a charity match, and the air raid wardens arranged matches against the local defence volunteers (home guard), the first aiders and the auxiliary fire service.

From 1941 the ground was rarely out of use. The police, air raid wardens, royal artillery, home guard, an army XI, special constables, the supporters' club and Dobroyd Castle Approved School all played matches. A comic match between the special constables and air raid wardens in June raised £60 from 'a crowd so large it was

Wings for Victory Week, baseball game on Centre Vale.

reminiscent of a Nelson match with Constantine'.

There was a greater opportunity for youngsters to play cricket and in April 1941 the Secondary School arranged to use Centre Vale for twelve house matches and three inter-school matches. An agreement with the Education Committee allowed elementary schools to play matches from 1.30pm to 4pm on Mondays and Wednesdays. The elementary schools were the all-age schools with children up to the leaving age of 14 years, the secondary school catering for those who passed the County Minor (11+) examination. By 1943 Todmorden Youth Centre and the Air Training Cadets had regular practice nights at Centre Vale.

In June 1943 a baseball match was played between US air force teams, Giants and Tigers. Despite poor weather 1500 turned out for the game and a second game was held a couple of months later. The base was in front of the score-box and a high net was erected to protect the crowd. This was part of the 'Wings for Victory Week' to fund ten wooden built Mosquito fighter planes at £200,000. As part of this Andrew Savage recalls that his section contributed to a display on Centre Vale Park, demonstrating the Home Guard machine gun.

> I joined the navy when I was 18 in 1942, only to be discharged shortly afterwards and listed grade 3 because of poor eyesight. It was suggested that I might join the army but when I returned to my job at Pickles's Portsmouth factory, making leather-cloth for Austin motors, I discovered that it was classified as a reserve occupation. I remained there throughout the war and joined the Home Guard. Our HQ was at Priestwell School, where we drilled once a week. We were equipped with Canadian rifles using 0.300 ammunition as opposed to the British 0.303. Our Home Guard comprised men from the 1st World War and those unfit for service or in reserved occupations. I became part of the elite machine gun section, made up of the younger men, and became a lance corporal. Our section officer was Bob Butterworth, the local masseur, and we were keen. When it was our turn to man the outpost at Bridestones, an ideal vantage point overlooking the whole district, we did it conscientiously. It was rumoured that other sections did part of their lookout duty from the nearby Kebs pub. This nightly vigil

continued into November 1944.

As we worked until Saturday lunchtime, manoeuvres were held on Sundays but not every week. One Sunday I used my rock-climbing skills to scale the face of Horsfall railway tunnel and 'flour bombed' our Priestwell HQ. My initiative was rewarded with the threat of Court Martial.

Todmorden Home Guard machine gun squad
L-R Row 3: John Mitchell, Joe Milnthorpe, Archie Jackson,
Row 2: Ronnie Greenwood, ____, Alwyn Carrington, ____,
Row 1: Fred Townend, ____, Andy Savage, Bob
Bullimore.

Manoeuvres involving rival neighbouring Home Guard companies became serious confrontations. On one occasion the Hebden Bridge Home Guard were instructed to capture Portsmouth Railway Station from the Todmorden company. Guarding the approaches to the station and posting look-outs on hillside vantage points, the Todmorden men waited in vain for signs of movement or attack. The 'enemy' cunningly arrived by train capturing the station unopposed, until a Todmorden soldier claimed victory for Todmorden as he had blown up the line at Eastwood - signified by scattering flour across the track. In the ensuing fracas blood was shed.

This incident occurred before Andrew joined the Home Guard but when they were finally 'stood down' at the end of the war, he was convinced that, along with other Civil Defence groups, the Todmorden 'A' Company of the 21st West Riding Battalion Home Guard had been good for morale and had played their part well.

Meanwhile the Todmorden cricket team, in common with other club teams, used an increasing number of players and on a few occasions the printed team sheet included A.N. OTHER. The club was fortunate when Jack Holt returned to the district and was able to spearhead the attack with his accurate in-swing bowling, capturing 208 wickets from 1940 to 44. The new medical officer of health, Dr AJ Muir also strengthened the team from 1941 to 44, becoming captain in his last season. In 1943 AL (Lenny) Moss returned after three years at Walsden and made an immediate impact as a true all-rounder, following in the footsteps of his father Ernest, Todmorden's professional in 1924 and 25, and his grandfather Sam.

1944 was the nadir of wartime cricket. Todmorden had to call on 36 players during the season and the average runs per wicket, which had declined steadily from 18.96 in 1939, was only 10.9. The team reached 100 just three times in nineteen attempts and at Enfield, having bowled Enfield out for 54, Todmorden collapsed from 7 for 0 to 13 all out! It remains the club's lowest-ever total and the annual report for 1944 acknowledged that the standard of play was:

> not even on a level with previous war years...which has meant our having to field elevens made up by almost any available player willing to turn out.

It was not only lack of playing depth which was responsible for poor results but also below standard ground maintenance and pitch preparation. In September 1944 the club became a member of the Board of Greenkeeping Research at a yearly subscription of £5 5s 0d, showing the serious need of treatment for the ground. The club did not spend five guineas lightly and acted quickly on the researchers' recommendations.

Playing without professionals during the war was not universally popular in the Lancashire League. Most of the pre-war professionals were still around. Indeed, with no jet passenger transport until 1952, many overseas players spent their winters working in England. Edwin St Hill, professional at Lowerhouse from 1931-33 and subsequently in the Huddersfield and Bradford leagues, served in the army at the start of the war and was one of the 330,000 rescued from Dunkirk in 1940. In 1941 Constantine was appointed welfare officer for north-west England by the Ministry of Labour to assist black West Indians who had been introduced to alleviate labour shortages.[5]

In June 1940 *The Cricketer* asserted that the Lancashire League would have to revert to professionals to increase the gate money, comparing the 1940 receipts for Burnley v Nelson of £14 to previous years when the fixture had attracted £200 to £250. At Burnley's AGM in December 1940 the influential League president, Edward Crabtree, clashed with Burnley's president, who contrasted the Lancashire League with 'the league over the border in West Yorkshire' - the Bradford League - which was traditionally an open league. The four clubs in the Burnley area, Burnley, Lowerhouse, Nelson and Colne, had desired, without forfeiting their loyalty to the League, to separate and carry on a programme of their own with professionals, but the rest of the League did not accede to their request. Crabtree's reply was:

> If Hitler attempted an invasion of this country in the spring, as was indicated, surely the time was not opportune to talk about professionalism. What the league had to do at the present time was to continue as quietly as possible.

In January 1941 the *Yorkshire Observer* considered that there had been few professional signings in the Bradford League because 'several prominent players' were awaiting 'the decision of the Lancashire League clubs on professionalism'. Some of them were said 'to favour a return to limited professionalism'. When the Lancashire League confirmed it was to be all amateur, Bradford League clubs announced a spate of new signings and the re-engagement of Constantine, who was at Windhill, and others from their 1940 season.[6] This pattern was reversed in 1945 when the Lancashire League reverted to employing professionals; Jim Smith moved from Yeadon to East Lancs, Ellis Achong from Windhill to Burnley and George Pope from Spen Victoria to Colne.

The Central Lancashire League also had doubts about playing without professionals and at a meeting in October 1942 a split vote resulted in seven being in favour of one professional per club, with a limit on payments, and seven for the suggestion going to further discussion. The Radcliffe club said the Central Lancashire League suffered in comparison with the Bolton League who still employed professionals. For example, Bradshaw's professional in 1940, 41, 44 and 45 was left-arm spinner Fred Hartley, originally amateur at Bacup and professional in Church's first championship-winning team in 1939. In his four seasons at Bradshaw he took 436 wickets and scored 2054 league runs.[7]

Royton's view was that their first priority should be 'winning of the war and not winning of matches'. In 1944 the Central Lancashire League agreed to allow professionals again but there was no compulsion.

Edward Crabtree had a second confrontation at Burnley's AGM in 1943 where it was reported that the four Burnley area clubs were again seeking to withdraw from the League during the rest of the war to form their own section with professionals. The criticism of Crabtree's views became so personal that the League committee called a special meeting at which a motion of confidence in the president's ability, sound judgement and unbiased and fair treatment of everyone and everything connected with the Lancashire League, was passed unanimously.

In June 1944 the Lancashire League Committee:

> ...had under consideration the fact that several clubs reported that their amateurs had been approached by Bradford League clubs to play, in some cases as pros and in others as so called amateurs to receive a scale of payments for expenses which in any other league than the Bradford League would brand them as pros.

Amateurs are free to play wherever they wish provided they comply with the rules of the league involved. Todmorden was one of the clubs affected when, part-way through 1944, John Crowther joined Bingley in the Bradford League, where Kenneth Fiddling Todmorden's pre-war wicketkeeper was already a professional.

The loss of Crowther was off-set in August 1944 by the arrival at Todmorden of Jack Threlfall. A forcing left-hand bat and medium-paced right-arm bowler, he was professional at Church from 1930 to 32 where he scored 1732 runs and took 147 wickets. Appointed Todmorden's District Welfare and Relieving Officer, his performances in the last few matches of 1944 whetted supporters' appetites for 1945. His first match, which Todmorden won scoring 103 for 6 against Accrington's 102 all out, coincided with the local reporter writing nostalgically:

> The setting and conditions were ideal and must have made many in the crowd think with fond remembrance of pre-war cricket with its strategic combats between pro's and a host of talented and lion hearted amateurs. Those were days when amateurs had to fight for their places on teams, when the appearance of pros stimulated interest and the competitive spirit and when players could play their games and the spectators could indulge in banter and wisecracks free from the encumbrances and worries of wartime.

In September 1944 the Lancashire League followed the Central Lancashire League, allowing clubs the option of employing a professional in 1945. There would be two points for a win in place of three but any club without a professional defeating one with a professional would gain three points.

Harry Langton, chairman of Burnley, in a final salvo on the professional question commented, perhaps with some justification:

> If we had professionals in the league earlier we might have retained players who had gone elsewhere. The league had suffered enormously during the war years and it was a pity that departures from the ranks had been fostered by the policy adopted by the majority of clubs.

By adhering, as far as possible during wartime, to its strict criteria, the Lancashire League had just about survived these trying years.

Todmorden began the search for a professional for 1945, advertising in the *Yorkshire Post* and *Nottingham Daily Post*. On 30 October the club minuted:

> Provided we do not receive a satisfactory reply from Bryn Howells or J Wardle by Friday morning post we sign Harold Haigh of Littleborough as professional for 1945 at a maximum of £5 per match.

How close Johnny Wardle was to becoming professional in 1945 we shall never know as Haigh was signed. A slow left-arm bowler he had played for Todmorden as an amateur for part of the 1930 season and during the war was a prolific wicket-taker for Littleborough, claiming 107 wickets in 1941. Haigh joined a weakened side as Muir and Holt had left the district and Billy Scott was unavailable. Haigh was no batsman, made little impression with his bowling and was obviously disheartened when, following defeat at Enfield by 111 runs, he offered to relinquish his wages for the match. The committee accepted!

With five games abandoned, the only real spark was Jack Threlfall's performances. With 617 runs for 10 dismissals, he topped the league batting and his 29 wickets were more than any other Todmorden bowler achieved, although Roy Whitham, Lenny Moss and Haigh all took more than 20. The season's highlight was Threlfall's unbeaten 105 against Haslingden at Centre Vale on Whit Friday, the *Todmorden Advertiser* commenting:

> Bowling which had been treated with the utmost respect was made to look less than ordinary by Threlfall, who smote it hip and thigh. We do not know why he omitted to hit one over the school for he certainly went in abundance in Burnley Road, the churchyard and the park. In fact youngsters were kept busy rooting about for lost balls in the churchyard.

Those youngsters, to whom he was already a hero, and who sat around the pavilion door ready to cheer when he came out to bat, longed for one of his soaring drives to hit the church clock.

As the war ended, so did an era in Lancashire League cricket. In October 1945, Edward Crabtree, League president since 1921, died in office. Todmorden's Central Lancashire League representative in the 1890s, he had served local cricket in official capacities for over half a century, including the role of Todmorden president since the death of EB Fielden in 1942, the first outside the Fielden family to hold this position.

The most influential administrator in the Lancashire League's history, Edward Crabtree always conducted affairs with determination, perseverance and utter integrity and fairness. The Lancashire League paid tribute to the man who:

> had drafted practically every rule in the handbook - a permanent memorial to his work for the league.

Chapter 14

Commonwealth Stars 1946 to 1960

'They suck it in with their mothers' milk,' said Dr John de Ville Mather, when presenting the prizes at the club's 1946 AGM. He was quoting his father, with whom he agreed that there was no better cricket outside the Lancashire League. President of the club from 1949 to 1968, Dr Mather often watched the cricket from his bedroom window at Calderside, across Burnley Road from the ground, or dodged from his surgery into his garden to check the score between appointments.

His enthusiasm was shared by many as cricket, one of the cornerstones of community life that signalled a return to normality, thrived in post-war Todmorden.

The Supporters' Club honoured their 1942 pledge to keep the cricket field 'in good order for when the war was over'. With cash reserves of £950, they paid for the repair of the old motor mower, and bought a new one costing £250. They also repaired or replaced much of the seating. A new Ladies' Refreshment Committee, formed in 1946, gave money to the club and the Ladies' Social Committee donated £100. The club ended 1946 with a bank balance of £25 16s 11d. Chairman Harold Sutcliffe, in proposing an increase in members' subscriptions by 25% from 10s 0d to 12s 6d for 1947, said that in all his 45 years as a member, the rate had been 10s. This increase began a trend, which was to continue.

Seeking new members and spectators, its only sources of income, the club advertised forthcoming matches on the screens at the Todmorden Hippodrome and Olympia cinemas - cinema-going boomed in 1946, with a total attendance of 31,000,000 across Britain. The initiative helped to increase the club's membership to almost 1100.

Todmorden Schoolboys 1947
L-R Malcolm Heywood, Donald Houghton, Keith Marshall, Colin Anker, Trevor Lumb,
Peter Brownbridge (c), Richard Sykes, Harry Hazeltine, Maurice Greenwood, Roger Moss,
Dennis Widdup.

Attendances received a further boost in 1946 when the Labour Government reduced the working week. Forty-five hours spread over five days meant an end to Saturday working in the mills. For the cricketers there would be no more working until 11.30am before the rush to play in a match starting at 2pm. Supporters, most of whom travelled by bus, could now get to away matches. It could take a full day to see Todmorden play at Ramsbottom, Colne or East Lancashire but many made the journey by service bus. The single-decker team bus was always full, a season's seat on it costing £1 5s, an amount which did not change from pre-war days to the 1960s.

With large crowds anticipated, a special committee meeting on Saturday 6 April considered 'means of control of boys at matches'. Youngsters were suffered rather than encouraged and a notice was posted decreeing that, 'Boys are not allowed on the twelve seats in front of the Players' Pavilion on Match Days', thus denying them the perfect stage from which to cheer their heroes as they came out to bat. More positively for the youngsters, Lancashire schoolboys' cricket was revived and the Todmorden team comprised boys from both the grammar and recently formed secondary modern schools. Todmorden was grouped with Littleborough, Rochdale and Heywood.

For the first time since 1939, the Lancashire League had a full 26 match programme, a 2nd XI league, and all the clubs would have a professional. Only the Worsley Cup was left in abeyance because it involved midweek or evening play when match pros may not have been available.

Todmorden once again aspired to an England international professional. They contacted Maurice Leyland, the left-handed Yorkshire batsman/spinner, before signing Morris Stanley Nichols, the former Essex and England all-rounder, whose powerful left-handed batting and right-arm quick bowling had realised an impressive 17,827 runs and 1833 wickets.[1] His contract of £16 per week for 22 weeks included £6 per week from December 1945 to tide him over the winter and, like the other professionals in the league, was for one year to keep the field open for potential professionals still to be demobilised from the forces.

Nichols, who played for Bradford League club Farsley in 1945,[2] was a formidable cricketer. Months before the 1932/33 Bodyline tour he had, according to John Arlott, batted Harold Larwood with 'no trouble whatsoever'.[3] EM Wellings, playing alongside Nichols in an end-of-war charity match at Imber Court, recalled that, even in his 44th year, he was 'still able to bowl fast', bowling unchanged for 22 overs and taking 4 wickets before lunch. His only concession to age was to instruct his skipper 'I don't mind how long I bowl but don't take me off and expect me to come back, because I can't do that now'.[4]

Dennis Compton and Morris Nichols, Army v a Lord's XI, at Lord's in 1941.

The stiffness of age cannot have been helped by Nichols's 500 miles round trip between his Essex home and Todmorden each weekend and perhaps explains his slightly disappointing return of 360 runs and 63 wickets. Nevertheless, Todmorden finished fifth and Nichols was offered terms for 1947. Instead, he signed for Littleborough, where he enjoyed two successful seasons. In August 1947 Walsden were bowled out for 77 by two former Todmorden professionals, Nichols 7 for 25 and Haigh 3 for 50.

Todmorden's amateur batting, led by Harold Dawson, Jack Threlfall and Billy Scott, was strong in 1946, whilst Alec Smith, Roy Whitham, Ivor Martin and Threlfall, all former club professionals, provided medium pace back-up to Nichols. Martin, a right-arm fast-medium bowler and hard hitting left-hand batsman, had

Todmorden CC Supporters' Club c1949

been Queensbury's professional in 1938 and 39. Prior to this he had had a trial with Warwickshire, where his chances may have been blighted when he bowled to RES (Bob) Wyatt in the nets and broke the England batsman's finger.

Competition for places and inept decision-making caused the unnecessary loss of Lenny Moss, Todmorden's leading all rounder in 1945. For the second match of 1946 the selectors contrived to pick him for the first team, then demote him to the seconds. Moss moved immediately to Walsden and was mainstay of the 1st XI with his forthright batting and medium-paced swing bowling until his retirement in 1968.

For 1947, Todmorden signed Frank Woodhead, a 34 year-old right-arm fast-medium bowler, who had been with Nottinghamshire since 1934. His salary was £475 for the 22 week season including an advance winter payment of £4 per week from 6 October. With most players now returned from the forces, Todmorden had high hopes of success in 1947, but this was not to be.

The counties were keen to reinforce their ageing and depleted staffs. Harold Dawson agreed terms with Hampshire and Richard Horsfall played one innings, scoring 51 against Lowerhouse, before joining Essex. In the same year Peter Greenwood became pro at Kendal in the Ribblesdale League, where his benefit match against a team of Lancashire League cricketers and Burnley footballers, captained by Billy Scott, raised £100. A talented sportsman, he played football for Burnley and Chester and signed for Lancashire CCC in 1948, making his debut against Kent. Staying with the county until 1952, he played seventy-five matches, scored 1270 runs and took 208 wickets with his right-arm medium/fast bowling - varied with off-spin.[5]

Wicketkeeper batsman Ken Fiddling, who made his championship debut with Yorkshire in 1939, had moved to Northants where he played until a persistent foot injury forced his retirement in 1953. With Derek Shackleton at Hampshire, Jack Threlfall joining Moss at Walsden and John Crowther pro'ing in the Bradford League, Todmorden had haemorrhaged almost a full team of cricketers.

Derek Shackleton played just one match for Todmorden in 1946, playing most of his cricket in the army where he caught the eye of Hampshire's Sam Staples, who travelled north to meet him via Todmorden chairman Harold Sutcliffe in April 1947. Eight of Hampshire's pre-war eleven were now over thirty and Derek signed for them after his demobilisation in July 1947, reportedly regarded as a batsman who bowled 'temperamental leg-spinners'. Such was Hampshire's shortage of pace-bowling that, prior to the 1948 season, club chairman WK Pearce, in search of hidden talent, ordered everyone on the staff to bowl quickly in the nets. Derek impressed, showing:

> ...extraordinary natural ability...uncoached, unspoilt...very straight with a natural high action and, although not genuinely fast, produced deliveries that were distinctly lively.

He made his debut alongside Harold Dawson. In their second match against the

Hampshire CCC with Viscount Montgomery 1948
L-R Row 2: 4th Derek Shackleton, 6th Harold Dawson.

Combined Services at Aldershot, both had the privilege of meeting Field Marshall Montgomery.

A steady, thoughtful and consistent character, always immaculately dressed, Derek soon earned popularity and respect. He took 100 wickets in his first full season 1949 and repeated this achievement for 20 consecutive seasons, the most accurate bowler of his era, missing only 13 matches through injury in that time. The key to Derek's longevity was a light-footed run-up and deceptively gentle style - the nip coming from a superb wrist action.

When Hampshire won the county title for the first time in 1961, captain Colin Ingleby-Mackenzie stated, 'He, above all, was the man who won us the championship'. Between 1962 and 65 Derek was the leading wicket-taker in the country for four consecutive seasons and in 1964, his fortieth year, he bowled 282 overs more than anyone else. In his last full season 1968, aged 44, he took 5 for 58 in 27 overs against the Australian tourists.

England batsman Tom Graveney says of Derek:

> You were aware that you were facing a bowler, so skilled, that there was absolutely no room for error. I played him off the front foot which was the only way but if you made a mistake you knew the chances were you would be back in the pavilion...he was the finest of his type in post-war cricket...in a class of his own.

Peter Lever tells of going out to bat at Dean Park, Bournemouth, against Hampshire. His partner, Harry Pilling, came to meet him and asked which of the two bowlers he preferred to face, the lively pace of Butch White or the old chap at the top end. Peter reminded him that this was the legendary Derek Shackleton, to which Harry replied, 'Well, don't spit on't pitch or it'll green up and he'll use it' - a professional's recognition of Shackleton's accuracy.

Derek probably lacked a couple of yards of pace to succeed in test cricket, where batsmen pick up the line and length more quickly, and his seven test matches were spread over thirteen years. In June 1950, he became the first Todmorden cricketer to play for England in the 3rd Test against the West Indies at Trent Bridge, where he opened the bowling with Alec Bedser. Derek top-scored with 42 in England's first

Derek Shackleton bowling to Colin Cowdrey,
the non-striker is Brian Luckhurst.

Shackleton, ever immaculate,
cleans his boots.

innings but took only one wicket. England won by 10 wickets and he was left out for
the next game.

Derek's final appearances were also against the West Indies when, after a gap of
eleven years, he played four test matches in 1963. He played a key role in the famous
draw at Lord's with match figures of 7 for 165 in 84.2 overs. His 15 wickets in the
series were achieved whilst conceding only two runs an over. At the age of 38 he
succeeded in frustrating the attacking flair of the best batting side in the world. Injuries
began to catch up with him and he moved on to play for Minor Counties' side Dorset
from 1971 to 74, finally hanging up his boots at the age of 50. He was a first class
umpire from 1979 to 81.

Derek married a Todmorden girl, Kathy at St Mary Church, Todmorden, in August
1950, and their son, Julian, was born in Todmorden in 1952. Julian played for
Gloucestershire from 1971 to 1978 and then followed his father to Dorset, where he
became one of the county's most successful bowlers. Although settling in the south, the
Todmorden family connections remained strong. Derek became known as 'Top End
Tod' on a 1950/51 tour of India by a Commonwealth XI which included several
Lancashire League professionals. The nickname stuck with him throughout his career.[6]

The start of the 1947 season came as a relief from a winter which remains the worst
in living memory. Snow fell early in February and stayed. Strong winds whipped snow
into drifts blocking roads as soon as they were dug out. With transport disrupted,
walking two or three miles to school became an adventure, whilst sledging over frozen
fields with no visible boundary walls was magical. Disruption to industry was serious
as movement of coal, the main source of power, was curtailed and working hours were
staggered to even out the demand for electricity.

Surprisingly, on 19 April the cricket season opened as scheduled, Todmorden
winning by six wickets against Lowerhouse, whose pro was Emmanuel (Manny)
Martindale, the veteran West Indian fast bowler. Todmorden's fragile batting, dismissed
for less than 100 nine times, relied heavily on Alan Cunliffe, Frank Saul and Billy Scott
in a season from which three things stand out. The first is Todmorden's complete
inability to cope with the left-arm spin of Church's pro, Bacup-born Fred Hartley, who
took 8 for 6 in Todmorden's 20 all out at Centre Vale and 9 for 19 in the return match.
Secondly, Alec Smith's bowling brought him 60 League wickets from almost 240 overs,
in what was virtually a two-pronged attack with Woodhead who took 73 wickets from
315 overs. Lastly was one of the most amazing matches, when Accrington visited

Fred Hartley, Church pro and scourge of Todmorden in 1947.

Todmorden on 30 August.

Accrington had first use of a good hard pitch but lost their professional, JH (Jim) Parks of Sussex (the only player to score 3000 runs and take 100 wickets in a county season), who was bowled for two by a Woodhead leg-cutter, and the innings subsided to 96 for 8 wickets. An unlikely partnership between Jackie Hope and Frank Rushton took the score to 160 before last man Les Hartley, dropped at slip before scoring, set about the bowling. With Hope he took the score to 230 for 9 when the declaration came, leaving Todmorden 2 hours 7 minutes to hit their highest total since 1939.

Undaunted, Billy Scott and Alan Cunliffe attacked the bowling; 100 was hoisted in an hour but with only 20 minutes left 50 runs were still needed. The club's record opening partnership of 179 was passed and extended to 196 when Scott was caught for 81, leaving 36 required in 15 minutes. Woodhead and Martin were out hitting and Cunliffe had reached 119 when Frank Saul 'fairly galloped to the wicket...5 runs needed in 3 minutes. The umpires looked at their watches and the crowd bobbed up and down on their seats'. Carter sent down a delivery with all he had but Saul turned his left shoulder to it and with a lovely drive to the school boundary 'set the lads in the enclosure to yelling their heads off'. Saul sealed victory for Todmorden with another single and wickets were drawn with a minute to spare. '462 runs had been scored in 272 minutes. Enthusiastic players carried Cunliffe shoulder high to the pavilion'.

The Worsley Cup knockout competition recommenced in 1947 using the pre-war zoning system. Todmorden, once again playing East Lancashire for a place in the semi-final, lost by 127 runs after the double-winning Blackburn side made 282 all out. From 1949 the competition became a straight knockout for all teams with the first round draw regionalized, Todmorden playing one of Burnley, Colne, Lowerhouse or Nelson, or receiving a bye in round 1. In 1957, and from 1964 onwards, there was a free draw for all rounds.

By mid-June Todmorden had decided not to offer Woodhead terms for 1948 but when the weather improved and pitches quickened from mid-July, he showed his quality. Five 6 wicket hauls helped Todmorden to win six of the last nine matches and climb from the re-election zone to eighth. By this time the committee, looking to strengthen the batting, was in negotiations with Stanley Worthington of Derbyshire, who signed for 1948 on exactly the same terms as Woodhead.

Frank Woodhead's value cannot be judged purely by his performances on the field. He coached the juniors during the long summer holidays, organising matches on the park side of the ground and teaching many skills and strategies, including: the correct stance; the need to bowl a

Alan Cunliffe and Billy Scott, record opening partnership of 196 against Accrington in 1947.

length; how to run between
wickets without turning 'blind';
and the importance of backing
up throws in the field. He
returned to Nottinghamshire in
1948 and when he clean
bowled Bradman, Hassett and
Miller of the touring
Australians, the Todmorden
lads basked in reflected glory.

Stan Worthington was a
cricketer of some distinction.
Born in 1905 at Bolsover, he
played 406 matches for
Derbyshire from 1924 to 47. A

Todmorden 1st XI 1948

'vigorous middle-order right
hand batsman and right arm
fast medium bowler', he toured
Australia and New Zealand in

L-R Row2: Harry Shepherd, Ernest Brooks, Ivor Martin,
Gordon Helliwell, Jim Moncrieff, Derek Grannon,
Row 1: Alan Cunliffe, Stan Worthington (pro), Billy Scott
(c), Clifford Potts, Tommy Carrick.

1929/30 and 1936/37 and was in Lionel Tennyson's party to India in 1937/38. He
played 9 test matches and in 1936 against India at the Oval scored 128 in a stand with
Hammond of 266 in just over 3 hours.[7]

In signing a batsman, the committee had not anticipated that their main amateur
bowler, Alec Smith, would sign as professional for Queensbury in the Bradford League.

Worthington batted with an easy style which lingers in the memory. A powerfully
built man attired in cream flannels and cravat, he was every inch the professional. In
the Worsley Cup, however, he was outwitted by East Lancs' substitute professional,
George Tribe, the Australian left-arm chinaman and googly bowler, who was pro at
Milnrow. Worthington on 33 was in no trouble, moving out to smother or drive Tribe's
spin. Suddenly, presumably by pre-arrangement with his keeper, Tribe bowled a full
toss over the advancing Worthington's head and had him comprehensively stumped.
Todmorden, 73 all out, lost by 8 wickets.

Collections were highly prized; they could easily be more than a week's wages and,
if achieved near the holidays, pay for a week at Blackpool. Until 1948 the home club
had the responsibility for deciding when collections should be taken. Most clubs had
reciprocal arrangements, a score of 50 warranting a collection, but there was no
standard for bowling collections until 1948. Then the League decided that an amateur
would qualify for a collection if at the end of an innings he had taken: 5 wickets for 40
runs or under; 6 for 48 or under; 7 for 56 or under; or 8 or more at any cost. For a
professional the figures were 6 for 30 or under; 7 for 35 or under; 8 for 40 or under;
or 9 or 10 at any cost.[8]

To narrowly miss a collection was a great disappointment, rarely more so than in
Todmorden's match at Bacup in May 1948 when Billy Scott, stricken by lumbago, had
to retire hurt on 46. Helped to the pavilion, he was vigorously attended by his wife, but
her attempts to massage him back to the middle were in vain. At the fall of the next
wicket he was still unfit to bat and his chance had gone, Todmorden declaring at 196
for 3. To add to Billy's disappointment, Bacup won by 4 wickets, led by 104 from
amateur Fred Cooper who later joined his brother Edwin at Worcestershire.

The post-war enthusiasm for cricket continued to expand. Todmorden were happy
with gates, which increased from £350 in 1946 to £650 in 1948 (the highest since

1921), a membership approaching 1200 and a bank balance of £151.

However, when Worthington intimated that he did not wish to renew his contract, Todmorden did not join the rush to sign an overseas professional, whose ranks in the League grew from four in 1948 to eleven in 1949. Amongst the newcomers were Everton Weekes, Cec Pepper, who moved from Rochdale to Burnley, Bruce Dooland and Vijay Hazare. Todmorden's search for an Englishman included Bill Lawton, pro at St Annes and husband of actress Dora Bryan. An off-spinner who played occasionally for Lancashire, he hit the headlines some years later as captain of Oldham when, batting second, he declared the innings closed to protect his players from the fearsome West Indian paceman Roy Gilchrist.

Todmorden signed 33 year-old Eric D Denison, professional at Werneth. A left-arm spinner and obdurate left-hand bat, Denison had topped the Yorkshire Council bowling averages at the age of seventeen with Rawdon CC, which was where Hedley Verity grew up and learnt his cricket. Pre-war Denison had been professional at Kendal and Middleton, helping the latter to the Central Lancashire League double in 1938, and he played for Yorkshire 2nd XI in 1939.

During the war Denison was taken prisoner in Italy. He escaped and spent almost three years on the run. Returning to England 'much greyer and thinner', Denison was only third in the post-war queue of Yorkshire left-arm spinners behind Arthur Booth and the mercurial Johnny Wardle. So he sought out Middleton who, not knowing his whereabouts, had already signed a pro for the coming 1946 season. Torn between a desire to honour their current contract and an obligation to an old servant, the club was in a quandary. They gave Denison a couple of games towards the end of the 1945 season, kitted him out with cricket equipment and, with great reluctance, helped him to secure a professional post at Werneth, who jumped at the chance.[9]

Eric Denison and John Crowther opening the innings.

In 1949 Todmorden signed Denison from Werneth on a two-year contract at £24 per week for the 22 week season. He dovetailed into a team strengthened in seam bowling by Alec Smith's return and the advent of medium pacer John Ingham. Every inch a professional, he led from the front in matches and in practice and made an immediate impact.

Another boost came in July when John Crowther returned to Todmorden, probably because of his work in the Fire Service. During five seasons in the Bradford League John played first for Bingley and then Windhill. In 1946 he was second in the league batting averages and topped them the following year with an average of 53.35, Eddie Paynter being 2nd.[10] John's 134 for Windhill against Spen Victoria, shortly before he returned to Todmorden, was the highest individual score in the league in 1949.

1949 was a good year. The sun shone, Denison with 1001 runs and 81 wickets was exceptional, Todmorden finished third in the League and gate money totalled £900. In the

League as a whole 325,999 spectators paid admission and crowds reminiscent of pre-war days ensured that matches had atmosphere.[11] Totally focused, these communities of experts anticipated every delivery and nuance as the contests unfolded. Fiercely partisan banter and barracking added to the entertainment; good play was applauded and mistakes, especially by the opposition, castigated. Applause could begin, for no apparent reason, and travel around the ground as news was relayed of some obscure record broken. There were well-known characters, who revelled in barracking and playing to the crowds. Tommy 'Longhair' travelled from Blackpool to every Todmorden home game. During the Denison era Tommy heralded his arrival with 'Bump 'im one Eric' and the entertainment had begun.

At East Lancs' Alexandra Meadows the banter and barracking came from the 'scratting shed', a wooden structure at the school end of the ground. Visiting players were reluctant to collect from this area and often went in twos. This aspect of the game has diminished as crowds have dwindled and matches, which were concentrated within a five hour period can now extend to seven.

The doyen either side of the war was Nelson's Alwyn Nightingale, whose 'full throated, pungent' offerings from behind the wicket at Seedhill earned him a chapter to himself, *A Nightingale Sang…*, in Noel Wild's centenary booklet *The Greatest Show on Turf*.

By the 1980s, Alwyn's mantle had passed to the Bacup trio, known improbably as Roy Rossendale, Clive of India and Gordon of Khartoum. Umpires, who gave opposition bowlers the benefit of the doubt on width, met instant retribution. 'Wide vampire! As ta' getten arthritic arms, vampire?' When Roger Harper struck Todmorden's Ibrar Ali for a huge straight six, Ibrar, who was a taxi driver at the time, was advised, 'Ali, taxi!' When Mike Whitney visited Bacup as Haslingden's professional in 1990, Roy was quick to exploit the Australian's shock of black, almost Afro-style hair. 'Hey, Whitney Houston!' heckled Roy, only changing his tune when Whitney dropped a sharp caught and bowled. 'He's not Whitney Houston, he's Whitney Useless!'[12]

Former players have not been averse to joining the fun. A dull end-of-season match on a sluggish, flood-affected pitch in 1982 saw Burnley crawling to an inevitable victory after Todmorden had posted a hopelessly inadequate 108 for 9. Opener Trevor Pickup was seemingly intent on taking most of the 46 overs to get the runs, amidst interminable delays as flocks of birds targeted the recently re-seeded wicket ends. As Pickup played out another maiden, former Todmorden wicketkeeper Albert Connor advised, 'I should keep an eye on that pigeon batsman. It's looking to nest in thee.'

Centre Vale has always been prone to flooding and the worst occurred on the evening of Wednesday, 6 September 1950, three days before the season ended. Heavy rain caused the River Calder to overflow and pour its waters onto the field to a depth of four feet. When the water subsided a two inch layer of a 'clay-like' deposit covered the entire ground and pavilion floors. Around 100 tons were shovelled and wheeled from the ground but the bad weather prevented this from being done immediately. Fear that the turf, especially on the square, had suffered was confirmed by specialist advice.

A decision to re-lay the square was taken. Voluntary labour dug out the square's 1200 square yards of turf. A similar amount was removed from the outfield on the school side and re-laid on the square by Conways of Halifax, whilst the volunteers reinstated the school side with new turf. The work was completed by mid-December and the public rallied round, a special appeal fund raising £936.

The ground was fit for the 1951 season but the pitch offered much assistance to the bowlers and always deteriorated. Of Todmorden's 13 home matches, five were

The flood of 1950, on the school side plank seats float and the sightboard has been washed from the edge of the field.

drawn and the other eight were won by the team batting first, including six Todmorden victories. Whilst the team batting first topped 150 eight times, the highest score by a team batting second was 126. In the circumstances, Denison's club record of 1027 league runs, which stood for 47 years, was a remarkable achievement and key to another successful season in which Todmorden finished third.

Garth Warren who had joined the club from Walsden in 1950 found the relayed surface to his liking. Over six feet tall and bowling fast-medium with a high action, he extracted considerable lift and movement. He took 63 wickets, finished top of the League bowling averages and earned a contract in the Ribblesdale League to begin an eleven-year professional career.

The desire to engage overseas professionals intensified and in April 1952 the local *Northern Daily Telegraph* commented:

> The number of overseas professionals had again been brought to mind with the news that a 'cargo' of Lancashire League pro's will arrive at Tilbury.[13]

Travel to England from Australia was still cheaper and more common by sea than air in 1952, and in that year Denison was the only English professional in the League pitting his skills against international stars such as Weekes, Pepper, Alley, Dooland, Walcott, Mankad, Roy Marshall and Lindwall.

Meticulous in his preparation, Denison analysed the opposition and sometimes discussed his plans after practice. When Burnley were due to visit Centre Vale on 2 July 1949 Denison predicted that his old Central Lancashire League rival, Cec Pepper, would try to clear the shortish leg-side boundary on the Burnley Road side and was likely to offer a chance. Todmorden batting first declared at 240 for 6 wickets and Burnley's hopes rested largely on an aggressive knock from their powerful professional. Sure enough, Pepper targeted Denison's leg-side boundary, skying the ball to deep square leg - where he was dropped twice on his way to 119 not out from Burnley's 226 for 5, the match being drawn.

Pepper was in his element in the Leagues. An attacking batsman and a fine leg-spin and googly bowler with a top-spinner and a vicious flipper, he loved playing centre stage. In 1949 he and Vijay Hazare, the Rawtenstall pro, became the first players to achieve the double of 1000 runs and 100 wickets in Lancashire League cricket. A fiery character, who could have played many Test matches but for his brush with the Australian authorities, and Bradman in particular, he worked both the crowds and the umpires. The spectators were rarely disappointed in anticipating some incident when Pepper was playing.

One midweek evening Pepper's car broke down near Ivor Martin's house in Halifax

George
Tribe

Everton Weekes

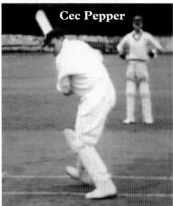

Cec Pepper

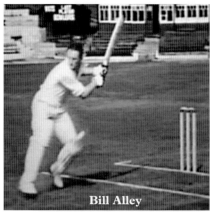

Bill Alley

Clyde Walcott

Vijay Hazare

OVERSEAS STARS
OF THE POST-WAR
RESURGENCE.
RARE ACTION
SHOTS TAKEN
FROM FILM

Road. Ivor and others helped to get it started and pushed it on its way. When Todmorden met Burnley shortly afterwards, Pepper greeted Ivor with a leg-side full toss and the comment 'that's for pushing my bl***y car'. Ivor gratefully hit the gift ball for four.

It has been said that Pepper's bark was worse than his bite but he could be very intimidating on the field. After an over of beating a bemused Colne batsman he shouted down the pitch, 'Right, you can open your eyes now – I've finished'. When a young Malcolm Heywood padded up to three consecutive leg breaks Pepper walked up the pitch, stood eyeball to eyeball and announced, 'If you pad up to me again sonny I'll bowl you round your f****** a***!'.

In 1953 East Lancashire replaced Bruce Dooland, who had joined Nottinghamshire, with another Australian leg-spinner, Colin McCool. Denison, again in a post-practice discussion, remarked that McCool had a high back-lift and that by holding the ball back slightly he could have him caught and bowled. The Todmorden scorebook for 8 August 1953 reads 'McCool c&b Denison 0'.

In 1950 Harold Dawson returned to Todmorden after three years in Hampshire. He played only briefly for the county but became a very popular professional at Paignton, scoring many runs and having a benefit in 1949. He took over the Todmorden captaincy from JC (Jim) Moncrieff in 1951 and held the post until his retirement 14 years later.

In the last home match of 1952 Denison (102 not out) and Dawson (104 not out) set a club record partnership of 214 against Haslingden and their spin bowling professional Vinoo Mankad. Mankad also played for India in their Test series against England that summer. At Lord's he top-scored with 72 in India's first innings total of 235, then bowled 73 overs, taking 5 for 196, as England scored 537. Going straight out to open the batting again, in the words of the *Daily Mirror's* Peter Laker:

> The 'Haslingden marvel' gave more than can be expected of any man during a

Todmorden 1st XI 1950, with the Mayor, club treasurer Alfred King
L-R Row 2: E Gregson (scorer), F Saul, J Crowther, J Ingham, G Helliwell, I Martin,
H Dawson, T Carrick, GE Haworth (sec),
Row 1: A Cunliffe, JC Moncrieff (c), Dr J de Ville Mather, Ald A King (treas),
H Sutcliffe (chair), W Scott, ED Denison (pro).

marathon innings of 184 in four hours twenty-five minutes, the highest individual score by any Indian in a Test - and the finest exhibition of fighting cricket ever seen at Lords.

Mankad was out at 270 for 3 but India crumbled for 378 and England knocked off the 77 which they needed for the loss of 2 wickets, Mankad bowling a further 24 overs. No wonder it is known as 'Mankad's Match'.[14]

Denison left Todmorden after 1953 to continue his professional career in the Central Lancashire League, playing for Royton, Littleborough and Walsden. In his enviable league career he scored 13,110 runs and took 1449 wickets. The search for Denison's successor began in June 1953 and a galaxy of county players were sounded out: Ellis Robinson (Yorkshire); Cliff Gladwin (Derbyshire); Arthur Jepson (Notts); Reg Perks (Worcestershire); Charles Groves (Warwickshire) and Todmorden's own Derek Shackleton at Hampshire.

The club minutes do not suggest that any of these enquiries reached the stage of a monetary

Harold Dawson (104*) and Eric Denison (102*), record partnership 214 against Haslingden, September 1952.

offer, but seemingly out of the blue, is written, 'We agree to sign J Burke (Australia) on his terms and he be cabled of our acceptance and sent an agreement form for his signature'. Burke, the 23 year-old New South Wales and Australian opening batsman and off-break bowler, was recommended 'by a very fine former Test match player' with considerable Lancashire League experience - probably Arthur Richardson who toured with the Australians in 1926 and was professional at Bacup from 1929-31 and Burnley 1932-34.

Signing Burke was a bold move by hitherto conservative Todmorden. They became the last Lancashire League club to break with the tradition of English professionals at a time when they owed the bank £276 and the Supporters' Club £200. 1953 had been wet and across the League support was declining. 1953 saw a drop in total membership of 1000 from its all-time high of 17,464 in 1952, and paying spectators dropped by 50,000 to 204,637, the last year in which 200,000 was reached.[15]

With travelling expenses, the professional's cost breached £1000 for the first time in the club's history and the season's final bank balance for 1954 of £1 5s 0d was only achieved with a further £200 loan from the Supporters' Club and £224 from the Social Committee.[16]

Burke announced himself by hitting 92 and taking 5 for 36 as Todmorden beat Colne by 103 runs on the opening day. His stylish batting was good to watch but, in a season of indifferent weather on largely uncovered pitches, Burke's off-spin bowling was the crucial element. Only Rishton pushed Todmorden hard in the first half of the season. Burke took a hat-trick as Rishton were dismissed for 72, but their Indian leg-spinning professional, Subhash Gupte (7 for 37) soon had Todmorden in a spin. Left-handed Kenny Walker stood firm, his unbeaten 32 steering Todmorden to victory on 73 for 8. Burke took another hat-trick at home to Colne and on 19 June demolished East Lancs

Todmorden 1st XI 'double team' 1954
L-R Row 2: John Ingham, Brian Fielden, Jim Burke (pro), Jim Moncrieff, Malcolm Heywood,
Row 1: Jack Hazeltine, Kenny Walker, John Crowther, Harold Dawson,
Frank Saul, Colin Sunderland.

with 97 not out and a spell of 8 for 14.

By this time Burke's action was a major talking point, especially when he bowled his faster ball and, frankly, he would be unlikely to pass scrutiny today. David Frith in *The Slow Men* writes of Burke's bowling:

> a blatant 'pusher' who, surprisingly was never called for throwing. A puckish and perhaps knowing grin spread over Burke's countenance when the matter was raised…A 'dart thrower' was the more common epithet used by opponents. This talented pianist and mimic . . . once took 4 for 37 in a Test at Calcutta, a feat which gave him quite as much satisfaction as his marathon innings of 161 in the previous Test at Bombay.[17]

Todmorden lost only once, to a Weekes-inspired Bacup in July, and the League title was assured with three matches to spare, the final margin ten points over Enfield.

Todmorden, drawn at home in every round of the Worsley Cup, took their revenge over Bacup in the semi-final to set up a tense final against Church on a rain-affected pitch. Todmorden slid to 28 for 3 before Burke (39) and Walker (19) added 43 for the fourth wicket. Once Burke had gone, Todmorden had their worst half hour of the season. Church's Indian professional Polly Umrigar ran though the lower order as Todmorden crashed from 81 for 4 to 84 all out. Church began steadily with a stand of 18 for the first wicket, before Burke and John Ingham got to work, reducing the visitors to 43 for 7. Resistance from the tail kept everyone guessing but Burke (6 for 25) and Ingham (4 for 28) prevailed as Church were bowled out for 70.

Todmorden had achieved the League and Cup double for a second time. In all

matches Burke contributed 817 runs and 118
wickets, Harold Dawson 813 runs and John
Crowther 603 runs and 30 wickets.

Burke retired from first class cricket at the age of
28 following a broken rib on tour to South Africa,
but he played grade cricket for another thirteen
years. He was an excellent golfer and a 'popular
and articulate cricket commentator with the ABC'
(Australian Broadcasting Corporation). The
Complete Who's Who of Test Cricketers writes of
Burke:

> Although he had domestic and financial
> worries, and was facing a major hip operation
> which threatened to prevent him from playing
> golf, a sport he loved, it was a great shock to his
> friends when he bought a gun one morning in
> Sydney early in 1979 and shot himself with it
> that afternoon.[18]

Jim Burke

In early June 1954 Todmorden offered Burke terms for 1955 but he did not wish for
another season and by August Neil Dansie of South Australia had been signed in his
stead. Dansie was full of enthusiasm, a positive batsman and useful spinner who
changed from leg-spin to a brisker off-spin style as it was better suited to slow
Lancashire League pitches. He was a keen coach and in the nets would mark on the
wicket parallel lines, one from each stump to where the length balls would pitch, which
helped both batsman and bowler. The nets had sides but no roof and sometimes he

Todmorden v Burnley, Worsley Cup June 1955
The scoreboard shows Todmorden have suspended their innings at 130
and Burnley are about to bat.

would conclude his batting session by announcing that he would hit every ball into the park (beyond the field on his leg side) - and he usually did.

His two seasons at Todmorden brought 1891 runs and 131 wickets and he is still remembered for his innings in the 1955 Worsley Cup Final where he confronted the Rishton pro, Gupte. Dansie hit an unbeaten 121 of Todmorden's 206 all out and described his battle against Gupte, who took 10 for 101:

> I watched the ball spinning through the air to see which way it was going. Then I played forward if it was up and back if it was short. Mainly I cut and swept him and in the end he couldn't bowl spin at me. He kept spinning it to the amateurs but just bowled medium-pacers to me.

Dansie farmed the bowling quite brilliantly in a last wicket partnership of 45 with wicketkeeper Jack Hazeltine. This ended when he played the last ball of an over for three runs so that he could keep the strike but the fielder allowed the ball to go over the boundary for four, thus exposing Hazeltine to

'Fergie' Gupte and George Walsh at Rishton

Gupte who trapped him lbw with the fifth ball. Rishton won the match by four wickets.

Tenth in 1955, Todmorden improved to 5th and reached the cup semi-final in 1956, the season beginning spectacularly when Colin Sunderland took a hat-trick in the first over against Lowerhouse. Todmorden were prepared to sign Dansie for a further two years but he needed to pursue his career in Australia.

Neil Dansie has visited Todmorden several times over the years. In 2004 he was pleased to be interviewed on his career. Asked about his earliest cricketing memories, he said:

> I used to go, as a very young boy to watch our team called 'The Dansies' which was made up of my father, uncles, cousins etc. At the end of practice I would get a little bat. They used to throw me some balls underarm.

Describing his all-round ability:

> I think I could have been good at most sports but not truly outstanding at any of them. I played Australian rules football for Norwood from 1946 to 49 but gave it up to concentrate on cricket. I also played 'A' Grade baseball, which helped me to throw fast and flat and I suppose helped my hand-eye co-ordination.

On his early South Australian cricket career:

> I had made a few runs in 'A' Grade, they had a look at me in the nets and selected me to play against New South Wales. That was in 1949. I went out to bat at 84 for 5 and made 36. I remember that Keith Miller was in the opposition and when I had got a few he walked past between overs and said to me, 'Keep going you're batting well'. That's

Cartoon by 'Tipping' (*Lancashire Evening Telegraph*), Todmorden at East Lancs in 1955

hard to believe from an opponent these days, isn't it? That generosity of spirit started to disappear when all the money came into the game. I remember a piece of advice I got from Don Bradman in my early days. He said, 'Son, you're a cutter and a hooker. These shots will get you out a few times but don't ever stop playing them because they'll get you thousands of runs'. I played against all the greats of that period - Arthur Morris, a wonderful opening bat, Sidney Barnes, Lindwall, Hassett, Bill Johnston - all great players.

He recalled that he was due to come to England by boat but was taken ill and hospitalised, so he had to come by plane which was quicker. It still took two or three days to get here. He bought a raincoat and a cloth cap, one of his proudest possessions, which he wore at the 2004 Worsley Cup Final.

Of the Lancashire League he said that every team had four or five exceptionally good cricketers. The pitches were slow, but quite good when they were dry and difficult to bat on when they were wet, but that was good too because it taught you to watch the ball and play it late. 'I definitely returned to Australia a much better player'.

He experienced snow for the first time at Bacup, and a snowball fight replaced the cricket.

After his first season at Todmorden, Dansie wintered at Alf Gover's Cricket School in London where he was coached and learned how to coach. The resident coaches were ex-county players Andy Sandham, Surrey, and Arthur Wellard, Somerset.

We had all sorts of players coming in but one who was there nearly every day was Jim Laker. He spent that winter perfecting his arm ball and disguising it so that it looked like his off-spinner - and of course the following summer he took his 19 wickets against Australia at Old Trafford.

Dansie played for South Australia until 1967 and was awarded honorary membership of the South Australian Cricket Association when he retired. He had the privilege of batting with Don Bradman of whom he says:

> He was in position to play his shots faster than anyone I have ever seen. He just picked up the line and length of the ball so quickly. I batted with him in his very last innings in Grade cricket. A crowd of 4000 turned up and when the umpire gave him out - quite rightly - they booed the umpire and then they all left.

Speaking of the pace bowlers he faced, Dansie considered Frank Tyson in 1954 to be the most formidable:

> He was the quickest. He wasn't that tall so he skidded at you and it was hard to get out of the way. Fred Trueman was a great bowler. I once had to bat out the last over against him for South Australia. I survived the first seven balls and Trueman only ran in four paces for the last one. It was the quickest of the lot, pitched leg and middle and hit the top of off. Great bowler!

Dansie has been a selector for South Australia since 1976 and the cricket academy is named after him and fellow long serving batsman Les Favell. When asked about pre-match preparation in his day he commented:

> We might do a bit of stretching if we felt stiff but nothing like they do now. When Don Bradman was asked how he kept fit he just said, 'Running between the wickets'.

On coaching at Todmorden, he says:

> I ran nets for the juniors from 4pm to 8pm and one man was always the first to arrive and the last to leave. I said at the time, 'with that determination and enthusiasm he will go a long way in the game', and fifteen years later he was getting off the plane to play against Australia. His name was Peter Lever.

Peter Lever was 'gently pushed into cricket' as a 'reluctant seven year-old' when his parents made him a member of Todmorden Cricket Club advising, 'You'll be better off there than loafing around street corners'. Peter recalls:

> There used to be a fight to get into the 'rag net' with sometimes over 30 wanting to get a bat. As my interest in the game grew, the next fight was to get in Eric Denison's coaching net and try and get noticed.

A fire precipitated Peter's 1st XI debut. The 2nd XI had already left for Colne, when opening bowler and fireman Colin Sunderland got a 'call out'. Thirteen year-old Peter, the only player available, was sent home for his kit. Batting alongside Dansie, Peter scored seven, including a boundary off Colne's Australian professional, Jack Manning.

There was friendly rivalry between Peter and his talented brother Colin. Colin enjoyed a prolific career with Buckinghamshire and is the only player to have topped the Minor Counties' averages in both batting and bowling. As professional for Heywood in the Central Lancashire League from 1968 to 76, Colin scored a record 6439 runs and took 771 wickets, assisting the club to four league titles and two Wood Cups. In 1965 he played his only first class match for the Minor Counties against South Africa.

Peter began to emerge from Colin's shadow after full seasons with Todmorden's 1st

XI in 1958 and 59. Initially selected as a batsman, Peter scored 222 runs and took 30 wickets in 1959. His bowling was coming to the fore and this caught the eye during trials at Old Trafford. Aged nineteen in 1960, he joined Lancashire CCC, where he learned his fast bowling trade watching and listening to two of England's best practitioners, Brian Statham and Ken Higgs. Peter patiently waited, steadily gaining experience and developing supreme levels of fitness - his winter cross-country runs were legendary.

Capped in 1965, his big opportunity came with the retirements of Statham in 1968 and Higgs in 1969. By the end of the following season Peter had earned international recognition and was selected to play for England in the 5th Test at The Oval against the Rest of the World. This magnificent team was a last minute replacement for South Africa, who were beginning their long isolation from test cricket, but these matches were later controversially expunged from Test Match records. This was cruel on Peter, who…

> bowled with heart and fire on an unresponsive pitch and quite astonishing success…his 7 for 83…included some of the finest batsmen currently to be found on the global circuit.

Peter's seven victims were Eddie Barlow, Graham Pollock, Mushtaq Mohammed, Gary Sobers, Clive Lloyd, Mike Procter and Intikhab Alam. Has there ever been a finer haul in a single innings? Thrust suddenly into the national spotlight, he said:

> More has happened to me in a fortnight than in ten years…I feel scared and delighted at the same time…To be picked as one of the best sixteen cricketers in the country must be a bigger kick than any drug could give you.

He had earned his place on the 1970/71 tour of Australia, where he took 13 wickets, despite having several slip catches dropped and often bowling from the least favourable end. He proved the perfect foil to the spearhead of the attack, John Snow, as England regained the Ashes. Captain Ray Illingworth fully appreciated his value as 'the perfect tourist', and John Arlott was also impressed:

> The spark which lifts Lever above the rest is his ability to make the ball, new or worn, which pitches on the right hander's stumps leave the bat late, and with all the life that the pitch will grant. These merits have made him an honest and respected performer on the highest level of cricket. He came to his Test standing through solid virtues rather than outstanding brilliance. He bowls at full effort. His stamina and application are such that he can, and does, bowl long spells without loss of control or enthusiasm.

Peter Lever bowls Sobers, one of his 7 victims for England v Rest of the World at the Oval in 1970.

In 1971 he enjoyed an outstanding match against India at Old Trafford, hitting 88 and taking 5 for 70 to set up a victory chance which was denied by rain. His best test figures, 6 for 38 at Melbourne, helped secure England's consolation victory in the final test of the ill-fated 1974/75 tour of Australia. Having suffered an injury in the 1st Test, Peter had missed most of the series. The most sickening moment of his career came on the New Zealand leg of the trip. He felled Ewan Chatfield with a bouncer and the Kiwi seam bowler was declared clinically dead before England physiotherapist, Bernie Thomas, resuscitated him.

Alongside his seventeen test matches, Peter played in the very first one-day international at Melbourne in January 1971 and bowled effectively in the first World Cup tournament of 1975. He was also a key member of the outstanding Lancashire team of this period, famed for its succession of one day triumphs. Jackie Bond, the county's astute captain, admired Peter's work ethic, concentration, determination and faith in his own ability:

> He has done a great deal to enhance the status of the game and, in the process, to carve out his own cause for pride, in the annals of top class cricket.

Fourth in the first class averages in 1975, a troublesome back injury persuaded Peter to retire from the game a little earlier than expected in 1976. Since then, in the mid-1980s, he coached at Lancashire and was appointed England's bowling coach in 1994, during Ray Illingworth's tenure as national manager.[19] Peter has retained his Todmorden links. In 1967, when his father was Mayor, he brought a Lancashire XI to play at Todmorden and he played in benefit matches in 1978 and 1980. He has always been ready to support the club and local schools.

With Dansie not returning in 1957, Todmorden signed Safdan Hamid (Jim) Minhas, who had played two seasons as an amateur with Lowerhouse and was a good prospect. Tall and powerfully built, he generated pace and lift from a short run and could cut the ball both ways; he was also an attacking batsman. His fee was a modest £400 plus £50 expenses and - a first for Todmorden - a series of incentive payments: 15s 0d for scoring 50 runs plus 5s 0d for every extra 25; £1 for a hat-trick or 3 wickets in one over; and £1 for 6 or more wickets in any match. These would be in addition to any collections he received for meritorious performances.

Minhas repaid the club's initiative with interest bowling a prodigious 425 overs, taking 84 wickets and scoring 449 runs. Todmorden were strengthened by wicketkeeper-batsman Albert Connor, whose move from Walsden was rewarded with 591 runs and 20 victims. Well led by Harold Dawson, who broke his own club record with 790 runs, their positive cricket was epitomised by 17 year-old Ewart Clayton in two breath-taking finishes.

In the second match of the season East Lancs' Pakistani paceman Fazal Mahmood had bowled his side to the brink of victory with Todmorden 92 for 9 in reply to the visitors' 112 all out. Many sides would have settled for a draw but Clayton (21 not out) continued to pursue the target and, when he struck Mahmood for the winning boundary, the cheers could be heard a quarter of a mile away in the town centre.

Clayton came to the rescue again at home to bottom club Colne. Chasing a respectable 172 all out Todmorden were 134 for 8, but again shunning the draw, Clayton struck 35 not out to secure another one wicket victory.

Whilst Todmorden chased victories and the title, Burnley set a League record with 21 draws and finished third from bottom. Their negative approach earned them 'the distinction of possessing the worst popular side in the north' and was well illustrated in their matches against Todmorden. At Turf Moor they replied to Todmorden's 158 for

8 declared with 78 for 5 in 32 eight ball overs, whilst at Todmorden they batted 49 overs in making 136 for 5 declared, Todmorden replying with 98 for 8 in 28 overs after tea.

Challenging for the title, Todmorden gained impetus from the availability of teenage left-arm spinner Bryan Davies for the last eight matches. His great grandfather, Johnny Horsfall, outstanding all-rounder for Todmorden from 1871 to 1900, would have been proud as Bryan's 19 wickets at an average of 6 lifted him to the top of the League's bowling averages. With one game remaining, Todmorden had joined one time runaway leaders Rishton on 53 points. The last match, at Rishton, was effectively the championship decider.

Todmorden, batting first on a damp pitch which cut up and gave increasing help to the bowlers, made Rishton pay for the error of not opening the bowling with Gupte. Albert Connor (38) and John Crowther (16) rattled up 45 in seven overs against some wayward amateur seam bowling before the little Indian was introduced. After that, batting became a struggle for survival. Richard Horsfall, in a brief spell back at Todmorden after ten years in county cricket with Essex and Glamorgan, added 23 for the 6th wicket with Richard Crabtree, but Todmorden subsided to 87 all out, Gupte 6 for 26, and Rishton were fully expected to clinch the title after tea.

They had reckoned without the considerable lift and movement Minhas could generate, bowling with a fierce wind behind him from the Blackburn Road end. He took 4 for 0 in his first four overs as Rishton collapsed to 2 for 5, a start beyond Todmorden's wildest dreams. Of Rishton's upper order only Jackie Chew, 'the straightest bat in the league', remained. Possessing an ice cool temperament, the former Burnley and Bradford City winger, led a recovery with the obdurate Stuart Ormerod, taking Rishton to 36 for 5. Davies took over from Crabtree, who had toiled manfully into the wind and, spinning the ball despite pushing it though, removed Ormerod and ran through the tail. Chew was left stranded on 29 as Rishton collapsed to 48 all out, Minhas 5 for 17, Davies 4 for 13. It was a remarkable victory to cap an unlikely League triumph, achieved with a professional plucked from the amateur ranks at Lowerhouse.

In early June Minhas was offered terms for 1958 but, when he played for time in making a decision, the club began to look elsewhere. Todmorden contacted Warwickshire leg-spinner Eric Hollies, Australians Peter Philpott and Norman O'Neill, and South African fast bowler Peter Heine. Johnny Wardle was approached but within hours of his dismissal by Yorkshire in July he signed for Nelson. The search for a big name proving fruitless, terms were agreed to retain Minhas.

The weather in 1958 was truly awful, 10 matches being partly or wholly abandoned. Minhas had little bowling support, the amateur batting fired only rarely and the team slumped to 11th equal in the League. Minhas left to become pro at Kirkburton in the Huddersfield League and, after a successful season he returned to Lowerhouse as pro in 1960.[20]

Minhas was replaced at Todmorden by Trinidadian Sylvester Oliver. He was recommended by Ellis Achong, the West Indian left-arm wrist spinner whose vast experience of the Lancashire leagues included a spell of 10 for 71 for Burnley at Todmorden in 1945. Oliver, a right arm medium-fast bowling all-rounder and brilliant fielder had been 12th man for the West Indies. He had a decent first season, scoring 662 runs and taking 52 wickets, and received good support from Bobby Marshall (52 wickets) and Peter Lever (30 wickets). 1960 was less successful. Oliver could only manage 40 expensive wickets, Lever had gone to Lancashire CCC and the team slumped to mid-table, despite 604 runs from Kevin Wilkinson and 831 from Harold Dawson, again breaking his own club record.

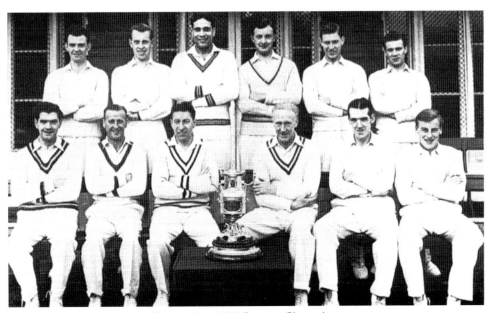

Todmorden 1957 League Champions
L-R Row 2: Peter Brownbridge, Bobby Marshall, SH (Jim) Minhas (pro), Richard Crabtree,
Bryan Davies, Ewart Clayton,
Row 1: Malcolm Heywood, Frank Saul, Harold Dawson, John Crowther, Albert Connor,
Colin Lever.

Missing were the all round abilities of John Crowther who retired at the end of 1959, aged 49. John went out on a high, contributing 597 runs, 24 wickets and 19 catches to Todmorden's title challenge that went to the final day when Colne visited Centre Vale, the top of the league table reading:

	Played	Points
Nelson	25	63
Colne	25	62
Todmorden	25	61

Neither Colne nor Todmorden could afford to draw the game, and a rapid unbeaten 58 from Wilkinson enabled Todmorden to declare at 168 for 7 leaving enough time for both sides to force a result. Colne professional, Ceylonese batsman Stanley Jayasinghe, who left the field injured during the Todmorden innings, returned to stroke a majestic 104 as the visitors replied with 172 for 5 to win the match and, as news arrived that Nelson had lost, the title. Todmorden were left to rue a two-run defeat to Nelson in July, and to say a fond farewell to John Crowther.

Jack Isherwood, Lancashire League secretary, in his annual report wrote of him:

> He could aptly be called 'Gentleman John' - his selfless approach to the game, his keenness, his immaculate attire, his true sportsmanship, his courtesy, have made him an example that I suggest all young cricketers should try to emulate...He was known all over the League, not only for the feats he performed, both with bat and ball, but for the sportsmanlike way he always played the game.

John was an exceptional club cricketer, who could have played county cricket. He was a stylish opening batsman with a fine technique, a leg-spin and googly bowler, and a very good close-to-the-wicket fieldsman. Born in 1911, he played originally with

Walsden CC, before making his Todmorden debut in 1931. Within five years he was playing as a professional at Darwen and then Millom, before returning to Todmorden as a key player in the 1938 double championship team.

Whilst at Windhill, John played alongside Constantine under whose captaincy they won the Bradford League in 1948. Constantine remembered John, '... against whom I bowled cannon balls when he played for Todmorden and I for Nelson.'[21]

His form remained consistent and, back with Todmorden, he hit 74 against a Nelson attack spearheaded by Ray Lindwall, in 1952. He recalled that, on 49 not out, Lindwall's (8 ball) maiden over was the best he had ever faced.

John along with Harold Dawson and more recently Stuart Priestley are the only batsmen to have scored 10,000 runs for Todmorden. In the club's two most successful periods, the 1930s and 50s, John and Harold formed the backbone of the team. In total John hit 10,028 runs at an average of 24, took 386 wickets at an average of 16, and held 195 catches. He won Worsley Cup medals in 1935, 38 and 54; and championship medals in 1933, 38, 54 and 57. He continued his links with the League as groundsman at Lowerhouse and then Rawtenstall. A sportsman to the end, John died during a match on Todmorden golf course in 1971, at the relatively young age of 61.

Ray Lindwall in action

Chapter 15

Fast and Furious 1961 to 1970

In October 1957, notice to quit was served on occupiers of allotments behind the pavilion, where a new pavilion was to be sited. It was ready for the start of the 1959 season, when the old wooden pavilion with its two changing rooms, one cold tap, one toilet and no artificial lighting was dismantled. The new facilities included a central entrance, two dressing rooms with showers, toilets, a kitchen, committee room and a function room with a hatch opening to a small bar in the far corner of the building and accessed from a rear outside door. There was no concept at this time that the bar could be a focal point or that it would extend the club's social life into the winter months; indeed, it had only been achieved against significant opposition. There had been no alcohol sold on the ground since the days of the 'old ale tent', over forty years earlier. Attitudes changed, and by early 1965 there were moves to extend the bar accommodation, which was completed by 1969. The function room was also well used and hired out and, by 1987, a full length extension along the rear had been built.

Not all changes were within the club's control. In 1963 the Borough Council implemented a plan, which had been on the agenda for years, to create a footpath along Burnley Road outside the ground. This entailed moving the cricket ground wall back and taking a similar strip of land, about five feet wide, from the playing area - making it significantly smaller.

By the end of May 1960 the Todmorden committee was scouring the county scene for a bowling professional for 1961. They sought permission from Lancashire to approach Malcolm Hilton and Roy Tattersall, telephoned Jim Laker (Surrey), Les Jackson (Derbyshire), and Don Shepherd and Jim McConnon (Glamorgan), and wrote to Fred Ridgeway (Kent) and Frank Tyson (Northants). Sonny Ramadhin and Subhash Gupte complete an impressive list.

During these negotiations the committee was uncharacteristically free from 'leaks' so that rival clubs were not alerted to the names in the frame, committee members adopting an air of 'I know something which you don't know'. Rumours circulated the town and no-one was disappointed when, in early August, Frank Tyson signed a one year contract for £800.

Born in Farnworth in 1930, Tyson played as a youngster for Middleton of the Central Lancashire League. Here he impressed John Kay who, in his book *Cricket in the Leagues*, recounts taking the young bowler twice for trials to Old Trafford, where he was rejected. Kay then recommended him as professional to Knypersley CC in the North Staffordshire and South Cheshire League, before the influence of Northamptonshire's Australian Jock Livingstone took him to that county in 1952.[1] Tyson played at Northants for seven years until his retirement from county cricket in 1960. Between 1954 and 1959 he took 76 wickets in 17 tests touring Australia and New Zealand, West Indies and South Africa.[2]

'Typhoon' Tyson rocketed to fame in the 1954/55 tour of Australia under Len Hutton's captaincy. After taking 1 wicket for 160 runs in the first Test at Brisbane, which England lost by an innings and 154 runs, he cut down his run without loss of pace at Sydney and took 10 wickets in the match, his 6 for 85 in Australia's second innings decisive in England's 38 run win.

Front and back views of Todmorden's new Pavilion 1959

An evenly-fought third Test at Melbourne was in the balance as Australia, chasing 240 to win, began the final day on 75 for 2. 60,000 spectators expected to see a full day's struggle but the 'Typhoon' was unplayable. In 6.2 eight ball overs he took 6 wickets for 16 runs and Australia were all out for 111 before lunch, Tyson's analysis being 7 for 27 in 12.2 overs. Over 50 years later, Tyson's bowling on this tour remains, by common consent of players and commentators, the fastest they ever saw. David Frith in *The Fast Men* writes:

> The batsmen had been no match. England's discovery, with his shuffling launch, giant, raking, steps, and spring-steel spine action, had, with his laser-beam bowling, given his side a victory weapon. Both sides had batsmen, bowlers and all rounders of established reputation, but the side with a bowler of 'Typhoon's' pace - so long as he remained fit - had to win.[3]

Tyson wrote of himself:

> Oh yes, there have been better fast bowlers. But I doubt whether there has been one who derived more pleasure from bowling fast. One of its greatest attractions for me is its straightforwardness. It is an honest pursuit whose rewards are gained by the sweat of the brow, and not by any underhand or surreptitious method.[4]

Tyson did not have things entirely his own way in the Lancashire League. On a perfect Centre Vale pitch in June, Burnley put Todmorden in to bat but showed no inclination to chase Todmorden's 186 for 7 declared. With 15 minutes less batting time, Burnley replied with 140 for 0.[5] There was more help for the bowlers at Turf Moor three weeks later, Burnley's West Indian test off-spinner Lance Gibbs taking 6 wickets as Todmorden declared at 154 for 7. Burnley lost early wickets, but opener Neil Whalley and the middle order steadied the ship. With ex-Lancashire wicketkeeper Jack Jordan at number 9 batting solidly, they were 120 for 7 when Tyson returned for a second spell at the Belvedere Road end. At this juncture a Burnley supporter made loud, unparliamentary remarks about Tyson's lack of hair. Visibly bridled, the paceman steamed in and finished the innings with 3 quick wickets for an analysis of 6 for 30 to bowl Burnley out for 128.

The following Wednesday at Accrington, the great West Indian fast bowler Wes Hall took 8 for 44 to tumble Todmorden out for 81. Hall then opened the batting with Derek Rushton and they were in little trouble until, with Hall's score on 21, Tyson bowled not only him but also the next 3 batsmen with consecutive balls. When Bob Marshall accounted for the next 2, also without scoring, the scorecard showed five consecutive ducks. However, this golden patch did not continue and Accrington gained a 3 wicket victory on their way to becoming League champions by a clear margin.

Tyson's most devastating performance was reserved for the mid-week match at Haslingden on 23 August. Todmorden's 115 all out on a bowler-friendly wicket was more than adequate as Tyson, moving the ball late, proved unplayable. Haslingden were reduced to 9 for 5 wickets; 20 for 8 and 34 all out, Tyson 7 wickets for 17 runs and Brian Whittaker 3 for 14.

Todmorden finished fourth in 1961, despite an unlikely one run defeat to bottom club Lowerhouse who won at Centre Vale for the first time since 1912, an incredible run of 51 League and Cup matches.

Tyson contributed an impressive 602 runs and 98 wickets in League and Cup. On good pitches he did not run through sides but was very effective in the second half of the season when, cutting down his pace, he found movement through the air and off the pitch. 19 of Tyson's wickets came in the Worsley Cup, Todmorden reaching the

Frank Tyson's action
in sequence

final, where they were beaten at home by East Lancashire (Todmorden 155, East Lancashire 158 for 5).

John Kay, in the 1962 *Playfair Cricket Annual*, wrote:

> Todmorden, whose gamble in signing Frank Tyson for one season was well rewarded, were always worth watching.

Tyson was only ever going to stay for one season as he had plans to emigrate to Australia. Here he took up a teaching post in Melbourne, became an eminent cricket coach, a radio and television commentator and writer. Playing alongside him was something to savour.

Tyson used his influence to secure a contract with Northants for talented all-rounder Ewart Clayton, who topped the League amateur bowling averages as well as scoring 626 runs. He also helped one of his old Northants colleagues to a contract at Todmorden.

Behind the usual wall of silence, Todmorden had approached Tony Lock, Cec Pepper, Subhash Gupte, Les Jackson and Brian Close before,

Wes Hall, West Indies opening bowler and pro at Accrington 1960 to 62, as the batsman saw him!

during the tea interval at the last match of the season, chairman Walter Scott brought a rather small, slightly rotund gentleman into the dressing room with the words, 'This is our professional for next season'. There was a short but marked silence as no-one recognised him except Tyson.

The 'unknown' was Des Barrick who had a county record of 20 centuries, around 14,000 runs and could also bowl leg-breaks and googlies. No-one realised how much humour he would inject into the club over the next two seasons, how much good cricket advice he would impart and how much pleasure his batting would give to both players and spectators. In two wet summers at Todmorden, he topped the League batting averages in both seasons.

Barrick's sense of humour had been experienced by Tyson during their Northants days. Following a hard stint in the field at Derby, Tyson plunged into the huge communal bath where Barrick poured a bucket of cold water over him. Intent on revenge, Tyson poured water over the fully dressed Barrick who, although soaked, was grinning from ear to ear - he had put Tyson's clothes on![6]

When Todmorden played Bacup, Barrick jokingly took guard against the notoriously hostile Gilchrist from behind the wicket. On encountering a Lancashire League umpire who announced the end of each over with 'hup', Barrick chose his moment during the innings to surreptitiously call 'hup' after the seventh ball, creating chaos as everyone started to change ends, leaving the bewildered umpire to wonder what was happening. Barrick's genial manner pervaded the dressing room at Centre Vale and the team by and large played relaxed and entertaining cricket.

The quality of Barrick's batting was particularly demonstrated in a match at Enfield in August 1962. There was a modicum of friction between Barrick and skipper Harold Dawson and, needing 140 to win, Todmorden lost an early wicket bringing Harold in to join Barrick. As the partnership developed Barrick skilfully manipulated the strike,

Johnny Wardle, supreme left-arm spinner, pro at Nelson 1959 to 62 and at Rishton 1963 to 68

calling loudly and with a hint of affectation 'Come one Harold', at or near the end of an over, to the amusement of his teammates. With the score on 137, Harold was 47. Barrick (75) had teasingly left him a boundary to win the match and reach his half century - which he duly hit!

In 1962 Barrick's only regular bowling support was Brian Whittaker's medium-pace outswing and Bryan Davies, the latter taking hat tricks against Enfield and Colne, but the batting prospered. Four amateurs topped 500 League and Cup runs, led by pugnacious left-handed opener Kevin Wilkinson with 812, as Todmorden finished fifth in the League and participated in a unique Worsley Cup final against Nelson at Seedhill.

The final started on Sunday 19 August but, owing to rain, was still unfinished when the League programme ended on 8 September. Todmorden, led by 67 from Wilkinson, had suspended their innings on 132 for 5 to which Nelson had replied with 119 for 7. Todmorden pressed for the match to be completed but Nelson's pro Johnny Wardle was out of contract after Sunday 9 September and would not play after that. Todmorden wanted to complete the match but Nelson didn't. Todmorden protested to the League that: finance had taken priority over cricket; Nelson had made no attempt to remove water from the ground at around 4pm on the final Sunday; the absence of some members of the League executive on that day had prevented a decision being made when required; and a 'knock out' competition by definition must be played until all but one team has been knocked out. This was to no avail and the League ruled that the Worsley Cup be shared, each club holding it for 6 months. It remains the only occasion when the cup competition has failed to reach a conclusion.

The following year, 1963, Todmorden slumped to twelfth in the League despite four bowlers each taking over 30 wickets. Garth Warren, on his return to the club after several years as professional in the Ribblesdale League, took 8 for 25, including a hat trick and the wicket of future Australian skipper Ian Chappell in the 10 wicket victory over Ramsbottom, one of only four League victories.

Todmorden saved their best form for the Worsley Cup, disposing of eventual League champions East Lancashire in round two on the way to a home final against Rishton. Once again they confronted Wardle, who had moved from Nelson to Rishton. Todmorden suspended their innings at 130 for 3 and were eventually all out for 214 in 70.7 eight ball overs. Barrick, playing against medical advice with a broken bone in his hand, scored 67 and Wardle took 5 for 112. Rishton collapsed from 113 for 3 to 137 for 7 as rain and bad light prolonged the contest to two Sundays and a final Tuesday evening, again well beyond its scheduled time. Future Accrington Stanley chairman Eric Whalley hit 36 to rally Rishton to 180 for 7 before a three wicket burst from Brian

Todmorden 1st XI 1963 Worsley Cup winners
L-R Row 2: Walter Southwell (scorer), Peter Brownbridge, Brian Whittaker, Garth Warren,
Bryan Davies, Keith Link, Clifford Stansfield (sec),
Row 1: Malcolm Heywood, Kevin Wilkinson, Des Barrick (pro), Harold Dawson, Albert
Connor, Michael Jowett.

Whittaker polished off the innings for 191. Whittaker took 6 for 50 from 27.5 overs and
was matched for stamina by Garth Warren, who took one for 41 in 31 overs.

After two years at Centre Vale Des Barrick moved on but always kept in touch. He
made his last visit to Todmorden during the 2007 season, only a few months before he
died on Christmas Day. The club was represented at his funeral.

Meanwhile, the days of timeless cup matches were over. At the cup presentation,
League chairman Jim Powis said that some form of 'limited' cricket would be
introduced into the Worsley Cup matches the following season, initially on an
experimental basis. Consequently, the Lancashire League followed the example of
county cricket which had introduced a limited overs knockout competition in 1963, the
Gillette Cup, itself a direct result of an initiative by Leicestershire's secretary Mike
Turner who had organised a financially successful one-day knockout tournament
between four Midlands counties in 1962. In 1964 Worsley Cup matches were limited
to 40 eight ball overs per innings.[7]

Limited overs cricket was the second major innovation by the Lancashire League
around this time. The other was to play on Sundays.

Before World War II, at least locally, the question did not arise. The Todmorden and
District League comprised, in the main, teams which were church or chapel-based and
the Protestant ethic, although in decline since World War I, was still relatively strong.
Many children went to Sunday School and for some, 'playing out' on Sunday was not
allowed. Sunday was different from the other six days of the week; a day of rest or
worship but certainly not for organised sport.

In February 1941, at both Enfield and Rishton cricket clubs' AGMs there was
discussion on the subject of Sunday cricket. Following this it was broached at the

Lancashire League meeting but was opposed. League chairman Edward Crabtree of Todmorden claimed that it would lose clubs a great deal of support without any compensation.

In May of the same year a plea was made to Todmorden Borough Council that special measures were called for in wartime because life was different. There were longer working hours, and exhortations to 'Dig for Victory' and to spend holidays at home. Opening the park for Sunday games would help morale. After much discussion the Council confirmed an original minute 'not to allow Sunday bowling and other sports in the park' by a vote of 13 to 7; the view that 'This agitation has been going on for years, by just a few', prevailed. This attitude was not unique to Todmorden. The *Rotherham Advertiser* 26/06/1943 reported that Rawmarsh Council voted 12 to 3 against opening Rosehill Park on five Sundays in July and August for bowls, tennis and golf, in support of the 'Holidays at Home' campaign. They argued the need 'to safeguard the sanctity of the Sabbath'.

The Sunday games issue rumbled on through letters to the local paper and, in April 1942, the Council agreed to allow Sunday bowling and tennis in Centre Vale Park from 2pm to 5pm on a three months' trial. From this point there was no going back.

In February 1945 Todmorden Park Bowling Club requested that the greens be opened on Sundays from 6pm to 9pm as well as in the afternoon but the Council rejected any extension of Sunday bowling. In June 1946 the Council's Parks and Recreation Ground Committee agreed that the golf course in the park should open on Sunday afternoons from 2pm until 5pm.[8] Five years later in 1951 the Council, as owners of the ground, allowed Walsden Cricket and Bowling Club to play bowls on Sunday evenings.[9] The gate was now open and when, in February 1952, Todmorden Park Bowling Club requested that the Council consider opening the bowling greens on Sunday evenings, it would have been difficult to refuse. So the bowling greens, tennis courts and golf course were opened on Sundays from 2pm to 9pm.

Post-war there was no immediate challenge to the Lancashire League's stance that no Sunday cricket could be played on the grounds of member clubs. Nor could a League club play anywhere else on a Sunday if it used the club's name. This was overcome by playing under the captain's name, so when on Sunday, 1 September 1946, Todmorden played Hickton Colliery it was as J Threlfall's XI. Similarly in August 1948 it was W Scott's XI v Paddock. Earlier that month a combined XI from Todmorden and Walsden played Littleborough in the first Sunday match on their Harehill ground, 'following a decision of club members to endorse the innovation'. Seemingly in the Central Lancashire League the decision whether or not to play Sunday cricket rested with the individual clubs.

In 1949 Todmorden were unable to accept Walsden's invitation to a match on Sunday 24 July and in 1951 Glossop CC were informed that 'We do not participate in any Sunday matches'. It is worth noting that Ted Lester's contract with Yorkshire in 1951 (to which every regular playing member of Yorkshire CCC was subject) contained the condition, that:

> No player, with or without a county cap, shall at any time during his engagement with the county club take part in any cricket match or cricket play of any description on a Sunday.[10]

Attitudes were changing, albeit slowly. At Todmorden's AGM in November 1952, a lengthy discussion on Sunday cricket was followed by a vote, but there were so many abstentions that no decision was resolved. At this all-male meeting (women were not full members as they paid a lower subscription) most were middle aged or elderly and the many abstentions point to minds torn between love of cricket and a reluctance to abandon the traditional Sunday. Many had ties with one or other of the churches or chapels of the district.

Eighteen months later in June 1954 the League referred the matter of Sunday cricket to the individual club committees for their consideration. Todmorden declared in favour of a certain amount of Sunday cricket but under the jurisdiction of the League, 'The matches to be non-competitive and controlled by us'. There was to be no free-for-all. The League would be in overall control and the club would decide whom it would play and when.

Jack Isherwood as secretary of the League in his report on the 1954 season stated:

> An important decision was taken during the year when, after much thought and discussion, it was decided to revise the ban on Sunday cricket, allowing clubs, if they so desired, to play friendly matches. Whether this was a wise move or not one cannot foresee. Only the future can tell of the wisdom or otherwise of the decision made.[11]

At Todmorden's AGM on 15 November 1954 it was resolved that Sunday cricket would be played at Centre Vale next season subject to the approval of the Lancashire League Committee and the club committee. As Todmorden leased its ground from the Municipal Borough Council its permission had to be obtained. This was granted and the League was notified of the club's intention to play four Sunday matches in 1955 against Littleborough, Kendal, Bolton Police and Walsden.

The following year the Town Clerk, realising that the terms of the lease on the ground had been broken, proposed amending the lease to legalise Sunday cricket, subject to the written permission of the Borough Council. Annual applications for six Sunday fixtures were granted by the Borough Council in each of the next seven years.

Todmorden always upheld the authority of the League and in 1957 opposed a proposal that grounds could be used at any time, except when there were Lancashire League fixtures, without permission from the League.

Having accepted that friendly matches could be played on Sundays, a demand for Sunday competitive cricket was inevitable, but as always the League moved cautiously. In October 1961 it sanctioned Worsley Cup matches on Sundays, providing both clubs were agreeable. The first competitive Sunday match under the auspices of the Lancashire League was played at Centre Vale on 13 May 1962 Burnley making 174 and Todmorden replying with 178 for 7. Reaching the 1962 final, Todmorden played all four Worsley Cup matches on Sundays.

There was some apprehension that the Lord's Day Observance Society might attempt to make an example of one of the matches, as there was a fixed admission fee for cup ties as opposed to the voluntary collections that had been taken at friendly matches. At a special League meeting in April it was agreed that if any club was fined as a result of the Society's intervention, all the clubs would pay a share. This was a real concern and as Keith Miller wrote in *Cricket From The Grandstand* (1960):

> You can pay to see a Sunday film in England or for a deck chair on a beach. But try to pay admittance to a Sunday afternoon benefit match and the police are compelled to intervene because the Lord's Day Observance Society choose to act as informers...If people swim and sunbathe and have picnics on Sundays, what's wrong with a few games of cricket?[12]

As far as the Lancashire League was concerned, the question of charging for Sunday cricket was taken up with the relevant Government minister by the MCC but in fact there was no action against any clubs in the League.

The following year, 1963, all Worsley Cup matches were officially scheduled for Sundays. The League rejected Todmorden's proposal to play two of the traditional midweek League matches on Sundays but agreed, in the interest of better gate money, to play the fixtures arranged for the FA Cup Final Saturday on the following Sunday. In so doing League matches on Sunday had been accepted.

The 1964 season fixture list comprised matches on 21 Saturdays, 3 Sundays and 2 midweek games on various dates to suit individual clubs, but by 1966 midweek fixtures had gone in favour of 20 Saturday and 6 Sunday matches. Fixtures continued roughly in these proportions until the 1980s when the number of Sunday matches began to increase and, by 1987, outnumbered those on Saturdays by 14 to 12. This had become 18 to 8 by 2007.

The move towards Sunday cricket was not solely owing to the increasing secularisation of the Sabbath. The League, after the heady days of the late 1940s and the early 50s, was losing support. Overall, society was more affluent as was aptly put by the Prime Minister Harold MacMillan in his 1957 statement, 'Let's be frank about it most of our people have never had it so good'.[13] More people were car owners and Saturday was a day free from work. When Todmorden's Hippodrome cinema closed in June 1956, the manager Cyril Nichols laid responsibility for its closure on competition from television and the trend of Todmorden's public to seek their entertainment out of town at weekends - as well as the cinema's burden of taxes and overheads. Similar sentiments were expressed when Cornholme's Gem cinema closed.

The League clubs soon discovered that Sunday matches attracted better gates than Saturday games, when attendances were further depleted by further encroachment of professional football at both ends of the season. The League had real cause for concern. From the peak in 1949, when 325,999 spectators paid at the gates during the season, there was a relentless decline to 71,775 in 1958. Brilliant weather in 1959 saw the number increase to 117,066 but it was not sustained and by 1969 had dropped to 49,487, since when the decline has continued.

Todmorden's gate receipts reflect the impact of these falling numbers on finances across the League.

Season	Minimum Admission Charge	Todmorden's Gate Receipts
1949	1s 0d	£900
1951	1s 3d	£690
1955	1s 6d	£683
1961	2s 0d	£438

No wonder the League executive urged the clubs to do all they could to encourage membership, which ensured a regular income season by season.

In 1949 the total League membership was 15,223 which rose to a record 17,464 by 1952. It dropped below 10,000 in 1963 and by the 1970s had steadied at around 9400. Todmorden traditionally had a strong membership, 1250 in 1950, and was held up as an example to the League of what a small town could do even though its population was declining. By 1963 the club's membership had dropped below 1000, and it steadily declined thereafter only levelling out at between 300 and 400 from 2008 to 2010.

Seeking a professional for 1964, club treasurer Alfred King went to Old Trafford in May 1963 hoping to sign Lance Gibbs, but the West Indies' off-spinner rejected a two year contract at £900 per year. Nasim-ul-Ghani the Pakistani left-handed all-rounder who toured England in 1962 was offered £725 plus talent money and in early

September, Brian Statham was contacted. Then, out of the blue, came a letter from Sylvester Oliver applying for the post of professional.

Syl had enjoyed three successful years in the Huddersfield League, one at Kirkburton and two at Marsden, where he topped the league batting averages both years. He was also considerably cheaper than others the club had contacted, and was quickly snapped up on a one year contract, a much improved cricketer since he last played for Todmorden in 1960. Interviewed by local reporter and cricket enthusiast John Graham, Syl was quite honest about his first spell in the League.

> The trouble was I had to learn a new technique for your wickets. Back home on the hard and fast wickets it was one thing; here, instead of the ball coming onto the bat, it does unpredictable things.
> I bowled too short of a length all the time and batsmen had plenty of time to play me. Now, I am bowling up to them and getting more movement in the air.

By 1964 Syl was the consummate League professional. His batting, still potentially explosive and always attractive, was also more selective. His bowling could still be pacy, but had become much more controlled. In League and Cup he scored 586 runs, took 98 wickets and held 23 catches. His fielding was brilliant whether in the slips or the outfield. His direct throw in 1959 which ran out Ramsbottom's Australian professional, Peter Philpott, who was cantering a seemingly safe single, is still remembered. A magnificent caught and bowled to dismiss Accrington's South African pro Eddie Barlow from a full-blooded drive - never more than a few inches off the ground – was reminiscent of Constantine.

In October 1963, the League minutes read:

It was reported that in view of the number of fast bowlers who had been engaged as professionals for next season, the state of certain grounds and wickets was causing some anxiety, and clubs were asked to ascertain before the next meeting whether or not their grounds were fit, or could be made fit, for such fast bowlers.[14]

This was triggered by the signing of Charlie Griffith by Burnley, Lester King by Rawtenstall and Roy Gilchrist by Lowerhouse, adding to Church's Chester Weston. There had been 'quicks' in the League before without such comment being made and undoubtedly the main concern was Griffith. Along with Wes Hall, Griffith formed a formidable opening attack on the West Indies' 1963 tour of England and their comparative statistics indicate the threat that Griffith posed to League batsmen.

Roy Gilchrist and Wes Hall (aged 19 the youngest on the West Indies team) arrive at Southampton for the 1957 tour of England.

	All Matches		Test Matches	
	Wkts	Ave	Wkts	Ave
Griffith	119	12.83	32	16.21
Hall	74	20.35	16	33.37

Wes Hall's three seasons at Accrington ended in 1962. In each season he took over 100 wickets, the best being his last with 123 wickets at an average of 10.21. Anyone who watched or faced him at Todmorden, where he began his run from near the sightboard at the park end, would agree with David Frith's description in *The Fast Men*:

> Hall had a magnificent bounding approach, eyes bulging, teeth glinting, crucifix flying, climaxing in a classical cartwheel action and intimidating follow through.[15]

He was never less than hostile but always bowled fairly, providing a real challenge for batsmen who, in that era, had little in the way of body protection. Hall took 8 for 65 and 7 for 60 on his first two victorious visits to Centre Vale, but for his third visit in 1962, Todmorden captain Harold Dawson took the pace out of the pitch by rolling dead grass cuttings into it. Todmorden declared on 174 for 9, Dawson 76, and bowled Accrington out for 126.

Compared to Hall, Charlie Griffith was a more menacing proposition altogether. A commonly-held opinion, terrifying for many League batsmen, was that Griffith threw his bouncer and his yorker, a jerking of the arm sometimes causing the batsman to lose sight of these deliveries. Bowling with a speed and hostility that fully justified his reputation, Griffith dominated the League like no professional before or since, devastating much of the batting, amateur and professional, and took 144 wickets at an average of 5.2 runs per wicket.

David Frith says that Griffith:

> ...in contrast to Hall, brought his large frame to the wicket at a fairly leisurely trot and swung his arm over at a low trajectory, the ball travelling at great speed and skimming towards the line of the batsman, making it hard for him to sway away from a short delivery.

Frith also writes of:

> ...the conviction shared by many of his opponents that he threw the ball at least some of the time.[16]

Fred Trueman in his book *Ball of Fire* is more specific as he writes of an incident during the Lord's Test of 1963:

> I was having a quiet soak in one of the individual bathrooms at Lord's. The place was otherwise deserted. Then I heard voices in the corridor outside. And I found myself listening to RWV Robins, chairman of the English selectors at the time, apparently talking to two umpires about the suspect action of Griffith and the complaints which had been coming in from various

Charlie Griffith from behind - the controversial action! His fast bowling terrorised League batsmen when he was the Burnley pro in 1964.

counties. I heard him say that the umpire should under no circumstances call Griffith for throwing. When they objected he explained that there was a lot of worry about racial tension in London and he feared a riot might be sparked off if Griffith was no-balled at Lord's. When I came out of the bathroom Mr Robins was waiting for me. He had heard me moving about. He asked me if I had overheard the conversation so I had to admit that indeed I had. Then he solemnly asked me to give my word never to disclose it. I promised I would keep silent for a time but told him that I thought it should be made public eventually if only to point out the handicap England had been playing under.[17]

Todmorden played Burnley with Griffith three times in four weeks in 1964. On 6 June at a dull Turf Moor, Burnley declared at 134 for 3 wickets. During the tea interval it rained and the Todmorden reply began in extreme murk. Skipper Harold Dawson edged Joe Fletcher onto his face and went to hospital for repairs. Syl Oliver and Keith Link each scored 11 runs. The umpires rejected appeals against the failing light and after the fifth wicket fell at 40 not another run was scored. The blood drained from the face of future Todmorden Mayor, Stanley Hollows on his return to the pavilion, bowled Griffith. He had forgotten to insert his abdominal protector. Batting that day was a frightening experience, most amateurs relieved that the ordeal was short-lived. Griffith took 7 for 17.

In the second round of the Worsley Cup a fortnight later Griffith took 8 for 28 as Todmorden were bowled out for 72, despite a spirited 26 from Peter Brownbridge, and Burnley won by four wickets. The following Saturday at Centre Vale Griffith took 8 for 40 as Todmorden improved to 107 all out, only the third side to top 100 against Burnley, who still won by 6 wickets. In this match Syl Oliver scored 49 not out, but the team had good reason to ask why Griffith had used the short ball less frequently against him than against the amateurs. Syl, always ready with an answer, replied, 'You know why he didn't bounce me? - Because he knows I won't hook him'. 'You mean he thinks we will!' was the chorused reply. 'He didn't bounce you because you're his mate.' By early June Syl was signed for 1965 and then on a yearly basis until 1968.

Burnley won the 1964 League title by a massive 13 points from Rishton, whom they met in the League's most famous Worsley Cup final. Before a crowd of 7,000, Jackie Chew emerged black, blue and victorious from his duel with Griffith as Rishton, to the delight of the rest of the League, denied Burnley the double. Three decades later Griffith still recalled with respect the way that Chew stood up to him and 'gave it everything'.

At the end of the 1964 season, 50 year-old Harold Dawson announced his retirement as a player and the last pre-war playing link was broken. Harold was an outstanding cricketer from an early age, captaining Todmorden Schoolboys in the 1920s and playing for Old Royd in the Todmorden and District League before joining Todmorden CC in 1931 aged 16. His first full season was in the League-winning team of 1933. An unbeaten 65 against Colne's Indian pace-man Amar Singh in 1935 marked Harold as an exceptional player of pace bowling. He had a wonderful eye and the ability to pull, hook and cut with timing and placement as the likes of Wes Hall and that ruthless terrorist of League batsmen, Roy Gilchrist, would testify. In 1960 Harold took on Gilchrist at his peak and hit an unbeaten 69 out of 101 for 5 before rain ended proceedings, and in 1963, aged 49, he made 71 whilst Gilchrist (8 for 51) ran through his team mates to bowl Todmorden out for 128.

Following his war service and a spell at Hampshire, Harold had returned to Todmorden in 1950 and captained the 1st XI from 1951 until his retirement in 1964. He set new club batting records in 1955, 1957 and finally in 1960 with 831 runs. These

Roy Gilchrist, a fearsome fast bowler, pro at Bacup 1960, 62, 63 and Lowerhouse 1964.

were the days of time cricket, when teams negotiated a match in the five hours between 2pm and 7pm. Batting first, Harold's initial target was to score 100 by 4pm, with wickets in hand to accelerate towards a 4.30pm declaration. Overs cricket, he thought was artificial and took many of the subtleties out of the game. After his retirement, he served on the Todmorden committee, was Chairman for many years and then President. He was President of the Lancashire League from 1985 to 87. In his younger days Harold was a fine amateur footballer, representing Walsden and then Rossendale United in the Lancashire Combination. He also had trials with Halifax Town. For almost 30 years after his retirement from cricket, his competitive nature was evident on the Centre Vale Park bowling greens, where he became a formidable opponent. He died in office as President of Todmorden Park Bowling Club in 1994, aged 79. His Lancashire League run-tally remained a League record until the early 1990s, by which time covers and improved pitch preparation made run-scoring significantly easier. The loss of almost a decade of his Todmorden career at his peak, makes Harold's club records of 12,329 runs and 204 catches even more remarkable. League president, Peter Westwell, described Harold's death as, 'the end of an era for the Lancashire League'.

On Harold's retirement the captaincy for 1965 was handed to Malcolm Heywood, and although Todmorden finished eleventh, this hides an eventful season. Well-placed after nine matches with four (including a Worsley Cup tie) won, four drawn and one lost, Todmorden lost their professional. Whilst acting as sub-professional at Almondbury in the Huddersfield League, Syl Oliver seriously injured his shoulder and was not fit to play again until 24 July, and even then he was unable to bowl flat out. Todmorden did not win any of their last 18 League matches.

Todmorden's sub-professional against Haslingden at Centre Vale on 11 June was Roy Gilchrist, and the gauntlet was laid down when the first ball of the match from Haslingden's West Indian professional Clairmonte Depeiza evaded Kevin Wilkinson's hook shot, hit him around the left eye and he had to be assisted from the field. Todmorden declared at 180 for 6 and the scene was set for a personal duel between Gilchrist and Depeiza, who clearly had little liking for each other. Depeiza grafted half an hour for 1 run and Gilchrist, due for a rest, asked for one more over at him. Expending all his energy, Gilchrist dug one in that Depeiza could only fend to leg-slip where, to Gilchrist's delight, Brian Whittaker held a brilliant catch. Haslingden struggled to 87 for 7 at the close.

For the second round Worsley Cup tie at Bacup, Syl secured the services of Garfield Sobers as his replacement, which ensured a good gate. An opening partnership of 93 between Heywood (52) and Wilkinson (39) was the foundation of Todmorden's 154, of which Sobers made 12. Sobers bowled fast left-arm over-the-wicket from the Greensnook Road end and took a wicket in his first over. Second slip felt certain that the ball was coming straight at him when suddenly it dipped and swung in late; the perfect in-swinging yorker. Bob Bennett, later to become chairman of Lancashire CCC, had received the unplayable ball. Stanley Hollows and Brian Whittaker chipped in, reducing Bacup to 32 for 5, but the middle order coped rather better when Sobers changed to wrist spin, lifting the total to 120 all out. Sobers bowled through the innings, taking 5 for 51.

In Oliver's absence, the amateur bowlers took their opportunities. Stanley Hollows and Albert Lowe, with 46 League wickets each, were joint runners-up for the Matthew Brown Amateur Bowling Prize and in all matches both had over 50 wickets.

A youthful Garfield Sobers bowling left-arm spin.

Restored to full fitness, Oliver's bowling was devastating in 1966. He took 114 wickets in all matches, as Todmorden finished third in the League and reached their fourth Cup final in six seasons. League champions East Lancs hosted the final and, after the start had been delayed by an hour, made Todmorden graft hard for runs in wet conditions. Peter Brownbridge's 45 led a recovery from 28 for 3 as Todmorden totalled 147 for 9 in their 40 eight-ball overs. East Lancs were 113 for 4 with 13 overs left when bad light stopped play, their Australian test batsman Bob Cowper making 42 and future Tottenham and Wales centre half Mike England 31.

A tense Monday evening brought two caught and bowled, and two run-outs for Oliver as Todmorden, contesting every run, reduced East Lancs to 145 for 8 with one over remaining. Wicketkeeper Ray Kelly scrambled a single before David Adams made a 'death or glory' swing at Stanley Hollows' fourth delivery 'to send it racing past the square leg umpire for four'. Todmorden received much praise for the sporting nature of the match, whilst the climax, 'one of the finest and most exciting finishes to the annual Worsley Cup Competition that has been seen for many a long day', further vindicated the limited overs format.

In 1967 Ewart Clayton returned to the club after a spell as professional in Scotland at Kilmarnock, Malcolm Heywood was runner-up to Enfield's Edward Slinger in the League's Lion Brewery Award for the highest aggregate runs in League matches by an amateur batsman and John Townend announced himself by topping the bowling averages as Todmorden finished a low-scoring season in fourth position.

Few amateurs are genuinely fast, but the youthful Townend's left-arm pace had amateurs and a number of professionals hopping around. On his day he was devastating and he twice won the Telegraph Tankard for the League's best bowling analysis, taking 8 for 23 against Rishton in 1972 and 8 for 33 against Nelson in 1973. He played briefly for Worcestershire 2nd XI and was a Ribblesdale League professional from 1974 to 1976.

1968 proved to be Syl's last season at Todmorden and, with 777 runs and 80 wickets, his personal best. He had played with a team of dedicated amateurs and although not winning any trophies, the team competed in the top part of the League. Syl, always keen and competitive, was meticulous in placing his fielders and also in moving them, sometimes more than once in the same over. His favourite instruction to 'stand by that patch of grass', caused mirth and bewilderment in equal measures. This was especially so when he decided to have a 'fly slip', which led to Peter Brownbridge wandering about between the slips and third-man, diligently trying to locate the exact patch of grass to which Syl was directing him. Always full of enthusiasm, Syl would instigate an argument on any subject with anybody, always convinced that he was right. Consequently the dressing room and practice sessions were never dull. Ronnie Wild, the local sports' reporter was fulsome in his praise:

> Oliver in form stamped himself as one of the most exciting cricketers in the Lancashire League. His period with Todmorden has been profitable and a pleasure. He has made his mark as a true professional - at Todmorden there have been few occasions when Oliver has not succeeded with either the bat or the ball.
>
> Next season Oliver commences a new era with Egerton in the Bolton League and many people from Todmorden will wish him well. There are many who are disappointed at his departure from Centre Vale - I am one of them.

In his seven years at Todmorden, Syl contributed 3942 runs, 504 wickets and 130 catches. He continued as a professional cricketer for many years including spells at Walsden, Almondbury (Huddersfield League), Winnington Park (Cheshire County League), Egerton (Bolton League) and Newton Heath (Manchester Association). He maintained his Todmorden connections, returning as coach in the 1980s and was never

Todmorden 1st XI Worsley Cup finalists 1966
L-R Row 2: Roger Lever, Peter Brownbridge, Robert Whitaker, Paul Thackray,
Brian Whittaker, Albert Lowe,
Row 1: Garth Stansfield, Stanley Hollows, Malcolm Heywood (c), Kevin Wilkinson,
Sylvester Oliver (pro).

happier than when invited to play in a charity, benefit or friendly match. Brian Heywood recalls, as a young batsman in 1981, partnering Syl in a tight run chase on a pre-season tour to Clevedon. Clevedon captain Bob Latham was bowling accurate in-swing and Syl advised:

> 'You should try to use your feet and, if you get near the pitch of the ball, hit him over the top. If it doesn't swing it will go back over his head and if it does you will hit it over mid-wicket.' It was simple, constructive, confidence-boosting advice, and he demonstrated what he meant with couple of blows. The shots Syl suggested were effective in pushing the fielders back and in the end we won quite easily.

Syl played for the Lancashire Over 50s Team and was still a formidable cricketer. In a friendly match at Todmorden in 1990, he took a sharp slip catch and pocketed the ball whilst most were scanning the third-man boundary for it. Todmorden professional, South Australian Brett Williams commented, 'Bobby Simpson would have been proud of that'. In 2001, still enjoying excellent health, Syl went on holiday to his native Trinidad, but he contracted a virus and died suddenly. A memorial service at St Mary Church, Todmorden, was attended by representatives of all his league clubs; there was standing room only. The inscribed board of professionals at Todmorden is simply dedicated 'To the Memory of Sylvester Oliver Professional and Friend'.

During the 1960s it became clear that the question of how to make cricket more attractive had to be addressed. Positive, match-winning professionals such as Syl Oliver were becoming rarer as the counties relaxed the qualifications for overseas players, thus leaving fewer current stars available to the leagues. This made it easier for league teams to play for a draw as fewer professionals were able to force a result.

The increasing number of drawn games was a major concern. A full season comprises 182 games of which, in 1961, 71 were drawn. This number increased, reaching 101 by 1967, and the average over the decade was 86, just over 47%. Of course, draws caused by bad weather were unavoidable but the public became increasingly intolerant of matches that were drawn because the risk of losing outweighed the desire to win. Limited overs had proved a success in the Worsley Cup competition but the clubs were loath to introduce them to League matches. Todmorden was amongst those supporting limited overs and when the majority were against this, Todmorden proposed awarding a 'bonus point' to the team with the best run-rate per over in a drawn match, providing at least twenty overs had been received by each team. This would give some incentive for positive play, especially when weather truncated a match. Todmorden's proposal was carried by 11 votes to 3. The following year, 1968, Accrington's proposal for limited overs received Todmorden's support but the vote was tied; 6 for, 6 against and 2 abstentions.

Syl Oliver would be a tough act to follow and the counties were scoured for a professional for 1969: Alan Oakman (Sussex), Jackie Birkenshaw (Leicestershire), Basil D'Oliveira (Worcestershire), Randolf Ramnarace (Surrey) who signed for Colne, and Johnny Wardle; were all contacted. Eventually in January 1969 Rushdie Majiet, a young cape-coloured all rounder from South Africa, recommended by D'Oliveira and approached by Burnley in a previous season, was signed. A talented medium-fast bowler and stylish batsman, Majiet had never played on grass before and did not flourish in Lancashire League conditions. An injury left him unable to bowl effectively in the latter part of the season. With John Townend also injured for eleven weeks, and the amateur batting (Kevin Wilkinson excepted) not performing, the team was fortunate to avoid re-election. Rushdie returned to follow his career in South Africa and the next time he visited Todmorden it was as a selector of the South African national side on their tour in 1994, a tangible sign of the end of apartheid - which had been pre-empted by mixed race cricket.

Todmorden again looked overseas in 1970 and signed Terry MacGill of Western Australia, following good reports of his leg-spin bowling from Tony Lock and of his batting from Colin Milburn. MacGill took a keen interest in the players and wrote pen-portraits about each of the first eleven which appeared weekly in the local paper. Unfortunately, new skipper Kevin Wilkinson missed several matches with a broken finger and only Garth Stansfield, with the bat, and vice-captain Brian Whittaker, with the ball, offered significant support to the professional. Todmorden finished equal bottom with Lowerhouse and Haslingden and had to apply for re-election for the first time since being admitted to the Lancashire League in 1897. The last two seasons had brought 20 defeats, 29 draws and just 3 wins. Things could only get better.

Todmorden CC Committee c1970, a complete all male committee.
L-R: Row 2: Derek Grannan, Clifford Greenwood, Bill Holt, John Lunt, Alec Smith,
Alan Dunkeley, Jim Lord, George O'Neill
Row1: Peter Brownbridge, Gordon Holt (sec), Walter Scott (chair), Harold Dawson,
Norman Stansfield.

Chapter 16

A Close Encounter 1971 to 1980

1970 was the last of Tommy Carrick's 47 seasons in Lancashire League cricket, 29 as a player and the last 18 as a formidable and much-respected umpire who officiated at several Worsley Cup finals.

Despite his lack of inches, Tommy was unafraid to confront even the most intimidating professionals. During a match at Bacup he had the temerity to no-ball Roy Gilchrist who rounded on him in a threatening manner, growling 'I don't bowl no-balls, Mr Carrick'. Next ball Gilchrist deliberately overstepped the crease and, hearing Tommy's distinctive high-pitched 'no-ball', turned with a gleeful expression - the ball still in his hand. A few balls later Tommy no-balled a legitimate delivery and, as Gilchrist reacted in fury, calmly said, 'You let go of that one didn't you'? At this time Tommy travelled to matches from Todmorden on his motor scooter and as Gilchrist was living in Walsden they would be taking the same route home. 'When you're riding home on that little scooter of yours tonight, I'm going to get you Carrick', threatened Gilchrist. 'He fley'd me' said Tommy. 'There weren't many cars on the road in those days. As I was riding home over Sharneyford, I kept looking behind me and every time I saw headlights in the distance I stopped and hid in bushes at the side of the road until they had gone passed'.

South African Peter Swart came fresh to the League as Accrington's professional in 1969 and early in the season wrote an article criticising the standard of umpiring. The following week Tommy was at Accrington and, as Swart handed him his sweater prior to opening the bowling, Tommy said 'Good afternoon Mr Swart. I believe you don't think much of our umpiring.' Swart made some placatory reply and commenced the opening over - which lasted for sixteen balls - as Tommy signalled a succession of wides and no-balls. When he relented and handed Swart his sweater, no words were spoken but each knew that the point had been made. Tommy held his own abilities and the standing of the League in high regard.

Tommy, ever approachable and helpful, umpired Todmorden's under 18s' evening matches during the 1970s.

A regular spectator at home matches for the next 20 years, Tommy was well entertained in the first four of these by Peter Marner, signed from Leicestershire, initially on a two year contract at £800 per year. Marner's county career spanned nineteen seasons from 1952 to 1970, during which he toured Pakistan with the Commonwealth Team in 1967/68, and at 35 years of

Peter Marner at catching practice, Todmorden pro 1971 to 74

age was still physically powerful and hugely talented.[1] He had played once before at Centre Vale as substitute professional for Nelson in 1961. On a wet wicket amidst islands of sawdust and an outfield so saturated that it was difficult to hit the ball off the square, Marner memorably thundered an on-drive past a startled mid-on, who turned to see the ball rebound from the school-side boundary boards.

Outspoken and with a temperament at times as belligerent as his batting, Marner's county career had not been without incident. Born in Oldham he played with Lancashire from 1952 to 1964 and won the first ever 'Man of the Match' in the Gillette Cup competition, playing in the preliminary round for Lancashire against Leicestershire in 1963.[2]

Marner's last season at Old Trafford coincided with David Lloyd's first and *David Lloyd the Autobiography* gives some insight into Marner's temperament, including an incident involving former Todmorden professional Stan Worthington, who was the authoritarian coach at Old Trafford from 1951 to 62.

> His (Worthington's) trademarks were blazer and cravat, trilby and cigarette holder. ... That trilby became a magnet to the more mischievous players.

Two of these, Marner and Geoff Clayton, were 'doing jankers in the second team' playing Northumberland at North Shields. Returning to their guest house late one evening, Stan's trilby was identified on the hat stand and used as a rugby ball in an impromptu game along the hallway. At breakfast the following morning Stan confronted them:

> 'Last evening I believe there was a game of rugby in the hallway featuring my hat. This evening you will all have another opportunity to play rugby with my hat - only this time my bloody head will be underneath it!'[3]

Lloyd also tells how protective he was of the new kit he acquired when he first went to the county.

> The sensitive seniors would understand this but Peter Marner thought he would have a bit of fun at my expense. He picked up the treasured new bat that had cost me £4 11s 0d from the sports shop in Accrington, threw it on the floor of the Old Trafford dressing-room and trod on it. 'You'll be able to get your oil in there now', he chuckled.

Lancashire was not a happy place at this time and at the end of 1964:

> The club dispensed with Peter Marner and Geoff Clayton because, so the statement read, 'Their retention was not in the best interests of the playing staff or the club' - diplomatic code for a dressing-room revolt with which the committee lost patience.[4]

Marner played the next six seasons at Leicestershire and in 1969 won a Ford Capri for hitting the season's fastest first class century. Marner's arrival at Todmorden gave the club a boost. He took a personal interest in preparing the practice wickets, marling and rolling them to make a good lasting surface. He encouraged the club to obtain covers to protect the match pitches and he coached the youngsters after school. One of these, John Brierley, recalls that when Marner offered to work with the youngsters, 'Many at the club took a sharp intake of breath. How would young players react to the larger than life, often cantankerous Marner? How would he interact with them?'

They need not have worried. He was a firm, knowledgeable, patient coach who insisted on good discipline and was popular with his young charges. The young Brierley regularly grabbed a quick tea or missed it altogether because 'Mr Marner will be cross with us if we are late'.

His impact was to prove immense, particularly on Brierley and Brian Heywood, who were to become stalwarts of the 1st XI throughout the late seventies, eighties and, Brian the nineties. Both have continued contributing to the game, Brierley as a high ranking professional ECB coach, both locally and as far afield as India, and Heywood who, in addition to being Todmorden's fourth highest run maker has, with spells in other senior leagues amassed over 14,000 runs and also meticulously documented the club's history. Brierley remembers Marner as his first direct contact with a real hero, who made him welcome. No longer was practice confined to matting over concrete wickets on what is now the car park:

> We were playing on the hallowed turf at last, we felt wanted; this man was taking time out to work with us! He was a hard taskmaster. I well remember Peter asking if he could bowl at me (a young 13 year-old). He was enormous and awesomely quick for a young player used only to Under 18 cricket. I was doing OK when a ball from Peter rose up and hit me in what can best be described as my exceptionally skinny ribs. Despite my best efforts the crocodile tears started to roll down my face whereupon Peter, walked slowly down the wicket, and asked if I wanted to carry on. Keen not to show any weakness I said 'Yes' and with some trepidation awaited the next ball. As I left the net, Peter took me to one side and quietly said, 'You'll do OK Tiger, you'll make a cricketer'.

John has taken these inspirational words with him on his cricketing journey as player and coach. Eleven year-old Heywood similarly revelled in the first professional coaching he had received, finding Marner's enthusiasm contagious and he assimilated technical advice on grip, stance, backlift and footwork which set him off on his amateur career. Marner stressed the importance of technique, anticipation and pride in fielding and it is no coincidence that, in their prime, Brierley and Heywood became two of the best outfielders in the League, whether saving one or on the boundary.

For the senior players, Tuesday and Thursday practice evenings regularly ended with fielding sessions. The players lined up with their backs to Marner who hit the ball in the air calling a player's name. The player had to turn, focus on the ball and move to catch it. Ground fielding and throwing were also practised in a competitive way; all good for team spirit.

Marner's eye for field placings in matches was apparent against Accrington in July 1971. John Townend, fast left-arm over the wicket, opened the bowling from the school end to Accrington's substitute professional, Lancashire's David Bailey. The pitch was hard and Todmorden's gully fielder had moved a yard or so nearer the slips anticipating that, because of the conditions, the ball would come off the bat a bit finer than usual. With a tap on his shoulder Marner indicated that he should stand finer still, and the first ball of the match clipped the edge of Bailey's bat flying straight to the fielder at chest height. Thankfully he held the catch.

Marner inherited a team most of whom had played together throughout the 1960s. The leading batsman was skipper Kevin Wilkinson who, during his career from 1953 to 71, scored 6559 runs. When he moved to Oldham after 1971, he was sorely missed. Ewart Clayton's return from professional spells at Barnoldswick and Clitheroe in the Ribblesdale League bolstered the team and along with Mike Jowett, Peter Brownbridge, Malcolm Heywood, Garth Stansfield and the emerging Ian Smith, gave solidity to the batting. In Brian Whittaker and John Townend the team had two of the League's best amateur bowlers, Whittaker being the leading amateur wicket-taker in 1971 with 77 wickets.

1971 saw the introduction of limited overs for Lancashire League matches - 32 eight-ball overs per side - on a two year trial. It was an attempt to achieve brighter

Todmorden 1st XI 1971 Holland Cup winners
L-R Row 2: Garth Stansfield, Malcolm Heywood, Michael Jowett, Paul Thackray,
Peter Brownbridge,
Row 1: Peter Marner (pro), John Townend, Kevin Wilkinson (c), Brian Whittaker,
Tom Alston (Lgue Exec), Ian Smith, Ewart Clayton, Walter Southwell (scorer).

cricket with a result in each game and to stem the drift away by spectators alienated by a succession of drawn games. To put this in perspective, in the 64 seasons between 1897 and 1962 Todmorden's number of drawn games in a season reached double figures on only eleven occasions but did so a further eight times in the 10 seasons of 'time cricket' between 1963 and 1974.

The Lancashire League's cricketing purists had been swimming against the tide for some time, and the success of the counties' John Player Sunday League, a 40 overs competition which began in 1969, tipped the balance in favour of limited overs cricket. The John Player League itself was inspired by the huge popularity of the International Cavaliers, a team of mainly retired test and county players that toured the country in the late 1960s, playing 40 over matches to raise money for good causes, often county beneficiaries. A Lancashire League XI played the Cavaliers in one such match at Alexandra Meadows in 1968. Many of these matches were televised on Sunday afternoons, the commentators being John Arlott and Learie Constantine. Enviously eyeing the Cavaliers' huge Sunday crowds, the counties copied their format, formed a league and, with BBC2 televising a game each week, raised much additional income by selling perimeter advertising.

The success of Lancashire's one-day side which was attracting huge crowds to Old Trafford and, according to David Lloyd, owed much to the competitive nature of league cricket in the county, had also raised the status of limited overs cricket locally. Meanwhile, the first one-day international - in which Peter Lever opened the England bowling - had been played at Sydney the previous winter.

In the Lancashire League's first limited overs season Todmorden challenged strongly for the title, Marner, one of the country's most experienced and effective one-day cricketers, transforming the team. Only in the last fortnight, did Enfield pull ahead, proving their superiority by defeating Todmorden at Centre Vale in the last match, having beaten them twice previously in the League and Cup. So Enfield were champions and Todmorden received the Holland Cup as runners-up. This was to be the high spot of the decade as only twice afterwards, in 1972 and 1976, did Todmorden finish in the top half of the League.

Marner maintained his consistency and in his four years at Centre Vale scored 2596 runs took 171 wickets and held 46 catches. His pull shot off Burnley medium-pacer Chris Rawstron, which struck half way up the mill wall some 80 yards beyond the Burnley Road boundary, remains one of the biggest hits ever seen on Centre Vale.

Only occasionally did Marner's maverick temperament get the better of him. When, not as part of a game-plan, he announced that he was going to open the batting and put the first ball out of the ground, the team feared the worst - and it usually happened. In the final match against Enfield in 1971, the newspaper report read:

> He was dismissed first ball as he tried ambitiously to lift Ryan into the park only to see his middle stump uprooted.

In a different scenario at Lowerhouse in August 1972, the home team had been bowled out for 27 in 16 overs on a terrible pitch (John Townend 7 for 10). Todmorden duly passed this score but, in accordance with League rules had to bat on until 5.30pm. Marner refused to bat on such a pitch and was already changed at the fall of the 9th wicket, thus allowing Lowerhouse to gain a bonus point. Todmorden, although they had already won the match, were deemed, at an emergency meeting of the League executive, to be all out. The following week at Haslingden a different aspect of his character was portrayed. Todmorden's 163 for 6 (Marner 78 not out) was being overhauled as aggressive batting from Bryan Knowles narrowed the gap. Marner took over and, with a series of virtual 'yorkers', bowled Knowles and contained the rest, to earn a victory by 5 runs.

After he left Todmorden he continued as 'mine host' at The Old Original, Saddleworth, where friends from Todmorden visited him, and on his death in 2007 they were at his funeral to pay their respects.

The Lancashire League, concerned that in limited overs cricket, bowling and field placings had become too negative and batsmen were too often denied the chance to build an innings, reverted to 'time' cricket in 1973 and 74 but this was so unpopular that limited overs cricket was re-instated in 1975 with 34 eight-ball overs per side.

Brian Crump of Northants was signed as professional for 1975. Cousin of David Steele, England's unlikely batting hero against Australia that summer, the diminutive Crump had played for the county from 1960 to 72 as a reliable batsman and economical medium-paced seam bowler.[5] The League wickets were probably too slow for his style of play and, although his figures were not far short of Marner's, they were accumulated steadily and did not include the match-winning performances needed from a professional. However, two bowlers came to the fore this season. Mike Hartley, who had made his debut in 1972, came to maturity taking 40 wickets with his fast-medium in-swing bowling delivered from a classical high action, and Bob Whitaker headed the bowling with 47 wickets from his slow-medium left-arm spin, many of his wickets clean bowled when batsmen played back to cut and the ball zipped through to hit off stump.

Although pitches were slowly improving, this was still an era when most Lancashire League batsmen looked to score primarily off the back foot. Pitches were often so slow that only the very full ball could be driven with safety and there were only a handful of amateurs whose strongest shot was the drive, Haslingden's Bryan Knowles and Todmorden's Ian Smith being two that spring to mind.

Mohsin Khan batting at Centre Vale, Todmorden's pro 1976, 77 and 81;
non-striker is Garth Stansfield.

No doubt feeling that the amateur bowling was strong enough and with Ewart
Clayton returning, the club looked for a specialist batsman as pro for 1976 and signed
21 year-old Pakistani Mohsin Khan, who was professional in the Bolton League at
Astley and Tyldesley. Born in Karachi in 1955, he played representative cricket in
Pakistan from his mid-teens onwards. Following his first season at Centre Vale, he
toured with Pakistan to the West Indies, England, Australia, New Zealand and India.
He is best remembered for his superb double century at Lord's in 1982,[6] later confiding
to team mates at Todmorden that batting in the Lancashire League was often more
testing than England's one-dimensional attack in that match. Without the injured Bob
Willis, whom Mohsin rated highly, England's attack of Ian Botham, Robin Jackman,
Derek Pringle, Ian Greig and spinner Eddie Hemmings who pushed the ball through
without much flight, lacked the necessary variety for a perfect Lord's pitch.

From the introduction of overs cricket, the Lancashire League awarded four points
for a win, with an additional bonus point for bowling out the opposition as an attempt
to encourage attacking bowling and field placings. In reality, teams quickly found that
if the run-rate could be contained by defensive bowling and field placings, wickets
would follow. The 10th wicket, which brought the bonus point, was more often gained
by pressurising the batting side into trying to score at a ridiculous rate than by attacking
bowling. To genuinely encourage attacking strategy in the field there also needs to be
an incentive, when the run chase is impossible, for the batting side to avoid being
bowled out. The Bradford League, for example, had a 6-0 points allocation if the losing
side was bowled out and a 5-1 allocation if they were not. Although taking wickets
remained the most effective way of curtailing run scoring the overall emphasis on
defence was not significantly affected by the bonus point, especially as more clubs had
effective covers and the number of bowler-friendly pitches, which allowed all out attack,
were becoming fewer.

The trend towards higher scores continued in the 1970s. In the decade beginning 1970, only 16% of Todmorden's totals were below 100, the lowest so far. For the first time, totals between 100 and 200 reached 75%, whilst scores of 200 or more saw no significant change.

Todmorden finished the 1976 season in a healthy fifth place in the League. Mohsin, whose athleticism enabled him to bowl quite rapidly with a slingy action, took 41 wickets, and the amateur bowling also performed well. The outstanding achievement was Mike Hartley's 9 for 13 against Bacup at Centre Vale, which not only won him the League's Telegraph Tankard but remains the best ever bowling analysis by a Todmorden amateur - made more remarkable in that he conceded 10 runs in his first over and then took 9 for 3.

Mohsin scored 890 runs, entertaining with his stylish batting. Captain Ian Smith, the club's leading amateur batsman, his opening partner Alan Fiddling and veterans Garth Stansfield and Brian Whittaker all passed 400 runs.

A major blot on the season came in the Worsley Cup quarter-final at Burnley, the classic example of snatching defeat from the jaws of victory. Batting first Burnley made a challenging 194 for 7 and Todmorden's reply, led by Mohsin (89 not out), stood at 194 for 6 with two balls remaining. With the scores level, Todmorden needed only to block out the remaining balls to win, as they had lost fewer wickets. Obviously the players did not know the rules as Mohsin was run out attempting, as he thought, to win the match. With scores and wickets level Todmorden would still win as they had scored more runs in the first 20 overs. Unlike Burnley, Todmorden were oblivious to this. Brian Whittaker and Mike Hartley went for an impossible single from the last ball and Hartley was run out, leaving Todmorden's score 194 for 8 and Burnley the winners.

It was symptomatic of a team that had the ability to beat any other in the League, but was often out-thought. Enfield stalwarts David Stanley and Ian Metcalf believed that Todmorden was the last side in the League to learn how to play overs cricket. The successful Lancashire League teams of the 1970s quickly got to grips with the containment strategies demanded by this new form of the game, such as starting with an extra cover. Todmorden still set attacking fields, often leaked cheap runs, then were frustrated by the containing tactics of the opposition's less talented but accurate bowlers.

In 1977 Todmorden were leading the League by early June, then lost five games in succession and finished in eleventh position.

In 1978 the club caused something of a shock by signing Brian Close, who had retired from county cricket as captain of Somerset. The agreement was made by telephone during a committee meeting and the news aroused quite a stir in the town and beyond. This indestructible 47 year-old was a legend in sporting circles. Having played for England when only 18 years old in 1949, he had captained Yorkshire from 1963 to 70 leading them to the County Championship four times in 1963, 66, 67 and 68 and the Gillette Cup twice in 1965 and 69. Following a dispute he departed Yorkshire and went to Somerset in 1971. He played for England 22 times, captaining them to six victories in seven test matches - the last test against the West Indies in 1966 and series against India and Pakistan in 1967. He was, however, not a figure of the establishment which found a reason to replace him following allegations of time-wasting in a county match, and the captaincy went to Colin Cowdrey.

Physically courageous and single-minded, his career, which yielded 34,911 runs including 52 centuries, 1168 wickets, 808 catches and 1 stumping,[7] was plagued by incident, as was his introduction to the Lancashire League. Close was a high class golfer who played off a single figure handicap either right or left handed, and prior to signing for Todmorden had accepted an invitation to play in South America, making him unavailable for one match. Under Lancashire League rules a professional had to play in all matches unless indisposed. Todmorden declared Close's prior golfing

Granada TV cameras on the school side filming 'A Good Do for Batters' in 1978
when Brian Close was pro.

commitment and was immediately given a fine of £250, which the club regarded as
more than a little harsh.

A large number of fans gathered to see him in action at the first practice of the season
and his presence enhanced the profile of the club. Granada TV based one of its 'This
England' programmes around Close, the club and the town.

On the eve of the 1978 season, skipper Brian Whittaker became ill and Ewart
Clayton took over the captaincy. Close, predominantly a front foot player, took time to
adapt to the slow early season wickets and six defeats in the first seven games ended
any hope of winning the League. With only the Worsley Cup left to play for, Close set
his stall out to win it, displaying more than a few flashes of his old brilliance. In the first
round his 54 runs and 3 wickets along with skipper Clayton's majestic 82 helped to beat
Church. In round two he was outstanding on a treacherous wicket at Accrington.
Following his own advice that no-one should play forward, he hit a magnificent 100 out
of Todmorden's 150 all out. When a Close six crashed through a car windscreen at
square leg, the dressing room voices, laughed as one, until opener Alan Fiddling
realised it was his car. John Brierley, who scored 14, recalls the innings:

> I had been batting with him for some time and he was on 96 but clearly tiring. He then
> struck the ball into the deep and we set off. As I was the one running to the danger end
> I, somewhat implausibly, called him back for a fourth run taking Brian to a well
> deserved century. As I walked down the wicket to congratulate him he was a purple
> colour and was on his haunches almost unable to breathe. Congratulations offered,
> applause acknowledged, he was out next ball and just about managed to reach the
> sanctuary of the dressing room unaided, a man utterly exhausted.

Accrington's reply quickly emphasized the quality of Close's knock. Reduced to 7
for 5, they were bowled out for 70.

The semi-final at Rawtenstall again saw Close at his most determined. Batting

Close bowling, batting, fielding and showing
the determination and enthusiasm which were
his trade-marks.

fluently, he had made 38 and looked set for a big score when he advanced down the pitch to young off-spinner Paul Riding, aiming for wide long-on. Unfortunately he missed and literally lost his grip - the bat, not the ball - sailed in that direction. Stumped by yards, Close stomped back to the pavilion in silence and once inside declared, 'That's the story of my b***** career. I'm just about to achieve something worthwhile and then something b***** ridiculous happens'. Garth Stansfield made 58 of Todmorden's 178 for 8 but Rawtenstall won by 5 wickets.

Close's sense of humour came out during the match with Enfield at Centre Vale in June. David Stanley, a talented all rounder, who played Minor Counties cricket, was discomfited by a ball from Mike Hartley which clipped his glove and flew up via his chest to shoulder and head. As he collapsed on the floor, Close, from short-leg bent over him solicitously, enquiring if he was all right and helping him to his feet. When Stanley said he thought he could carry on Close said, 'Well you can **** off then, I've just caught you'.

Todmorden finished a disappointing 11th. Speaking in 2010, Close believes that he could have contributed much more if, as he requested, he had been granted the captaincy. Ewart Clayton - 'a lovely fella' - was always receptive to his ideas, but Close found it restrictive having to go through someone else. 'We had some talented cricketers in that side and we should have done much better, but they were tactically very naïve.' Having the professional as captain was, however, not the done thing, even if he was Brian Close! It was a missed opportunity for a team that needed to learn how to play overs cricket.

The successes of Rawtenstall with Abid Ali and Enfield with Madan Lal added to mounting evidence that the route to success in the Lancashire League at this time was a bowling professional who could control one end for most or all of the opposition's innings. Todmorden, meanwhile, continued to employ professionals who were predominantly batsmen and signed one of the most naturally talented cricketers to come from Pakistan, Aftab Baloch. Born in Karachi in 1953, he toured with the Pakistan Under 25s to Sri Lanka in 1973/4 and to England in 1974. His scores include a massive 428 for Sind against Baluchistan at Karachi in 1973.[8] In the first of his two seasons as Rishton's professional in 1975, he destroyed Todmorden in consecutive matches with scores of 137 and 85, both not out.

Aftab came to Todmorden in 1979 on a two-year contract. His approach to the game and to life was casual, exemplified when, complaining of being bored, he declined an invitation from a couple of the players to a round of pitch and putt in the nearby park because, it was 'too far to walk between hits'. He never took guard when batting, just took his stance and was ready - but he oozed talent.

Aftab Baloch, Todmorden pro 1979 and 80, batting at Centre Vale with an eye on the scorebox.

Perhaps success came too easily to him; in 1979 he scored 1000 League runs and his batting, including two centuries, was decisive in five of Todmorden's nine victories. His underrated and under-used off-spin bowling won one match when he took 6 for 44 against Rawtenstall. Todmorden were second in the League after 16 matches but won only one of the last ten to finish 8th. In 1980 Aftab's batting sparkled less often and the team slumped to twelfth.

All teams need a nucleus of dedicated stalwarts who throughout their careers are its backbone and provide continuity, whilst others come and go. 1980 seems a pertinent time to reflect on three such cricketers. This was Garth Stansfield's last season, having been wicketkeeper since his debut in 1959. A pugnacious competitor, he scored 5165 runs, many with his favourite square cut and square drive, and had 354 victims behind the stumps. He was captain in 1974, 75, and 80, and, despite or perhaps because of his no nonsense approach to the game, was well regarded throughout the League and instantly recognisable as his small sturdy figure strode purposefully out to bat.

1980 saw the death, at a tragically early age, of Peter Brownbridge. A brilliant schoolboy batsman, he played in the inaugural Lancashire Federation Team of 1949 under the legendary Jim Gledhill. He was awarded the Todmorden 1st XI captaincy in 1972 and 73 but, whilst batting in the opening match at Rawtenstall in 1973 he collided with a fielder when going for a run and received a severe blow to the temple. He played no more that season and did not have another full season with the 1st XI but captained the 2nd XI from 1977 until he succumbed to a brain tumour.

A committee man from 1975 he, along with Malcolm Heywood, was responsible for forming a 3rd XI in 1979 which played in the Halifax Association. Sustained by long-serving captains Duncan Sutcliffe and Tony Gledhill, the 3rd XI has played continuously since then and joined the Lancashire League 3rd XI Division in 2001. This team has been vital in providing depth to the club's playing strength.

Peter Brownbridge was a gentle person, which would surprise opponents from his footballing days with local team Lydgate where he was a rugged 'thou shalt not pass' centre-half. Not so for those who played cricket with him, where he could show a certain naiveté. Who else would play a classic cover drive straight to cover-point and, on his return to the pavilion, run out, declare 'That shot was worth one' receiving the reply, 'Yes Peter, but not when cover point is Clive Lloyd'. Facing Wes Hall in 1960 Peter, not quite ready, stopped him in his run-up. Wes trudged back to the start of his long run, set off and was stopped again as Peter withdrew. This time Wes went back only four paces, let go a fierce ball and Peter was on his way back to the pavilion. The following season, when Todmorden played Accrington twice on consecutive midweek days during the town's July holidays, Peter contrived to be moving house on both days. Typically, he was quite happy to play along with the team's view that this was not entirely coincidental.

The career of Brian Whittaker, which began in 1958 was drawing to an end by 1980. Succeeding to the captaincy in 1978, he was taken ill on the eve of the season. He played a few games with the 2nd XI before bouncing back as captain of the 1st XI in 1979. In July 1980 he celebrated his testimonial season by organising a star-studded match, the proceeds of which were shared between Calderdale Society for Continuing Care and the cricket club, each receiving £240.

Brian's batting, which could be explosive, was matched by his temperament which would flare spectacularly if he felt aggrieved. He won the Telegraph Tankard for the League's fastest 50 three times. In 1966 Enfield's sub-professional Sonny Ramadhin had reduced Todmorden to 100 for 8, when Brian came in at number 10. He immediately set about the bowling and, when the innings was declared 33 minutes later, he was 50 not out and the score 182 for 8. The match was drawn and would have been lost but for this amazing innings. Seven years later against Haslingden at Centre Vale, again batting number 10 and coming in with the score 144 for 8, he rattled up 50 in 28 minutes, taking the score to 213. On a good pitch Haslingden's reply of 172 for 3 would have been a winning score, without Brian's fireworks.

In 1975 at Rishton, he surpassed himself hitting 50 in only 17 minutes, helping the team to declare at 224 for 6. Unfortunately, Rishton led by Aftab Baloch's 137 not out, won by 5 wickets. He was set for a fourth award the following year when against Nelson he hit 50 in 29 minutes, going on to score 98 not out in 40 balls as Todmorden won by 55 runs. This feat was unbeaten until the last home match of the season, when Rawtenstall were the visitors to Centre Vale and George Croisdale raced to 50 in 26 minutes. Thoroughly miffed by this and blaming it entirely on what he considered to be faulty tactics in the field, Brian retired to his car in a black mood, only emerging four places lower than scheduled to bat at number 10. He set about the bowling with such ferocity that he raced to 34 in 23 minutes in a brave attempt to snatch back the record.

A rain stoppage during a Worsley Cup tie at Burnley in 1979 saw Brian at his most confrontational. Burnley were well placed at 84 for 2, professional Mudassar Nazar 31 not out, but Mudassar was due to join the Pakistan World Cup squad and if the game was delayed for a fortnight he would take no further part in it. The rules required the captains to agree when the conditions were fit to re-start but, in the circumstances, there was no prospect of any agreement between Brian and the equally determined Roland Harrison. It was then left to the umpires, but Brian imposed himself on proceedings by point-blank refusing to take to the field until the outfield was dry. So there was no more play that day, nor the following Sunday when the players hung around for 4½ hours. Relishing every inspection, Brian beamed as he returned victorious to the dressing room, having harangued the officials into a further delay.

The match eventually resumed four weeks later with the World Cup underway.

Burnley, minus Mudassar, made 171 for 8 and bowled Todmorden out for 150!

One rainy day at Rawtenstall, time was hanging heavily and Brian wandered into the home dressing-room to make conversation. Skipper Brian Payne said that they were passing the time by selecting a League 'Sods XI'. Whitt thought this a great idea and eagerly asked 'Who's in this team?' Payne chuckled, 'Well, you're the captain Brian!'

Brian's career statistics, 3262 runs, 628 wickets and 148 catches, are testimony to his fiercely competitive nature, and he is second only to Walter Leslie Greenwood in the club's list of wicket-takers. Statistics alone cannot do justice to Brian's impact on Todmorden cricket for which he worked tirelessly on and off the field, raising money and organising matches and teams. He was

Brian Whittaker bowling; the action which brought him 628 League and Cup wickets.

primarily responsible for the pre-season trips to Clevedon, often reciprocated by the Somerset club, which began in 1979 and ran for most of the next ten seasons.

On 23 December 1990, Brian attended a committee meeting which selected the captains for 1991. Two days later, on Christmas Day, he passed away, aged 50. The Parish Church next to the cricket ground was full for his funeral, one of the last services held there before it closed. The congregation included many familiar faces from across the Lancashire League.

Brian Whittaker's Testimonial
Seated: Garth Stansfield, Peter Lever, Brian Whittaker, Brian Close, Javed Miandad.

Chapter 17

Floods and Finals 1980 to 1989

The start of the 1980s was a time of change. In cricket, the establishment was under challenge at international, league and club level. In 1977 cricket's national boards had been rocked to their foundations by the Kerry Packer 'Circus'. Locally, Lancashire League clubs 'were no longer prepared to...be submissive' to an executive which was still 'applying the old Victorian ethics'.[1] Indiscipline and gamesmanship on the field and occasional crowd violence off it showed increasing disrespect for the game's traditional values.

The Lancashire League executive backed cricket's establishment by banning clubs from engaging Packer players as professionals. This further limited the pool of available stars, which was contracting through the increasing demands of international cricket. In 1978 Madan Lal (Enfield), Mohinder Amarnath (Lowerhouse) and Karsan Ghavri (Ramsbottom) were recalled by the Indian Board of Control to prepare for a test series. The League's rules allowed for a substitute professional only if the regular pro was injured and the three Indians were banned from the League for life. Subsequently Amarnath, who had a medical certificate, was reinstated, and the other bans were reduced to substantial fines. Enforcing a rule that was no longer fit for purpose made the League look out of touch and dictatorial. International cricketers could not be expected to prioritise the Lancashire League over playing for their country and, increasingly, clubs were going to need substitute professionals.

The executive allowed professionals to be released only to play in world cups, regarded as special, isolated events. In 1983, one week after appearing in India's shock victory over the West Indies in the Lord's final, Lowerhouse professional Kirti Azad returned from celebrations in Delhi, with an unused dinner invitation from Mrs Ghandi, to score a match-winning century against Todmorden.

With test commitments increasingly overlapping the start and end of the English season, League secretary Jim Clarke, in his annual report of 1980, asked: 'Should the moral obligation towards a player selected to play for his country transcend the legal validity of a contract between the player and the club?' Answering his own question, he continued '...for the league to alter its rules...after more than 80 years of administration...is surely too simple an answer to be readily accepted and considered satisfactory.'

It took further examples of professionals flouting contracts, not all related to international cricket, before, in 1984, the rule about substitute professionals was relaxed so that professionals could be released to play for their country. It was a sign of the times when the League felt a need to appoint former Enfield and Lancashire 2nd XI captain, Eddie Slinger, as its first Honorary Solicitor in 1985. Slinger's suggestion, in 1987, that 'a disproportionate amount of salary should be paid on conclusion of the contract'[2] - written in as 10% since 1994 - has eased the League's legal and disciplinary burden, whilst the need for clubs to engage substitute professionals has increased.

In 1979 and 1980 inconsistent enforcement of the rule that a 'sub pro' must not be superior to the regular pro, created further problems. Burnley, barred from replacing injured 24 year-old South African state bowler Greg Hayes with one-time England bowler, 42 year-old Harold Rhodes, were fined £50 when captain Roland Harrison refused to apologise for an exasperated outburst to the press. Colne were ordered to re-play a cup-tie they had won because England batsman David Lloyd had substituted for journeyman League professional David Halliwell. Yet Australia's premier spin bowler, Ray Bright, was allowed to substitute for both Accrington's home-grown professional Alan Worsick, and for East Lancashire's then rookie and uncapped Australian leg-spinner, Peter Sleep.

Bright's appearance for East Lancs was against Todmorden, and he took one for 16 in 17 eight-ball overs as East Lancs won by 4 wickets. The rain-affected pitch was ideal for his left-arm spin, but it was his prodigious swinging arm-ball that most impressed the Todmorden batsmen - at least until he took out his handkerchief and a tube of lip-salve fell out onto the popping crease, right in front of the umpire, who appeared totally oblivious to its significance.

In 1980 Accrington's Peter Westwell made the League's first ever challenge for the chairmanship, putting up against vice-chairman Tom Ward. Westwell eventually became chairman in 1990 and under him the League became much more democratic.

Meanwhile, in 1980 relations at Todmorden had degenerated into 'a total lack of liaison between the committee and members'. Additionally it was suggested that 'the club was inventing special occasions just to get extra drinking time' - 'a totally unwarranted allegation'.[3] Led by Chairman Bob Marshall, the committee reappraised the running of the club, forming a players' committee, which had involvement in selection, appointment of the professional, purchase of cricket equipment, preparation of practice wickets and coaching of juniors. This initiative mended bridges and spread the workload.

The first team had a new captain in 1981, 46 year-old Phil Morgan, who had played for the club since moving to live in Todmorden in 1977. A positive left-hand batsman, his front foot technique was redolent of the harder Leicestershire pitches on which he had played much of his cricket. Morgan faced a baptism of fire. Whilst the League paraded the most formidable battery of fast-bowling professionals in its history,

Phil Morgan batting 1983

Morgan had inherited a much-weakened team.

In addition to Garth Stansfield's retirement, left-arm spinner Bob Whitaker, who lived in Burnley, had finally responded to Burnley's overtures to play for them, and Brian Whittaker had played his last full season of first team cricket. Second team captain Mike Jowett, whose magnificent innings had snatched victory from East Lancs in the 1980 Junior Knockout Cup final, had retired, and was replaced by Ewart Clayton. Clayton had been much under-used in the first eleven. In 1980 he had rarely batted higher than eight and was restricted to just 45 overs with the ball. Yet he took two five wicket hauls, finished top of the bowling averages and, in the last match against Colne, scored 53 and took 5-22 to become the first Todmorden amateur for 19 years to earn two collections in the same game - the last being Clayton himself in 1961. To remove him from the first team at this time was a mistake, which was confirmed in 1983 when, aged 43, he returned to the first eleven, scored 404 runs, took 33 wickets and was the League's leading amateur all-rounder that season.

Another significant absentee in 1981 was Ian Smith, who opted to play for Halifax in the Yorkshire League. At the 1980 AGM he had insisted that 'a bowling professional is a must', but Todmorden re-signed Pakistan's opening batsman Mohsin Khan.

Writing in the new and short-lived players' newsletter, Morgan was realistic, 'We certainly will need all of our abilities and confidence to challenge some of the best professional quick bowlers in international cricket.' Andy Roberts, Michael Holding (West Indies), Ian Callen (Australia), Kapil Dev, Madan Lal (India) and Gary Robertson (New Zealand) had all taken the new ball for their countries. Added to these were the rapid if erratic Ray Winter from Jamaica, and the most hostile and hungry of them all, Franklyn Stephenson. The first equipment order from Todmorden's new players' committee included helmets and lacrosse-style chest protectors. Most batsmen never wore helmets except as a necessity in 1981, but this began the gradual increase in wearing them as a matter of course. The first League rule about helmets - that they should be off the field when not in use - applied mainly to the fielding side and appeared in 1984.

With Rawtenstall's Franklyn Stephenson first up, the new helmets were soon in evidence. Stephenson took 4 for 36 and young off-spinner Roger Watson 6 for 31 as Todmorden failed to meet the challenge of forcing the pace at the other end and collapsed to 91 all out. Stephenson took 8 for 24, demolishing Todmorden for 60 in the return at the end of May, but in terms of humiliations, this was as bad as it got. Although Stephenson, Wynter, Callen and Roberts all bowled spells that tested the Todmorden batsmen's physical courage, and Kapil Dev demonstrated his wonderful all-round ability, a wet summer blunted much of the pace and Michael Holding nursed an injured back for both of Todmorden's mid-season matches against Rishton.

Roberts was at his most hostile on an unpredictable pitch at Haslingden, his mood not improved when Morgan twice hooked him off the front foot for four. After a short pitched barrage at Brian Heywood and Mike Hartley, which included the fastest bouncer either player saw in their careers, umpire Chris Metcalf asked: 'Do you think we could see a few pitched in their half please?' 'You want me to bowl off-spinners umpire?' Roberts replied.

Hartley, who made 40, responded by backing away to use Roberts' pace, carving the ball over gully. Roberts remembered, and in the return match at Todmorden asked his captain for 'seven gullies' when Hartley came to the crease. Although Roberts seemed able to nip the ball either way off the pitch at will, Todmorden's batsmen had their moments against him. At Todmorden, Morgan hit 51 and big hitting fast bowler John Townend struck him for 17 in one over, including a six onto the school roof.

Mick Hartley

Albert Ross

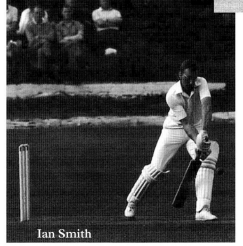

Ian Smith

John Brierley

Brian Heywood

**Some Key Amateurs
in the 1980s**

Todmorden nevertheless lost both matches, albeit narrowly at Haslingden, where the home side, ahead on run rate, survived the last over with nine wickets down.

An early season win over Colne, four magnificent Mohsin centuries that produced four wins, and a late-season double over Bacup, which lifted Todmorden off the bottom for the first time in three months, were just enough to avoid re-election. The team finished twelfth and that, in the circumstances, was a minor triumph.

The season had, to a degree, been one of transition. Morgan, an approachable and democratic captain, ran a happy ship which eased the considerable pressure on his young charges. John Brierley had come of age as a batsman, benefiting a great deal from batting with Mohsin. Their partnership of 196 against Church featured some breathtaking running between the wickets, and this would become a strong feature of Brierley's game. 23 year-old David Whitehead, who returned to the club from Walsden in 1980, developed into a genuine wicket-keeping all-rounder. He was only denied a maiden half century at Bacup when, 49 not out, he rejected several singles so that he could keep the strike with Todmorden ahead on run rate and nine wickets down.

Todmorden began 1982 in much better shape. Smith returned from Halifax, and on his recommendation, Todmorden signed as professional 21 year-old Roderick Orville Estwick, a six feet four inches genuinely fast bowler from Barbados whom Smith had encountered in the Yorkshire League at Bradford. For the first time since 1968, the attack had a professional cutting edge.

Another significant arrival was Albert Ross, a determined left-handed opening batsman who had topped 500 runs in seven of the last eight seasons at Walsden. Todmorden were well aware of his ability and his highly competitive nature from annual challenge matches played between the two clubs since 1976.

There had been a significant increase in 'verbals' on the field since the 'sledging' of the Australians under the captaincy of Ian Chappell, particularly on England's 1974-75 tour of Australia. Professionals give league clubs a hotline to the latest developments in the international game and the Lancashire League's first suspension for dissent was administered in 1975. Todmorden was on the receiving end in 1977 when Ramsbottom captain/wicketkeeper Dally Brooks and Australian professional Trevor Laughlin launched a barrage of 'provocative and obscene comments'[4] at both players and umpires throughout the Todmorden innings. Brooks became the first Lancashire League cricketer found guilty of bringing the game into disrepute and was given a four match ban. One of the umpires was so appalled that he vowed never to umpire in the League again. Not all on-field comments about the opposition's batsmen qualified as sledging. Jack Highley reduced a Church 2nd XI batsman to tears of laughter when he remarked: 'I can tell this bugger can't bat. He left that divot on a length alone all last over and it stood out like a turd on a billiard table'.

Albert Ross's hotline to the international game was Ian Chappell's younger brother, Trevor, Walsden's professional in 1975. The villagers won the Wood Cup, Chappell became the first Walsden pro to do the double of 1000 runs and 100 wickets and he was a strong influence on Ross's vocal approach to the game.

Ross's uninhibited encouragement of his colleagues, vocal pressurising of opposition batsmen and, at times, winding up of opposition bowlers, helped to make Todmorden much more competitive. Described by the *Lancashire Evening Telegraph* as 'a great enthusiast in the field', Ross's comments were usually within earshot, directed at his own players, and calculated to build up the confidence of his own side and undermine that of the opposition. 'It's a psychological battle,' he said. 'You've got to let them think you're on top.' Mike Hartley, manfully shouldering the amateur seam bowling after the loss of John Townend to Lucas in the Ribblesdale League, commented that he had 'never had so much encouragement'.

With the younger players inspired by Ross's example and Estwick firing the bullets, Todmorden were transformed from a quiet team to one of the most vocal and obviously competitive in the League. There is no doubt that they became much less pleasant to play against. They also became more successful.

An early season trip to the altitudes of Bacup tests the mettle of any professional used to warmer climes, and Estwick passed with flying colours. After Smith had been run out - 'his thermal underwear too great a handicap against the gale' - Estwick struck a rapid 53 and followed that with 4 for 53 in 17 overs. Following two wins, it was a shock when, chasing Nelson's 119 for 9, the third match was lost by nine runs, even though South African Neal Radford had reduced Todmorden to 17 for 5.

Nelson and holders East Lancashire were Todmorden's opponents in a tricky group in the Cup. East Lancs recovered from 89 for 6 to make 191 for 6 at Centre Vale, but a century opening partnership by Morgan and Ross set Todmorden on their way, the two left-handers repeatedly cutting Australian Ian Callen to the pavilion rails. Although Morgan fell for 55, Ross's 83 not out steered Todmorden to victory by 6 wickets. Nelson lost so heavily to East Lancs in the group's second game that they had little left to play for when they came to Todmorden. Estwick (7 for 33) demolished them for 91 and Todmorden won by 8 wickets to qualify for the semi-final.

An effective team pattern was emerging, not least because Todmorden batted second in 15 consecutive matches. Mike Hartley took 50 wickets, and Terry Makin - bowling his off-spin more quickly and effectively than previously - took 31, keeping one end tight whilst Estwick attacked at the other. Morgan usually gave the innings a fast start before Ross and Heywood, who scored over 1400 runs between them, laid the platform. Criticised for slow scoring at times, the pair ran well together, Heywood's confidence benefiting enormously from Ross's belief and encouragement as he came of age as a first team batsman. Todmorden were most successful when one of them anchored the innings, allowing the stroke-making middle order of Brierley, Smith and Estwick, who all topped 400 runs, Whitehead, who struck his maiden half century, and Hartley to play with freedom.

Estwick had a typical West Indian fast-bowler's approach to batting. On seeing one of the League's slowest ever bowlers, East Lancs' canny leg spin and googly veteran, Brian Bowling, he stomped around the dressing room remonstrating: 'Look at that! How can this man bowl? I'm going to hit him over de moon.' Despite pleadings to hit Bowling for long safe ones rather than big risky sixes, Estwick's patience lasted one ball, the most studious, slow motion forward defensive. His second ball landed in the hands of long off. This was the longest of Estwick's first three innings against Bowling. In the return match at East Lancs Bowling had him stumped first ball swishing at thin air, and the following season Estwick connected, but was caught at long on. In subsequent meetings Estwick hit Bowling on the ground for ones, part of a learning curve that saw his batting become more selective and productive during his three seasons at Todmorden.

Whitehead and Hartley were involved in an extraordinary incident on a dreadful pitch at Ramsbottom. Replying to Ramsbottom's 118 for 7, Todmorden were 68 for 7 when a nasty lifting delivery from Sri Lanka's opening bowler Ashantha de Mel struck Whitehead in the mouth. Hartley's eyes followed the ball but, as he completed a single, he found Whitehead next to him, prostrate and bloodied. Whitehead was carried off, Hartley was run out and Todmorden's ten and eleven, Terry Makin and Jack Highley, walked out to bat together.

Despite occasional setbacks, Todmorden were well positioned in the League as they

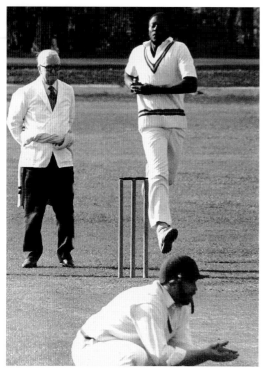

Friendly match; Rod Estwick bowling, Tommy Carrick umpiring, Tony Greenwood at short-leg.

entered a crucial weekend. Unfortunately, the cup semi-final at Burnley was overshadowed by the visit to League leaders Lowerhouse 24 hours earlier, which produced the worst crowd violence ever seen at a Todmorden Lancashire League match.

Occasional crowd violence was not new to the League, but violence fuelled by alcohol - a spin-off from the social facilities that now provided vital income - was. The police had intervened at Enfield in 1977, and at Colne in 1979 where brawling Nelson fans overturned a sightscreen. More disturbing than these isolated examples, was a distinctly 'unfamily' atmosphere in the vicinity of the bar as matches progressed.

The trouble at Lowerhouse was foreshadowed when Lowerhouse were soundly beaten at Centre Vale three weeks earlier. Making a lack-lustre 133 for 5, they failed to punish a number of deliveries that drifted down leg side and accused Todmorden of negative bowling, even though Estwick and Hartley bowled throughout the innings to six fieldsmen on the offside. Lowerhouse skipper Alan Holden's criticisms appeared in the *Burnley Express*, adding 'we are a better batting, bowling and fielding side'.

With Lowerhouse in contention for their first ever trophy, the return match attracted a large crowd. Todmorden were struggling at 60 for 5 when Estwick emerged to unsavoury insults that included reference to his colour from a contingent of about 100 who had been drinking outside the bar. Estwick silenced them with three huge sixes off New Zealand left-arm spinner Evan Gray, but the crowd erupted again when the West Indian stomped off after a highly controversial lbw decision. Estwick's 37, Whitehead (22), and Tony Greenwood (15 not out) lifted Todmorden to a barely adequate 144 all out.

Needing early wickets, Estwick bowled to two slips, a gully and, again, just three men on the leg side - a short leg, backward square leg and fine leg - but the first delivery that slipped down leg side sparked 'disgusting and foul-mouthed abuse' about negative bowling.

Estwick's enthusiastic appealing - described by the *Burnley Express* as 'constant leaping about down the wicket as he screamed for lbw at every conceivable opportunity...total hysteria' - was fired by the atmosphere and a sense of injustice at his own dismissal, and only wound the crowd up further.

Todmorden's intensity was evident in 'dramatic scenes of celebration at the fall of every wicket', but whilst the cauldron inspired Todmorden, it intimidated Lowerhouse. Estwick (5 for 24) and Hartley (5 for 21) bowled with great pace and hostility. Six batsmen were bowled and a seventh lbw as Todmorden dismissed Lowerhouse for 57.

By then, however, events off the field were out of hand. A section of the crowd took exception to Bob Brierley's interview by BBC Radio Lancashire and violently rocked the broadcast van, failing to overturn it but successfully cutting the transmission.

Harold Dawson, taking Mike Hartley's collection, was 'hustled, abused, pushed around and finally had to be rescued by club chairman Richard Crossland'. 'NEVER in my life did I expect to see a Lancashire League club official go round with a collecting box...and be greeted with snarling boos, jeers and even threats of violence,' wrote Ronald Kennedy in the *Sunday Express*. The *Burnley Express* concurred: 'The saddest sight of all was Harold Dawson, who has given a lifetime's loyal service to the Centre Vale club, being booed, insulted and even threatened by the mindless mob'.

As the match ended the mob moved towards the pavilion. The Todmorden players were booed, jeered and jostled as they left the field, home players and committeemen forming a cordon to keep the more hostile spectators at bay. Once in the relative safety of the dressing rooms, Todmorden's team locked themselves in and stayed there for over an hour whilst a large section of the mob remained outside hammering on the dressing room door and hurling abuse at players and officials.

Whilst admitting that some sections of the home crowd behaved 'very badly', Lowerhouse secretary Joe Waterworth 'put the blame firmly on the Todmorden players for sparking off the angry reactions'. Lowerhouse captain Holden agreed: 'What happened on the field in this match was all wrong...in our opinion, the amount of appealing by the Todmorden players was ridiculous...and it unnerved our lads quite a lot.' Phil Morgan responded:

> We have been in the doldrums for some years, but now we have a good team, and a fine and competitive professional in Rod Estwick. We go out determined to win every time and I have no doubt that our attitude showed through in this match. We know that Lowerhouse think we bowl negatively. Our answer is that six of their batsmen were clean bowled and we got them all out for 57.[5]

Perhaps the most pertinent comment came from the *Todmorden News*:

> Lowerhouse must seriously question the wisdom of allowing supporters to consume alcohol outside the bar whilst matches are in progress.

By comparison, the Martini Trophy semi-final at Burnley had a serene and anti-climactic feel, despite the £797 gate. Quietly spoken to by the League Executive about their exuberance, Todmorden's conduct was exemplary as, in perfect batting conditions on a sweltering afternoon, Burnley totalled 187 for 8 in their 48 overs. Estwick bowled through to take 4 for 92, the amateurs, led by Hartley (2 for 32 in 13 overs) kept the score in check, and Todmorden's fielding, with John Brierley and Tony Greenwood both responsible for run-outs, was superb.

Brian Heywood's 79 not out anchored a purposeful Todmorden reply against accurate bowling, particularly from New Zealander Gary Robertson. When Brierley was dismissed with seven overs remaining Todmorden were 152 for 5 but David Whitehead struck off-spinner Joe Edmondson for 18 in the 43rd over and Heywood square drove Robertson for successive boundaries to send Todmorden into their first final since 1966.

Five days before the cup final several Todmorden players enjoyed valuable extra practice with a victory over Scottish touring team Poloc and their cape-coloured professional Omar Henry. Almost 450 runs were scored and conditions at Centre Vale have never been more perfect. No-one would have believed the condition of the ground less than 24 hours later.

Around 3.30pm on 4 August a torrential storm swept through Todmorden. An inch

4 August 1982,
Leslie Forrester and
Clifford Greenwood
glumly survey the
aftermath of the
flood.

Urgent clearing of
the flood's residue

of rain fell in 15 minutes. At Portsmouth torrents tumbled down Ratten Clough, Greens Clough opposite the Roebuck Inn, and Tower Clough above Carrfield Mill. Rivers, streams and culverts quickly became blocked as the water, carrying debris and silt, thundered down the valley bottom. In places the rubble and silt on Burnley Road was five feet deep. Cars were washed down the road, preventing fire engines reaching rescue sites. A house collapsed at Cornholme, and hundreds more were flooded and muddied. The bowling greens on Centre Vale Park were ripped up and opposite the cricket ground, furnishings at Tony's chip shop and the Freemasons Arms floated out into the road. At the end of Victoria Road, water shot geyser-like out of the subterranean culvert, powering a manhole cover twenty feet into the air. The trail of havoc stretched three miles from the Roebuck Inn to the bus station. Within an hour Todmorden was a disaster area.

On the cricket ground David Hatton and Stuart Priestley were in the dressing rooms, their afternoon practice abandoned, when, Hatton recalls:

> The line of grass cuttings at the bottom of the hedge at the park end started to march onto the ground. It was surreal. Then a massive wave of water followed them and it started to pour through the gate. In no more than a minute the ground was a lake. Debris was tumbling through the gate into the ground.

The ground was flooded to a depth of 4 feet 6 inches, but as the water began to recede from the park end, three to four inches of thick, porridge-like mud remained. The following evening the fire service hosed the mud off the square. Local companies were generous in loaning a pump, dumper trucks, barrows, shovels and squeegees. A veritable army - committeemen, players, members and non-members, young and old, male and female - literally 'mucked in', some working 12-13 hours a day to remove the mud, every second increasing the risk of permanent contamination.

Minister for the Environment and Sport, Neil MacFarlane, visited the town with local Tory MP Donald Thompson the following day and immediately contacted the National Sports Council for assistance on the club's behalf. 'League cricket must go on in Todmorden,' he said.

With some equipment written off and damage to the ground's three buildings, the club started an appeal, chairman Richard Crossland stating: 'Without minimising the need for cash at the club I want the appeal to be in proportion to the rest of the damage in the town'. Members of the Lancashire League Executive, initially sceptical about the scale of the problem, were 'horrified' at what they saw and the League donated £250.

By the following Tuesday an estimated 200 tons of mud had been removed and the club anxiously awaited a report on the condition of the ground from Rigby-Taylor horticulturalists. When it came it was good news. The turf was healthy.

The team, meanwhile, had a cup final to play. Walsden allowed practice at their Scott Street ground on Friday evening, and Saturday's League match was switched to Colne, where Todmorden overcame the threat of West Indies all-rounder Collis King to win by 19 runs.

Sunday's cup final at Haslingden began in gloom. Mike Hartley removed Zimbabwean professional Rob Bentley, but the home side had progressed to 32 for 1 after 8.4 overs when rain ended proceedings. The break suited Todmorden as Estwick, over-striding in his run up, was struggling for rhythm and had already conceded 27 runs.

Play resumed seven days later but the Haslingden innings was interrupted by four further rain breaks, enabling Morgan to bowl a much improved Estwick (3 for 96) and the reliable Hartley (5 for 61) through Haslingden's 48-over innings. On a dry but slow

The Martini Trophy winners 1982
L-R Row 2: John Brierley, Stuart Priestley, Tony Greenwood, Rod Estwick (pro),
Michael Hartley, Brian Heywood,
Row 1: Terry Makin, David Whitehead, Phil Morgan (c), Albert Ross, Ian Smith.

wicket that rewarded accuracy, the home side were restricted to 168 for 8.

After a slow start against Haslingden's three-pronged medium pace attack, the Todmorden innings gathered momentum with Heywood's 58 and bursts of acceleration from Smith (27) and Estwick (14), but when Estwick fell at 144 for 6, Todmorden still needed 24 from 4 overs. Brierley and Hartley scrambled 15 before Hartley skied one to Haslingden wicketkeeper Tony White but, at 8.45pm the light had almost gone.

The street lights outside The Woolpack shone brightly through the darkness as the experienced Rod Taylor began the final over. Todmorden were 160 for 7, needing nine. Brierley scrambled a single and Greenwood somehow saw enough to slap a two and a three on the leg side. A dot ball was followed by a bye to the keeper, leaving Todmorden on 167 for 7, needing 2 to win, with one ball remaining.

Keeper White came up to the stumps and Taylor bowled a length ball outside off stump. Greenwood swung and missed. White took the ball and removed the bails in an instant. Just for good measure, he put ball to stump and removed the stump, breaking the wickets for a second time. Haslingden celebrated. The cup had been won - or had it? Brierley had set off as the ball was delivered and completed 22 yards. Greenwood had raced up to the other end. Square leg umpire Joe Collier was shaking his head. Pandemonium and confusion reigned. The decision contradicted what most people, including the players, thought they had seen. Result and emotions switched in an instant. As the Haslingden team surrounded Collier, Brierley sprinted to the pavilion, arms raised, shouting 'He's given not out. He's given not out!' The final run had counted and tied the scores on 168. Todmorden were the winners as they had lost fewer wickets - seven to Haslingden's eight.

Collier adjudged that when White removed the bails Greenwood still had his back foot grounded, and that when the stump was removed, Brierley had completed the run. This was the first Todmorden match to be videoed, and the video confirms that Collier was right. Given the awful light and the state of the game, Joe Collier had made arguably cricket's most brilliant and bizarre umpiring decision.

Todmorden had won its first trophy since 1963 and it was Tony Greenwood's finest hour. Most club teams have at least one player who rarely gets the chance to bat or bowl; throughout 1982 Greenwood had batted at number nine, hit a few quick runs when required, fielded with great energy and enthusiasm, and never

Tony Greenwood, Jack Highley and Terry Makin celebrate being runners-up in the Lancashire Junior League 1987

complained. An unorthodox fieldsman, he put his body on the line, his hands often the second line of defence. On more than one occasion he aqua-planed headlong into the stumps, demolishing them in his eagerness to prevent a single. Yet he was highly effective, had a powerful throw, a safe pair of hands and was a real asset to the side.

In 1987 Greenwood captained the second team to become runners-up in the Junior League, its highest position for over 60 years and in 1988 he shared a joint benefit match with Terry Makin, awarded for their 21 years' unbroken service to the club. The match attracted some of the leading amateur and professional players from the Lancashire and Central Lancashire leagues and raised over £1000 for Cancer Research, Ferney Lee Junior and Infant School and the Special Baby Care Unit at Halifax General Hospital.

Prize and gate money from the 1982 cup final totalled over £1000, vital to Centre Vale's restoration following the flood damage. Todmorden played two more 'home' matches on opposition grounds, winning at Enfield and Ramsbottom, but their title challenge floundered on an incredible 179 by Collis King at Colne and a shortened match at Burnley, after Todmorden had mopped up the Burnley ground with flood equipment brought from Centre Vale.

Rawtenstall retained the title by one point over Lowerhouse whom they played in the last match. Intent on preventing Lowerhouse gaining the bonus point for bowling them out, Rawtenstall contrived 50 for 6 in their 34 overs - and all with barely a murmur about negative cricket.

Although Todmorden finished fifth, the return of cricket to Centre Vale for the last two home matches, notwithstanding the soft surface, the flies and the smell, was a triumph in itself.

Fund-raising specifically to pay for flood repairs continued into 1984. Donald Thompson MP donated 'The Donald Thompson Trophy' for the winners of a six aside

Donald Thompson MP and Sports Minister Neil MacFarlane send the 'Turf Push' on its way
from the Grace Gates, Lord's; Andy Harvey pushing the barrow.

The Lord's turf arrives at Centre Vale.
L-R: Terry Makin, Rod Estwick, Tommy Farry, Stuart Priestley, Jeremy Ward,
Richard Crossland.

Borough Centenary Celebration Match, President's XI v Parliamentary XI, 5 June 1996.
L-R Row 2: Malcolm Thomas (Bridgeholme CC), Ben Johnson (S Australian pro Colne CC),
Ian Smith (TCC), John Garland (Walsden CC), Duncan Parker (TCC), Simon Barker
(TCC), Mrs Ena Marshall (Mayoress), Cllr Albert Marshall (Mayor), son of Roger Stott MP,
Sir Donald Thompson MP (Calder Valley), Robert Atkins MP (S Ribble), Philip Walters
(TCC), Darren Walters (TCC), Dan Marsh (S Australian pro TCC), Stuart Priestley (TCC).
Row 1: Martin Hinks (TCC), Peter Brennend (Bridgeholme CC), Kenneth Gale (Walsden
CC), Trevor Bailey (Walsden CC), John Brierley (TCC), Roger Stott MP (Wigan), James
Davidson (CVCA AG sec) Mark Clayton (TCC).

tournament at Centre Vale, entered by twelve of the 14 Lancashire League clubs and
won by Lowerhouse, who defeated Todmorden in the semi-final. The competition
almost brought further financial complications when, with the ball flying to all parts,
a Mrs Ashworth from Rawtenstall was struck in the face, but the Albion Insurance
Company declined her claim for compensation under public liability insurance.

Thompson and his parliamentary colleague Neil MacFarlane were at the Grace
Gates, Lord's, to send off a 225 mile Turf Push, Lord's to Todmorden. Pushing round
the clock, the nine-strong team, which included professional Estwick, took 70 hours
and raised over £3000. The turf remains planted as part of the lawn in front of the
pavilion.

Thompson, who was knighted in 1992, remained a friend of the club but lost his
Calder Valley seat in the Labour landslide of 1997. In 1996, Todmorden's Centenary
as a Municipal Borough, a match was arranged between 'Sir Donald Thompson's
Parliamentary XI' and a 'Todmorden Select XI' made up of players from the town's
three clubs Bridgeholme, Todmorden and Walsden. In the celebratory spirit of the game

Sir Donald manfully heaved himself out to bat, but as he set off for a run one of his colleagues warned, 'For God's sake don't go for two Donald. We can't afford a by-election'.

Todmorden made a disastrous start to 1983. Three separate break-ins cost the club over £1000. Of the first six League matches, three were lost and three rained off and the team were bottom of the League. The first round cup tie at East Lancs spilled over to the reserve date when several players were unavailable and that too was lost. After the fourth match Phil Morgan resigned the captaincy and retired from the game owing to pressure of work and Terry Makin took over the reins.

Makin himself had received 'special commendation' in another complaint about Todmorden's conduct in the third match of the season at Bacup. Following a rain delay, one of the umpires took umbrage when outvoted on whether to resume and announced 'I'm going to count the balls and do bugger all else'. Despite clear frustration when a palpable lbw was turned down, Makin took 5 for 18 as Bacup collapsed to 97 all out.

Todmorden were 11 for 1 when more rain ended play, but were still padded up in the changing room hoping for resumption, when Bacup's players emerged showered and changed. Disgusted, Morgan commented on both umpire and the home side in his captain's report.

Todmorden's players thought little more about it and were frankly amazed to read the headline 'Todmorden 'aggression' under fire' in the *Lancashire Evening Telegraph*. Bacup captain Phil Lord had written an 'unofficial letter of complaint' to the League, to the press and to Todmorden chairman Richard Crossland, whilst the umpire in question, unsupported by his colleague, had reported Todmorden's 'aggression' to the League. As at Lowerhouse the previous season, no action was taken, but the incident reinforced Todmorden's reputation for being, in the words of Lord, 'too aggressive and intimidatory'.

The only light early-season relief came from a seven-a-side floodlit competition at Horwich RMI Football Club, small-scale but influenced by the success of floodlit cricket in the Kerry Packer Circus and subsequent one day cricket in Australia. Todmorden were one of 16 invited teams, which also included Burnley, Haslingden, Rawtenstall and Walsden. The 12 overs per side matches were a qualified success and a new experience for the players and spectators. Estwick in particular found the short square boundaries to his liking, as Todmorden beat Westhoughton and Rawtenstall to progress to the semi-finals when, fielding a much-weakened team, they lost to Horwich.

In the Lancashire League Todmorden gradually recovered from their dreadful start. Although Ross lost form, Ewart Clayton and Ian Smith thrived as a new opening partnership, Smith hitting a century in the win at Nelson. Estwick's haul of 77 wickets was 22 fewer than in 1982, but he was once again the League's leading wicket-taker and the team again finished fifth. Unlike in 1982 however, they never threatened the leaders. In the last match under eight-ball over rules, Bacup were 116 for 8 needing 62 from four overs, but won by one wicket, as Neil Hammond struck Estwick for 34 in one over and 18 off the next to record the season's fastest 50.

From 1984 the Lancashire League fell in with the rest of the cricketing world and played six-ball overs - 46 per side, two fewer than the knockout cup competition which had been 48 overs per side since 1981. Brian Close, who disliked eight ball overs because they gave the fielding captain less flexibility and restricted opportunities for youngsters, would have approved.

In 1984 Estwick returned for a third season to a team now shorn of Ross, who had returned to Walsden, and Heywood who was working and playing cricket in Surrey. Although Smith, Hartley and Estwick produced brilliant if isolated match-winning

Todmorden 1st XI 1985
L-R Row 2: T Farry, D Whitehead, J Townend, I Smith, J Wadsworth, I Ali
Row 1: J Brierley, D Scott (pro), A Fiddling (c), A Ross, G Duffield.

performances, the team failed to function as a unit. In July, Terry Makin resigned the captaincy and finished the season on the second team. Alan Fiddling took over, but the rot had set in and, with five wins and 19 defeats, Todmorden finished equal bottom with Bacup. For only the second time in its history, Todmorden had to apply for re-election to the League.

In the spring a contract was sent to South Australian Jamie Siddons. At the last minute he was unable to come, but found a colleague who could and, with the season impending, Todmorden had little choice but to sign unknown all-rounder, Darryl Scott.

The return of Albert Ross to open the batting and John Townend to open the bowling added resilience and experience to both departments. Scott was soon to demonstrate the ability and personality to dominate opponents with his hard hitting batting and his surprisingly hostile fast-medium bowling. As John Brierley recalls, 'Darryl brought his typical aggressive Australian manner to all aspects of his cricket and this complimented the team perfectly'.

Scott invariably performed with bat or ball and was never more dangerous than when defending a target after he had failed with the bat. A first round cup win at Rishton instilled enormous belief. Chasing Todmorden's 158 for 8, the home side were cruising at 140 for 4, their South African professional Martin van Vuuren 57 not out, but Scott, supported by young Tommy Farry, induced panic and a collapse to 155 all out.

The second round was even more remarkable. Todmorden made 180 for 7 and, with Scott unfit to bowl, Church recovered from 79 for 7 to 178 for 8 with one ball remaining. The final ball appeared to be heading for the winning boundary, but Scott dived full length, stopped it, hurled it in and Nick Westwell was run out going for the third and winning run. With the scores tied, Todmorden won by losing fewer wickets.

Church supporters insist to this day that Scott fielded the ball with one foot dangling in the Centre Vale gutter, and their incensed scorer was reported for bursting into the umpires' room, accusing them of bad signalling and generally abusing them. To Todmorden eyes, however, there seemed little their professional could not achieve.

The team was playing with zest and belief, and although mid-table after eight games, embarked on a fourteen match unbeaten run of eleven wins - still a club record - and three no results.

Time and again opposing teams were overwhelmed. In the cup semi-final at home to Bacup, Todmorden recovered from 69 for 5 to 162 for 8 before Scott (7 for 28) bowled Bacup out for 70. The following week, defending a barely adequate 132 for 9 at Bacup, Scott took 5 for 30 in twenty overs and along with Mike Hartley (4 for 19) destroyed the home side for 73. When Church restricted Todmorden to 131 for 9, Scott and Townend reduced the visitors to 10 for 5 and eventually 85 all out, Scott taking 5 for 11 in 20.3 overs of unremitting accuracy.

As other challengers were overhauled and fell by the wayside, Todmorden chased down League leaders Haslingden, who had established similar momentum. The two sides were due to meet twice in the last four games but dreadful August weather put paid to four of the last seven matches, including both against Haslingden, and Todmorden had to settle for the runners-up spot on 78 points, eight points adrift.

The cup final, away to Rawtenstall, was played at the fifth attempt on 7 September, and only then after extensive mopping up and a late start. In a match reduced to 42 overs per side, Rawtenstall set a stiff target of 187 for 8 and although Smith (28) and Ross (35) gave Todmorden a positive start, the pace of West Indian Tony Merrick (5 for 61) proved too much in the gathering gloom and Todmorden were bowled out for 153.

Todmorden fully expected a trophy when Scott returned in 1986. After winning only three of the first seven games, they closed in on top spot with 14 wins from 15 matches, the highlight when leaders Accrington collapsed from 10 for 0 to 11 for 7, including ducks for David and Graham Lloyd and Tasmanian professional Rod Tucker. Scott (6 for 22) and Townend (4 for 20) bowled them out for 48 and Todmorden won by ten wickets.

In the cup Todmorden progressed to a semi-final at home to title-chasing Nelson. Despite Ross's 45, Todmorden were in trouble at 107 for 7 before captain Alan Fiddling (43 not out) and young Gareth Duffield (22 not out) added 59 in the last eight overs. On a wicket of pace and bounce, Scott responded to the goading of a feisty Nelson contingent with increased pace and aggression. The Nelson players pleaded in vain with their supporters to 'stop winding him up', but it was too late. Scott (5 for 37), Townend (1 for 12) and Hartley (4 for 19) were rampant and dismissed Nelson for 67.

The final at Accrington was played on a much slower surface. Before a crowd approaching 3000 paying, then, record receipts of £1750, only Ross with an obdurate 42 and Mike Hartley with a hard hit 28 not out made anything of the conditions. Accrington skipper and former professional Alan Worsick ducked the ball late into the pads for 23 overs to take 6 for 55, and David Lloyd took 3 for 33 as Todmorden were dismissed for 121. Pre-match, Scott had confessed that this was his seventh final, he had never scored runs in any of them and his team had lost the lot. Worsick's victims included Scott, caught and bowled second ball for 0.

As the pitch dried, Rod Tucker drove his way to a fluent 48, leaving 38 needed from 19 overs with seven wickets left. Fiddling switched his bowlers round and found his best combination in Scott and Ian Smith's off-spin. The pair all but strangled the life out of the Accrington innings, but David Lloyd (22 not out) survived Accrington's middle order wreckage to clinch a three wicket victory with two balls to spare.

Todmorden still had the League title to play for and victory over Lowerhouse on 24 August took them five points clear with four games to play. The following day, the considerable remnants of Hurricane Charley battered Britain, causing at least eleven deaths, and Centre Vale was once again flooded to a depth of over four feet. The fire service pumped a million gallons off the ground but thankfully there was no silt residue and, although mopping up replaced practice, the ground was just about fit for the weekend.

The pitches across a sodden League had now changed in nature and, on the back of the hurricane, Todmorden's title challenge ran aground. Three exceptional bowling performances from Winston Davis (6 for 38), Tony Dodemaide (3 for 25 in 23 overs) and Hartley Alleyne (9 for 25) secured low scoring victories for their respective teams, Rishton, Lowerhouse and Haslingden in very difficult and, at Haslingden, treacherous batting conditions.

While Todmorden lost at Haslingden, the excitement of the title race proved too much for some Nelson and Rishton supporters at Blackburn Road. Rival fans battled, there were six arrests, two were taken to hospital and the game was halted for ten minutes as fighting spilled onto the outfield. A pram was knocked over and the fighting continued on top of it as the baby was dragged clear. Police officers, kicked and punched, called for reinforcements and the police van was damaged as the men arrested were carted away.

The brawl was a microcosm of violence in society that peaked in the 1980s, headlined by the miners' strikes of 1984, the Heysel Stadium disaster and the Luton Town/Millwall riot of 1985, and locally by Burnley fans, who rioted at Ewood Park following heavy handed tactics by the Blackburn police in 1983. The Rishton brawl was the worst crowd violence the Lancashire League has ever seen.

When play resumed, Nelson won the match and entered their final match at home to bottom side Bacup, five points clear of Todmorden and Rishton who were joint second and playing each other at Centre Vale. It was Darryl Scott's final match for the club and, determined to go out in style, he demolished Rishton with 5 for 35 and an unbeaten 59 as Todmorden strolled to a seven wicket victory.

The runners-up spot was secured, the five points briefly putting Todmorden level with Nelson. Then, remarkably, news came through that Bacup had beaten Nelson by four runs. A play-off for the title was needed and hastily arranged for Turf Moor the following Sunday.

Darryl Scott – Cheers!

With both Darryl Scott and Nelson professional, South African Eric Simons, leaving on pre-arranged flights, both clubs engaged their professionals of 1982, Rod Estwick and Neal Radford. Estwick was professional at Farnworth Social Circle in the Bolton League, and Radford, one of *Wisden*'s five Cricketers of the Year after taking over 100 wickets in 1985, was at Worcestershire and had recently made his test debut for England.

Another significant absentee was Mike Hartley, abroad on holiday. Hartley had a good record in big matches and without him Todmorden's amateur bowling was patchy. Although Estwick bowled with fire, pace and bounce to take 4 for 52 in 23 overs, Nelson posted a challenging 171 for 7. Todmorden's reply was always just off the pace. Radford (2 for 71) was tamed, but his taller amateur partner, Peter Cockell (5 for 61), troubled all the batsmen with his bounce. Lacking a substantial innings, Todmorden fell 13 runs short on 158 for 8.

For the fourth time in his tenure as League president, Harold Dawson presented a runners-up trophy to Alan Fiddling. The four trophies of 1985 and 86 had been won by four different teams - Haslingden, Rawtenstall, Accrington and Nelson.

John Brierley has no doubt that in Darryl Scott's two seasons Todmorden were 'far and away the best side in the League', adding:

> Work hard, play hard doesn't even come close to describing Darryl as he embraced with relish all the club, League and town had to offer. On the field he was someone the opposition, players and supporters alike, loved to hate, but once the game was over he was the first person in the bar, sharing a drink with the opposition and his demeanour would win them over no matter how tough the game had been.
>
> He brought his remarkable charisma to all aspects of his role as pro, ensuring that tea ladies, groundstaff, juniors and even the cynical bar-flies loved him from his first day at the club to his last. Darryl had the charm to win even the hardest heart and he will linger long in the memory of all who met him. His presence lifted the side, and individuals within it, to play some stunning cricket with a smile on our faces. To the membership he was simply adored by one and all.
>
> Pros come and go. Some leave a mark on the field, others off the field, but very few both. Darryl is still in touch with us after all this time, and still says, to anyone willing to listen, that those two summers were the best of his life. They were for us all!

1987 was believed to be the club's 150th anniversary season* and extensive celebrations were organised by a separate committee, the 'Friends of Todmorden Cricket Club'.

A souvenir booklet was produced and a week-long Festival of Cricket included a team of distinguished MPs brought by Donald Thompson, whilst England batsmen Graham Fowler and Bob Woolmer, and ex-Lancashire and Gloucestershire batsman David Green entertained. A special lunch featured on BBC2's *Food and Drink* programme and two editions of BBC Radio 2's annual *Brain of Sport* quiz, chaired by Peter Jones, were recorded in a packed function room.

Yorkshire granted Todmorden their 2nd XI county match against Kent. 1000 runs were scored and 25 wickets taken in three days, and the county were so impressed by the pitch and the hospitality that they awarded Todmorden an annual fixture which has continued unbroken since. Lancashire too have used the ground for 2nd XI and U19s fixtures.

A new and bizarre record was set at Todmorden during the 2nd XI Roses match in 1993. Trying to set up a contest, Lancashire took 'declaration bowling' to new levels as Burnley's Mark Harvey gifted Yorkshire 18 consecutive wides which were allowed to go for four. His figures of 0 overs, 0 wickets for 108 runs remain unique.

Chairman of cricket Brian Whittaker was keen to make it another special year on the field and contacted both Geoff Boycott and Clive Lloyd before signing as professional 22 year-old pace-bowler Fanie de Villiers. De Villiers' state, Northern Transvaal, paid his air fare as they regarded a year in the League as good experience.

* It would be 15 years before an account book detailing entries from 1835, setting 1985 as the 150th anniversary, was discovered.

Todmorden U18s 1984 winners of their League and Cup
L-R Row 2: A Barker, R Priestley, I Ali, M Gledhill, T Farry, G Duffield,
Row 1: J Barker, M Clayton, D Hatton, R Eastwood, S Priestley.

De Villiers joined a team in transition. John Townend had retired on a high with 37 wickets in 1986 and would be hard to replace. Unrest at Walsden had brought their two leading amateur batsmen, Richard Eastwood and Stephen Bailey, to Todmorden. Reading the runes, Stuart Priestley, still establishing himself in the Todmorden side, went to Walsden where he played the next two seasons.

Priestley was one of a rich crop of youngsters reaped from an improved youth policy made necessary by the collapse of the Todmorden and District League in 1959 and of cricket in the local secondary schools. The U18s won their league in 1966 and an annual junior schools competition had been established in 1971, but by 1974 only Mike Hartley and Ian Smith of the younger brigade had made a real impact at first team level. The eight-match U18s season was not bringing enough youngsters through and in 1975 Todmorden established an U15s team. This was followed by an U13s team alongside a junior cricket committee in 1977. The better youngsters played open-age cricket from 1979 when a 3rd XI was re-introduced after a gap of 20 years. The club's teams expanded to seven in 1992 when John Brierley established the U11s.

A particularly fine crop of juniors won the U13 and U15 leagues in 1982, and the U18 Lancashire League and Cup double in 1984. Another group containing seven future first team cricketers won the Halifax U18s' League in 1990 and helped the 3rd XI to the Halifax Sunday League title. This group included Stuart and Duncan Parker, sons of former Ashton and Nelson professional Derek who moved to live in Todmorden in the early 1980s.

The 1984 juniors included batsmen Stuart Priestley, Gareth Duffield and Andrew Barker, all rounder Mark Clayton, medium pace bowlers Tommy Farry and John Barker and left-arm spinner Ibrar Ali. By 1987 most of these were beginning to make their mark in the 1st XI. With 26 year-old Brian Heywood returning north in mid-season after four years in Surrey, competition for places was strong.

Several of these players experienced county representative cricket. Heywood and Eastwood played for both Yorkshire Schoolboys and Lancashire Federation, the local schools being in Yorkshire whilst the Todmorden and Walsden clubs both play in

Todmorden 3rd XI Collinson Cup winners and Halifax League Division 2 Champions 1982
L-R Row 2: J Barker, J Ward, A Gledhill, J Kaye, A Mitchell, D Sutcliffe, M Clayton, P Kaye,
T Farry, D Hatton,
Row 1: J Wadsworth, R Brownbridge, I Highley, G Payne, G Duffield.

Lancashire leagues. Heywood never played on a losing side for Yorkshire Schoolboys, topping the batting aggregates and averages in each of his three seasons and opening the batting with future Yorkshire and England opener Martyn Moxon. He also performed well for Lancashire Federation, for whom Eastwood scored 729 runs from 1983-85, and formed a formidable opening partnership with future England captain Michael Atherton.

Clayton bowled effectively for Yorkshire Schoolboys and toured Barbados with Yorkshire's first U16s' team in 1986, where he shared the new ball with future Gloucestershire and England left-arm seamer Mike Smith. Stuart Parker bowled economically for Lancashire Federation in 1993, when his younger brother Duncan was sharing all-rounder duties in Lancashire U16s with Andrew Flintoff.

The Parkers were the last young county cricketers to come through Todmorden's youth teams for many years. As spontaneous cricket on street corners, school yards and Centre Vale Park almost disappeared in the face of counter-attractions, children who once joined the cricket club if they had some ability, were now joining to find out if they had any ability. Some even arrived for their first taster sessions fully equipped. It was style over substance or, as Stuart Parker succinctly put it, 'All the gear and no idea'. In an increasingly commercial, affluent and materialistic age, the sports' marketing men had won. Indeed, in 1992 a new League rule allowed advertising logos of the manufacturer and club sponsor on players' shirts and sweaters in line with county guidelines.

The best young player to emerge from Todmorden in this era was Ibrar Ali. Between 1986 and 88 he took 35 wickets for Lancashire Federation at an average of 11.50, his record comparing favourably with contemporaries, future Lancashire bowlers Gary Yates and Peter Martin. In 1987 Ali took 5 for 84 in 34 overs for Lancashire 2nd XI against Derbyshire at Old Trafford, and in 1988 he was the leading U19s wicket-taker in the country. He had no further county opportunities, being told at a succession of county trials that his bowling was first class standard but he needed a second string to his bow - either batting or fielding.

Ali's quality was never better illustrated than in encounters with West Indian Test players, Phil Simmons and Roger Harper, in 1992. At Haslingden his first delivery, a beautifully dipping arm-ball, completely deceived and bowled Simmons, whilst at Bacup he bowled two balls which turned and lifted then, with Harper playing for the spin, pierced his defence with another quality arm-ball. In 1995 the *Todmorden News* wrote:

> It really is a joy to watch Ali bowl. His flight and spin variations never allow even the best professional batsman to settle. And for the purist a maiden he bowled at Centre Vale to East Lancs' [pro] Allan Dawson, who tried to attack every delivery, but was out thought and deceived throughout, was cricket of the highest class.

Ali won Telegraph Tankards for spells of 8-23 in 1995 and 7-40 in 1997, both against Accrington, and was the League's leading amateur wicket-taker in these seasons. In 1998 he played the first of eleven seasons as a club professional - six at Widnes in the Cheshire County League, three at Spring View in the Bolton Association and one each at Huddersfield League clubs Holmfirth and Honley.

Born in Rawalpindi in 1969, Ali was the first in Todmorden's growing Asian population to make his mark in League cricket. His great grandfather had played against the British Raj before the partition of India in 1947 and his father and father-in-law both joined the thousands who were offered vouchers to work in Britain after the British Nationality Act was passed in 1948. This Act gave British citizenship to the 800 million people of the Commonwealth, and was designed to alleviate the labour shortage as Britain was rebuilt after World War II.

When the first Asians arrived in Todmorden there was mutual cultural ignorance, as Ibrar's father-in-law explains.

> I came in 1957. We came for a few years to earn money to send back to our families in Pakistan, but most of us ended up staying and our families came over to join us. When we arrived we wanted to fit in. The Englishmen all seemed to wear suits, waistcoats and ties when they were out of their houses, so we did the same. It was like a sort of uniform. There were few leisure clothes like there are today. We lived in a street of terrace houses near to the town centre and none of the houses had toilets. There was one toilet for everyone in a shed at the end of the street. I thought when I went out I had better wear my suit and tie, so even if I needed the toilet in the middle of the night I would change out of my pyjamas into my suit and tie to go to the toilet at the end of the street.
>
> But the English also knew nothing of our culture. In the 1950s there was much less variety in English food. Fish and chips, steak and kidney pie and rice pudding are usual ones I can remember from that time. I remember the first time we cooked a curry. Our house did not have good ventilation so we opened the windows to let out the smoke and steam. Before we had finished cooking there was a blue flashing light outside the house. It was a fire engine. Our English neighbours had never smelled curry before. They thought the house was on fire and had called the fire brigade.

Outside the schools, integration of the Asian part of the community has been slow. Talat Mahmood, Todmorden's 12th man at the 1982 Martini Cup Final, was the first to become a playing member at Todmorden in 1980. But by the end of the decade only two others had played for the open age teams. This number increased through the nineties as Ali rose to prominence in the 1st XI, but tailed off immediately when Ali moved to play professionally for Widnes in 1998.

Todmorden cricketers, end of season outing 1952, suits or smart jackets and flannels
were the fashion
Cricketers pictured L-R: J Crowther, E Denison, H Shepherd, B Ashworth, I Martin,
H Dawson, A Cunliffe, W Scott, F Saul, G Warren,
Front right J Holmes (groundsman).

The number rose again when Indian Gyanendra Pandey was professional from 2003-05. The club's Asian players and their families organised Pandey's leaving party and for one night there was a genuine multi-cultural feel to the function room. When, in the early hours, Gyan was collected for his flight home, the Scoreboard-flat was heaving. Gyan eventually became more alert en route but check-in confirmed over £200 of excess baggage. He proceeded to empty everything onto the airport floor, selecting what to take or leave for the next season - fortunately the airport was comparatively quiet at this early hour. Since 2005 Asian involvement has declined and in 2009, of the 41 players who appeared for Todmorden's open age teams, only four were Asian.

Meanwhile, a Todmorden Asians' team has played occasional matches against Asian teams from Burnley, Keighley and Halifax, home and away, their home matches played on Centre Vale Park next door to the club. The ball used in these matches, symbolic of the cultural divide, is a tennis ball wrapped in tape, as in most recreational cricket played in Pakistan.

The cricket club has made occasional overtures to the local Imam. Ibrar Ali, has helped to establish and organise 'Integrate', which looks to tackle social cohesion more widely. He cites the bar culture as a major stumbling block to integration through cricket. Yet there has been an increasing Asian presence in other Lancashire League teams, particularly in the Hyndburn area.

History suggests that eventually cultures will merge, but at Todmorden Cricket Club the degree of integration has merely reflected the wider social pattern, when cricket could be the catalyst for both the club and the Asian part of the community to accelerate the integration process.

For all Todmorden's anniversary celebrations, one issue overshadowed all others in 1987. Viv Richards, the world's greatest batsman, had signed for Rishton. As he arrived for his first match by helicopter amidst a hail storm, Rishton was 'the focus of the cricketing world'.

Rishton were thankful for generous sponsorship because the weather was truly awful. Todmorden had a club-record nine abandonments and with damp, slow pitches allowing batsmen time to adjust to de Villiers' main weapon, the outswinger, the professional did well to take 67 wickets.

Richard Eastwood stroked 619 runs, including 77 in a thrilling last ball win over Nelson and their then relatively unknown professional, Steve Waugh. But the success of the season, in every sense, hinged on the first weekend of July, a home double header to Rishton in the League and East Lancs in the Cup semi-final.

Channel 4 were in attendance, filming a documentary on West Indians in the Lancashire League for the *Bandung File*, and for once the sun shone. Huge crowds filled the coffers, but Todmorden were abysmal. The weekend began well when de Villiers clipped the top of Richards' off stump after he had made just 40, but Rishton still totalled 227 for 7. Todmorden spluttered to 129 for 8 in reply. A similar match unfolded 24 hours later - East Lancs 244 for 5, Todmorden 137 all out.

In the return match Richards made 127 of Rishton's 210 for 7 before he played on to Ian Smith's off-spin. Smith (5 for 72 and 51) enjoyed a fine game, but Todmorden (173 for 8) lost narrowly on run rate.

1987 witnessed Todmorden's most remarkable limited overs match. Haslingden's opening bowlers Alan Barnes and Zimbabwean Eddo Brandes reduced Todmorden to 43 for 8 before David Whitehead (56 not out) and Tommy Farry (37 not out) shared a club record ninth wicket partnership of 93, the innings closing on 136 for 8. De Villiers then took 7 for 39 as Haslingden, the eventual champions, were dismissed for 111. The result further enhanced Todmorden's reputation as Haslingden's bogey team in a period when the League title went to Bent Gate seven times in eleven seasons. Victories in the last three matches lifted Todmorden to seventh and Alan Fiddling, stepping down as captain to be replaced by Ian Smith, could be satisfied with his three seasons in charge.

Two visits to Haslingden provided rare highlights in 1988. In the cup semi-final Todmorden reduced Haslingden to 44 for 5, before the home side recovered to 165 all out. With Australian paceman Geoff Lawson firing at one end, Todmorden were 90 for 6 before Fiddling (30) and Hartley (36) took Todmorden to the brink of victory - 160 for 7 with two overs remaining. Somehow Lawson (2 for 53) and Mick Tracey (6 for 51) restricted Todmorden to 163 for 9. Three weeks later Todmorden's young Barbadian professional Sherlon Greaves hit an unbeaten 92 there, a match winning knock of the highest class, as Todmorden inflicted one of only three defeats on the champions.

Greaves contributed a highly respectable 882 runs, including a

Viv Richards leads Rishton out at Todmorden

wonderful unbeaten 124 against Church's Australian off-spinner Peter Taylor. He also took 47 wickets with a mixture of medium pace and leg-spin, but he was unable to control one end for long periods in the field and, although never hammered, Todmorden were often 20 to 30 runs short. Notwithstanding the Cup semi-final and runners-up spot in the 2nd XI knockout cup, 1988 was a season to forget. The return to a batting professional, despite much stronger amateur resources than seven years previously, had brought a return to twelfth place in the League.

'It's Hot Toddy!' announced the *Lancashire Evening Telegraph*, headlining Todmorden's signing of Sri Lankan Ravi Ratnayeke for 1989. One of the world's leading all-rounders, Ratnayeke had played 19 test matches and appeared for the Rest of the World against England in the MCC's bicentenary celebration match at Lord's in 1987.

Todmorden, among the favourites for the title, were soon in turmoil. Despite wholehearted performances from Ratnayeke, the first three matches were all lost, the only cheer coming when the professional led a makeshift team to runners-up spot in a six-a-side tournament at St Annes on May Bank Holiday Monday.

Victory over Enfield in the fourth match came at a huge cost. Ratnayeke injured his shoulder whilst batting and played only one more match, leaving inexperienced captain David Whitehead to accommodate the strengths of a variety of substitute professionals, ten in total. These include Sri Lankan test batsman Athula Samarasekera and a nostalgic return for Mohsin Khan. The most successful was Hartley Alleyne who produced lightning spells of 8 for 56 against Bacup and 6 for 40 against Nelson to help Todmorden to their fifth consecutive Worsley Cup semi-final.

Semi-final weekend brought West Indian paceman Ian Bishop to the town. He took 1 for 50 in 18 overs in a two-run victory over Church in the League, and gave Accrington's early order batsmen a torrid time in the semi-final, hospitalising Billy Rawstron who was hit in the mouth and fell onto his stumps. Although Accrington professional Robert Haynes and David Lloyd fell cheaply, gutsy knocks by Andy Barker (40) and Paul Barratt (55) lifted the visitors to 195 for 9, Bishop taking 4 for 74 in 24 overs.

Ian Smith and Albert Ross began confidently against the medium pace of Haynes and Neil Holmes, but the match changed the instant Haynes (6 for 64) switched to leg spin, partnered by the slow left arm of Lloyd (3 for 59), Todmorden sliding to 144 all out.

Popular Australian Brendan McArdle, signed for nine matches, brought much-needed stability to the side. Bailey and Brierley both hit form to play influential innings. With the ball, Hartley returned to form and 14 year-old slow medium out-drift bowler Stuart Parker made his debut, bringing a new and effective dimension to the attack and taking 20 wickets to win the club's bowling prize. Bottom of the League after 12 matches, Todmorden won five of the last eight to finish tenth.

In 1990 Todmorden signed another batting professional, young South Australian Brett Williams. Williams struggled to adapt to League pitches until July, when he was visited and advised by Todmorden's former professional, the South Australian selector Neil Dansie, who was also casting his eye over Rawtenstall's Colin Miller and Rishton's Peter Sleep.

Renewing old friendships, Dansie recalled visiting Todmorden's schools in 1955-56 to tell children about life in Australia:

> They couldn't believe that there were roads 300 miles long without a single bend or that people did their shopping from a train which passed through once a week with the groceries.

Of Todmorden he said, 'There are more car-parks and the place looks cleaner but the atmosphere is still the same'.

Leslie Forrester and son Trevor's view from the Scorebox 1982

One face familiar to Dansie was that of 76 year-old Leslie Forrester, who was synonymous with Centre Vale. 1990 was the inaugural year of the *Todmorden News* Trophy for services to sport, given in memory of former sports' editor Ron Wild, and Leslie was the first recipient. He had 'put up the tins' on the Todmorden scoreboard since 1926, been the club's baggage man for many years and performed a multitude of other thankless tasks, including painstakingly whitewashing the boundary boards twice a season.

Leslie's pride and joy was the tackle store, which he nurtured to the point of sanding down the poly-armour covered bats. Fiercely protective of the equipment and of the committee's rules, he was adamant that 'practice doesn't start while half past six' and, holding the storeroom keys, usually ensured that it didn't. Although the tackle store is now relocated, the name 'Fort Knox', chalked onto its door in the early 1970s by Rod Howard, is still used today.

One of the sponsors for the Ron Wild Trophy summed up Leslie's many contributions to the club:

Pack the bag, raise the flag,
Climb the wall, retrieve the ball,
Paint the gate, don't be late,
Oil the bat and all of that
Clean the mower. What's the score?
Put up the nets, brew the tea,
He's done it all, whatever you name,
And been 'tin boy' at every home game.

Leslie, a life member at both the cricket club and the Hippodrome theatre, retired from his voluntary roles in 1992. In 1997, unwell for some time, he died on the same weekend as Princess Diana. His obituary in the *Todmorden News*, commented:

> Leslie was very proud of the presentations made to him by the cricket club and operatic and dramatic society...They showed the affection in which he was held and it is with affection that he is remembered.

Chapter 18

Brickbats and Bureaucrats 1990 to 1999

The ten years leading up to the millennium were not dull either on the field or off it. Wednesday, 2 May 1990, saw the first of two major fires when the old timber tackle shed burnt down. Built by Samuel Fielden in 1874 as a refreshment pavilion for the North of England v South of England match, it was the last of the original buildings on the ground. Luckily, the heavy roller and the mower were in use at the time and were saved. Rebuilt in Yorkshire stone, it incorporated a scorebox, a flat for the professional and an umpires' room as well as the tackle shed. Most of the work was done by volunteers led by Richard Crossland and Jack Highley, a long-serving player who worked in the building trade.

Opening of the new Scoreboard complex by chairmen Bob Bennett of Lancashire and Sir Laurence Byford of Yorkshire CCCs, 11 June 1991.

It was officially opened on 11 June 1991 by the chairmen of the Lancashire and Yorkshire County Cricket Clubs, Bob Bennett and Sir Laurence Byford, during the County 2nd XI Roses match.

The second fire occurred on Sunday, 19 July 1998, just before lunchtime, when the 2nd XI were due to play Haslingden. Starting in the kitchen area, where the electrical wiring was, it seriously damaged the kitchen, function room, and away team dressing room, whilst other areas were smoke-damaged. Alan Fiddling, ex-captain of the 1st XI, was a retired chartered surveyor. He gallantly supervised not just reinstatement but improvement of the building, including re-roofing. This was costed at the insurance money plus an additional £13,000, which was raised by an 'Ashes Appeal', bumper raffle, sponsored run, Dinner Dance at the Town Hall and a Sports' Memorabilia Auction.

The refurbished pavilion was officially opened in January 1999 by guest of honour, Yorkshire Television presenter John Helm.

Todmorden, like other clubs in the Lancashire League and beyond, became increasingly proficient at fund-raising in the 1990s. As memberships and gate receipts continued their downward trend, clubs had

Pavilion fire 19 June 1998

supplemented income from bar and function room-hire, by persuading local firms to place advertising boards around their grounds, and encouraging the sponsorship of matches and match balls. As each club sought salvation according to its local situation, committeeman Ernest Greenwood had the inspired idea of using the land next to the pavilion as a caravan park. The Caravan Club agreed to a five-pitch site being created in 1992. In 2010 the site has much improved facilities, including electric hook-ups, a shower room and the use of club facilities. The site is rarely empty and has contributed

John Helliwell, of the internationally renowned musicians 'Supertramp'

£80,000 to the club's income, rising from £1000 in 1992 to £15,000 in 2009.

At the caravan site's inception the club's current assets were £8700 a decline from £20,000 in 1990 two years earlier. An 'Action Group' was formed specifically to reverse this trend and organised events such as indoor car-boot sales, winter bowls, target golf, annual sports quizzes and treasure hunts. Concerts by, among others, the popular Belvedere Dance Band, the big band Sounds 18, and a rhythm and blues group assembled and led by Supertramp's Todmorden saxophonist John Helliwell, were sold out. Annual bonfires attracted family crowds of up to 4000. The club was packed for a talent contest which was organised by gregarious Australian professional Scott Williams in 1994, and for a choreographed strip routine by a four-strong players and

supporters group, inspired by the film *The Full Monty*, in 1997. Popular race nights, organised by player and long-serving committeeman Tony Gledhill, continued from the 1980s, the runners, riders and form guides revealing members' considerable talent for cryptic innuendo. Supported by catering and bar staff, these events kept morale high and, over six years, raised almost £30,000. By 1998 the current assets were approaching £25,000.

Unfortunately, in 1997 there was an accident when one of the professional stunt team, who lit the annual bonfire, was severely burnt. The club, as owners of the land, were held culpable by the local Environmental Health and Safety Department and faced a criminal charge. The barrister, employed by the club's insurance company, regarded this

Buiding the bonfire, with Philip Walters, Lee Montague, Andrew Sutcliffe and Matthew Brierley

Doreen Storey, Sue Whitehead and Val Smith at work in the 'tea tent'

Celebrating the Lottery Grant 1995: Ian Highley, Richard Crossland, Malcolm Heywood
and Jo Sugarman (Camelot Office)

as a test case for all voluntary organisations/clubs and advised the club to opt for trial by jury, which it did at the Magistrates' Court hearing at Halifax. The Environmental Health Authority dropped its charge just six days before the trial was due at Bradford Crown Court. Subsequently a civil action against the club was taken by the injured party, which he won, the club's insurers meeting the costs. The bonfire, whilst very popular with the community, required a great deal of effort both in preparation and in clearing up in readiness for the caravans. In 1999 it was replaced by a Beer Festival, which has become increasingly successful as both an event and fundraiser.

During the winter months the Scorebox Flat is rented out at a reasonable cost. Catering on match days is done by generous and hardworking volunteers whose home-baking is particularly appreciated and makes a healthy profit for the club.

Most clubs borrow from a brewery to fund improvements and the debt is paid off by barrelage (selling that brewery's produce). In 2002 Todmorden CC paid off a loan from JW Lees Ltd, thus writing off a £13,000 bar refurbishment bill. Since 1997, JW Lees have been generous sponsors of the club, currently contributing £6000 per year. The club treasurer is responsible for handling around £170,000 annually, including the bar's gross turnover of over £100,000, which rarely realises a final surplus of more than £3000.

In 1995 the National Lottery burst onto the scene and on 4 January, its first day, the club applied for a grant to renovate the premises. Peter Lever, a professional consultant, helped to compile the bid which realised £26,000, the maximum available. The club contributed a further £14,000, mostly in voluntary labour and expertise. New showers were installed, the function-room toilets were redesigned to provide access for the disabled and baby-changing facilities, and the Redbrick tea pavilion was upgraded.

As town clubs such as Todmorden devoted thousands of man-hours to sustaining major league cricket, the English Cricket Board (ECB) attempted to impose a national plan that took no account of local circumstances. Each county, regardless of its size or number of clubs and leagues, was to form a Premier League which, as the apex of a pyramid structure, would prepare young cricketers for the county game.

The Lancashire Cricket Board (LCB), formed in April 1996, had as one of its objectives the formation of a Lancashire Premier League. Over 30 clubs showed initial interest, including Accrington, Rishton, Haslingden and Burnley from the Lancashire League, but as arguments for and against such a league raged, these clubs withdrew. In August 1998 John Brewer, Chairman of the LCB, argued the case for a Premier League in the *League Cricket Review*, but confessed that the Confederation of Lancashire Cricket Leagues, a body formed to consider the Premier League issue, had broken off discussion with the LCB 'because the Leagues were totally against forming a Premier League in the County'. The following month the journal had a reply from Brian Heywood in which he expressed concern about the bad press received by local leagues for their opposition to Premier League proposals:

> It is an easy option to stereotype the leagues' executives as stubborn, dyed-in-the-wool traditionalists, whose resistance to change is born more from memories of past glories than hopes for positive progress.
> By comparison, the England and Wales Cricket Board in insisting on one system for all counties, regardless of local circumstances, has escaped unscathed. The failure of the powers that be at Old Trafford to impress on Lord's the wholly inappropriate nature of these proposals in terms of club cricket in Lancashire shows a staggering lack of understanding of their own nursery.

Drawing on his own experience he continued:

Having experienced club cricket in Surrey, Yorkshire and Lancashire over the last two decades I believe that the appropriateness or otherwise of Premier League proposals lies in the geographic and demographic aspects of the individual county, its consequent number of clubs and the structure of league cricket as it currently exists.

In 1986 Mickey Stewart...was the driving force behind setting-up the equivalent of premier league cricket in Surrey. Over the past decade the 'Surrey Championship' has unquestionably been a success. It has made club cricket in Surrey more competitive and has helped to develop good players for the county side.

But the circumstances which made a premier league...painless to set up in Surrey do not exist in Lancashire...Surrey is quite small and very densely populated...Its major conurbations and teams are quite close together...journeys to away matches are much shorter than many of those necessary in a league covering the whole of Lancashire.

...Club cricket in Surrey is financed mainly by the players and major sponsors, both contributing around 500% more than their Lancashire League equivalents in 1986. There are no gate receipts and bar takings are relatively small, so there was no fear of losing lucrative local Derbys - all important in the Lancashire League.

Whereas Surrey already had an unofficial hierarchy of leagues, Lancashire had many more clubs and leagues, including several of similar quality. What would happen to the clubs left behind once the best were creamed off? Many only survived because of a handful of selfless, hard-working individuals. Michael Parkinson commenting in the *Daily Telegraph* wrote:

> ...what they have in common is they survive, not because of any Government policy...or the help of an enlightened council, but because of bloody minded citizens with an instinct for preserving something good, beautiful and full of character.

Stimulation for the proposed 12 club Premier League, Thwaites Brewery sponsorship of £100,000 over 3 years - less than £3000 per year for each club - did not change many attitudes. As the chairman of Lancaster CC commented at the sponsorship launch at Old Trafford, 'The greatest pyramid builders in the world were the Egyptians and they did not start at the top'. Indeed, the one issue which the LCB consistently failed to address was how, in practice, it was going to work, particularly with regard to transport, payment of players, and restructuring of the leagues for those clubs left behind. In response to the question of who a club's 2nd XI and youth teams would play if the 1st XI was travelling far and wide, Dave Edmundson of the LCB stated, 'That is a very difficult question'.

Support for the existing structure came from former Rishton and Church professional Brendan McArdle, who had sub-proed for Todmorden in 1989. He said:

> One of the greatest charms of English cricket is its parochialism - a super league would nullify this. You have a unique club set-up...and can be justifiably proud of it.

By January 2000 the ECB and LCB had publicly acknowledged the desirability of at least two Premier Leagues in a county the size of Lancashire, the Liverpool Competition and the Northern League taking the plunge. In 2010, the Liverpool Competition is still operating as a Premier League but the Northern League, unable to set up a pyramid system of feeder leagues, has lost this status. Clubs in industrial Lancashire still function outside the Premier League blueprint, and continue to produce their fair share of county cricketers, as they always did.

The Premier League debate had an indirect effect on the Lancashire League, League chairman Peter Westwell stating:

> Rumblings over the proposed Premier League in Lancashire have fuelled the momentum for a move from overs cricket back to a form of time cricket...But it has to be played in the right manner.

The reversion to time cricket in 1998 was not to make the game more exciting or attractive for spectators but to improve the quality of play, specifically the bowling. Twenty-three years of overs cricket had produced an emphasis on containment rather than attacking strategies to bowl out the opposition.

Matches would last 100 overs. The team batting first could face a maximum of 55 overs but could declare at any time. Points available were, for a win 10, a tie 5 and a draw 2. In the second innings, the batting side gained 2 bonus points on reaching 90% of its opponent's total runs, and the bowling side gained 1 point for taking 5 wickets and another for taking 7 wickets.[1]

This worked against Todmorden in 1998. Unusually, the club had splashed out on a high profile professional, Vasbert Drakes, a 28 year-old Barbadian, who had performed well for Border in South Africa and as a substitute professional in the Lancashire League, including a spell of 5 for 26 for Enfield against Todmorden in 1997. A hostile bowler capable of late away movement, a natural striker and timer of the ball, and athletic fielder, the players agreed that Vasbert was the most talented all-round cricketer with whom they had ever played. Despite missing 10 matches owing to rain and Commonwealth Games commitments, his 753 runs and 63 wickets in League and Cup matches were very respectable.

He worked hard at his fitness and offered quiet, constructive advice in the nets. On one occasion he told an amateur that he was not watching the ball closely enough and span off breaks, leg breaks and top spinners at him from ten yards, demanding to be told which way each ball was spinning before it pitched. After five minutes he asked: 'What are you watching?' On receiving the reply, 'The ball,' he advised, 'Now watch the middle of the ball - that's what Desmond Haynes does'. The amateur's success rate improved immediately, an example of league cricketers learning from playing alongside top class professionals. Sadly, Vasbert had little interest in the social side of the club and did not really settle in the town. If relationships between Vasbert and the club had been warmer, he would have been held in greater regard.

Todmorden found it a frustrating season. Seven matches were abandoned, nine were drawn of which Todmorden dominated eight, yet they won only 3, lost 5, tied 2 and finished ninth in the League, because points for a win significantly outweighed all others.

A loophole in the rules - that the side batting second did not have to be bowled out for a match to be tied - was exploited by Todmorden and Church at Centre Vale. Church declared at 206 for 7 and with one ball remaining Todmorden were 200 for 4. The teams would take two points each for a draw unless Todmorden could tie the game with six from the final ball, in which case both sides would take five points. Following a discussion between bowler Nick Westwell and batsman Brian Heywood - friendly rivals since under 15s Roses matches in 1975 - and the two captains Peter Gilraine and Richard Baigent, the 6 runs were scored by way of 2 wides and 4 byes, despite the best efforts of Hussain at fine leg who dived full-length trying to stop the final ball from reaching the boundary.

For the first time in the League's history opposing players were called before the disciplinary committee for being too friendly with one another. The charge was 'bringing the League into disrepute and specifically contriving a result by agreement which is contrary to the spirit of the game'. In the end no action was taken against the players or the clubs - no rules had been broken.

The new rules proved unpopular with players and spectators. Rain wrecked many matches, and even in a wet summer, the pitches were good enough to prevent bowlers from forcing victories.

An improved format of 50 overs per side has been in place since 1999. There are 10 points for a win, 5 for a tie and 3 for a no result. There are 2 bonus points for bowling out the opposition and further bonus points for the losing team - 1 each for taking wickets 5, 6, 7, 8, and 9 if bowling second, and 1 each for scoring within 50, 40, 30, 20, and 10 runs of the opposition's total if batting second. The rule that at least four fieldsmen must be within a 25 yard radius from the pitch at all times, adopted for the Worsley Cup in 1991, was also brought in. This attempt to encourage positive cricket and give each side something to play for throughout the match has, overall, been successful.[2]

Cricket Despite Bureaucracy

During the 1990s clubs began to feel pressures from central authority, which had increasingly pervaded Local Government since World War II. Todmorden had become a Municipal Borough in 1896 and many of its leaders had developed their skills whilst helping to administer the democratic and financially sound institutions of the Co-operative Society, the chapels and the Friendly societies. Here the rewards for serving were not financial, but gave the opportunity to exercise talent, extend experience and influence, and enhance reputation. These independent organisations were no threat to anyone, people could be enthusiastic or indifferent to them, but their leaders aspired to improve and benefit society. With this background Local Authority councillors put the interests of the citizens foremost - party politics were largely irrelevant as there was little dependence on Whitehall. Todmorden controlled its own services - gas, electricity and water etc. and could plan for the future. Sport flourished supported by the chapels/churches and people trained to run their own affairs.

During WWII, of necessity, the Government assumed control in defence of the country and the safety of its citizens. Post-war, although wartime restrictions were lifted, Whitehall gradually spread its influence and control, starting with nationalisation. At town level, however, many things were still run locally until Local Government reorganisation in 1974 saw Todmorden absorbed into Calderdale. The Town Council lost most of its executive powers but, as a final throw, it ensured that Todmorden acquired its own swimming pool and that Centre Vale cricket ground became the property of the club. Since then Local Authorities have weakened as power has been stripped away by Central Government through imposition of initiatives such as The National Curriculum for education and 'targets' for the police - regardless of their relevance to the local situation. In effect intermediate levels of government, such as Calderdale, have become agents of Whitehall and thereby diminished. Bureaucracy and fear of litigation has grown. Red tape appears to increase in proportion to the capacity of communications technology to produce it. As a cult of regulation for its own sake has developed, sports clubs have also felt the hand of central bureaucracy. But despite this, and with the welcome support of Lottery funding, they survive.

Overseas professionals, unless in possession of a British or European passport, have required a work permit from the late 1970s. In 1994 the Todmorden minute book records that work permits would only be granted for professionals who had played First Class cricket within the previous 12 months. This ruling lasted until 1999 when The Department for Education and Employment decreed that a professional should have played a minimum of one Test or five First Class matches in the preceding 18 months - significantly tighter criteria.

Allan Stuttard, chairman of Walsden CC, led a campaign against the new criteria arguing, correctly, that 'many excellent players starting out on their careers and those coming to the ends of their careers were barred'. Darryl Scott, for one, would not have qualified under these rules. Letters to MPs and a meeting of the LCB, attended by the ECB's Recreational Cricket Manager, Frank Kemp, failed to achieve any change. It became very clear that no-one was able or willing to fight the league clubs' cause. In autumn 1998, Frank Kemp and Neil Edwards, secretary of the League Cricket Conference, attended the annual meeting with the Department for Education and Employment officials at Lord's to discuss criteria for the coming season. Afterwards, Edwards wrote:

> It was quite clear that we were to be told what the criteria were to be, and negotiation was not on the agenda.[3]

In 2004 it was announced that league clubs could sign a young overseas professional between the ages of 17 and 27 years, who did not require First Class cricket qualifications, but he could only stay two seasons. Was this the dawn of an age of enlightenment? No! In February 2005 this concession was rescinded, catching out some clubs like Walsden, whose contract for their intended young professional had been sent out but not yet returned. The Work Permits Agency had opposed this rule as cutting across their criteria and the Home Office backed down.

Matters have not improved. Neil Edwards, writing of his meeting with Work Permits UK at Lord's in the autumn of 2005 to discuss criteria for 2006 says:

> Traditionally we (League Cricket Conference) have been invited to sit in on the meeting and have some input. However as the years have progressed many of the criteria have been imposed upon us and it is now very much a case of 'this is a Government policy' and our input has been limited. ECB also have their own agenda in which they wish to see limitations on overseas players, and greater use of those players in a developmental role. As it happens these aspirations fit the Work Permit UK philosophy and tie in with their attitudes.[4]

Mike Atherton, in the January 2010 *Wisden Cricketer*, writes:

> The ECB was established in 1997 - combining the old TCCB and the National Cricket Association - and, in a sleight of hand little commented upon, the voice of the recreational game was instantly diminished. Its ability to profit from the funds that flowed in, once Sky and Channel 4 became competitors to the BBC, was diminished to the benefit of the professional hordes riding the gravy train.

Other bureaucratic pressures have descended on league clubs as the Government controls them through the grants system. To qualify for grants the club has to achieve the status of 'Club Mark' or 'Focus Club' and fulfil conditions ostensibly laid down by the ECB but which, in fact, are set by the Government. The origin of many of these conditions is to be found in the European Union, and specifically in the charter of the European Non-Governmental Sports Organisation which advises the Council of Europe on all sports matters.[5] In turn, the Council of Europe's recommendations have been adopted to form a very large part of our own Government's policies on sport which, via the Sports Minister, are passed to Sport England (a government quango) which controls the governing sports bodies in this country. For cricket this is the ECB from whom policies filter down to the county cricket boards and thence to local clubs via the leagues. This is a typical 'Top-Down' system beloved of governments, who increasingly seek to control the lives of ordinary people.

Health and safety legislation and child protection requirements are laudable concepts but can be carried to extremes. Clubs, often struggling to find enough volunteers to administer their open-age and junior teams, are in danger of being submerged by paperwork. It may look good on paper that junior coaching sessions can only take place if a Level II coach is present, or that those under 16 years should have separate changing/showering facilities from adults, but compliance at club level can create enormous practical difficulties. At league level most clubs are family clubs, where everyone knows and looks out for everyone else. They do their best to cater for all, caring for juniors, boys and girls whether they play cricket or not. They provide a safe environment and are not helped by policies which in effect say 'unless you jump through our hoops you will not receive any financial help' or, 'you cannot give voluntary help because we do not trust you without your Criminal Records Check' - even though there is no criminal record to check! This is erosion of trust by Government policy and 'trust' is the basis of so much that is essential in life.

None of this has any bearing on the game of cricket and the skills it requires. Cricket appears to be the least of the priorities. How much better it would be if those involved in recreational cricket at club level were asked for their views on what help the game needs. If only the Government would turn to those involved with the game, who know it like the backs of their hands and who would be more than willing to give advice, then those at the top would get information that is sound, accurate and costs nothing.

Chancellor Gordon Brown, in an article about volunteers in hospitals on the front page of *The Times* of 11 January 2001, declared:

> Politicians once thought that the man in Whitehall knew best. Now we understand that the woman from the WRVS, the mother from the play-group movement or the local volunteer bringing in their own expertise might know better.

Too true! The same applies to club cricket.

Cricket is Paramount

Amidst all the pressures surrounding the League during the 1990s, the game itself carried on. Using position in the League as a bench mark, Todmorden had a mediocre decade, finishing no higher than seventh but only three times lower than eighth.

In 1991 Clint Yorke, of Tobago, came to Todmorden from Evenwood in the Durham County League and became the first of many to occupy the new 'Scoreboard Flat', which most professionals have found adequate for their needs. Australian, Dan Marsh, professional in 1996, commented 'it's a bit small but comfortable... and I haven't any neighbours so I can play my music as loudly as I want. I'm having a great time. I couldn't be happier'.

Clint Yorke was a hard-hitting, left-hand batsman, right-arm pace bowler and brilliant fielder. His younger brother Dwight was also in England starting to make his name as a professional footballer with Aston Villa.

Yorke's power and grace was evident in a magnificent 135 at Burnley as he and Stuart Priestley, who had come of age as the side's most fluent amateur batsman, added 209 for the second wicket, only five short of the club record. Todmorden totalled 250 for 3 to win by 97 runs, and almost matched that the following day at home to Rishton when captain Brian Heywood hit an unbeaten 54 in 32 balls to win the Telegraph Tankard for the League's quickest 50.

Although Yorke was no strike bowler, he had pace and complemented a balanced amateur attack of Tommy Farry's outswing, Stuart Parker's accurate slow medium, Ian Smith's off-spin and Ibrar Ali's slow left-arm. Todmorden were well placed as they

Todmorden 1st XI, 1991
L-R Row2: S Bailey, I Ali, C Yorke (pro), S Priestley, S Parker, T Farry,
Row 1: A Barker, I Smith, B Heywood (c), M Hartley, D Whitehead

entered two mid-season matches against Accrington and their leg-spinning professional, the then relatively unknown Shane Warne.

At Accrington, on a pitch which deteriorated, Tommy Farry (3 for 28) and Ibrar Ali (3 for 31) restricted Accrington to 123 for 7 in their 50 overs. Yorke made 50 out of 78 for 2 and was replaced by Heywood who has clear memories of batting against Warne.

> Warne was bowling well and started to run through our middle order. He bowled far more googlies than later in his career and we decided the best way to pick him was to watch where the ball pitched. He was very accurate and turning the ball a long way, so his googly had to pitch well wide of off stump and his leg-break on or outside leg stump. His weakness in that match was a lack of patience. Accrington hadn't many runs to play with but we were collapsing and, with Ian Birtwistle keeping it tight at the other end, Warne should have kept the pressure on by bowling as he was. Instead, he began to experiment. He fired in a couple of quicker balls, which shot passed everyone for eight byes, runs they could ill afford. He also placed a fieldsman for a mishit behind square on the leg side and deliberately bowled a high full toss, which went over the fieldsman for four.
>
> Another of his strategies was to try to rush us, because he was on top. I had a run in with him when I wasn't quite ready and he had to stop in his run up. At that point he stopped to tie his bootlace to keep me waiting, so I went out to do a bit of gardening to pass the time. As soon as I was out of my ground he leapt up to bowl, protested that I still wasn't ready and bent to tie his other bootlace. So to wind him up further I continued gardening and again he leapt up protesting that I still wasn't ready. This pantomime went on for a minute or two until the square-leg umpire, Bryan Murray, wandered in and asked laconically, 'Excuse me you two, do you think there might be a chance of seeing a bit of cricket?'
>
> We lost our 6th wicket still needing 17 runs to win, then Tommy Farry came in and knocked off the runs in three overs. Using his feet to Warne, he played a glorious cover drive for four to win the match.

At Centre Vale, having bowled Accrington out for 146, Todmorden's reply was of a different nature. Heywood recalls:

> He bowled me three balls to cut, but had
> protected that area well. The fourth was shorter
> still, I went back to cut again and hadn't got the
> bat down when it shot through and trapped me
> lbw. I thought it was just a quicker ball. It was
> only a couple of years later, watching Warne on
> television that I realised the ball was a flipper.
> We were 15 for 3 at that point. The pitch was
> much firmer than at Accrington, spinning less
> far and making Warne more difficult to read. I
> remember Brian Close telling us to sweep when
> we couldn't read Colne's leg spinner Rakesh
> Shukla in 1978 and that's what David
> Whitehead decided to do against Warne. He
> repeatedly slog-swept him into the seats in front
> of the pavilion.

Warne took 2 for 70, Whitehead struck a
memorable unbeaten 70 and Todmorden won by 5
wickets.

Shane Warne, Accrington pro 1991

The victory put Todmorden four points clear at the top with eleven wins from 14
matches. Then the season fell apart. Five consecutive defeats, Ian Smith's retirement
and a group of the younger players setting off for an Australian holiday with five
matches left to play, meant the dream of winning the League evaporated. Late season
wins over champions Haslingden and runners-up East Lancs showed what might have
been, but Todmorden finished seventh, just 6 points behind East Lancs.

Sadly, illness curtailed Tommy Farry's career and Mike Hartley, a mainstay of the
attack for almost twenty years until 1990, was coming to the end of a career that
brought him 608 wickets, second only to Brian Whittaker post-war.

In 1992 the bowling attack was built around Yorke's pace and slower bowlers, Stuart
Parker and Ibrar Ali. This was reflected in a season of three parts, Todmorden winning
the first four and the last four completed matches, when conditions were soft and in their
favour, but losing eight out of 12 on drier pitches in mid-season. On the most sodden
'puddings' in the first two matches, 'Pudding' Parker took 13 wickets for 82 runs in 39
overs and Ali - known as 'Sheriff' as he kept things on a tight rein - 4 for 50 in 32.

A win at Bacup ended controversially when the home side's number 11, Neil
Wilkinson, was given out 'obstructing the field'. Wilkinson was well out of his crease
when the ball deflected off his bat and prevented his being run out. There was an
investigation by the League as to how the umpires came to be locked in their changing
room after the game!

Todmorden were again seventh in the League, but had a say in the destination of the
centenary title by finding a novel way of frustrating Haslingden in the season's
penultimate game. Chasing Todmorden's 166 for 9 on a squelching outfield in
increasingly heavy rain, Phil Simmons powered Haslingden to 109 for 1 in 24 overs,
ahead of the run rate, but until 27 overs had been bowled there could be no result.
With the title at stake the umpires were reluctant to go off, even though conditions
were deteriorating by the minute. Simmons had already lost two balls when Heywood
put himself on to bowl and deliberately bowled a waist high full toss to the short leg-
side boundary. Simmons predictably despatched the ball out of the ground, many yards
up Victoria Road, and lost it. The umpires had no more balls. They retreated to their

Paul Allott signs for Todmorden 1993, with
President, Norman Stansfield and
Chairman, Richard Crossland

room to find another one but, with puddles appearing, a re-start was impossible, the match was abandoned and Ramsbottom were confirmed as centenary champions.

The popular Yorke was replaced as professional by Paul Allott, just retired from county cricket. He took over the captaincy when knee injuries forced Stephen Bailey into retirement, but Allott too had injury problems. He persevered conscientiously but troublesome calves reduced his effectiveness at times and Todmorden finished a disappointing eleventh.

Via Queensland chief coach Dave Gilbert, Todmorden agreed terms with young pace-bowler Andy Bichel for 1994 until Bichel withdrew citing a better deal in the Central Lancashire League. As a replacement Gilbert recommended fast-medium outswing bowler Scott Williams, but added 'he's a bit fiery'. Ironically, Bichel's 'better deal' did not materialise and he signed for neighbouring Walsden for less than Todmorden's original offer.

Despite a double over Haslingden, the batting frequently misfired and Todmorden were third from bottom with four wins from the first 13 matches. In the team warm up at Nelson an exasperated Ibrar Ali instructed the batsmen: 'I want you all to take responsibility today and think "a hundred"', adding 'and that's not a team total!'

By contrast, heavy scoring in the Cup took Todmorden to a home semi-final against League leaders and eventual champions Nelson. A £1000 gate saw Williams (68) lead a Todmorden recovery from 107 for 7 to 176 all out. He then took 6 for 41 and, with Ali (2 for 16 in 11 overs) trapping the dangerous Joe Scuderi caught behind cutting an arm ball, Nelson were dismissed for 106.

A few days before the final Williams injured his hand following an argument in the White Hart. Although he played in the Saturday League match at Burnley, he was clearly unfit. By a twist of fate, Bichel took his place but, batting first on a heavily cracked, concrete-based pitch, Todmorden could only muster 119 for 9. Bichel made 0, unluckily playing on to Haslingden's vocal professional Brad MacNamara, who took 5 for 52 and made 55 not out, as Haslingden won by 8 wickets. Bichel bowled a lightning-fast spell but had difficulty keeping the ball below stump height.

A fortnight later, most of the Todmorden team had to race back from Headingley to play against East Lancs. In the morning they were representing the White Hart, winning the semi-final of the Tetley Bitter Pub Challenge, and in the afternoon beat East Lancs by 64 runs. Seam bowler John Barker, one of the first back, opened the batting and hit 67, his maiden half century. Barker's batting prowess had been evident in a 10th wicket stand of 61 in 6 overs with left-hander Heath Kennedy against Bacup. Kennedy hit Roger Harper for 25 in one over, including 4 sixes, the most expensive over Harper ever bowled in competitive cricket.

The White Hart Wonders won the Headingley final of the pub competition, and Todmorden's League form improved as they finished eighth, Williams contributing 85 wickets and 812 runs, but off the field problems prevented him from being signed for a second year. Instead, he had a successful season at Colne, but his temperament surfaced in an outburst at Church, earning him the *Lancashire Evening Telegraph* headline 'Scott of the Rant Antics'. He confessed 'I'm working on improving my temperament...In Australia I can go for a surf or a buck ride and head down to the beach whereas here most leisure time seems to revolve around the pub'.

In 1995 the efforts of Otago seam bowler Aaron Gale were not enough to lift the team above eleventh place in the League. Gale's best performance, 7 for 43 in the win at East Lancs, helped David Whitehead to the best ever all-round performance by a Lancashire League wicketkeeper - 82 not out, 6 catches and a stumping. The seven victims won Whitehead the Telegraph Tankard for the most dismissals in a match by a wicketkeeper, which he won four times in his career. He also won the League prize for most victims in the seasons 1996 and 97.

As pitches have become firmer, particularly at Centre Vale, more edges have gone finer to the wicketkeeper instead of to the slips, and Whitehead pulled off spectacular catches standing back throughout his career. His 674 career victims for Todmorden, over

Scott Williams,
Todmorden pro 1994

240 more than anyone else, will take some beating. Respected throughout the League, Whitehead's combative demeanour set the tone for the team, whilst his frustration when he felt a decision had gone against Todmorden betrayed his passion to succeed. Following a series of such decisions at Accrington in 1998, he became the first Todmorden player to be suspended, receiving a two-match ban, when the umpire in question overheard his sardonic rhyming couplet, 'The circus is in town, And we've got the clown'. His batting was determined, pugnacious and aggressive, cutting and hitting powerfully on the leg side with a strong bottom hand, whilst rarely throwing his wicket away carelessly. Also a skilful amateur footballer, and later a manager of local teams, Whitehead approached all his sport in a committed and competitive manner, and in 1997 he became the third cricket club member to win the Ron Wild Trophy for services to sport in Todmorden. He captained the second eleven for five seasons from 2004 and, on announcing his retirement at the 2008 annual presentation evening, was given a standing ovation by the members.

In 1996 Dan Marsh, son of Aussie wicketkeeper Rod, was a very popular and successful professional. Despite troublesome tendonitis of the knee, he scored 1000 runs and took 68 wickets with his left arm spin. The power of Marsh's stroke play was apparent in a wonderful unbeaten 82 at Haslingden. Todmorden won by nine wickets with 24 overs to spare and one immense six was still rising as it cleared the scorebox on the distant mid-wicket boundary.

Although pace bowlers John Barker, Gideon Foster and Alex Scholefield took nearly 70 wickets in total, opponents often countered plans to bowl spinners Marsh and Ali in tandem by preparing pitches on the edge of the square. But, in League cricket, a team is entitled to seek its own advantage.

The big name in 1996 was Rishton's South African professional, Allan Donald, the world's fastest bowler, man-of-the-series against England the previous winter and, at 29 years of age, close to the peak of his powers. Pre-season, he commented:

Lots of great names have played in the Lancashire League and many Australian state cricketers go there every year. So it's an excellent league...I'm not a man to shy away from work. I've always given 100% to anyone I've played for.

Donald was true to his word. Treating the League with great integrity and respect, Donald gave his all for Rishton and his 106 wickets brought them the League championship.

Todmorden played Rishton twice in mid-May and should have won both games. At Blackburn Road Rishton were bowled out for 97. Priestley and Heywood, who cut and hooked Donald for successive boundaries, added 35 in eight overs before Priestley ran himself out. Then, changing ends, Donald (8 for 38) ran through an insipid middle order as Todmorden capitulated to 70 all out, Heywood, 29 not out, carrying his bat.

Todmorden's bowlers were again restrictive in the return match at Centre Vale, Rishton totalling 134 for 8 in 49 overs. Priestley (55) and Heywood (44 not out) then added 102 as Donald went wicketless for the only time all season. The *Halifax Evening Courier*'s Ian Rushworth, under the headline, 'The Great Wall of Tod' wrote:

> ...Battling amateurs Stuart Priestley and Brian Heywood were the toast of Todmorden today after succeeding where England failed last winter - by taming demon Donald...Tod's openers withstood everything the Springbok could throw at them in 14 lightning quick overs to compile a match winning century stand...Priestley was the more confident of the pair, moving confidently to 55 before running himself out going for a suicidal third run, while for Heywood it was a long, brave and ultimately a highly successful battle of survival...Donald tried everything he knew. Over the wicket, round the wicket, the yorker, the short ball, the slower one and the away-swinger but all to no avail...The match was as good as won when Priestley ran himself out but Heywood and Marsh, who lost part of his bat to a Donald delivery, completed the task and left the shivering South African without a wicket.[6]

Alan Donald bowling to Brian Heywood at Centre Vale, Stuart Priestley is the non-striker and Clifford Ashworth the umpire.

Stuart Priestley had exceptional reactions for an amateur. His ability to play pace bowling was apparent in 1983 when, aged 17, he withstood a ferocious barrage from Hartley Alleyne at Haslingden. In 1994 he played a superb match-winning 86 not out in Todmorden's 164 for 9 against Burnley's 6 feet 8 inches Australian test bowler Jo Angel. Such experiences develop the know-how and confidence to cope with challenges such as Donald.

Stuart Priestley unleashing a straight drive

Brian Heywood, who lacked Priestley's natural ability and power, practised assiduously, relying heavily on technique and a rhythm of playing the ball very late. This made him strong square of the wicket, difficult to dismiss and able to score runs in difficult conditions, but less strong driving in front of the wicket when the ball is played earlier. Playing against Donald, Heywood believed that the greatest danger was to be caught on the crease and this guided his thought processes for each ball: 'On your toes; this is going to be quick; play the length, forward or back.' He added: 'Batting Donald was a fantastic privilege and experience. How many amateurs, in whatever hobby, get the chance to take on the best in the world?'

Donald commented: 'I feel I'm bowling pretty well...Todmorden's batsmen got stuck in today and did very well.' This reflected his view of the League. 'The amateurs are well capable of handling themselves. There are some good batters and the overall standard is quite good.' He would 'definitely send batters over...to teach them how to play on slow wickets'.

His views supported those of East Lancashire's Paul Reiffel, writing in the *Daily Mail* on 26 June 1990:

> Sometimes they [the amateurs] can be a bit unorthodox, but week in week out they are the ones who cause the problems...You know what to expect from the professionals. Every now and then one of them is going to have a good day against you. But with the amateurs it is different - they know this league inside out, they know all about the conditions. It's not that standards are particularly high...if these guys came over and played on Australian wickets it would be no contest. But it's a different story here.

Todmorden professional Dan Marsh agreed.

> Over there you have nine or ten players of very similar quality, whereas in England the standard is much more varied, so I would think it's a fair bit better in Australia.

In1990 Haslingden's professional, Mike Whitney, told the *Lancashire Evening Telegraph*:

> League cricket is a unique game. It's totally different from any other kind of cricket for a number of reasons. Reputations mean absolutely nothing. You can be the best player in the world and a number nine batsman, who perhaps works on Bolton fish market, can come in and take a ball that's a foot outside off stump and pull you behind square for four. The wickets bring you down to earth as well ... bowling when there are deep footholds and wickets are slow.

Donald too had trouble with the footholds at times.

> ...conditions and footholds have obviously not been what I'm used to...I quickly found the line and length to bowl in this league - you've got to get the ball right up there for it to swing. The yorker has worked better than anything else. The wickets are not conducive to just banging in a quick ball...but... If the wicket's wet and unplayable matches should be cancelled.

Marsh was less critical of the playing conditions.

> ...it's tremendous how these guys just go out and play their cricket whatever the conditions. Three of the four games so far would not even have started back home but here they just get on with it.

Despite some impressive performances in 1996, Todmorden again finished seventh. Marsh furthered his first class career by transferring from South Australia to Tasmania, but he kept in touch with friends in Todmorden via email which led to his return for a second season in 2000.

A recurring theme with any voluntary organisation is continuity. In 1996 Richard Crossland stood down from the Todmorden CC committee after 17 years, 15 of them as chairman. For Crossland the club was, and still is, a way of life, having devoted almost all his spare time to working on the ground. He had overseen almost all the major projects on the ground, co-ordinating recovery from the floods of 1982 and 1986 and the building of the scorebox/flat. President of the club, Bob Brierley, who had served as club secretary for 16 years, said he 'could not imagine anyone working with greater dedication and commitment to a voluntary organisation'. In 1996, Crossland was awarded the Ron Wilde Trophy for services to sport in the town.

The 1990s saw ladies become full members of the committee and serve as officers, reflecting the wider trend as more women increasingly took prominent roles in public life and in private companies. In 1990 Sue Whitehead was the first lady to be elected onto the committee and served until 1996. In 1992 Freda Heywood became the first lady club secretary, followed in 1995 by Betty Whittaker, who became, and is still, the membership secretary. Parity in membership subscriptions between men and women was achieved by 2001. Attitudes have certainly changed since the League secretary, in his annual report for 1982 commented:

> Ladies Committees...are examples of perfect support...Apart from the occasional enquiry as to why a relative or boyfriend has not been selected for one of the teams they make no attempt to influence Club policy.

Two more substantial assets came to Centre Vale in 1997. Richard Baigent brought his Minor Counties experience with Buckinghamshire and, after acclimatising to League pitches, played some superb innings during his six years at the club. Frans Cronje, from the Border Club in South Africa, was the most committed of professionals. Working hard on team spirit, epitomised by the 'huddle' at the fall of a wicket, he demonstrated positive qualities similar to those that had made his younger brother, Hansie, an icon as captain of the South African team. Frans persuaded even the least energetic to participate in fitness runs through the park woods and was always ready with his physiotherapy skills when needed. He said:

> I have played for Westhoughton in the Bolton League, but this standard is higher. It is the best team spirit I have ever come across in league cricket in England.

As evidence of his commitment he donated his collections towards the purchase of mobile practice nets and, thus encouraged, the players did likewise. Described by Andrew Collomosse in the *Daily Telegraph* of 17 May 1996: 'as uncompromising on the field as he is amiable off it', Cronje ended the season with 1183 League and Cup runs and 67 wickets.

Richard Baigent, eyes following the ball as he sweeps

The Lancashire and Central Lancashire Inter-League Cup competition began in 1997 but, after great initial enthusiasm, Todmorden were soon disillusioned. With the fixture list now crammed there were no replay dates, leaving outcomes at the mercy of the weather and devaluing the competition. Reaching the quarter-final Todmorden were in command, 121 for 2 on a difficult pitch at Werneth, when the rain came and the result was decided by bowling at the stumps. Todmorden lost 5-1. Both semi-finals were decided in the same way. As Todmorden also reached the Worsley Cup semi-final, which they lost by three runs chasing 232 in 'one of the most thrilling finishes seen at Turf Moor for many a long year', the players had only one free date, Saturday or Sunday, in eleven weeks.

Defeated by Haslingden in the 1998 quarter-final, Nelson in 1999, and losing in another bowl-out at Norden in 2000, Todmorden did not lose a match to a Central Lancashire League team until 2001. By then, many clubs were fielding weakened teams in the early rounds. Copying the county game, both leagues introduced a midweek Twenty20 competition in 2006. This pushed demands on the players too far and the inter-league cup was discontinued.

With ten matches left in 1997 Todmorden were fourth, but only two more matches were won as the team's legendary inconsistency re-asserted itself. In one of these, at Rishton, Cronje (159 not out in 102 balls) hit Todmorden's highest individual score in the Lancashire League, and with Heywood (80 not out) added 230 in 29 overs, a new club record partnership, as Todmorden compiled 283 for 1.

Despite defeat by bottom club Rawtenstall in the final match, Cronje left the field to a resounding ovation. Alan West of BBC Radio Lancashire summed up the season: 'If Todmorden can beat Haslingden and East Lancashire [the top two] twice each what on earth are they doing in eighth place?' At least

Cronje and Heywood's record partnership of 230 at Rishton

Todmorden 1st XI 1997
L-R Row 2: A Scholefield, G Foster, H Kennedy, I Ali, M Clayton, R Baigent,
Row 1: A Sutcliffe, S Priestley D Whitehead (c), F Cronje (pro), J Barker, B Heywood.

the 3rd XI gave Todmorden a trophy to celebrate, winning the Halifax Courier Cup by beating Halifax in the final at King Cross.

Frans's Todmorden friends felt immense sadness as they witnessed on television his unconditional support for Hansie through the tortuous months of match-fixing investigations, and as he carried Hansie's coffin following his death in a helicopter crash at the age of 31.

Towards the end of the 1998 season, Lamphey Cricket Club in Pembrokeshire telephoned to speak to Vasbert Drakes. Drakes had already departed with Barbados for the Commonwealth Games in Kuala Lumpur, but during the conversation Lamphey recommended Brendan Nash to Todmorden. A 21 year-old Queenslander with no first class experience, Nash had a British passport and would not require a work permit. He was a friend of Littleborough professional Clinton Perrin and had been advised to seek a higher standard of club cricket by Ian Healey, the Australian wicketkeeper, who also played for Brendan's club side in

Brendan Nash bowling at Centre Vale 1999.

Queensland. Before the end of the season, Brendan had visited Todmorden and signed for 1999.

From a sporting family - his father had swum for Guyana in the 1968 Mexico Olympics - Nash was slightly built, a brilliant fielder, a medium-slow left-arm swing bowler and an impressive left-hand batsman. He had a wide range of scoring areas and was a swift runner between the wickets. 1999 was a season of remarkable matches but unremarkable results as Todmorden clung tenaciously to the mid-table position. High scoring was the order of the day with more runs being scored at Centre Vale than ever before. A bizarre fixture list, including two replayed matches and Cup ties, provided Todmorden with 11 out of 14 matches at home in mid-season when the weather was dry and often glorious. A new grass-cutting machine produced some wonderful pitches, the outfield was fast and the summer was characterised by the prolific batting of Nash and skipper Baigent who broke the club's professional and amateur records. At home to Ramsbottom, Todmorden hit their highest score in a one day Lancashire League game, 301 for 3. Nash beat Cronje's record score with 176 not out and with Baigent set a new club partnership record stand of 252. However Todmorden's lack of bowling resources was cruelly exposed as Ramsbottom, also revelling in the perfect conditions, raced to 303 for 7, a new League record for a club batting second. 604 was also a League record for runs scored in a one-day game.

Haslingden too enjoyed the Centre Vale conditions, scoring 284 for 6, but centuries by Baigent and Nash saw Todmorden achieve a remarkable tie. When another Baigent century helped Todmorden to 237 for 3 against Church, Todmorden winning by 18 runs, he became only the third Todmorden amateur after John Crowther (1951) and EB Shackleton (1916) to score two centuries in the same season. Nash finished the season in style, hitting 311 runs in his last four innings. He was so popular and his batting so pleasurable, that criticisms were long and loud when the committee reluctantly decided not to re-sign him.

Lacking Ibrar Ali, who had joined the professional ranks at Widnes in 1998, the bowling needed to be strengthened. Despite the avalanche of runs, only an unexpected win with a much depleted team in the last match at Ramsbottom lifted Todmorden from eleventh to eighth in the League - and provided Todmorden supporters with a last chance to revel in Nash's stroke play.

Nash and Baigent's record partnership of 252 v Ramsbottom 1999.

Chapter 19

The Millennium and After

The new Millennium brought a first for Todmorden Cricket Club. An Australian, Nigel Hunter was invited to the club, specifically to be first team captain. Hunter came to England in the 1980s, had been professional at Stockport in the Central Lancashire League, Greenfield in the Saddleworth League and had last played at Rochdale in 1998. The professional, Dan Marsh, was also Australian, returning for a second season at Todmorden four years after his first.

Highlight of the season was a Worsley Cup run spearheaded by Marsh, whose 294 runs in the competition included 50 or more in every round. He kept Todmorden's Cup hopes live in round one with a brilliant 100 not out from Todmorden's 183 all out, as eventual League champions Bacup were beaten by 24 runs.

The weekend before the second round Todmorden was flooded once again. Walsden Water burst through the roadside river wall at Shade and Rochdale Road became the river. The Calder also burst its banks, flooding properties close to the cricket ground and the terraced streets behind the Hippodrome theatre. Damage to the town was estimated at £12 million and Centre Vale cricket ground was submerged under three feet of clear water. Recalling the flood of 1982, some members took it as an omen of success in the Cup, whilst the Environment Agency drew up plans to alleviate the problem.

Todmorden's 2000 Worsley Cup winning team with supporters
L-R Standing: K Sutcliffe, L Crossland, D Sutcliffe, P Walters, H Crossland, C Sutcliffe,
A Gledhill, B Heywood, N Sutcliffe, R Baigent, J Vickers, J Morgan, S Scholefield,
N Stansfield, M Clayton, H Kennedy, J Barker, C Barker, D Campbell, A Scholefield,
A Claxton, W Storey, L Hinks, R Crossland, M Claxton, P Montague, J Claxton,
S Whitehead, M Heywood,
Seated: I Marshall, S Priestley, D Parker, N Hunter (c), D Whitehead, D Marsh (pro),
B Clayton, J Whitehead, H Whitehead.

The Centre Vale pitch was undamaged and surprisingly firm seven days later when Todmorden beat Rawtenstall by nine wickets to progress to the semi-finals, Marsh, Baigent and Priestley all hitting half centuries. Marsh made a further 69 as Church were comfortably despatched in the semi-final and, after five consecutive finals away from home - 1966, 82, 85, 86 and 94 - Todmorden at last received a home draw. Centre Vale was to stage its first Cup final since 1963.

As in 1982 and 94 the opposition was Haslingden. The sun shone and in front of a large and extremely partisan crowd Todmorden began well. Priestley (52) and Marsh (66) laid a solid platform and earned respective collections of £193 and £111, before Alex Scholefield (44) and Duncan Parker (27) led the final assault. Haslingden and their Zimbabwean professional Paul Strang wilted, and 68 came from the last eight overs as Todmorden accelerated to a formidable 236 for 5.

During the 2000 season the Todmorden attack relied heavily on Marsh's economical left-arm spin and Scholefield's skiddy, attacking fast-medium, but the lesser lights stole the show in the final. Chris Barker (2 for 20) broke the opening partnership of Paul Blackledge - cast as pantomime villain for the day by Todmorden's more raucous followers - and Mark Griffin, and Haslingden never recovered. The visitor's innings, punctuated by regular wickets and two male streakers, spluttered and subsided. Mark Clayton (3 for 25) and man-of-the-match Duncan Parker (5 for 24 and a £112 collection) destroyed the middle order as Haslingden were dismissed for 111.

Alex Scholefield joined Todmorden from the Halifax League club Sowerby Bridge Church Institute as a sixteen-year-old in 1996. Protected from the pace of Rishton's Allan Donald at the start of that season, he made his first team debut once those matches had been played and he was nurtured in 1st XI and junior teams over the next four seasons. An athletic and agile fieldsman, he worked hard at his game and in 2000 blossomed to become the League's leading all-rounder with 533 runs and 71 wickets, winning the League's best young player award. He took 8 for 29 against Enfield, and upstaged Australian paceman Jason Gillespie with figures of 8 for 15 in a nine wicket win at Rishton, to claim the *Lancashire Evening Telegraph* tankard for the best bowling performance of the season. It was no surprise when Ribblesdale League club Earby signed Scholefield as professional for 2001. Since then he has played as one of the paid men at Mirfield Parish Church in the Yorkshire Council and at Barkisland in the Huddersfield League.

Scholefield was able to play for Todmorden because, in 1993, the League extended its qualification rules, allowing in players who represented a club's junior teams, even if they did not fulfil the established criteria of birth, residence or business within a five-mile radius of the ground. These rules, the best and most rigidly enforced of any league in the country, had for decades compelled Lancashire League clubs to produce their own talent. The best of this talent had, like Scholefield - and before him the likes of Garth Warren, Ewart Clayton, John Townend and Ibrar Ali - often moved on to play professionally in other Leagues. Such movement had been largely one-way because most potential imports did not qualify under Lancashire League rules.

In 1997, faced with fewer youngsters playing cricket as leisure interests continued to diversify, and an impending Premier League, which might tempt even more of the better players away, the Lancashire League relaxed its rules about the importation of players. The birth, residence and business qualification radius was extended from five miles to ten for up to three amateurs per club.[1] This rule lasted one year and in 1998 the floodgates were opened. The qualifications remained but now any club could sign any player from 'within a 10 mile radius of the outermost clubs'.[2] In practice it meant that a player who lived in Halifax, within 10 miles of Todmorden, could travel thirty miles to play for East Lancs in Blackburn. This gave players greater freedom of movement both within the League and from outside its traditional confines.

Unlike other leagues, the Lancashire League still maintained the principle of only one paid man per club, the professional, and it was still not completely open to anyone, but the rules no longer enforced the League's keystone objective, 'to foster and develop local amateur talent'. The extent to which this objective was compromised would depend on the individual clubs.

Todmorden, exploiting its edge-of-League geographical position, became the first to take significant advantage of the new freedoms. Reinforced by the successes of Scholefield and the thrilling innings of Richard Baigent - who hit the highest ever Lancashire League score by a Todmorden amateur, 147 not out against Accrington in 2000 - new signings appeared to be the way to go. Invitations to play at Todmorden increased significantly after Nigel Hunter arrived as captain. In 2001 Steve Oddy, an experienced, brisk outswing bowler came from Rochdale to fill the gap left by Scholefield, and for two years did a good job. In 2003 Simon Newbitt, an immensely powerful and at times devastating left-hand opening batsman, joined from Sowerby Bridge Church Institute. At Todmorden he tightened his defensive technique whilst retaining his power and in 2009 broke Baigent's club records by scoring 892 runs in the League and 1115 runs in all matches. In 2010 he took over the captaincy from another effective import, Jon Henderson, a former England U19s international who had played for Lancashire 2nd XI and Shropshire. A medium-paced bowler and middle order batsman, Henderson became the eighteenth Todmorden amateur to score 1000 runs and take 100 wickets for the club. He came to Todmorden from Rochdale in 2005 with his good friend Mohammed Bux, who combined the sustained accuracy of his seam bowling with belligerent late-order hitting. Both stayed for five years and Henderson, captain from 2007-09, brought much-needed stability which helped to develop some of Todmorden's younger players.

In 2009 the Barker brothers, batting all-rounder Nick and pace-bowling all-rounder Stevie, joined from Walsden and have strengthened the team, effectively occupying the places left by Henderson and Bux in 2010. The Barkers' cricketing lineage dates back to the 19th century as their father, Chris, grandfather, Bill, and great-great grandfather, Frank Scott, all played with distinction for Walsden. Frank Scott remains the only amateur to score 5000 runs and take 500 wickets in the Central Lancashire League.

A total of twenty cricketers - four from Walsden and 16 who did not live in Todmorden - were invited to play for the club in the first decade of the 21st century. The successful imports improved the team because there was a role for them that Todmorden's existing players could not fulfil. Others stayed for a mediocre season or two, caused local, and in some cases better, players to be sidelined, and then left, leaving the team weaker than it would otherwise have been.

The club faced a mini-crisis in 2003 when a number of short-term players left simultaneously. The first job of new captain Mark Clayton was to raise a team. Reverting to home-grown talent, he persuaded Ibrar Ali to return from Widnes in the Cheshire County League, along with Brian Heywood, who was also at Widnes in 2002. Ali and professional Gyanendra Pandey bowled almost 1000 overs between them, each taking 70 wickets, and the 'Tod lads' finished seventh, equalling the best of the previous three seasons. Unfortunately, after one season Clayton resigned the captaincy and Ali returned to Widnes. In 2005 Ali moved on to Spring View in the Bolton Association where, in 2006, with Todmorden importing further players, he was once again joined by Heywood, who severed connections with Todmorden that began as an 11-year old in the U18s in 1972.

More serious than the sidelining of experienced players was the stagnation of Todmorden's younger talent. The progress of young wicketkeepers Paul Brierley and Danny Brown was delayed for a season. Brierley's considerable abilities as a batsman were consistently overlooked, and his brother Matthew rarely occupied a batting position for long. Late-developer James Morgan, who took 180 first team wickets in the last four seasons of the decade, might have performed to this standard sooner given an extended opportunity. Cousins Ben and Andrew Sutcliffe made their first team debuts in 2001, but it was 2009 before they contributed with any consistency. In 2010 Ben hit 762 runs in all matches, including an unbeaten 120 against Lowerhouse, whilst at Rawtenstall Andrew joined the select list of amateurs who have contributed 50 and 5 wickets to the same game.

Alongside the amateur comings and goings, Todmorden found out just where leagues stand in cricket's pecking order. Dan Marsh re-signed as Todmorden's professional for 2001, but early in the New Year, an item on BBC Ceefax announced that he had signed for Leicestershire. No approach had been made to Todmorden to release Marsh from his contract. If it had, the club would not have stood in his way. Eventually, Leicestershire paid some compensation, but there was no one to take up the cause of club or League, or to decry the high-handed way in which the club and contract were totally disregarded. Nor was this an isolated incident. In 2004 Colne's Australian professional Matthew Cleary played for one month and then decamped, also to Leicestershire. That this was sorted out to Colne's financial satisfaction is not the point. If the ECB was really concerned about cricket as a whole, as they would claim to be, they would take action. Such incidents do little to assuage the extreme scepticism about the motives of the ECB that exist in the recreational game.

Todmorden found an able replacement for Marsh in Australian pace bowler Matthew Nicholson, but after a good start - eight wins from 12 matches - eleven of the last 13, including all of the last seven, were lost. To compound Nicholson's frustrating end to the season, he was in mid-air, returning to Australia, when al Qaeda terrorists flew two planes into New York's World Trade Centre and a third into the Pentagon. In the ensuing pandemonium at the world's main airports, he was severely delayed at Singapore.

Meanwhile, back at Todmorden, the committee report lamented that 'effort was not sustained at "the nets" and thus on match days towards the end of the season'. Practising every Tuesday and Thursday helps to develop team spirit as well as skills, but sustaining practice through the season takes more commitment from players who do not live in Todmorden and have to travel. At times, work pressures made practice impossible for some of these players. A pattern was developing. In nine seasons from 2000 to 2008 there were only two - 2003 and 2005 - when results in the second half of the season equalled or bettered those in the first.

Net practice, along with ground infrastructure, quality of outfields, fielding and pre-match warm-ups, are aspects in which the Lancashire League remains superior to other leagues. In 2010 South African professional David Weise was impressed by practice at Todmorden, commenting that in his previous appointment at Darwen, recently a LCB Premier League club, there was hardly any practice. Pre-match warm-ups have progressed since the 1970s when players just turned their arm over and had a gentle hit. In 1993 injured professional Paul Allott and his substitute, Lancashire's Steve O'Shaughnessy, were amazed and impressed in equal measure to see the jogging, stretching and fielding drills of both Todmorden and Colne before the opening match of the season, and such routines remain an integral part of match preparation.

As knowledge of sports science has filtered down from the professional game, most amateur sportsmen are physically stronger than their counterparts of thirty years ago, and cricket has become more macho. Better and heavier bats, better pitches and the influence of Twenty20 cricket, have all contributed to harder hitting and a faster, higher scoring game, whilst modern bowlers generally hit the pitch harder. Skill levels do not appear to have kept pace. Batting records are surpassed regularly, partly because fewer bowlers can cope when conditions are heavily in favour of the batsmen, and partly because there are now far fewer international match-winning professional bowlers in the League than previously. In 2007, the wettest summer on record, batsmen's techniques were also found wanting in bowler-friendly conditions when Todmorden bowled Enfield out for 42 and were themselves bowled out for 46 by Ramsbottom, the first sub-50 totals in Todmorden's matches since 1974.

The increasing need to find substitute professionals continued into the new Millennium and Todmorden faced a season of them when Queenslander Jerry Cassells was injured in the first match of 2002. The most successful of Cassells' replacements were Barnoldswick professional Clinton Peake, who scored 340 runs in five innings, and Tushar Arothe, who hit a club record score of 189 not out at Accrington, setting a new club record 4th wicket partnership of 187 with Matthew Brierley. Cassells' most notable replacement, however, was a young batsman who arrived from Nottinghamshire 2nd XI to play in a second round Worsley Cup tie at Nelson. He took one wicket for 57 in 10 overs of off-spin, a catch and made seven. Todmorden nevertheless cantered to a seven-wicket win, and as the players watched the last rites from the Nelson balcony, the sub-pro announced, somewhat surprisingly given his contribution, 'I'm going to be the best player in the world'. His name was Kevin Pietersen.

Todmorden's 2002 Cup run ended at the hands of another future test star in the semi-final, Ramsbottom's Australian Michael Clarke hitting 178 as the home side totalled 307 for 4 to win by 192 runs.

From 2003-05 Todmorden were grateful to have the services of a reliable and talented professional in Gyan Pandey. Captain of his Indian state Utter Pradesh, he

worked in a bank from 11am to 1pm, after which he played cricket. A non-driver (in India he had a chauffeur) Gyan did not require a car. An orthodox spinner, with beautiful control of flight, and a very correct left-handed batsman who never played a cross-bat shot, Pandey shouldered a full burden. In total he bowled 1340.5 overs, took 200 wickets and in his 78 innings scored 3136 runs, including 24 half centuries and 5 centuries. In each of Pandey's seasons Todmorden won more than they lost and beat the respective League champions, East Lancs, Haslingden and Lowerhouse - although Haslingden exacted considerable revenge in the return match at Todmorden in

Gyan Pandey and Neil Dansie (TCC pro 1955 to 56) meet at the Worsley Cup Final at Lowerhouse 2004

2004. The inexperienced Hurr Abbass had everyone's sympathy when recalled to bowl the penultimate over of Haslingden's innings to their professional, New Zealander Chris Harris, who was in full cry. Balls disappeared deeper and deeper into the graveyard as the ensuing carnage yielded five sixes, a two and a four. Including a no-ball, the over cost 37 runs, a record for the League in a six-ball over.

The following seasons found an increasing number of league professionals unable to complete their seasons. In 2006 Todmorden's pro Morne van Wyk, a talented South African batsman, was recalled to join an 'emerging cricketers' squad at the end of June. His replacement, Jacques Rudolph, played two innings before South Africa recalled him for test duty, and the season was completed with substitute professionals. Todmorden won just two of the last 17 games, and only avoided the re-election zone with a one-wicket victory at Colne on the final day of the season. By then five of the League's 14 clubs were without their original professionals. Todmorden's 2007 professional, Francois du Plessis, was recalled to South Africa at the end of June, returned in early August but left again with four matches to play.

The demands of state and national boards paled besides government interference that plunged unchartered depths in 2009. The season opened with ten Lancashire League professionals languishing in their home countries awaiting the completion of paperwork. Of the other four professionals, two were English.

This totally unacceptable situation was caused by a new immigration scheme. In April 2008 the UK Border Agency was formed by merging the Border and Immigration Agency, UK Visas (which handled work permits), and the port of entry functions of HM Revenue and Customs. In an attempt to simultaneously prevent terrorism and address growing discontent about immigration figures, the new agency's remit included dealing with all immigrants. Immigration figures, which weighed in at 170,000 net in 2008, had rocketed since eight Central and Eastern European countries were admitted to the European Union in 2004, allowing their citizens freedom of movement within member states. The Government seems not to have anticipated the impact this would have and, as with an increasing number of Government schemes in the new Millennium, when reality dawned, the response - in this case setting up the Border Agency - was rushed and shambolic.

For league cricket professionals, the immediate impact of the Border Agency's wide remit was an increase in the paperwork required. Club and professional had to assemble a veritable portfolio of forms and licences from the ECB, Border Agency and the professional's home state before professionals could be granted entry. That this paperwork could not be processed in time for ten of the League's 12 overseas professionals to start the season - and some not until June, illustrates what a disorganised, unco-ordinated morass the Border Agency was in.

A more sinister side to the new agency was revealed by the experience of Luke Woodcock, Church's experienced 27 year-old professional from New Zealand, who arrived with some of his paperwork incomplete. He was placed in secure holding accommodation at Heathrow for around nine hours, with no opportunity to seek legal help, and the Church representative, who was there to meet him, was not allowed to see him. Luke was returned to New Zealand, having to surrender his mobile phone and passport to the aircraft captain. The message was clear. Until proved otherwise, everyone is a terrorist suspect. It then took the Border Agency in Canberra six weeks to complete Luke's paperwork.

Many other leagues were without their professionals, but there was no help from higher authorities in cricket or government to speed things up or, indeed to acknowledge that a problem existed. Professionals dribbled in as the season progressed.

Jon Henderson wins the 2005 Worsley Cup Semi-Final against Rishton with a six from the last ball

James Morgan, reliable medium-pace bowler

Below left:
Ben Sutcliffe, an established opening batsman

Below right:
Simon Newbitt, Todmorden captain 2010 and a fierce striker of the ball

Todmorden's Sri Lankan international, Chintha Jayasinghe, arrived in mid-June, and was not the last. Substitute-professionals were at a premium and a few clubs in the League were driven to name one of their amateurs as pro. The League hurriedly amended its rules to allow these players to retain their amateur status providing they played as pro only in the Lancashire League.

Faring better in the Worsley Cup than the League, Todmorden reached the final in 2005, 2008 and 2009. The 2005 semi-final had a thrilling conclusion. Chasing Rishton's 234 for 3, Todmorden needed 30 from ten overs with seven wickets left, but collapsed to 229 for 9 with one ball remaining. Jon Henderson then hit Sri Lankan test off-spinner Kumar Dharmasena for six over wide long-off to put Todmorden through. In the final Todmorden were well beaten by 5 wickets at Ramsbottom, but enjoyed another remarkable run in 2008. In the first round South African professional Gulam Bodi struck 182 not out, as Todmorden chased an improbable 283 to win at Rawtenstall. Mark Clayton's unbeaten 79 turned the semi-final on its head after Ramsbottom appeared to be coasting to victory. Defeat followed in the final at home to Accrington after the visitors made 290 for 6, a new record score for a limited overs final, but it was a crowd disturbance between rival supporters and two arrests that attracted regional television news.

The best final of the three was at Ramsbottom in 2009. Chasing 187 for 7, Alistair Harrison brought Todmorden to the brink of victory with a rapid 34, but the innings fell just short on 182 all out. Harrison is one of several players who promise a bright future.

Third in 2009 and fourth in 2010 represent Todmorden's best League seasons since the days of Darryl Scott in the mid-1980s. Simon Newbitt, the longest serving, most successful and only remaining out-of-town import still in the first eleven, led a young and vibrant team of Todmorden-based players to eight consecutive victories at the end of 2010. The club has once again aligned itself to the keystone objective 'to foster and develop local amateur talent'. The U15s and U13s teams are also strong, and 15 year-old Freddie Priestley is the club's first schoolboy county cricketer for almost 20 years. Could the second decade of the new Millennium see Todmorden win the Lancashire League title for the first time since 1957?

The Wider Leisure Scene

As leisure activities continued to increase and diversify, the first decade of the 21st century brought significant new opportunities for the young and the old.

More people have retired early and are living longer in reasonable heath, enjoying more years of active retirement. They also have more free time than previous generations because of labour-saving devices in the home and, in some cases, because families are more dispersed, responsibilities, such as child-minding, are fewer.

Catering for this age group, a branch of the University of the 3rd Age (U3A) began in 2008 and within two years had over 200 members. It holds monthly meetings with a speaker at the Central Methodist Church and utilises membership expertise to run over twenty special interest classes at various venues around the town.

The U3A Bridge Class has boosted membership of the Bridge Club, which meets at Todmorden Golf Club. Established about 30 years ago, the Bridge Club has over 50 members.

OAK, a community group, whose concerns are the health and well-being of the over 50s, sprang from a meeting to consider the needs of older people, organised by the local Health Authority at the Town Hall in 2007. OAK's funding ceased in spring 2009, but by then the group was self-sufficient. Its membership, almost 100-strong, continues

Upper Calder Valley Walking Group on the 'Barlick Circular', 2004

to enjoy an established pattern of activities, based mainly at the newly refurbished Central Methodist Church.

Founded 45 years ago, Todmorden Antiquarian Society attracts an audience of about 50 to its winter programme of fortnightly talks at the Town Hall. During the summer, trips are organised to places of historic interest. Over the years the society has painstakingly recorded all the gravestones from the burial grounds within the borough. Among the society's excellent publications are founder member Betty Savage's *Murder at the Vicarage, Sam Banks - His Life and Times*, and *Stoodley Pike*; Dorothy Dugdale's *Portrait of a Town - Mid-19th Century Todmorden*; and J Crowther's *Walsden: A Century of Change*.

A branch of the Women's Institute meets regularly at the Oddfellow's Hall, and the ladies' Probus, a group at which professional and business people listen to visiting speakers, attracts around 50 members to its meetings in the Masonic Hall.

In 1984 Marjorie and Peter King of Hebden Bridge started the Upper Calder Valley Leisure Group. Its activities included Monday afternoon tea dances at Todmorden Town Hall, which are still popular, and a walking group, which thrived and in 1995 became the Upper Calder Valley Walking Group, led by Brian Binns. Since then walks have been organised on alternate Wednesdays, and include summer coach trips to such places as Windermere, Derbyshire, Cheshire, Scarborough and Whitby. Walks are planned at levels to suit differing abilities and regularly attract over 30 of the group's 70-strong membership.

Since 1997 the Calderdale Walking Festival, now part of the South Pennine Walking Festival and occupying a fortnight in September, has organised about 70 walks of varying severity. These are very popular, as is the annual Todmorden Boundary Walk. This was originally organised by the Calder Valley Mountain Rescue Association and then in 1981, after a ten year lapse, revived by the Todmorden Rotary Club and Inner Wheel to raise money for charity.

Incredible Edible is a community group whose object is to make Todmorden self-sufficient in food. It arose from a conference attended by Pam Warhurst and Mary Clear where the speaker advised, 'Stop growing flowers and start growing food instead'. The Todmorden group's first meeting attracted 60 people and the concept has mushroomed. Local schools participate, not least the High School, where food is grown in polytunnels, and an aquaponic unit for fish farming will soon be operable. Spare land throughout the town has been utilised and raised beds have been installed on less fertile sites. Vegetables, herbs and/or fruit trees grow in various unlikely locations - on

'Incredible Edible Todmorden', students planting in a boat at the High School

IET Fielden Wharf seen
through corn-cob stalks

Prince Charles holds a
marrow at Todmorden
Market, September 2010

HYT's production of *Wizard of Oz* December 2006

the station platforms, under the viaduct, around the recreation ground, outside the new health centre, by the community college, in the grounds of the residential home, at the supermarket, at Fielden Wharf and outside the police and fire stations. People are invited to help themselves to any of the produce. A further initiative encourages poultry keeping to produce local free-range eggs. Incredible Edible's 'Egg Map' of January 2010 shows 32 producers covering an area from Portsmouth to Blackshaw Head, Mankinholes and Ramsden Wood.

Incredible Edible's unique scheme is bringing the community together and has raised the profile of the town nationally and internationally. It was visited by Prince Charles in September 2010, featured on Michael Portillo's BBC2 television series *Great British Railway Journeys*, and has hosted a National Conference at Todmorden High School, which attracted over 170 people.

The number of organised activities for children has also snowballed in recent years. The Choral Society, for example, started a junior choir in 2009. Springing from a choir created by Daniel Bath, which had performed regularly at the society's Town Hall Christmas concerts, it is led by Richard Pomfret, who has returned from the north-east where he ran successful junior choirs.

A young angler's catch on the Angling Society's 'Taster Day' 2010

The Hippodrome, as well as hosting the Gang Show, has its own Youth Theatre (HYTs), which caters for around 90 children from 9 years upward. Meeting weekly in the Hippodrome foyer in two different age groups, they explore various aspects of theatre, performing informally. The year culminates in a full-length Christmas show, and recent excellent musical productions of *The Wizard of Oz*, *Seusical* and *Peter Pan* have shown why there is a waiting list to join HYTs.

Todmorden Angling Society, which celebrated its 75th anniversary in 2010, has 200 juniors among its 350 members. The society has nine still-water fishing ponds - New Mill (Folly) Dam on Woodhouse Road, Portsmouth Reservoir, Ramsden Wood Fishery, two more at Cliviger and four in Littleborough. It also has fishing rights to parts of the River Calder and over 13 miles of the Rochdale Canal, from Callis Lock in Hebden Bridge to Manchester Road at Castleton. Twice yearly it holds 'Taster Days' when anyone may fish free for half an hour instructed by a coach. Junior members can attend coaching sessions on the canal throughout the summer on Saturdays and Sundays, and junior matches take place on Friday nights.

At Todmorden Karate Club children enjoy the expert tuition of Bob Smith. Smith's sport was judo until a knee injury prevented him from competing. He joined Rochdale Karate Club when it began missionary work in Todmorden at Priestwell School in 1969, and has been an instructor for 40 years. In 1984 Smith achieved his ambition to represent Great Britain and enjoyed victories over Japan at Kyoto, Tokyo and Gifu. He also had the pleasure of seeing his pupil Dave Stafford selected for the British team in 1981-82. Since 1984 Smith has

Bob Smith, seen in Sweden celebrating 40 years as Karate Instructor

regularly instructed in Germany and Sweden. At Todmorden he uses facilities at the high school and the sports' centre and instructs a mixed class of 25, aged 10 or over. Karate, recognised as a Japanese art, originated and developed as a form of self-defence among monks in India who were not allowed to use weapons, and through it children learn discipline, leading to self-discipline, and gain confidence and pride in their ability to take care of themselves and to help others. There is a moral as well as physical dimension to Karate.

With a Tae Kwon Do club at Ferney Lee School, Kick Boxing at Todmorden Sports' Centre and Judo at the Oddfellows' Hall and the cricket club, Todmorden is well served by the Martial Arts.

Todmorden Harriers, formed in the late 1960s, continues to flourish with a membership of around 130, including about 30 youngsters, who train weekly under the supervision of well-qualified coaches at Todmorden High School. The seniors train on Todmorden's rugged terrain and have enjoyed recent individual and team successes in both national fell and long

Tae Kwon Do class at Ferney Lee School 2010.
Inset: Tae Kwon Do Instructor Keith with student Nathan

Inaugural run of Todmorden Harriers, Top Brink, 1968

Junior run Dec. 2007 in conjunction with the 'Hot Toddy Race'

distance running. The club organises six annual races of which five - the Noon Stone, Hebden Bridge, Stoodley Pike, Shepherd's Skyline and Hot Toddy - are local. The arduous Shepherd's Skyline run, from the Shepherd's Rest Inn at Longfield, covers 6.25 miles and includes an ascent of 1150 feet. The minimum entry age is 18 but there are curtailed courses for the U8s, 10s, 12s, 14s and 16s age groups. The 'Hot Toddy' race, run over 5.8 miles every December, starts and ends in Dale Street and attracts runners from far and wide. On the same day there is a one-mile off-road fun run from Todmorden Station car park, which is popular with junior runners. The sixth race organised by the club is the 'Isle of Jura' in Scotland, one of the classic British fell races, covering 16 miles with an ascent of 750 feet.

Cornholme Vale Youth Club (part of Calderdale Young People's Service) working towards a
Duke of Edinburgh Bronze Award

For youngsters the football scene is vibrant, although in 2010 there is no girls' team. Todmorden Borough FC runs eight junior teams, ranging from U7s to U16s, each with a qualified coach. The two oldest junior teams play at Bellholme, whilst the other teams use Centre Vale Park, where extra pitches were provided as part of the Environment Agency's flood alleviation area that followed the summer flood of 2000. The club has 100 to 120 junior members, some age groups playing in the Burnley or East Lancashire leagues but most in the Calderdale League.

Of the town's senior cricket clubs, Walsden is the furthest along the trail of ECB accreditations. They have progressed from 'Club Mark', to 'Focus Club', to the 'Chance to Shine' status that accesses grants to pay coaches who can formally link the club with local schools. Todmorden has recently achieved 'Club Mark' status and runs junior teams for under 9s, 11s, 13s, 15s and 17s, playing clubs within the Lancashire League.

For children whose families commit the time and can afford the cost, the unprecedented number of youth sections in leisure and sporting organisations at Todmorden and elsewhere has filled a physical activity breech. Simultaneously, there has been an alarming reduction in children's spontaneous outdoor play and an increase in sedentary leisure activities.

Today few children adventure onto Todmorden's hillsides, where once summer holidays were passed roaming and chasing, damming streams to create pools in which to play, climbing trees and making dens, all quite free from adult interference. There are fewer spontaneous games of football or cricket on the park or on patches of spare land, and school playgrounds are no longer available but are surrounded by high security fences. Children enjoy a wider choice of leisure activities than ever, but most recent additions are technology-related, indoor and sedentary. Communicating with friends via email and mobile phone has, in many cases, replaced playing out with them.

Walsden Cricket Ground from the Scorebox 2010

The computer, mobile phone, television, DVDs and screen games accounted for almost one third (32.3%) of the boys' leisure-time and two-fifths (41.6%) of the girls' time, in the 2009 survey. Over the years from 1930 girls' participation in sporting activity is seen to have decreased whereas for boys there has been an increase. In 2009 girls are shown to spend less than 6% of their leisure-time on sporting activities whereas boys engage in sports for over 23% of their time. Running parallel to these trends is increasing concern about childhood obesity.

Is society justly protective of its children, or damagingly over-protective? Restrictions on playing out have arisen, partly from legitimate concerns about increases in road traffic and drug abuse, and partly because of a 24-hour news media which, whilst increasing awareness of various crimes, creates an exaggerated perception of their frequency, generating public outcries that demand a Government response. On 26 October 2010 BBC Home Affairs Editor Mark Easton commented on:

> ...a growing list of what experts call 'signal crimes' - incidents which receive a huge amount of media attention and come to be seen as indicative of the state of society...their emotional power has become the central driver for criminal justice reform...The murders...in Soham created a vetting culture which some argued proved heavy handed and counter-productive...the innocent face of Baby P demanded a political response on child protection, even though such deaths have been regular events for decades...the 'signal crimes'...drive public debate, perhaps because they allow us to conduct our conversations in black and white - callous villains, incompetent officials and blameless victims.

Government has responded with blanket checks on anyone who has regular contact with children, regardless of circumstance, implying that everyone could be a threat until proven otherwise, reinforcing fear and mistrust.

Children's play is regulated and supervised like never before; spontaneity, inventiveness and the ability for self-organisation have suffered. In the 1930s, for five

Todmorden Choral Society and Orchestra, Director Anthony Brannick, performing *Elijah* at
the Town Hall, April 2009

shillings membership, a boy could practise all summer on the cricket field in the 'rag
net', often with twenty or more others. There was no supervision but the rule when
batting was 'ten minutes or three times out'. Today a cricket net session cannot be held
without a Level 2 coach in charge. Bob Smith has had to modify his Karate teaching
as child protection regulations now prevent the pairing of an adult (over 18) with a
junior for teaching purposes. Nor can an instructor use contact to guide a junior into
the correct position. As coaches and instructors in other sports would agree, the
regulations have gone too far. The fear that blame will be attributed for genuine
accidents, in a growing culture of litigation and insurance claims, is a further powerful
incentive to comply, no matter how irksome, expensive or impractical the regulatory
requirements.

Qualified supervision applies to all junior activities in any society or club, and whilst
fewer skills are developed through informal play, the quality of formal coaching has
vastly improved. Children are welcomed as organisations seek to develop their youth
sections and ensure their futures. Gone are the Victorian notices on the cricket field
'Children under 16 not admitted'.

The burgeoning of societies and clubs for all ages has, in part, filled the void left by
the decline of the churches and chapels, which at one time provided most organised

Recent match at Bridgeholme.

leisure activities - and the attendant security and comfort of belonging to groups of like-minded people.

The population of Todmorden has decreased by about 42% since 1900. It is no longer an industrial cotton town but retains its beautiful hillsides and distinctive identity, and has attracted people of talent bringing with them new energy and ideas.

How would Todmorden Cricket Club's Victorian figureheads, the Jonas Cleggs, Edward Crabtree and John Craven feel about the current scene: dismay at the demise of cotton, church, co-op and children's spontaneous outdoor play; astonishment at the wide variety of organised leisure activities for all ages; and, overwhelmingly, delight that through the myriad of changes, the threads of music, football and cricket remain continuous, woven into the social fabric of Todmorden.

Centre Vale amidst the hills.

Todmorden High School Year 9 in 2009
Leisure-Time Pursuits : Allocation of Time

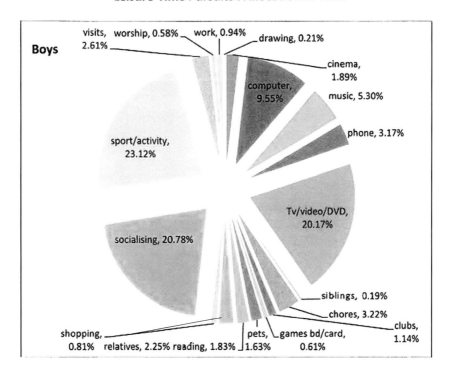

Boys

visits, 2.61% — worship, 0.58% — work, 0.94% — drawing, 0.21%
cinema, 1.89%
computer, 9.55%
music, 5.30%
phone, 3.17%
sport/activity, 23.12%
Tv/video/DVD, 20.17%
socialising, 20.78%
siblings, 0.19%
chores, 3.22%
clubs, 1.14%
shopping, 0.81%   relatives, 2.25%   reading, 1.83%   pets, 1.63%   games bd/card, 0.61%

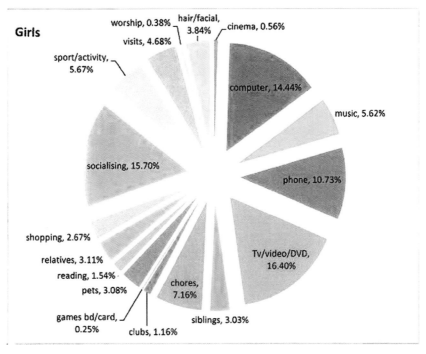

Girls

worship, 0.38% — hair/facial, 3.84% — cinema, 0.56%
visits, 4.68%
sport/activity, 5.67%
computer, 14.44%
music, 5.62%
socialising, 15.70%
phone, 10.73%
shopping, 2.67%
relatives, 3.11%
reading, 1.54%
pets, 3.08%
Tv/video/DVD, 16.40%
chores, 7.16%
games bd/card, 0.25%
clubs, 1.16%
siblings, 3.03%

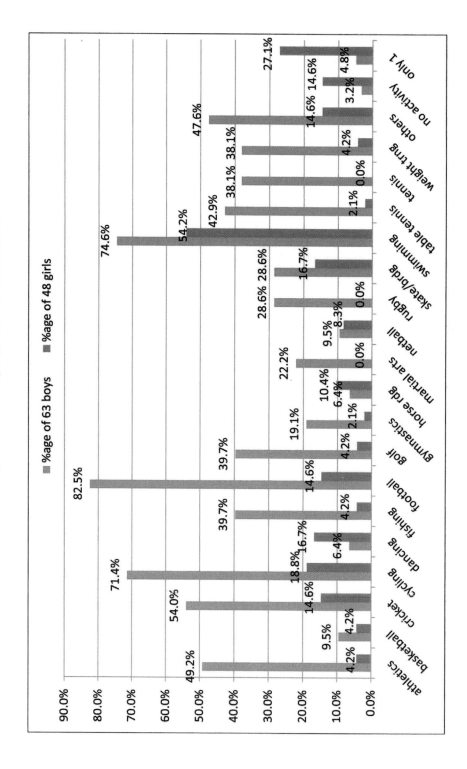

Todmorden High School: Year 9 Sport/ Activities in Leisuretime

■ %age of 63 boys ■ %age of 48 girls

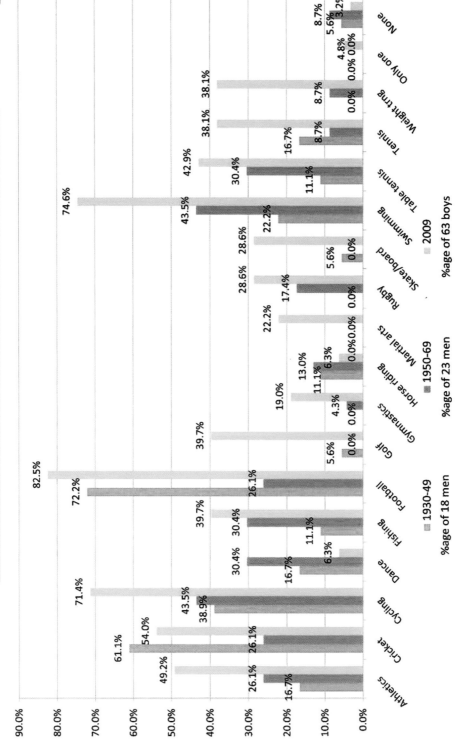

Sport/Activity Participation by 14 year-old Boys in 1930-49, 1950-69 and 2009

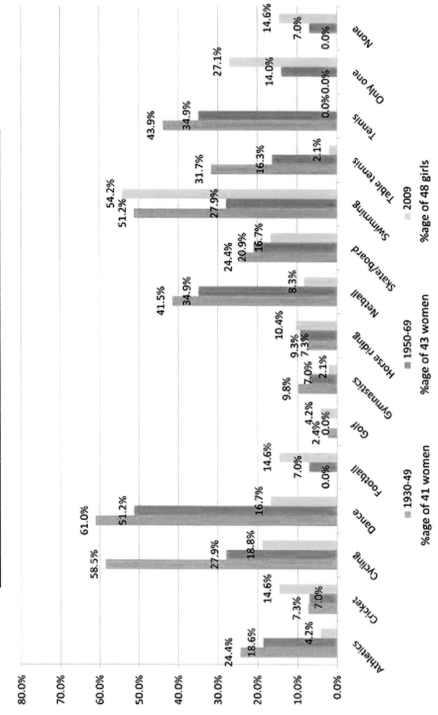

Sport/Activity Participation by 14 year-old Girls in 1930-49, 1950-69 and 2009

Todmorden Cricket Club

Statistical History

1. Club Honours

First XI: **Central Lancashire League (1892-1896)**
Champions: 1896
Runners-up: 1893, 1894, 1895

Lancashire League (1897-2010)
Champions: 1927; 1933; 1938; 1954; 1957
Runners-up: 1914; 1926; 1929; 1971; 1985; 1986

Lancashire League Knockout Cup (1920-2010)
Winners: 1935; 1937; 1938; 1954; 1962; 1963; 1982; 2000
Runners-up: 1925; 1926; 1931; 1955; 1961; 1966; 1985; 1986;
             1994; 2005; 2008; 2009

Colne Trophy (1996-2010)
Winners: 2009
Runners-up: 2001

Second XI: **Central Lancashire Junior League (1892-1896)**
Champions: 1894; 1895; 1896

Lancashire Junior League (1897-2010)
Champions: 1897; 1899; 1902; 1908; 1920
Runners-up: 1973; 1980; 1987; 2009

Lancashire Junior League Knockout Cup (1972-2010)
Winners: 1980
Runners-up: 1988; 2005; 2006

2. Average Runs per Wicket Decade-by-Decade
(Lancashire League Matches 1897-2009)

Decade	Todmorden	Opponents	All Innings
1897-99	13.67	14.94	**14.30**
1900-09	14.82	14.91	**14.87**
1910-16,19	14.42	13.55	**13.99**
1920-29	13.63	11.92	**12.75**
1930-39	17.75	14.42	**15.90**
1940-49	15.20	14.58	**14.89**
1950-59	21.15	16.77	**18.83**
1960-69	16.68	15.89	**16.29**
1970-79	17.01	18.29	**17.64**
1980-89	20.96	20.79	**20.87**
1990-99	21.84	21.27	**21.56**
2000-09	22.13	22.16	**22.15**

3. Playing Record Club-by-Club:
Lancashire League Matches 1897-2010

Club	Home						Away						All Matches					
	P	W	L	D	T	NR	P	W	L	D	T	NR	P	W	L	D	T	NR
Accrington	111	42	33	15	0	21	111	44	39	18	0	10	222	86	72	33	0	31
Bacup	112	44	29	29	0	10	112	38	42	17	0	15	224	82	71	46	0	25
Burnley	112	38	35	27	1	11	112	35	43	22	1	11	224	73	78	49	2	22
Church	111	41	40	10	1	19	112	40	43	17	0	12	223	81	83	27	1	31
Colne	111	46	33	23	0	9	111	43	33	23	1	11	222	89	66	46	1	20
East Lancashire	112	38	43	15	1	15	110	21	48	23	1	17	222	59	91	38	2	32
Enfield	108	37	29	24	0	18	110	45	44	12	1	10	220	82	73	36	1	28
Haslingden	111	32	29	19	3	28	112	37	39	17	2	17	223	69	68	36	5	45
Lowerhouse	111	45	23	26	0	17	112	47	36	17	0	12	223	92	59	43	1	29
Nelson	113	32	49	15	1	16	113	28	42	31	0	12	226	60	91	46	1	28
Ramsbottom	109	43	28	22	0	16	113	38	33	21	0	21	222	81	61	43	0	37
Rawtenstall	111	41	27	27	1	15	110	39	38	15	0	18	221	80	65	42	1	33
Rishton	112	47	25	25	1	14	111	43	36	19	0	13	223	90	61	44	1	27
Totals	**1444**	**526**	**423**	**277**	**9**	**209**	**1451**	**498**	**516**	**252**	**6**	**179**	**2895**	**1024**	**939**	**529**	**15**	**388**

N.B. Table includes 74 seasons of time cricket and 38 seasons of limited overs cricket.
Rain-affected time matches in which the second innings did not commence are counted as 'No Results'.
Uneven numbers in home and away matches are explained by additional play-off matches - all those on neutral grounds recorded as 'away' - and by seasons 1941-45 when 22 matches were played instead of the usual 26.

Lancashire League Knockout Cup Matches 1920-2010

Club	Home						Away						All Matches					
	P	W	L	D	T	NR	P	W	L	D	T	NR	P	W	L	D	T	NR
Accrington	4	2	2	0	0	0	5	3	2	0	0	0	9	5	4	0	0	0
Bacup	11	7	4	0	0	0	7	4	3	0	0	0	18	11	7	0	0	0
Burnley	10	5	5	0	0	0	12	4	8	0	0	0	22	9	13	0	0	0
Church	5	5	0	0	0	0	4	1	3	0	0	0	9	6	3	0	0	0
Colne	8	6	2	0	0	0	4	3	1	0	0	0	12	9	3	0	0	0
East Lancashire	13	6	7	0	0	0	13	4	9	0	0	0	26	10	16	0	0	0
Enfield	5	3	2	0	0	0	2	1	1	0	0	0	7	4	3	0	0	0
Haslingden	8	4	4	0	0	0	6	2	4	0	0	0	14	6	8	0	0	0
Lowerhouse	5	3	1	0	1	0	5	4	1	0	0	0	10	7	2	0	1	0
Nelson	9	8	1	0	0	0	10	5	4	0	0	1	19	13	5	0	0	1
Ramsbottom	5	4	1	0	0	0	4	1	3	0	0	0	9	5	4	0	0	0
Rawtenstall	3	2	1	0	0	0	2	1	1	0	0	0	7	3	4	0	0	0
Rishton	8	5	3	0	0	0	2	2	0	0	0	0	10	7	3	0	0	0
Totals	**94**	**60**	**33**	**0**	**1**	**0**	**78**	**35**	**42**	**0**	**0**	**1**	**172**	**95**	**75**	**0**	**1**	**1**

N.B. The 6 first round matches from 1920 to 1925 doubled as a league fixture and are included in the 'League' but not the 'Knockout Cup' table above. Todmorden won 5 and lost 1 of these matches.

4. Career Records

Competitive Matches 1897-2010
(Lancashire League, Lancashire League Knockout Cup,
Lancashire and Central Lancashire Inter-League Challenge Cup
and Colne Trophy Matches)

Player	Career Span	Batting		Bowling		Fielding		
						Fds	Wktkprs	
		Runs	Ave	Wk	Ave	Ct	Ct	St
H Abbass	1997-2005	89	8.90	3	78.33	3	-	-
Nisar Abbass (s-p)	2009	12	12.00	2	26.50	0	-	-
Hasan Adnan (s-p)	2003	150	150.00	2	13.50	1	-	-
Shabbir Ahmed (s-p)	2006	12	12.00	1	41.00	0	-	-
W Akroyd	1901-09	316	12.64	4	24.00	14	-	-
Graham W Aldridge (s-p)	2007	3	3.00	5	15.80	0	-	-
I Ali	1985-2010	604	7.84	564	19.62	102	-	-
Hartley Alleyne (s-p)	1989	29	7.25	20	13.65	2	-	-
Paul JW Allott (p)	1993	340	17.00	58	16.33	11	-	-
Tushar Arothe (s-p)	2002	432	86.40	19	15.00	1	-	-
Bilal Asad (s-p)	2006-09	97	19.40	14	12.43	2	-	-
Naved Ashraf (s-p)	2006	6	6.00	1	19.00	1	-	-
B Ashworth	1929-45	1935	13.63	-	-	24	-	-
R Ashworth	1999	0	0.00	-	-	0	-	-
W Ashworth	1919	34	5.67	5	23.60	0	-	-
E Astin	1943-44	23	5.60	-	-	3	-	-
J Astin	1943	34	5.67	-	-	1	-	-
Graham Atkinson (s-p)	1969	24	24.00	1	2.00	0	-	-
John Atkinson (p)	1902	246	12.30	61	13.79	13	-	-
Parvez Aziz (s-p)	2009	11	11.00	8	5.40	0	-	-
R Baigent	1997-2004	4410	33.16	2	35.00	45	-	-
S Bailey	1987-93	2733	22.04	13	27.69	50	-	-
Aftab Baloch (p)	1979-80	1834	39.87	84	17.90	21	-	-
A Barker	1989-2000	1613	13.91	0	-	42	-	-
C Barker	1999-2000	21	10.50	12	21.75	1	-	-
J Barker	1988-2000	988	10.08	146	24.64	50	-	-
M Barker	2004	-	-	1	21.00	0	-	-
N Barker	2009-10	1050	29.17	27	20.74	14	-	-
S Barker	1989-2004	329	10.61	-	-	12	-	-
SP Barker	2009-10	351	19.50	69	21.12	11	-	-
W Barker	1941-42	7	3.50	-	-	2	-	-
A Barnes	1916	0	0.00	0	-	0	-	-
JW Barnes	1943	6	2.00	-	-	-	0	1
N Barratt	1919-20	131	7.71	7	21.14	3	-	-
Des Barrick (p)	1962-63	1383	46.10	91	19.21	13	-	-
CW 'Bob' Bartells (s-p)	1962-65	2	1.00	10	7.80	1	-	-
EL Bentley	1916-19	-	-	-	-	2	-	-
WA Bentley	1942-44	13	3.25	-	-	0	-	-
Andy Bichel (s-p)	1994	0	0.00	1	60.00	0	-	-
Ian Bishop (s-p)	1989	32	16.00	5	24.80	2	-	-
FA Blakey	1897-1900	900	12.16	110	14.92	24	-	-
D Blanche	1998	3	1.50	-	-	2	-	-
Gulam Bodi (p)	2008	913	53.71	43	16.86	14	-	-
Frank Booth (s-p)	1927	33	-	2	12.00	0	-	-
D Bowyer	2004	-	-	-	-	1	-	-
J Brierley	1976-99	3957	16.56	-	-	85	18	1
M Brierley	1999-2010	1623	12.88	1	60.00	48	-	-
P Brierley	1999-2006	499	10.62	1	4.00	5	63	24
E Brook	1940-53	768	10.11	2	6.50	20	-	-
A Brown	1932	15	3.75	-	-	1	-	-
A Brown	1958	9	4.50	3	14.67	2	-	-

Player	Career Span	Batting		Bowling		Fielding		
						Fds	Wktkprs	
		Runs	Ave	Wk	Ave	Ct	Ct	St
D Brown	2003-10	512	8.83	-	-	-	135	28
P Brownbridge	1951-76	4248	15.62	1	31.00	89	-	-
R Brownbridge	1990-99	45	11.25	-	-	7	26	16
Jim Burke (p)	1954	817	45.39	118	7.29	7	-	-
E Burkes	1957	-	-	-	-	0	-	-
M Burns	2003	36	5.14	-	-	-	8	14
D Burton	1956	2	0.50	3	26.33	1	-	-
JRD Butterworth	1969-70	16	1.60	55	17.75	2	-	-
M Bux	2005-09	782	11.33	176	21.80	16	-	-
J Campbell	2003-2009	241	16.07	49	32.08	12	-	-
T Carrick	1924-52	414	3.91	-	-	-	336	97
Lee Carseldine (s-p)	2002	36	36.00	1	56.00	0	-	-
Jerry Cassell (p)	2002	21	21.00	-	-	1	-	-
R Cherry	1935	3	3.00	-	-	0	-	-
EW 'Nobby' Clark (p)	1931-32	103	6.87	176	8.34	11	-	-
N Clark	1945-49	36	3.60	12	16.50	6	-	-
P Clark	1955	13	3.25	-	-	-	12	4
JE Clayton	1953-85	3747	14.75	197	20.08	91	-	-
M Clayton	1983-2008	2858	14.01	82	32.90	44	-	-
J Clegg jnr	1897-1903	1095	15.21	-	-	20	-	-
D Brian Close (p)	1978	657	29.86	37	22.03	4	-	-
Werner L Coetsee (s-p)	2007	57	57.00	4	8.25	0	-	-
J Collinge	1932-34	43	8.60	-	-	1	-	-
A Connor	1957-63	1760	17.78	-	-	-	122	30
JT Connor	1939-44	245	10.21	-	-	4	22	2
H Cockroft	1948-53	8	2.00	0	-	0	-	-
J Coupe	1940-41	20	7.67	2	23.00	0	-	-
J Crabtree	1952-53	14	7.00	0	-	0	-	-
JA Crabtree	1919	0	0.00	2	18.00	0	-	-
JW Crabtree	1897-1910	3433	18.76	45	20.84	83	-	-
R Crabtree	1944-59	1413	17.44	93	24.24	17	-	-
Ernest Creighton (p)	1900-01	591	14.07	204	12.86	28	-	-
Frans C Cronje (p)	1997	1183	49.29	67	16.03	11	-	-
DG Crossley	1942	2	2.00	-	-	0	-	-
E Crossley	1923	1	1.00	-	-	0	-	-
F Crossley	1907	55	11.00	-	-	1	-	-
J Crossley	1898-1902	1517	18.50	3	18.00	25	-	-
J Crossley	2006-10	88	8.00	-	-	1	-	-
JW Crossley	1900-04	190	10.00	7	29.00	15	-	-
A Crowther	1943	10	3.33	-	-	0	-	-
J Crowther	1931-59	10028	24.70	386	16.34	195	-	-
Brian Crump (p)	1975	611	38.19	41	19.56	6	-	-
JA 'Jack' Cuffe (p)	1919	462	19.25	83	13.61	7	-	-
A Cunliffe	1938-53	2102	16.82	34	22.44	37		-
Aaron Daly (s-p)	1989	21	21.00	4	5.25	1	-	-
Neil Dansie (p)	1955-56	1891	47.28	131	15.60	22	-	-
Kevin Darlington (s-p)	1995	-	-	5	12.00	1	-	-
A Davies	1966-68	58	6.44	-	-	7	-	-
B Davies	1953-64	183	6.10	147	18.02	9	-	-
Harold Dawson	1932-64	12329	28.67	12	21.00	204	-	-
Hiram Dawson	1926-45	302	7.55	-	-	13	-	-
WR Day	1961	-	-	0	-	1	-	-
S Dean	1947-54	125	7.81	-	-	2	-	-
C Dearden	2001	559	19.96	26	23.54	4	-	-
Eric D Denison (p)	1949-53	4134	42.62	367	12.28	57	-	-
Fanie S de Villiers (p)	1987	290	16.11	67	15.33	7	-	-
J Dewhirst	1925-29	219	9.13	-	-	14	-	-

Player	Career Span	Batting		Bowling		Fielding		
						Fds	Wktkprs	
		Runs	Ave	Wk	Ave	Ct	Ct	St
E Dobby	1953	17	-	-	-	-	-	-
G Dobby	1972-73	128	10.67	-	-	5	-	-
Vasbert C Drakes (p)	1998	753	37.65	63	15.33	8	-	-
T Driver	1967	2	1.00	-	-	0	-	-
Francois du Plessis (p)	2007	429	33.00	38	14.47	6	-	-
G Duffield	1984-92	634	13.49	2	23.50	13	-	-
H Duffield	1940-41	21	2.63	1	67.00	4	-	-
S Dunkley	1975-79	8	1.60	-	-	-	4	4
F Eastwood	1904-09	155	8.16	66	18.53	20	-	-
H Eastwood	1939-47	35	3.89	-	-	0	-	-
P Eastwood	1951-60	0	0.00	-	-	-	-	-
R Eastwood	1987-94	975	22.67	0	-	9	-	-
R Eccles	1916	107	6.29	-	-	5	-	-
Rod O Estwick (p), (s-p)	1982-86	1634	24.39	260	17.12	31	-	-
C Eynott	1944	1	0.50	1	23.00	1	-	-
T Farry	1984-92	413	10.07	128	23.36	24	-	-
EFM Upul Fernando (s-p)	2009	11	11.00	2	11.50	0	-	-
A Fiddling	1962-90	2943	12.80	26	17.12	108	-	-
D Fiddling	1930	0	0.00	-	-	1	-	-
K Fiddling	1935-60	535	14.46	-	-	0	62	23
B Fielden	1949-56	562	13.07	4	28.25	6	-	-
J Fielden	1944-45	2	1.00	-	-	1	-	-
J Fielden	1900-04	258	10.75	-	-	3	-	-
JE Fielden	1898-1903	39	3.90	4	19.75	2	0	3
K Fielden	1965-75	887	12.15	-	-	21	-	-
R Fielden	1934-35	10	3.33	2	36.50	1	-	-
E Firth	1945-47	17	2.83	-	-	-	11	4
F Foster (p)	1908	166	9.76	76	15.45	10	-	-
G Foster	1995-97	66	6.60	40	29.90	14	-	-
S Frewin	2003	1	0.50	-	-	1	-	-
Aaron Gale (p)	1995	391	19.55	55	19.05	11	-	-
Jason Gallian (s-p)	1993	28	28.00	1	23.00	0	-	-
J Garland	1989	44	11.00	-	-	1	-	-
T Gibson	1944-48	44	4.00	3	53.00	1	-	-
Roy Gilchrist (s-p)	1965	1	1.00	3	10.67	0	-	-
George C Gill (p)	1911-12	685	16.31	147	13.47	17	-	-
A Girling	1898	6	3.00	0	-	0	-	-
A Glasse	1915-19	50	3.85	0	-	3	-	-
A Gledhill	1973-81	228	9.50	-	-	11	-	-
P Gledhill	2004-08	1	1.00	-	-	1	-	-
P Godsman	1987	-	-	2	24.00	1	-	-
A Grannon	1969-70	263	11.43	0	-	2	-	-
D Grannon	1945-49	120	8.00	-	-	2	-	-
R Grannon	1944	20	4.00	-	-	1	-	-
M Gray	1960-61	89	12.71	-	-	1	-	-
Sherlon Greaves (p)	1988	882	42.00	47	23.79	10	-	-
Tommy Greenhough (s-p)	1965	6	3.00	4	16.75	0	-	-
A Greenwood	1941	6	3.00	-	-	0	-	-
A Greenwood	1974-84	469	9.57	-	-	22	-	-
FL Greenwood	1945	0	0.00	-	-	0	-	-
H Greenwood	1919	0	0.00	0	-	1	-	-
J Greenwood	1897-1906	318	8.37	0	-	10	-	-
J Greenwood	1927-29	357	13.22	46	12.35	18	-	-
M Greenwood	1995	73	14.60	-	-	0	-	-
P Greenwood	1940-45	810	18.41	110	13.08	26	-	-
S Greenwood	1916	-	-	4	9.00	0	-	-

Player	Career Span	Batting		Bowling		Fielding		
						Fds	Wktkprs	
		Runs	Ave	Wk	Ave	Ct	Ct	St
Walter Greenwood	1900-21	3062	14.38	29	21.45	40	-	-
Walter Leslie Greenwood	1897-1923	1988	7.56	683	14.39	166	-	-
Wilfred Greenwood	1904-16	1829	16.19	-	-	29	-	-
E Gregson	1909-11	72	7.20	26	13.04	4	-	-
William Gregson (s-p)	1907	0	0.00	4	12.50	0	-	-
Oliver J Griffin (p)	1898	388	20.42	49	15.76	9	-	-
E Grindrod	1934	30	10.00	-	-	0	-	-
B Grundy	1961-62	19	9.50	10	29.00	4	-	-
Harold Haigh (p)	1930	534	26.70	40	16.38	8	-	-
Herbert Haigh (am, p)	1930-45	60	6.67	40	18.13	3	-	-
I Hague	2009	3	3.00	-	-	0	-	-
Alfred E Hall (s-p)	1924	4	4.00	5	7.40	0	-	-
Edwin Hall (p)	1897	463	23.15	48	16.48	16	-	-
Walter Hall (p)	1906-07	374	12.47	178	8.78	20	-	-
E Halliwell	1897	125	6.94	-	-	11	-	-
N Halstead	1975-78	6	3.00	3	80.00	1	-	-
W Halstead	1929-30	666	23.79	-	-	8	-	-
Edward Hargreaves	1905-24	2413	11.49	19	17.95	37	16	13
Ernest Hargreaves	1925-44	5666	25.41	12	17.83	60	-	-
Alistair Harrison	2003-10	877	13.92	-	-	40	-	-
Andrew Harrison	1984-85	38	6.33	-	-	0	-	-
AE Hartley	1903	0	0.00	-	-	0	-	-
J Hartley	1897	6	6.00	-	-	0	-	-
M Hartley	1972-92	3988	13.99	608	21.54	133	-	-
W Hartley	1912-25	1123	10.59	4	9.75	21	-	-
A Harvey	1981-86	35	3.89	-	-	2	-	-
Jonathan Harvey (s-p)	1998	55	27.50	9	12.00	1	-	-
D Hatton	1992-2007	509	10.60	11	36.64	19	-	-
J Hazeltine	1951-59	144	7.20	-	-	-	40	13
G Heard	1924-25	29	3.22	3	8.67	5	-	-
C Helliwell	1911-28	2398	12.05	18	22.39	78	-	-
F Helliwell	1897-1901	748	10.25	-	-	24	-	-
G Helliwell	1948-51	123	4.73	57	20.54	15	-	-
M Helliwell	1961-62	18	9.00	-	-	1	-	-
J Henderson	2005-09	1921	20.01	109	22.67	53	-	-
K Henfrey	1944	30	5.00	-	-	0	-	-
S Heyhirst	1923-27	1578	19.01	23	13.35	11	-	-
B Heywood	1976-2005	9451	26.04	49	21.59	180	-	-
M Heywood	1953-72	4391	16.14	11	17.45	96	-	-
R Heywood	1911-12	9	2.25	0	-	0	-	-
A Highley	2003-07	4	4.00	-	-	1	-	-
I Highley	1983-88	6	2.00	-	-	1	-	-
J Highley	1973-92	107	10.70	17	30.12	13	35	2
W Hill	1928-29	89	8.90	-	-	3	-	-
Colin Hilton (s-p)	1963	0	0.00	4	11.25	0	-	-
H Hinchcliffe	1958	11	11.00	-	-	0	-	-
JW 'Bill' Hitch (p)	1926-29	1183	14.79	305	11.45	40	-	-
C Hitchen	1925-26	54	13.50	-	-	1	-	-
Brad J Hodge (s-p)	1996	36	36.00	0	-	0	-	-
A Hodgson	1943	12	6.00	8	8.75	1	-	-
F Holden	1916	10	5.00	-	-	2	-	-
U Holland	1904-10	19	6.33	-	-	0	-	-
JF Hollinrake	1901-03	592	16.00	0	-	10	-	-
P Hollinrake	1897-1901	231	7.97	158	13.81	24	-	-
W Hollinrake	1910	7	7.00	-	-	0	-	-
K Hollows	1962-74	243	7.59	43	15.28	23	-	-
S Hollows	1951-68	672	9.33	138	28.71	29	-	-
G Holt	1958-65	356	10.79	-	-	3	-	-

Player	Career Span	Batting		Bowling		Fielding		
						Fds	Wktkprs	
		Runs	Ave	Wk	Ave	Ct	Ct	St
J Holt	1940-44	162	4.66	208	10.88	23	-	-
W Horne	1919	18	4.50	-	-	3	-	-
Johnny Horsfall (am, p)	1897-1900	962	13.94	1	46.00	15	-	-
R Horsfall	1936-57	1345	15.46	0	-	19	-	-
D Houghton	1952-59	117	4.33	50	23.00	21	-	-
R Howard	1973-75	20	2.50	41	18.73	21	-	-
N Howarth	1942	3	3.00	-	-	1	-	-
P Howley	2010	13	4.33	-	-	2	-	-
William Huddleston (p)	1903-05	1499	24.57	249	11.88	54	-	-
H Hudson	1905-26	3129	12.57	-	-		173	99
S Hudson	1897-1905	301	4.93	-	-	-	65	43
N Hunter	2000-02	1216	18.71	36	25.67	23	-	-
I Hussain	2003-10	63	12.60	12	31.58	3	-	-
M Hussain	2004	-	-	0	-	1	-	-
M Ingham	1904	0	0.00	-	-	1	-	-
J Ingham	1942-55	915	18.63	163	17.48	26	-	-
N Jackson	1942	84	8.40	-	-	4	-	-
R Jackson	2001	53	4.82	20	28.20	5	-	-
Asfandyar Jafri (s-p)	2006	20	20.00	0	-	0	-	-
J Jameson	1944	1	1.00	-	-	0	-	-
Chinthaka Jayasinghe (p)	2009	569	35.56	52	14.62	12	-	-
M Jowett	1956-78	3289	14.00	0	-	65	-	-
J Kay	1947-48	24	3.00	7	31.29	2	-	-
H Kennedy	1991-2000	734	11.29	3	40.00	13	-	-
Alex Kermode (s-p)	1904	11	11.00	2	28.50	0	-	-
J Kershaw	1926-29	1331	19.29	1	35.00	1	-	-
R Kershaw	1919	0	0.00	-	-	1	-	-
J Kettley	1971	-	-	-	-	-	-	-
Ameer Khan (s-p)	2009	67	33.50	2	30.00	1	-	-
Jannisar Khan (s-p)	2007-09	1	1.00	3	10.33	2	-	-
Mohsin Khan (p, s-p)	1976-89	2644	42.65	112	22.08	43	-	-
E Kilner	1940	3	3.00	-	-	1	-	-
J Kimber	1990	14	-	2	55.00	1	-	-
J Knowles	1897	1	1.00	-	-	0	-	-
Keith Knox (s-p)	1965	-	-	1	26.00	0	-	-
Jack F Knutton (s-p)	1907	5	5.00	9	1.22	2	-	-
W Law	1899-1920	4373	13.93	103	19.61	75	-	-
R Laycock	2001	0	0.00	0	-	0	-	-
D Leach	2002	20	4.00	5	18.40	0	-	-
C Lee	1913-14	119	9.92	-	-	5	-	-
C Lever	1956-61	893	15.14	13	28.08	15	-	-
P Lever	1955-59	314	11.63	30	22.53	9	1	0
R Lever	1956-68	237	6.97	-	-	10	-	-
K Link	1960-81	260	6.50	42	18.45	22	-	-
Graham Lloyd (s-p)	1993	39	39.00	1	18.00	1	-	-
EW Lord	1904-19	105	7.50	6	14.67	6	-	-
GR Lord	1919-25	754	9.54	-	-	24	-	-
J Lord	1899-1924	91	5.69	9	27.67	6	-	-
J Lord	1953	21	7.00	-	-	-	1	2
J Lord	1967-69	50	3.85	-	-	7	-	-
P Lord	1923-33	121	10.08	27	9.52	10	-	-
A Lowe	1963-68	434	11.73	79	12.39	17	-	-
George C Macauley (p)	1938-39	192	7.11	155	11.94	9	-	-
Terry MD MacGill (p)	1970	511	26.89	51	19.39	10	-	-

Player	Career Span	Batting		Bowling		Fielding		
						Fds	Wktkprs	
		Runs	Ave	Wk	Ave	Ct	Ct	St
T Mahmood	1983	1	0.50	-	-	3	-	-
Y Mahmood	1996-2003	54	9.00	5	29.60	0	-	-
Rushdie Majiet (p)	1969	438	21.90	31	20.10	9	-	-
T Makin	1968-88	378	6.75	133	24.86	32	-	-
Shehzad Malik (s-p)	2009	29	29.00	-	-	1	-	-
M Malone	1985-88	8	1.60	31	20.77	2	-	-
Peter Marner (p)	1971-74	2696	32.45	171	15.10	46	-	-
P Marrow	2009-10	55	11.00	-	-	0	-	-
Daniel Marsh (p)	1996-2000	2126	51.85	139	17.04	23	-	-
T Marsh	2006-10	807	16.81	1	37.00	11	-	-
A Marshall	1907-28	4095	13.25	180	17.69	121	-	-
H Marshall	1911	3	1.50	3	22.33	1	-	-
R Marshall	1916	-	-	-	-	1	-	-
R Marshall	1955-70	233	7.52	153	21.21	22	-	-
T Marshall	1919-23	76	4.75	-	-	8	-	-
Bryan P Martin (s-p)	2008	47	47.00	3	23.33	0	-	-
I Martin	1936-55	633	8.22	131	22.50	24	-	-
JW Martin	1938-40	253	10.54	0	-	7	-	-
M Mashimbyi (s-p)	2010	34	34.00	1	47.00	0	-	-
A Matthews	1974-76	124	10.33	-	-	4	-	-
J May	1981-82	11	2.20	-	-	0	-	-
Brendan McArdle (s-p)	1989	191	31.83	12	21.25	5	-	-
Richard McArthy (s-p)	1989	38	19.00	5	16.60	4	-	-
Ross D McMillan (s-p)	2008	19	19.00	2	31.00	1	-	-
James W Meads (p)	1909	250	14.71	31	21.87	5	-	-
A 'Tony' Merrick (s-p)	1989	10	10.00	6	10.83	0	-	-
N Metcalf	1969-70	58	6.44	1	16.00	4	-	-
T Mills	1921	19	9.50	-	-	0	-	-
A Milnes	1935-45	841	12.01	17	15.00	22	6	5
Safdar H 'Jim' Minhas (p)	1957-58	892	25.49	143	14.42	19	-	-
A Mitchell	1979-81	13	3.25	6	19.33	0	-	-
E Mitchell	1923-37	3262	14.18	4	22.75	145	3	2
Ian Mitchell (s-p)	2003	0	0.00	0	-	0	-	-
J Mitchell	1941	1	1.00	-	-	1	-	-
JW Mitchell	1898-1900	99	5.82	-	-	-	8	9
W Mitchell	1944	4	-	-	-	-	0	2
JC Moncrieff	1948-57	1713	17.84	-	-	72	-	-
J Montague	2004	-	-	0	-	0	-	-
AP 'Tony' Moore (s-p)	1978	-	-	-	-	-	-	-
Pat F Morfee (p)	1920-21	769	15.08	224	9.13	35	-	-
Bertie F Morgan (p)	1923	368	16.73	85	10.96	11	-	-
J Morgan	1990-2010	348	6.11	313	22.23	34	-	-
P Morgan	1977-83	1383	17.07	-	-	30	-	-
AL Moss	1943-46	682	17.05	93	12.06	19	-	-
Ernest Moss (p, am)	1924-32	216	6.17	143	11.21	16	-	-
AJ Muir	1941-44	560	12.44	53	15.42	20	-	-
Asif Mujtaba (s-p)	2002-07	85	28.88	11	17.64	3	-	-
Brendan Nash (p)	1999	1342	55.92	47	21.87	14	-	-
S Newbitt	2003-10	4570	31.09	4	26.00	47	-	-
P Newell	1942-43	1	0.50	-	-	1	-	-
G Nichols	1941	85	8.50	12	14.67	4	-	-
Morris S Nichols (p)	1946	360	20.00	63	9.94	2	-	-
Matthew Nicholson (p)	2001	609	29.00	79	19.44	12	-	-
William Oakley (p, s-p)	1898-1907	370	11.21	154	10.51	16	-	-
S Oddy	2001-02	307	10.59	81	27.70	9	-	-
WH Oldroyd	1900	1	1.00	-	-	0	-	-
Sylvester Oliver (p)	1959-68	3942	27.96	504	12.38	130	-	-

Player	Career Span	Batting		Bowling		Fielding		
						Fds	Wktkprs	
		Runs	Ave	Wk	Ave	Ct	Ct	St
A Ormerod	1911-12	771	18.36	0	-	23	-	-
M Ormerod	1959-61	52	17.33	-	-	2	-	-
Steve O'Shaughn'sy (s-p)	1993	21	21.00	3	15.00	0	-	-
A Ottewill	1942	9	4.50	-	-	0	-	-
Gyanendra Pandey (p)	2003-05	3199	52.44	203	20.20	21	-	-
Derek Parker (s-p)	1978	29	29.00	6	8.83	0	-	-
Duncan Parker	1993-2002	872	13.84	41	26.12	23	-	-
S Parker	1989-2005	621	9.55	249	24.63	45	-	-
Clinton Peake (s-p)	2002	366	91.50	15	22.87	1	-	-
L Pearson	2004-10	55	6.11	36	28.67	6	-	-
J Peavoy	2008	2	1.00	-	-	0	-	-
G Ruwin P Peiris (s-p)	2002	126	63.00	4	19.00	1	-	-
Cec W Pepper (s-p)	1963	24	12.00	8	9.75	0	-	-
Clinton Perrin (s-p)	2002	24	12.00	4	37.75	1	-	-
N Pettingell	1979	12	12.00	0	-	0	-	-
Neil Phillips (s-p)	1984	39	39.00	4	21.50	0	-	-
G Pickles	1966-67	133	14.78	1	1.00	2	-	-
H Pickles	1935-36	100	9.09	-	-	4	-	-
R Pickles	1978-85	136	6.80	-	-	9	-	-
Kevin P Pietersen (s-p)	2002	7	7.00	1	54.00	1	-	-
D Pilkington	1976	2	2.00	-	-	0	-	-
Leonard Pitchford (s-p)	1922	0	0.00	5	14.60	0	-	-
C Potts	1941-49	589	11.55	8	36.75	14	-	-
Henry Preston (s-p)	1927	-	-	6	12.00	3	-	-
F Priestley	2010	2	2.00	-	-	0	-	-
R Priestley	1984-87	9	9.00	-	-	0	-	-
S Priestley	1981-2010	10880	23.15	64	22.15	133	1	1
G Proctor	1993-96	251	8.66	2	21.50	8	-	-
JC Pullan	1955	0	0.00	0	-	0	-	-
Will RJ Purser (s-p)	2010	26	26.00	4	20.00	0	-	-
W Raby	1935-46	377	7.69	203	16.10	25	-	-
I Ramsbottom	2003	-	-	-	-	0	-	-
Ravi Ratnayeke (p)	1989	153	30.60	12	16.00	2	-	-
A Ratcliffe	1913-22	335	8.82	-	-	24	-	-
John Ratcliff	1904-20	3645	20.14	8	23.38	56	-	-
Jack Ratcliffe	1898-1910	760	13.33	3	20.00	41	-	-
A Rawsthorn	1940	23	4.60	-	-	1	-	-
Akram Raza (s-p)	2002	33	33.00	0	-	0	-	-
Bernard Reidy (s-p)	1984	14	14.00	1	57.00	0	-	-
JW Richards	1901	0	0.00	-	-	0	-	-
S Roberts	1897	31	5.17	-	-	-	2	3
Fred Root (p)	1933-37	2829	23.97	533	9.79	42	-	-
J Roscoe	1939	63	15.75	-	-	1	-	-
AE Ross	1982-90	3355	23.63	0	-	57	-	-
C Ross	1999	3	1.50	-	-	3	-	-
Jacques Rudolph (s-p)	2006	14	14.00	1	50.00	2	-	-
Nisitha S Rupasingh (s-p)	2008	1	1.00	0	-	0	-	-
WCH 'Bill' Sadler (p)	1922	325	15.48	70	12.76	14	-	-
M Saleem	1995-96	305	16.05	3	30.67	5	-	-
Athula Samarasekera (s-p)	1989	21	21.00	2	28.00	0	-	-
F Saul	1938-63	4174	17.53	3	21.33	54	-	-
Chris P Schofield (s-p)	2002-06	85	28.33	1	85.00	2	-	-
A Scholefield	1996-2000	1832	19.91	163	22.16	56	-	-
Darryl Scott (p)	1985-86	2101	45.67	165	15.31	36	-	-
W Scott	1931-52	7212	19.28	1	29.00	91	-	-
G Seel	1919-26	12	1.50	39	13.69	0	-	-

Player	Career Span	Batting		Bowling		Fielding		
						Fds	Wktkprs	
		Runs	Ave	Wk	Ave	Ct	Ct	St
D Shackleton	1940-46	951	19.41	22	9.77	10	-	-
EB Shackleton	1903-24	6981	20.06	1	53.00	86	-	-
H Shackleton	1942	1	1.00	-	-	0	-	-
H Shepherd	1947-52	218	5.89	135	16.00	22	-	-
Brandon Shinnick (s-p)	2002	0	0.00	0	-	0	-	-
C Shuttleworth	1932	0	-	-	-	0	-	-
Lendl MP Simmons (s-p)	2006	196	39.20	8	25.88	2	-	-
Peter Skuse (s-p)	1995	17	17.00	3	21.00	0	-	-
Daryn Smit (s-p)	2009	17	17.00	0	-	0	-	-
A Smith	1936-50	283	5.66	311	13.57	23	-	-
H Smith	1967-68	21	5.25	0	-	1	-	-
I Smith	1965-91	8551	19.00	171	22.28	165	3	0
N Smith	1997-98	7	1.00	-	-	1	-	-
Garfield S Sobers (s-p)	1965	12	12.00	5	10.20	1	-	-
AW Spencer	1961-63	47	6.71	-	-	6	-	-
HE Stanley	1901-03	1491	26.63	11	18.00	23	-	-
E Stansfield	1908-44	1440	10.51	514	13.25	55	-	-
G Stansfield	1959-80	5165	15.33	-	-	1	307	47
JM Stansfield	1898-1907	862	10.91	4	6.00	28	-	-
W Stansfield	1899-1903	79	3.43	80	13.24	4	-	-
Richard Steeples (p)	1910	57	3.56	48	15.71	5	-	-
A Stephenson	1908-34	5257	14.13	-	-	93	-	-
J Stocks	1952	10	2.50	-	-	1	-	-
F Storah	1929-36	115	7.67	34	18.32	11	-	-
W Storah	1905-26	64	6.16	586	12.21	39	-	-
F Stott	1937-48	532	18.34	3	44.33	4	-	-
W Stott	1902	5	5.00	-	-	0	-	-
Chris BP Street (s-p)	2006	-	-	-	-	-	-	-
Pieter C Strydom (s-p)	1998	-	-	-	-	-	-	-
John Sullivan (s-p)	1972	24	24.00	7	2.75	0	-	-
J Summerscales	2002	407	19.38	6	55.00	10	-	-
L Summerscales	1943	34	5.67	-	-	-	4	1
C Sunderland	1953-58	39	2.29	129	14.92	10	-	-
JW Sunderland	1919-30	951	9.61	380	10.36	48	-	-
A Sutcliffe	1903-05	130	6.84	-	-	6	0	1
A Sutcliffe	1939-52	126	6.63	-	-	1	-	-
A Sutcliffe	2001-10	1560	12.68	54	33.61	79	-	-
B Sutcliffe	2001-10	2420	16.29	1	5.00	43	9	4
D Sutcliffe	1987	-	-	-	-	1	-	-
DA Sutcliffe	1940-41	40	10.00	-	-	0	-	-
DT Sutcliffe	1899	0	-	-	-	-	0	1
E Sutcliffe	1942-47	31	5.17	-	-	-	2	3
G Sutcliffe	1907-10	19	2.38	-	-	2	-	-
J Sutcliffe	1940-42	17	5.67	6	16.00	1	-	-
JE Sutcliffe	1900-10	194	10.78	1	15.00	4	-	-
JW Sutcliffe	1919	3	3.00	-	-	0	-	-
LA Sutcliffe	1932-43	50	6.25	3	33.00	4	-	-
PW Sutcliffe	1941	6	3.00	-	-	0	-	-
R Sutcliffe	1916-34	2967	11.50	-	-	63	-	-
TG Sutcliffe	1921-29	116	4.00	32	17.75	2	-	-
V Sutcliffe	1934	4	4.00	2	18.50	0	-	-
W Sutcliffe	1897-1908	521	6.95	81	21.59	40	-	-
W Sutcliffe	1931-46	3173	14.76	169	20.76	67	-	-
JM Sykes	1950-52	44	6.29	-	-	3	-	-
T Sykes	1944-47	146	7.68	0	-	6	-	-
Imran Tahir (s-p)	2006	3	3.00	6	8.33	1	-	-
S Tamblin	1944	3	3.00	0	-	2	-	-
D Taylor	1960-62	44	5.50	0	-	3	-	-

Player	Career Span	Batting		Bowling		Fielding		
						Fds	Wktkprs	
		Runs	Ave	Wk	Ave	Ct	Ct	St
F Taylor	1897-1913	263	13.15	1	44.00	7	-	-
L Taylor	1944	0	0.00	-	-	1	-	-
P Thackray	1963-75	1637	11.37	6	31.00	76	13	3
AC Thomas	2007	-	-	-	-	0	-	-
J Thomas	1930	-	-	3	19.33	0	-	-
T Thomas (p)	1899	247	13.72	49	13.80	5	-	-
J Threlfall	1944-46	1082	40.07	52	15.63	12	-	-
J Townend	1965-86	1103	9.51	499	17.76	54	-	-
E Travis	1953	38	5.43	-	-	0	-	-
G Travis	1914-20	800	11.59	27	14.81	28	-	-
Frank Tyson (p)	1961	602	26.17	98	10.86	11	-	-
RD Uttley	1958	29	-	-	-	0	-	-
W Uttley	1931-34	21	2.63	12	20.42	3	-	-
D Wadcock	1993-2000	132	6.60	-	-	9	-	-
H Wadsworth	1936-40	15	3.00	-	-	0	-	-
J Wadsworth	1983-93	300	11.54	-	-	10	-	-
H Walker	1935-36	41	4.56	15	20.60	4	-	-
K Walker	1952-57	1325	17.67	1	103.0	16	-	-
A Walton	1944	1	0.50	-	-	0	-	-
Darren Walters	1995-2004	102	5.67	-	-	10	1	5
David Walters	1980-89	154	10.27	34	30.62	5	-	-
David Ward (s-p)	1989	19	19.00	-	-	0	-	-
G Warren	1950-64	116	4.64	132	14.77	28	-	-
J Webb	2006	156	13.00	9	35.56	2	-	-
Sajeewa Weerakoon (s-p)	2009	10	10.00	7	6.29	0	-	-
G Weir	2001-03	447	18.63	1	119.0	5	-	-
Amila Weth'asinghe (s-p)	2006	18	-	3	18.00	0	-	-
R Whitaker	1965-80	171	5.18	264	15.57	34	-	-
D Whitehead	1980-2009	6365	19.00	2	28.00	16	546	128
J Whitehead	2010	22	7.33	-	-	-	9	1
RS Whitham	1929-47	941	11.07	262	16.81	29	-	-
B Whittaker	1958-83	3262	11.82	628	18.97	148	-	-
N Whittaker	1944-48	13	3.25	5	9.40	0	-	-
D Widdup	1969	5	1.67	3	13.33	2	-	-
David Wiese (p)	2010	1051	52.55	66	16.32	9	-	-
AC Wilcock	1944	0	0.00	-	-	0	-	-
HD Wilcock	1942	0	0.00	-	-	0	-	-
J Wilkins	1978	15	7.50	0	-	7	-	-
E Wilkinson	1937-38	3	3.00	0	-	0	-	-
H Wilkinson	1947-58	772	13.54	5	43.60	32	-	-
K Wilkinson	1953-71	6559	22.62	6	72.00	163	-	-
William Wilkinson (p)	1897	195	15.00	55	17.42	9	-	-
Ambrose C Williams (p)	1915	281	15.61	82	12.61	6	-	-
Brett Williams (p)	1990	695	28.96	38	28.63	10	-	-
Scott Williams (p)	1994	812	31.23	85	18.89	10	-	-
George Wilson (p)	1913-14	713	16.58	201	10.84	18	-	-
H Wood	1912-16	374	9.12	-	-	17	-	-
O Wood	2003-10	150	10.71	47	31.98	22	-	-
Frank Woodhead (p)	1947	164	8.63	77	12.25	15	-	-
Duncan Worsley (s-p)	1965	20	20.00	3	12.00	0	-	-
Stan Worthington (p)	1948	776	33.74	24	26.88	4	-	-
G Wrench	1967	-	-	1	18.00	2	-	-
Morne van Wyk (p)	2006	615	68.33	12	38.83	8	-	-
K Wynn	1944-53	38	2.92	0	-	6	-	-
F Wynne	1903-05	58	4.46	50	16.40	4	-	-
Clint Yorke (p)	1991-92	1976	42.96	77	24.79	23	0	0

5. Leading Career Totals

Competitive Matches 1838-2010

(Challenge Matches 1838-1896; Central Lancashire League 1892-1896;
Lancashire League 1897-2010; Lancashire League Knockout Cup 1920-2010;
Lancashire and Central Lancashire Inter-League Challenge Cup 1997-2006;
Colne Trophy 2001; 2009)

Superscript = number of matches player probably played for which figures unknown;
@ = approximate bowling average; U = bowling average unknown

Batting (qualification 4000 runs)

Player	Career Span	Runs	Ave
Harold Dawson	1932-64	12329	28.67
S Priestley	1981-2010	10880	23.15
J Crowther	1931-59	10028	24.70
B Heywood	1976-2005	9451	26.04
I Smith	1965-91	8551	19.00
W Scott	1931-52	7212	19.28
J Clegg jnr	1875-1903	7021	16.33
EB Shackleton	1903-24	6981	20.06
JW Crabtree	1885-1910	6726	17.70
J Horsfall (am, p)^2	1871-1900	6686	14.63
K Wilkinson	1953-71	6559	22.62
D Whitehead	1980-2008	6365	19.00
Ernest Hargreaves	1925-44	5666	25.41
A Stephenson	1908-34	5257	14.13
G Stansfield	1959-80	5165	15.33
S Newbitt	2003-10	4570	31.09
R Baigent	1997-2004	4410	33.16
M Heywood	1953-72	4391	16.14
W Law	1899-1920	4373	13.93
P Brownbridge	1951-76	4248	15.62
F Saul	1938-63	4174	17.53
ED Denison (p)	1949-53	4134	42.62
FA Blakey	1886-1900	4098	15.29

Bowling (qualification 250 wickets)

Player	Career Span	Wk	Ave
E Creighton (p)	1887-1901	918	8.96
WL Greenwood	1894-1923	683	14.39
B Whittaker	1958-83	628	18.97
J Clegg snr^{15}	1851-80	619	@12.50
M Hartley	1972-92	608	21.54
W Storah	1905-26	586	12.21
I Ali	1985-2010	564	19.62
F Root (p)	1933-37	533	9.79
E Stansfield	1908-44	514	13.25
S Oliver (p)	1959-68	504	12.38
J Townend	1965-86	499	17.76
J Horsfall (am, p)^2	1871-1900	437	14.46
W Wilkinson (p)	1892-97	434	10.57
J Crowther	1931-59	386	16.34
FA Blakey (a,p)	1886-1900	382	13.05
JW Sunderland	1919-30	380	10.36
ED Denison (p)	1949-53	367	12.28
J Morgan	1990-2010	313	22.23
A Smith	1936-50	311	13.57
JW Hitch (p)	1926-29	305	11.45
J Crossland (p)^{13}	1850-61	277	U
T Knowles^{15}	1852-74	276	@14.00
R Whitaker	1965-80	264	15.57
F Steph'son (am, p)	1871-90	262	11.49
RS Whitham	1929-47	262	16.81
RO Estwick (p)	1982-86	260	17.12

Fielding (qualification 100 catches)

Player	Career Span	Ct
Harold Dawson	1932-64	204
J Crowther	1931-59	195
B Heywood	1976-2005	180
WL Greenwood	1894-1923	169
JW Crabtree	1885-1910	168
I Smith	1965-91	165
K Wilkinson	1953-71	163
J Clegg jnr	1875-1903	155
J Horsfall (am, p)^2	1871-1900	151
B Whittaker	1958-83	148
E Mitchell	1923-37	145
M Hartley	1972-92	133
S Priestley	1981-2008	133
S Oliver (p)	1959-68	130
E Halliwell	1884-97	122
A Marshall	1907-28	121
A Fiddling	1962-90	108
I Ali	1985-2010	102

Wicketkeeping (qualification 30 victims)

Player	Career Span	Ct	St	Total Vcts
D Whitehead	1980-2009	546	128	674
T Carrick	1924-52	336	97	433
G Stansfield	1959-80	307	47	354
H Stansfield	1865-95	161	153	314
H Hudson	1905-26	173	99	272
D Brown	2003-10	135	28	163
A Connor	1957-63	122	30	152
TN Stephenson	1875-91	23	88	111
S Hudson	1897-1905	65	43	108
P Brierley	1999-2006	63	24	87
K Fiddling	1935-39	62	32	85
J Hazeltine	1951-59	40	13	53
R Ashworth	1867-93	31	11	42
R Brownbridge	1990-99	26	16	42
J Highley	1973-92	35	2	37

6. Club Records

Competitive Matches 1838-2010
(Challenge Matches 1838-1896; Central Lancashire League 1892-1896;
Lancashire League 1897-2010; Lancashire League Knockout Cup 1920-2010;
Lancashire and Central Lancashire Inter-League Challenge Cup 1997-2006;
Colne Trophy 2001; 2009)

Runs in a Season

	All Matches			**Lancashire League Matches**		
Am	S Newbitt	1115 runs	2009	S Newbitt	892 runs	2009
Pro	B Nash	1342 runs	1999	B Nash	1200 runs	1999

Wickets in a Season

	All Matches			**Lancashire League Matches**		
Am	JW Sunderland	102 wickets	1928	JW Sunderland	95 wickets	1928
Pro	E Creighton	169 wickets	1890	P Morfee	131 wickets	1920

Wicketkeepers: Victims in a Season

	All Matches			**Lancashire League Matches**		
Am	TN Stephenson	52 (7ct, 45st)	1890	D Whitehead	42 (34ct, 8st)	1995

Fieldsmen: Catches in a Season

	All Matches			**Lancashire League Matches**		
Am	E Mitchell	23	1934	E Mitchell	21	1934
Pro	S Oliver	26	1964	S Oliver	23	1964

Highest Totals

	All Matches		**Lancashire League Matches**	
For	411 v Haslingden	1938	411 v Haslingden	1938
Against	394 by Rochdale	1870	326(4) by East Lancashire	2005

Lowest Totals

	All Matches		**Lancashire League Matches**	
For	13 v Enfield	1944	13 v Enfield	1944
Against	8 by Walsden	1889	19 by Ramsbottom	1905

Highest Individual Innings

	All Matches		**Lancashire League Matches**	
Am	J Clegg jnr, 178 v Milnrow	1896	R Baigent, 147* v Accrington	2000
Pro	T Arothe, 189* v Accrington	2002	T Arothe, 189* v Accrington	2002

Most 50+ Scores in Career

	All Matches		**Lancashire League Matches**	
Am	H Dawson	89	H Dawson	84
Pro	E Denison	34	E Denison	31

Record Partnership

252 by R Baigent (94) and B Nash (pro) (176) v Ramsbottom   1999

Best Bowling Performance

	All Matches		**Lancashire League Matches**	
Am	M Hartley, 9-13 v Bacup	1976	M Hartley, 9-13 v Bacup	1976
Pro	W Hall, 10-46 v Haslingden	1906	W Hall, 10-46 v Haslingden	1906

Most 5-Wicket Performances in Career

	All Matches		**Lancashire League Matches**	
Am	W Storah	51	W Storah	50
Pro	E Creighton	101	F Root	54

7. Test Match Records of Cricketers who have played for Todmorden (to 1 February 2011)

Player	Test Debut	Mts	Batting		Bowling		Fielding
			Runs	Ave	Wkts	Ave	Catches
Australia							
Andy Bichel	1997	19	355	16.90	58	32.24	16
Jim Burke	1951	24	1280	34.59	8	28.75	18
Brad Hodge	2005	6	503	55.88	0	-	9
Matthew Nicholson	1998	1	14	7.00	4	28.75	0
England							
Paul Allott	1981	13	213	14.20	26	41.69	4
Thomas Armitage	1877	2	33	11.00	0	-	0
RG 'Dick' Barlow	1881	17	591	22.73	34	22.55	14
W 'Billy' Bates	1881	15	656	27.33	50	16.42	9
Johnny Briggs	1884	33	815	18.11	118	17.75	12
EW 'Nobby' Clark	1929	8	36	9.00	32	28.09	0
Brian Close	1949	22	887	25.34	18	29.55	24
Willis R Cuttell	1899	2	65	16.25	6	12.16	2
Tom Emmett	1877	7	160	13.33	9	31.55	9
Jason Gallian	1995	3	74	12.33	0	-	1
Tommy Greenhough	1959	4	4	1.33	16	22.31	1
Allen Hill	1877	2	101	50.50	7	18.75	1
George Hirst	1897	24	790	22.57	59	30.00	18
JW 'Bill' Hitch	1911	7	103	14.71	7	46.42	4
Percy Holmes	1921	7	357	27.46	-	-	3
Peter Lever	1970	17	350	21.87	41	36.80	11
George Macaulay	1923	8	112	18.67	24	27.58	5
Arthur Mold	1893	3	0	0.00	7	33.42	1
Morris Nichols	1930	14	355	29.58	41	28.09	11
Kevin Pietersen	2005	71	5566	48.42	5	116.80	44
Dick Pougher	1892	1	17	17.00	3	8.66	2
Wilfred Rhodes	1899	58	2325	30.19	127	26.96	60
Fred Root	1926	3	-	-	8	24.25	1
Chris Schofield	2000	7	67	22.33	0	-	0
Derek Shackleton	1950	2	113	18.83	18	42.67	1
Jack Sharp	1909	3	188	47.00	3	37.00	1
Arthur Shrewsbury	1891	32	1277	35.47	0	-	29
Frank Tyson	1954	17	230	10.95	76	18.56	4
George Ulyett	1877	25	949	24.33	50	20.40	18
Stan Worthington	1930	9	321	29.18	8	39.50	8
Pakistan							
Shabbir Ahmed	2003	10	88	8.80	51	23.03	3
Naved Ashraf	1998	2	64	21.33	-	-	0
Aftab Baloch	1969	2	97	48.50	0	-	0
Mohsin Khan	1978	48	2709	37.10	0	-	34
Akram Raza	1989	9	153	15.30	13	56.30	8
Asif Mujtaba	1986	25	928	24.42	4	75.75	19
South Africa							
PS 'Fanie' de Villiers	1993	18	359	18.89	85	24.27	11
AE 'Alf' Hall	1923	7	11	1.83	40	22.15	4
Jacques Rudolph	2003	35	2028	36.21	4	108.00	22
Pieter C Strydom	2000	2	35	11.67	0	-	1
Sri Lanka							
Ravi Ratnayeke	1982	22	807	25.21	56	35.21	1
Athula Samarasekera	1988	4	118	16.85	3	34.67	3
West Indies							
Ian Bishop	1989	43	632	12.15	161	24.27	8
Vasbert Drakes	2002	12	386	21.44	33	41.27	2
Roy Gilchrist	1957	13	60	5.45	57	26.68	4
Brendan Nash	2008	18	1049	38.85	2	108.50	6
Lendl Simmons	2009	3	87	14.50	1	139.00	3
Sir Garry Sobers	1954	93	8032	57.78	235	34.03	109

The following played in one day and/or Twenty20 internationals only:
Graham Lloyd (England); Gyanendra Pandey (India); Gulam Bodi; Francois du Plessis;
Morne van Wyke (South Africa); Chinthaka Jayasinghe (Sri Lanka)

References

Abbreviations

TCC   Todmorden Cricket Club
HBT&CVG *Hebden Bridge Times and Calder
           Vale Gazette*
TA   *Todmorden Advertiser*

Note
Present day refers to 2009/10.

Books are attributed to authors and publishers on first mention but afterwards are referred to by titles only.

All references are from the *Todmorden Advertiser* or Todmorden Cricket Club minutes/archive unless otherwise stated.

References

Chapter 1

1 Barker Tony, *Cricket's Wartime Sanctuary*, Association of Cricket Statisticians and Historians, Cardiff 2009, p45
2 Ibid, p104
3 *HBT&CVG*, 30/04/1897
4 Ibid, 03/08/1900
5 Ibid, 12/09/1902
6 Ibid, 12/10/1897
7 *Todmorden Herald*, 23/05/1900
8 Ibid, 16/05/1900
9 *HBT&CVG*, 07/04/1899, 13/04/1900
10 *Todmorden Herald*, 17/04/1901
11 *HBT&CVG*, 25/09/1899, 11/08/1899
12 Ibid, 23/06/1899
13 Ibid, 09/08/1901
14 Ibid, 11/08/1899
15 Ibid, 11/08/1899
16 Ibid, 24/05/1901
17 Ibid, 13/09/1901
18 *Todmorden Herald*, 09/05/1900
19 Ibid, 23/05/1900
20 Ibid, 05/09/1900, 12/09/1900;
   HBT&CVG, 24/08/1900, 07/09/1900
21 *HBT&CVG*, 30/08/1901
22 Searle Andrew, *SF Barnes*, Empire Publications, M/c 1997, p2
23 *Todmorden Herald*, 12/06/1901
24 Ibid, 12/06/1901
25 *HBT&CVG*, 14/06/1901
26 Ibid, 14/06/1901
27 Ibid, 28/06/1901
28 Ibid, 12/07/1901
29 Ibid, 12/07/1901
30 *Todmorden Herald*, 14/08/1901
31 *HBT&CVG*, 09/08/1901
32 Ibid, 06/06/1902
33 *Todmorden Herald*, 09/05/1900, 15/08/1900
34 *HBT&CVG*, 22/06/1900
35 Ibid, 04/01/1901, 19/07/1901, 05/01/1906
36 *People's Century*, Prog 1 *Age of Hope*, BBC/WGBH, Boston 1995
37 *Todmorden Herald*, 12/06/1901

Chapter 2

1 *HBT&CVG*, 31/05/1901
2 Ibid, 08/06/1900
3 *Todmorden Herald*, 07/06/1901
4 *HBT&CVG*, 26/06/1903
5 Ibid, 05/09/1902
6 Ibid, 14/07/1902
7 Ibid, 22/05/1914
8 Ibid, 01/05/1903
9 Ibid, 04/12/1903, 27/05/1904
10 Ibid, 01/07/1904;
   Edmundson David, *See the Conquering Hero*, Mike McLeod, Litho Ltd 1992, p 27;
   www.cricinfo
11 *See the Conquering Hero*, p27
12 *Golden Moments : Accrington CC Record of Achievements* 1846-1995, p13
13 *HBT&CVG*, 01/06/1906
14 Ibid, 08/06/1906, 22/06/1906
15 Ibid, 30/08/1907
16 Ibid, 10/07/1908
17 Ibid, 21/10/1910
18 Law Brian, *The Fieldens of Todmorden*, Kelsall, Littleborough 1995, p250
19 *HBT&CVG*, 20/10/1911

Chapter 3

1 *HBT&CVG*, 01/07/1910
2 Ibid, 25/10/1912
3 *See the Conquering Hero*, p29
4 Lumbutts CC Treasurer's Book 1892-1912
5 *Who's Who of Cricketers*, Newnes Bks in assoc with the Association of Cricket Statisticians, p1112
6 *HBT&CVG*, 04/07/1913
7 *See the Conquering Hero*, p32
8 *HBT&CVG*, 26/06/1914
9 *Cricket's Wartime Sanctuary*, p90
10 *See the Conquering Hero*, p35
11 www.chrishobbs.com/henryhughes1918.htm Notes on conscription in World War I
12 Root Fred, *A Cricket Pro's Lot*, Edward Arnold & Co, London 1937, p180
13 Pickup Peter, *1903-1988: The History of the Bradford Cricket League*, Fairhaven Books, Pudsey 1988, pp53-55

Chapter 4

1 *Who's Who of Cricketers*, p254;
   Frith David, *Silence of the Heart: Cricket Suicides*, Mainstream Publishing 2001
2 *The Cricketer*, 23/08/1931, p108;
   See the Conquering Hero, pp32,33
3 Ibid, p23
4 Ibid, p36
5 *The Independent on Sunday*, 15/09/2002
6 *See the Conquering Hero*, p39
7 *Who's Who of Cricketers*, p716;
   Lancashire League Handbook, 1923, p80
8 *The Cricket Statistician* Issue 2 (1928), pp15-20
9 *Church & Oswaldwistle CC, West End Ground Centenary 1890-1990*, p27

10 *Who's Who of Cricketers*, pp723,724;
    Lancashire League Handbook, 1924, p76
11 *The Cricketer International*, April 1977, p17; May
    1977, p15; July 1977, p17
12 Ibid, June 1977

Chapter 5

1   Heywood F&M & Jennings B, *A History of
    Todmorden*, Smith Settle Ltd 1996, p216
2   www.cricketarchive.com
3   *Sunday People*, 29/07/1928
4   Green Benny (compiler), *The Wisden Book of
    Cricketers' Lives*, Queen Anne Press, Macdonald
    Pub, London 1986, pp177-179
5   Hitch Alan (W Hitch's nephew) MSS, p64
6   Constantine Learie, *Cricket in the Sun*, Stanley
    Paul & Co Ltd, London, p38
7   *See the Conquering Hero*, p41
8   *The Wisden Book of Cricketers' Lives*, p178
9   Birley Derek, *A Social History of English Cricket*,
    Aurum Press, London 1999, p241
10 Wild Noel, *The Greatest Show on Turf*, Hendon
    Pub Co Ltd, Nelson 1992, p7
11 *The Wisden Book of Cricketers' Lives*, p178
12 Ibid, p179
13 *A Cricket Pro's Lot*, p187
14 *Cricket in the Sun*, p38
15 *The Greatest Show on Turf*, p10
16 Ibid, p11
17 Ibid, p10
18 *Cricket in the Sun*, p84
19 *Lancashire Evening Telegraph*, 06/09/1997
20 *Cricket's Wartime Sanctuary*, p160
21 Ibid, p52
22 *The Wisden Book of Cricketers' Lives*, p177
23 *The Greatest Show on Turf*, p11
24 *Todmorden and District News*, 07/04/1933

Chapter 6

1   www.ycb-yca.org.uk/a-history-of-womens-
    cricket.html
2   *The Encyclopaedia of British Football*
3   Butler Bryon, *The Official History of the Football
    Association*
4   Burnley Central Library, *Burnley Chronicle* 1895
5   Harris Cath, *A Potted History of Women's Cricket*,
    http://users.ox.ac.uk/~beth/wca/insid.htm
6   www.ckcricketheritage.org.uk
7   Jacobs Barbara, *The Dick Kerr's Ladies*
8   www.thesun.co.uk
9   *A Potted History of Women's Cricket*,
10 Bishop Martin, *Bats, Balls and Biscuits*, Cricket
    Heritage Project, University of Huddersfield 2008,
    p120
11 Davies Peter J, *Bowling Maidens Over:1931 and
    the Beginnings of Women's Cricket in a Yorkshire
    Town*, Sport in History, 28:2, 280-298
    www.ckcricketheritage.org.uk
12 www.cricinfo - England/Players/Mona Greenwood
13 www.cricinfo - England/Players/Betty Snowball
14 www.ECB.co.uk:women'scricket
15 *Bowling Maidens Over:1931 and the Beginnings
    of Women's Cricket in a Yorkshire Town*, Sport in
    History, 28:2, 280-298

Chapter 7

1   www.rawtenstallcc.co.uk
2   *The Wisden Book of Cricketers' Lives*, p162
3   Ibid, p162
4   *Wisden Cricket Monthly*, June 1982, p39
5   Martin Jenkins Christopher, *Cricket's Lighter Side*,
    Simon & Schuster, London 1988, pp77,78
6   *Playfair Cricket Monthly*, Nov 1968, p18
7   *Derbyshire CCC Year Book 1955*, pp83,84
8   *A Cricket Pro's Lot*, p35
9   *Worcestershire CCC Year Book 1954*, pp93,94
10 *Derbyshire CCC Year Book 1955*, pp83,84
11 *A Cricket Pro's Lot*, p186
12 Ibid, p193
13 Ibid, p194
14 Ibid, pp186,187
15 Ibid, pp105,106
16 *Lancashire League Handbooks*, 1938
17 Ibid, 1939
18 *Todmorden Advertiser*, 06/08/1937
19 *Wisden Cricket Monthly*, Jan 1982, p24
20 Ibid, Sept 1986, p9
21 *A Cricket Pro's Lot*, p220

Chapter 8

1   *HBT&CVG*, 24/09/1909
2   *Todmorden Herald*, 12/09/1900
3   *HBT&CVG*, 21/06/1901
4   Ibid, 30/06/1899
5   Ibid, 08/09/1899
6   Ibid, 16/04/1897
7   Ibid, 20/09/1991
8   Ibid, 04/04/1902/, 19/07/1901
9   Ibid, 05/09/1902
10 Ibid, 10/07/1903, 19/08/1904
11 Ibid, 13/09/1912
12 Ibid, 16/09/1908, 03/08/1900, 10/05/1901,
    12/09/1902
13 *Hebden Bridge Times*, 03/01/1958

Chapter 9

1   *HBT&CVG*, 08/03/1901
2   Ibid, 11/01/1907
3   Ibid, 26/03/1909, 23/04/1909
4   Ibid, 04/01/1907, 25/09/1908, 05/02/1909
5   Heywood B, F & M, *Cloth Caps and Cricket
    Crazy*, UCVP, Todmorden 2004, p152
6   *HBT&CVG*, 23/04/1897, 07/05/1897
7   Ibid, 20/08/1897
8   Ibid, 24/09/1897
9   Ibid, 03/10/1897
10 Ibid, 10/12/1897, 25/03/1898, 01/04/1898
11 Ibid, 22/04/1898
12 Ibid, 13/05/1898, 27/05/1898, 22/07/1898
13 Ibid, 09/09/1898, 20/01/1899
14 Ibid, 24/02/1899, 17/03/1899
15 Ibid, 28/07/1899
16 Ibid, 01/12/1899
17 Ibid, 13/04/1900, 20/04/1900
18 Ibid, 20/04/1900, 11/05/1900
19 Ibid, 11/01/1901, 23/03/1901, 29/03/1901,
    03/05/1901
20 Ibid, 02/08/1901, 04/10/1901
21 Ibid, 13/12/1901
22 Ibid, 04/04/1902

23 Ibid, 15/08/1902, 19/12/1902
24 Ibid, 24/07/1903, 12/02/1904
25 Ibid, 06/09/1907
26 Ibid, 28/08/1910, 04/08/1911, 01/09/1911,
     08/12/1911
27 Ibid, 25/04/1913, 25/07/1913, 29/08/1913,
     05/12/1913, 08/05/1914, 23/05/1914
28 *HBT&CVG,* 24/05/1901;
TA, 04/09/1903
29 *HBT&CVG,* 23/06/1905, 21/07/1905, 20/04/1906,
     04/05/1906
30 Ibid, 31/08/1906, 07/09/1906, 11/01/1907
31 Ibid, 04/01/1907, 03/05/1907, 24/05/1907,
     02/10/1908, 20/03/1908, 26/02/1909, 06/05/1910
32 Ibid, 29/04/1910, 06/05/1910, 07/04/1911,
     30/06/1911, 16/02/1912, 05/04/1912, 08/05/1914
33 Ibid, 18/09/1908, 19/08/1910
34 Ibid, 16/07/1909, 25/03/1910, 16/08/1912,
     29/05/1914, 12/06/1914, 19/06/1914, 26/06/1914
35 *HBT&CVG,* 03/04/1925;
TA, 05/09/1924, 26/09/1924, 15/10/1926,
     07/01/1927, 29/07/1927, 10/08/1928
36 *A History of Todmorden,* p221
37 Issi Shannon (edit), *Milltown Memories,* Hebden
     Bridge, vols 4,5

Chapter 10

1 *HBT&CVG,* 10/07/1903, 26/06/1901, 17/07/1903,
    24/07/1903
2 Ibid, 09/07/1909
3 Ibid, 25/06/1909
4 Ibid, 04/06/1909, 13/08/1909, 17/12/1909
5 Ibid, 19/07/1901
6 Ibid, 14/10/1898
7 *Todmorden Herald,* 05/04/1905
8 *HBT&CVG,* 21/10/1911, 11/10/1912
9 *Todmorden Herald,* 06/03/1901
10 Ibid, 06/03/1901
11 *HBT&CVG,* 02/02/1906
12 Ibid, 06/02/1914
13 *Todmorden Herald,* 06/03/1901
14-29 *HBT&CVG,* 21/06/1901 to 29/09/1911
30 *Todmorden Herald,* 14/04/1905, 08/05/1905
31 Ibid, 17/06/1909
32 *HBT&CVG,* 17/06/1898
33 Ibid, 20/05/1898
34 Ibid, 12/06/1908
35 *Todmorden Herald,* 25/04/1900
36 *HBT&CVG,* 06/06/1902, 20/07/1906
37 Ibid, 17/06/1910
38 *Todmorden Herald,* 06/06/1900
39 Ibid, 26/08/1898
40 Ibid, 24/03/1911
41 *HBT&CVG,* 02/08/1900
42 Lee John A, *Todmorden, The Great War 1914-18,*
     Waddington & Sons 'News' Office, Todmorden
     1922, p81
43 *Todmorden Herald,* 28/12/1904
44 *The Fieldens of Todmorden,* p207
45 *Annals of Todmorden 1552-1913,* compiled and
     published by Dorothy Dugdale, 2002, p48
46 *HBT&CVG,* 08/09/1905
47 Birch Roger, *Todmorden Album* vols 1,2,3,4,
     Woodlands Press, Todmorden 2006, vol 4,
     pp29,64,66
48 *Todmorden Advertiser,* 16/03/1867

49 *Todmorden Album,* Vol 4, p118
50 *Todmorden Album,* Vol 1, 1983, p45
51 *Todmorden Album,* Vol 3, 1993, p111

Chapter 11

1 *Todmorden Herald,* 23/05/1900
2 Ibid, 01/08/1900
3 Ibid, 29/08/1900
4 Ibid, 22/05/1901
5 *Todmorden Album,* Vol 3, p40
6 *HBT&CVG,* 18/08/1905
7 Ibid, 17/02/1899
8 Ibid, 05/06/1908
9 Ibid, 26/02/1909
10 Ibid, 02/07/1909, 30/07/1909
11 Ibid, 17/09/1909
12 Ibid, 29/08/1913
13 *Todmorden Album,* Vol 1, p112
14 *HBT&CVG,* 10/08/1899, 01/06/1900, 10/08/1900,
     20/06/1902
15 *Borough of Todmorden 75th Anniversary Souvenir
     1971,* p29
16 *HBT&CVG,* 17/04/1903
17 *Todmorden Herald,* 06/11/1903
18 *HBT&CVG,* 06/11/1903
19 Ibid, 22/06/1905
20 Ibid, 17/09/1909
21 Ibid, 02/02/1912, 07/06/1912, 19/07/1912
22 Ibid, 22/08/1913

Chapter 12

1 *Todmorden and District News,* 04/12/1896
2 *Todmorden Album,* Vol 4, p81
3 Horsfall Ben, *The Autobiography of Ben Horsfall,*
     Badger Publishing, Halifax 1992, p178
4 Ibid, pp178-180
5 Ibid, pp186,187
6 Ibid, p185
7 *A History of Todmorden,* p217
8 *Todmorden Public Library Journal,* 1934
9 Heywood M & F, *Todmorden Hippodrome: One
     Hundred Years of Theatre,* UCVP, Todmorden
     2007, p8
10 Ibid, p9
11 *Todmorden Cameos,* Todmorden Antiquarian
     Society, 1999, p85;
     Todmorden Album, Vol 3, p112
12 *Todmorden Album,* Vol 3, p121
13 *A History of Todmorden* , p220
14 Ibid, p221
15 Thomas Peter, *Seeing it Through: Halifax and
     Calderdale During World War II,* Peter Thomas,
     Woodleigh, Savile Rd, Hebden Bridge 2005, p131
16 McKeever Rob, *On The Right Track With
     Northern Soul DJ Ginger Taylor,* Furness
     Peninsula Press 2009,
     pp19,20,22,24,27,33,34,43,62,65,69,111
17 Dr Ben Horsfall's letter to the Chairman of
     Todmorden Civic Entertainment Committee Feb
     1973.
18 *Todmorden Hippodrome,* p47
19 Ibid, pp47,50
20 Ibid, p110
21 *A History of Todmorden,* p228

Chapter 13

1 Hodgson Derek, *The Official History of Yorkshire CCC*, The Crowood Press, Marlborough 1989, p109
2 Robert Duffield's Diary
3 TCC Balance Sheets, 1940, 41, 42
4 Matthews David, *On the Spot Derek Shackleton, A Biography*, Blackberry Down Bks, Lincombe, Lee, Devon 1998, p31
5 *Cricket's Wartime Sanctuary*, pp116,131
6 Ibid, p122
7 *Church & Oswaldwistle CC West End Ground Centenary 1890-1990*, p31

Chapter 14

1 *Who's Who of Cricketers*, p747
2 *Cricket's Wartime Sanctuary*, p126
3 *Wisden Cricket Monthly*, Jan 1980, p35
4 Ibid, Dec 1986, p10
5 *Who's Who of Cricketers*, p408
6 *On the Spot Derek Shackleton, A Biography*
7 *Who's Who of Test Cricketers*, p150
8 *Lancashire League Handbook*, 1948
9 Kay John, *Cricket in the Leagues*, Eyre & Spottiswoode Pub Ltd 1970, pp74,75
10 *1903-1988;The History of the Bradford Cricket League*, p86
11 *Lancashire League Handbook*, 1950
12 Whitney Mike, *Whiticisms*, Pan Macmillan Australia Pty Ltd, Sydney 1995, p110
13 *Northern Daily Telegraph*, 02/04/1952
14 *The Daily Mirror*, 24/06/1952
15 *Lancashire League Handbooks*, 1953, 1954
16 TCC Annual Report 1954
17 Frith David, *The Slow Men*, George Allen & Unwin, London 1984, pp139,140
18 *The A-Z of Australian Cricketers*, The Australian Society of Sports History, OUP, Melbourne 1987, p42
19 *TCC 150th Anniversary Souvenir*, p5;
Central Lancashire League Centenary Year 1892-1992, Heywood CC;
The Cricketer, June 1952;
Playfair Cricket Monthly, Oct 1970, Feb 1971, Oct 1971;
Wisden Cricket Monthly, June 1985;
The Cricketer International, May 1974, Apr 1975, July 1975, Nov 1975, Nov 1976;
Who's Who of Cricketers, p611;
The Complete Who's Who of Test Cricketers, p83
20 *Lancashire League Handbook*, 1960;
Cricket's Wartime Sanctuary, p163

Chapter 15

1 *Cricket in the Leagues*, pp64,65,168
2 *Who's Who of Cricketers*, p1036
3 Frith David, *The Fast Men*, Corgi bks, London 1984, p184
4 *A Typhoon Called Tyson*, Sportsman's Bk Club, Phoenix House Ltd, London 1962, p23
5 TCC Scorebook 1961
6 Bird Dickie, *White Caps and Bails*, Hodder & Stoughton, London 2000, pp180,181
7 *Lancashire League Handbook*, 1964

8 Todmorden Municipal Borough Council Minutes, 05/06/1946
9 Ibid, 04/04/1951
10 *The Cricketer International*, May 2001, p11
11 *Lancashire League Handbook,*1955
12 Miller Keith, *Cricket From the Grandstand*, Sportsman's Bk Club, 1960, pp25,26
13 MacMillan's speech at Bedford, 20/07/1957
14 Lancashire League Minutes, Oct 1963
15 *The Fast Men*, p191
16 Ibid, p191
17 Trueman Fred, *Balls of Fire*, Bk Club Associates by arrangement with JM Dent & Sons Ltd 1976, p117

Chapter 16

1 *Who's Who of Cricketers*, p670
2 *Lancashire Cricket Year Book*, 2004
3 *David Lloyd The Autobiography*, Collins Willow, London 2001, pp36,37
4 Ibid, pp34,35,40
5 *Who's Who of Cricketers*, p253
6 Ibid, p710
7 Ibid, p210
8 Ibid, p18

Chapter 17

1 *See The Conquering Hero*, p106
2 Ibid, p122
3 *TA*, 05/12/1980
4 *See The Conquering Hero*, p112
5 *TA*, 30/07/82;
Lancashire Evening Telegraph, 26/07/82;
Burnley Express, 27/07/82

Chapter 18

1 Lancashire League Handbook 1998
2 Ibid 1999
3 Letter to A Stuttard 16/08/1999
4 Letter to CLL 28/03/2006
5 European Sports Charter (Article 3)
6 *Halifax Evening Courier* 20/05/1996

Chapter 19

1 Lancashire League Handbook 1997
2 Ibid 1998

Index